Ships of the Great Lakes

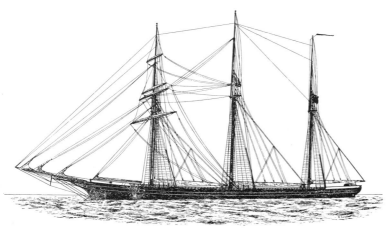

FULL-RIGGED SCHOONER MICHIGAN.

WOODEN ORE CARRYING STEAMER MASSACHUSETTS.

SIDE WHEEL STEEL PASSENGER STEAMER FRANK E. KIRBY.

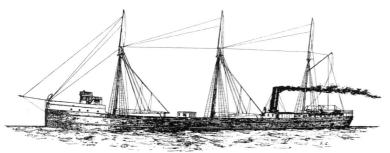

COARSE FREIGHT WOODEN STEAMER C. A. EDDY.

COARSE FREIGHT STEEL STEAMER PIONEER.

Ships of the Great Lakes

300 years of navigation

by James P. Barry

Thunder Bay Press

Holt. Michigan

The part of this book dealing with the sloop *Detroit* first appeared in
Inland Seas, Spring 1970, Great Lakes Historical Society, and is
reprinted here by permission of the society.

Title Page: One of the ghosts of the Great Lakes, the steamer
Bannockburn. Painting by Rev. Edward J. Dowling, S.J. *(Dossin
Great Lakes Museum)*

Frontispiece: Sketches reproduced from Detroit Dry Dock catalog of
the 1890s, *Around the Lakes.*

Printed in Canada

02 01 00 99 98   9 8 7 6 5 4

ISBN 1-882376-26-9

Thunder Bay Press
Holt, Michigan

Contents

Acknowledgements

*T*his revised and expanded edition owes much to the help and guidance of Daniel J. Cornillie, Manager, Fleet Operations, Inland Steel Company; Robert Graham, Archivist of the Institute for Great Lakes Research, Bowling Green State University; C. Patrick Labadie, Director of the Canal Park Marine Museum, Duluth; and Maurice Smith, Director of the Marine Museum of the Great Lakes at Kingston.

Grateful thanks also go to Mark J. Barnes of the Institute for Great Lakes Research, BGSU; Peggy Bechtol of the Great Lakes Historical Society; Sandy Calemme of the University of Detroit-Mercy; Wayne Farrar, photographer; Christine R. Hillston, Interlake Steamship Company; Joan Kloster, Wisconsin Maritime Museum; Suzette Lopez, Milwaukee Public Library; Robert J. Macdonald, Great Lakes historian; John Polacsek, Curator of the Dossin Great Lakes Museum; George J. Ryan, President of the Lake Carriers' Association; Ned A. Smith, President and CEO of the American Steamship Company; and William Smith of the Huronia Museum, Midland, Ontario.

For the original edition on which this one is based, I am greatly obligated to Miss Janet Coe Sanborn of the Cleveland Public Library (and editor of the invaluable *Inland Seas*), who not only provided information and pictures for this book but also gave guidance and even did detective work in locating such materials in other collections. Mrs. Ruth Revels of the Milwaukee Public Library very kindly furnished information and many pictures from the library's collections. Miss Edith G. Firth, head of the Canadian History and Manuscript Section, Metropolitan Toronto Central Library, gave extensive help, including provision of manuscript materials, pictures and the addresses of other sources of material.

Robert E. Lee, Director of the Dossin Great Lakes Museum, Detroit, provided a number of pictures from his files and suggested possible sources of others. Richard J. Wright, Director of the Northwest Ohio-Great Lakes Research Center at Bowling Green University, devoted a day of his busy schedule to a discussion of marine matters and made his extensive picture collection available.

John L. Lochhead of the Mariners Museum, Newport News, Virginia, kindly furnished pictures from the collections of that museum. Stanley G. Triggs, of the McCord Museum, McGill University, Montreal, provided guidance to material in the Notman Photographic Archives and arranged for me to obtain photos from the collection.

Malcolm MacLeod generously furnished guidance and information on early French and British naval vessels on the Lakes, to include unpublished material he had written. John Gardner, of Mystic Seaport, presented me with a quantity of materials on bateaux, guided me to others and discussed the craft at much length.

The Rev. Edward J. Dowling, S.J., supplied copies of his paintings of various ships, as well as photographs from his own collection, from those in the University of Detroit Marine Historical Collection, and from the collection of the Marine Historical Society of Detroit. Elizabeth Stanton Anderson gave gracious permission to use drawings by her father, Samuel Ward Stanton. Gordon R. McKean, editor of *Imperial Oil Fleet News*, gave help in finding information on and pictures of Great Lakes tankers.

Mrs. P. C. Band and Robert A. Zeleznek both very generously provided pictures from their collections. John R. Sloan, Director of the Ontario Historical Sites Branch, furnished pictures of the reconstructed bateau at the Marine Museum of the Upper Lakes.

Rowley W. Murphy gave kind permission to use his drawing of the *Eureka* and to quote the passage from his article, "Ghost Ships."

Phrixos B. Papachristidis graciously invited me on a three-week voyage aboard the *Grande Hermine*. Oliver T. Burnham, of the Lake Carriers' Association, gave pictures and information. Lawrence A. Pomeroy, Jr., of the Great Lakes Historical Society, freely provided advice and guidance. R. C. McDowell, of McDowell Wellman Engineering Co., most kindly furnished information about the rare pictures of Brown hoists, Huletts and other unloading equipment.

Certain people gave expert advice on specific vessels and areas. F. Clever Bald guided me to most of the references about the sloop *Detroit*. Robert C. Berger, furnished pictures and an extensive file on the U.S.S. *Waxwing*. Keith Denis, President of the Thunder Bay Historical Society, provided information about the history of shipping at the Canadian Lakehead and went to considerable effort to obtain for me a copy of that society's William Armstrong painting, "The *Rescue* at Fort William." J. L. Haskell of the Port of Milwaukee furnished material on the *Manchester Mercurio*. The late Fred Landon provided much information on the steamer *United Empire* and Mrs. Landon very kindly made available photos of that vessel and of the *Asia* from her husband's collection. Mrs. Irene McCreery of the Toledo Public Library furnished copies of many of the references on the *David Dows*.

Captain H. C. Inches, of Vermilion, Ohio, offered guidance on historical matters and kindly permitted me to use pictures from his collection and drawings from his book, *The Great Lakes Wooden Shipbuilding Era*. The late Captain Frank Hamilton set me straight, in his forthright style, on several matters that I raised with him. Harry J. Wolf provided pictures and led me to other picture sources.

This book leans heavily on a number of materials from the Public Archives of Canada; without them and without the interested help of the Archives staff it could not have been written. The U.S. National Archives also provided information. The National Gallery of Canada helped to find pictures. The Michigan State Archives and the Archives of Ontario were also helpful. The Ontario Department of Lands and Forests gave information and photographs on such diverse subjects as fishing boats, timber rafts and bateaux. The Hudson's Bay Company provided material on fur-trade canoes.

Information about their vessels and photographs of them were provided by Bethlehem Steel Corporation; Don Mummery Fisheries; Imperial Oil; the Papachristidis Co.,; Pickands Mather & Co., and United States Steel Corporation. Information on the pictures of U.S. naval vessels came from the Director of Naval History, U.S.N., Washington, and the Library, U.S. Naval Academy, Annapolis. Information and pictures of U.S. Coast Guard vessels came from the Commander, 9th U.S. Coast Guard District, Cleveland. Information about British naval vessels and the picture of the H.M.S. *Britomart* came from the Imperial War Museum, London. The Public Records Office, London, also provided copies of documents dealing with British warships on the Lakes. Information about the *Stewart J. Cort*, including an inspection tour of the vessel and of the plant in which she was built, was graciously provided by Erie Marine, as were some of the pictures of her.

The Port of Cleveland, Port of Milwaukee, Port of Toledo and Port of Toronto gave freely of materials concerning their operations past and present. The St. Lawrence Seaway Authority (Canada) and St. Lawrence Seaway Development Corporation (U.S.) furnished information and pictures of the Seaway and the vessels that have used it.

The staffs of the Ashtabula County District Library, the Buffalo and Erie County Historical Society, the Burton Historical Collection of the Detroit Public Library, the Chicago Historical Society, the Chicago Public Library, the Historical Society of Pennsylvania, the Marine Museum of the Upper Lakes, the Marquette County Historical Society, the Metropolitan Toronto Central Library, the New York Public Library, the Racine County Historical Museum, the Rochester Historical Society, the Rochester Public Library, the State Historical Society of Wisconsin, the Thunder Bay Historical Society Museum, the Toledo Public Library and the Library of Congress have all extended themselves to provide information, pictures or guidance thereto.

Heartfelt thanks go to the staff of the Ohio Historical Society Library in Columbus, where I did much of the research on the book. They were unfailingly helpful in the face of constant requests for what must eventually have totaled several tons of materials.

Finally, the contributions of my wife, Anne, ranged from literary criticism to proofreading, not to mention protection from interruption and encouragement during adversity. But for her help the book would not be here.

In memory of my father
Paul A. Barry
Who taught me to sail in a Mackinaw boat

Foreword

From Montreal to Duluth the St. Lawrence-Great Lakes complex stretches a thousand miles toward the heart of North America. It is the most obvious natural highway on the map of the continent, and those who have controlled it have moved farther and faster than any of their competitors. When the French held it in the 1620s they were able to establish missions on Georgian Bay, at roughly the same westing as the present city of Toronto. New England, New Amsterdam, and Virginia then still clung feebly to the Atlantic shore. When the British held it in the 1780s they had a major trading fort at Grand Portage, at the western end of Lake Superior. The United States then had nothing west and north of Cincinnati. Today it remains a major commercial artery for both Canada and the United States.

The vessels that men used on the Great Lakes reflect the men themselves and their purposes. The Indian paddling his canoe evokes a whole culture, the master of a bulk freighter scanning his radar screen a completely different one. The story of the people and the ships that sailed the Lakes is the story of developing America.

Large vessels on the Lakes are not always called ships. When steam first came, its promoters referred to their vessels as steamboats, probably because their ideas developed from river steamers that bore that name, and soon it was general practice to call all Great Lakes vessels boats. Sir Richard Bonnycastle, writing in 1846, referred to "these boats, as they call them, but which ought to be called ships." Today shipping lines and shipbuilders often do speak of ships, but the sailors themselves talk still of boats.

The pages that follow tell of the ships—or boats—of the Great Lakes and of the people who used them. They tell of voyageurs and fur traders, of battle and shipwreck, of families travelling to new lands, of pleasure cruises, and of cargoes sent to market. They tell of the growing life that has channelled through the Great Lakes for over three hundred years.

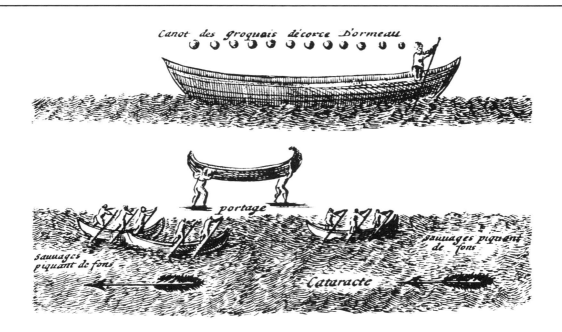

Canot des Jroquois d'ecorce D'ormeau

portage

sauuages piquant de fons

sauuages piquant de fons

Cataracte

Sauvages voguant de bout dans un grand canot

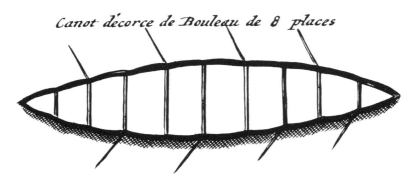

Canot d'ecorce de Bouleau de 8 places

Rame ou auiron

Some of the earliest European pictures of Indian canoes appeared in a book by
Baron de la Hontan published in 1703. (—*National Archives of Canada C 99061*)

1
The Fur Trade

Fur traders explored, penetrated, and for a time dominated the Great Lakes region before they were swept on by the tide of settlement. But fur remained an important economic force on the Great Lakes until the end of the War of 1812; after that the trade soon moved westward.

Settlement was embodied in the English colonies scattered along the Atlantic Coast. The fur trade stemmed mainly from Quebec and later from Montreal. The gathering of fur and the taking of land represented two conflicting visions of the North American continent; the fur trader would keep the country and its native people much as they were, but the settler would remake the country and drive the Indians out. The French garrisoned the area west of the Alleghenies while the British colonists established a land company to settle it.

Once the British won North America there was a strange reversal; the British Government at home decided to keep the lands west of the mountains an Indian country, even though colonial settlers were beginning to move into them. The official British position shifted almost to the old French one. But the attitude of the British colonists along the Atlantic Coast remained the same: the land to the west was theirs to take as they wished. The first seeds of the American Revolution thus were sown.

After the Revolution the headquarters of British North America moved to Quebec and the reversal of roles became complete. The Atlantic colonies, now the new United States, continued to push westward. The British permitted some settlement along Lake Ontario, largely by British sympathizers expelled from the former colonies, but they kept their forts on the southern shores of the Lakes and encouraged the Indians to oppose in every way American settlement west of the Alleghenies.

The vessels that appeared on the Great Lakes during these two centuries were used in the fur trade, in battle, and in carrying the first few settlers.

THE INDIAN CANOE

An 18-year-old French lad, Étienne Brûlé, came riding down the swift waters of French River to Georgian Bay in 1610. He was probably the first European to reach the Great Lakes, and he came as passenger in an Indian canoe.

The Huron Indians with whom he travelled followed an ancient trade route up the St. Lawrence and Ottawa Rivers, across Lake Nipissing, and down French River to Georgian Bay, where the Hurons lived. On this route there were thirty-five portages and at least fifty places where everyone had to get out of the canoes and pull them upstream through the rapids. The only craft known that could make such a trip were bark canoes.

Samuel de Champlain was the governor of New France and a man with a vision of future empire in the unexplored reaches of the Great Lakes region. He had sent Brûlé with a group of Hurons who were returning home from their annual trading expedition to the French colony on the St. Lawrence. Frenchmen had heard many Indian stories of the great inland seas; now the first European actually saw them. There he stayed for several years, making love to the Indian girls and making journeys such as the one that led him to Lake Superior before any other European.

Five years after Brûlé first arrived, Champlain himself came to the Lakes by canoe. A stream of traders, explorers, and missionaries followed, then fanned out across the Great Lakes. Among them were men such as Nicolet, who discovered what now is Wisconsin while looking for a trade route to the Orient, Brébeuf and Lalemant, the Jesuits who were tortured to death when the Iroquois overran the

Huron country and forced the French to abandon the Huron missions, and Radisson and Groseilliers, brothers-in-law who dared come back to the Lakes after the Iroquois victory and who then went on to discover the upper Mississippi and to explore the length of Lake Superior. Afterward came more explorers, missionaries, and *couriers de bois*, all of whom travelled by canoe.

We do not know the exact part of North America in which the canoe first evolved or the tribe that first developed it. By the time the white man arrived, many tribes were using canoes made of bark—usually birch bark—and each had its own tribal peculiarities of design. There were also different kinds of canoes for different purposes, according to the number of people who were to travel in them and the waters in which they were to be used, but they all had similar characteristics. They were light and readily carried. Because they were light they could be paddled, rather than rowed, and the paddlers faced forward—a necessity on fast streams and in narrow passages. They were all rather similar in general appearance, despite some striking variations in shape. And they were so well suited to the waters in which they were used that the Europeans promptly adopted them for their own use.

A French officer, Baron de Lahontan, writing in 1684, gave one of the best early descriptions of the Indian birch-bark canoe. The canoes he saw, if we translate his measurements into modern terms, ranged in length from 13 to 30 feet. They were sheathed inside, between the bark and the ribs, with cedar splints; the paddlers might kneel, sit, or stand; poles were used to push the canoes in shallow water. The normal life of such a canoe was five or six years.

GRIFFON

On the pleasant day of August 7, 1679, a small vessel put bravely out from the entrance to the Niagara River. Her sails filled and she headed up the wide and largely unknown blue-gray expanse of Lake Erie. Among those on board was a lean, aquiline man, her owner, Robert Cavelier, Seur de La Salle, a dreamer with the energy of a zealot and the organizing ability of a businessman. She was the *Griffon*, the first vessel to sail the Lakes above Niagara, and this was her first, and her last, trip.

As a young man, La Salle had come to Canada from his native Rouen, France, and bought a feudal seigniory on the St. Lawrence. While he developed his holdings, he planned exploration and trade farther west, and made an extensive canoe trip through the Lakes region to gain more knowledge of it. In 1674 he was granted the seigniory of Fort Frontenac, at the foot of Lake Ontario. In this the French government was not overly generous. He had to agree to buy the fort the government had built there, to maintain and garrison it, and to bring in colonists and provide for them.

In 1677 La Salle was given a charter to build vessels on the Great Lakes and the Mississippi and to trade in the great areas of the West. This brought him the immediate enmity of the jealous merchants of New France and the powerful Jesuit order which felt that organized trade in the Great Lakes region would hinder its missionary efforts. In order to build his vessels he recruited shipyard workers in Europe and bought shipbuilding materials there. He also had plans drawn for a vessel to be used on the upper Lakes. To accomplish all this he borrowed money at the interest rates of the day—some of them as much as forty percent.

At least two of the four small sailing vessels he planned for Lake Ontario had been launched by 1678; they were the first on the Great Lakes. No exact description of them has been found, but they seem to have been two-masted craft about forty-five feet long. That autumn La Salle had these vessels and a number of canoes take men and supplies to Niagara. The men cut a portage trail from the mouth of the river to a point above the falls, carried the supplies over it, and set up a shipyard, probably at the mouth of Cayuga Creek, on what is now the New York bank of the Niagara River. There, despite hostile Indians and mutinous workmen, a ship was built during the winter and launched in the late spring or early summer. This was the *Griffon*.

Although La Salle was at Niagara during part of her building, he spent most of the time at Fort Frontenac, combating the efforts of some of his credi-

The building of the *Griffon*, as shown in Hennepin's book. Historians have supposed that the author provided a sketch of the vessel upon which this illustration was based, and they have hoped that it was more accurate than the fanciful landscape. (*—National Archives of Canada C 1225*)

tors who wanted to seize his property there. He came back in August, having been reasonably successful in his fight, and soon afterward the new vessel set sail.

That first night out the *Griffon* almost became the first of the many ships that have been wrecked on Long Point, a finger that projects from the northern shore of Lake Erie far into the Lake. La Salle described the incident:

> Night came on, and a thick fog concealed the shore, from which we supposed ourselves some ten leagues distant. I heard breakers about a league ahead of us. Everyone thought it was but the ordinary sound on the lakes when the wind changes, which is always heard from the side it comes from, and the pilot wished to crowd on sail to gain an anchorage before we stranded ahead; but as I knew that these two sand banks extended out very far, and as I was of the opinion we were near the one which in fact was just ahead of us,

> I ordered, notwithstanding everybody, that we change the course and bear east northeast, instead of as we were going, west northwest with a light wind from the southeast. We sailed two or three hours, sounding constantly, without finding bottom; and still we heard the same noise ahead of us. They all insisted that it was only the wind, and I, that it was the sandbar which made a circle and surrounded us on the north side, from west to east. In fact, an hour later, we suddenly found only three fathoms. Everyone worked ship, I tacked and bore to the southwest, always sounding without finding bottom. At length the fog lifted, my conviction proved true, and they all saw that they owed their escape from danger to me.

Evidently the *Griffon* had sailed blindly into Long Point Bay, found herself trapped between the mainland and the point, and was barely saved by her owner's navigation.

The *Griffon*, as conceived by artist-historian George A. Cuthbertson, shown landing at Green Bay. (—*Canada Steamship Lines Collection of Canadiana*)

Three days after she left the Niagara, the *Griffon* reached the Detroit River. She worked her way through the narrows and Lake St. Clair, and entered Lake Huron. After she was well out on the open lake a wild storm swept over her. She ran before it under bare poles while most of those on board prayed; an exception was the pilot, a Dane named Lucas, who railed and cursed at La Salle for bringing him here to perish in a nasty lake after a long and glorious career on salt water. The storm abated, however, and Lucas and his ship were safe for the time. They sailed on to Mackinac, where there was a Jesuit mission and an Indian village. There La Salle discovered that some of the advance party he had sent ahead by canoe the preceding autumn had deserted and that others had squandered his supplies; so he sent his lieutenant, Henri de Tonty, to the Sault to apprehend two of the deserters and recover the goods in their possession. Tonty was an

Italian, a man with an iron hand to replace one that he had lost in battle and with a spirit to match it; he supported La Salle valiantly through the disappointments and disasters of a decade.

Without waiting for Tonty to return, La Salle sailed the *Griffon* westward into Lake Michigan. On what today is called Washington Island he found the faithful remainder of the advance party, who had assembled a quantity of pelts. It might have been wiser to keep the little ship there through the winter, but La Salle thought of the hungry creditors waiting in Montreal and Quebec, and he decided to send the *Griffon* back to the Niagara with a full cargo of furs. On September 18, 1679, she set sail, while he remained behind to go on and explore the Illinois country. A few hours after the vessel sailed a violent storm descended on the Lakes and continued to blow for four days. The *Griffon* was never seen again. Probably she perished in the storm, but it may also be that she was scuttled by her crew, so that they could steal her cargo or because they were in the pay of La Salle's enemies.

La Salle managed to survive this loss and others, and he went on to greater feats of exploration. It was not until March 19, 1687, somewhere in what now is Texas, that he was murdered by one of his followers.

The exact appearance of the *Griffon* is largely conjecture. Scholars have even questioned her name, which comes down to us only in the writings of Father Hennepin; to be sure, he sailed on her, but he has been shown as a good deal of a rascal and much of his writing as something approaching fiction. It is convenient to use that name, however, and it now is applied universally to the vessel. The best description of her is based on fragmentary reports from those who saw her, on an old (and possibly inaccurate) picture of her when she was being built that appeared in Hennepin's book, and on European shipbuilding practice of that day. She was evidently a small galleot, a type much used in Holland to carry large cargoes in shallow waters. Her hull was rather tubby, with the high stern then common. She was probably about seventy feet long. Such a vessel could have two or three masts. In the latter rig two would be square rigged and the third, the mizzen, lateen rigged; this rig is indicated by the spars shown in the old picture of her on the stocks.

THE BATEAU (I)

Jacques de Denonville took office as governor of New France in 1685. Once again the Iroquois were threatening to overwhelm the Indian allies of the French in the West, and now they were in league with English traders who were pushing westward from Albany. In the summer of 1687 Denonville took strong action; he embarked a French army from the head of the St. Lawrence while Tonty, Duluth, and other French leaders brought warriors eastward from the western tribes. Both converged on the Senecas, in what today is upstate New York.

To carry his army across Lake Ontario, Denonville used 142 canoes and 198 transports; the two largest transports were built at Cataraqui, near the foot of Lake Ontario, but most of the smaller ones were brought laboriously up the rapids of the St. Lawrence to join the expedition. They were the type of boat that came to be called a bateau. (*Bateau* in French, of course, simply means boat, but in colonial North America it early came to mean a boat of a particular kind.)

As the flotilla of over three hundred small craft, many of them under sail, moved across the lake a gentle summer wind rippled the surface which reflected a bright blue sky. Some two thousand men rode in the craft. Ahead of the main body sailed the two transports that were larger than the rest; each mounted a small cannon and carried a crew of fifteen.

When the flotilla reached a point near the present-day city of Rochester, N. Y., the craft followed the difficult waterways inland to reach the Seneca country. The expedition burned villages and disgraced the Senecas in the eyes of the western tribes, but it scarcely pacified them; soon they counterattacked the French posts violently. It also disturbed the British colonial governor of New York, Colonel Thomas Dongan, and when the Frenchmen returned to their base at Cataraqui they found waiting for them an emissary from Dongan bearing a strong protest. The troops returning to Quebec shot the St. Lawrence rapids in their bateaux, apparently the first time this was done in anything but a canoe.

The kind of boat known as a bateau was used by the French on the Great Lakes at least as early as 1687. It was used thenceforth by the French, British, Americans, and Canadians from Lake Champlain to Lake Superior, and it survives today in lumber camps from Quebec to Minnesota. It is a form of boat closely related to the dory of the North Atlantic, its bottom flat or nearly so with longitudinal planking, its sides curved, and both ends pointed. The history of the bateau has been traced to medieval European craft. Probably the French brought the type directly to the colonies, but the British colonists seem to have inherited it from the Dutch. French and English colonial types were somewhat different: evidently the French craft were more heavily built while the English ones were somewhat larger; but in time the national differences disappeared and the French name was applied to all similar craft.

OSWEGO AND LA MARQUISE DE VAUDREUIL

Under Iroquois pressure the French abandoned Lake Ontario in 1688, burning or sinking the few vessels they had maintained there. Then as they later pushed the Iroquois back again they reoccupied Fort Frontenac in 1694, raised one of the vessels, and apparently built several more. It was not until the Seven Years War began to loom, however, and it was evident that the British might try to seize the Great Lakes, that the French began serious efforts to establish a naval force on Lake Ontario. War between France and England did not become official until May of 1756, but in 1755 the French, under the direction of Montcalm, built two new vessels, thus bringing the total then in commission on the lake to four. One of the new ones was the topsail schooner *La Marquise de Vaudreuil*, carrying a complement of eighty men and measuring 120 tons gross.

Meanwhile during the winter of 1754-55 William Shirley, governor of Massachusetts and acting commander-in-chief of British forces in North America, established a dockyard in the remote wilderness at Oswego, on Lake Ontario. There, despite hostile Indian raids, a quantity of timber was cut dur-

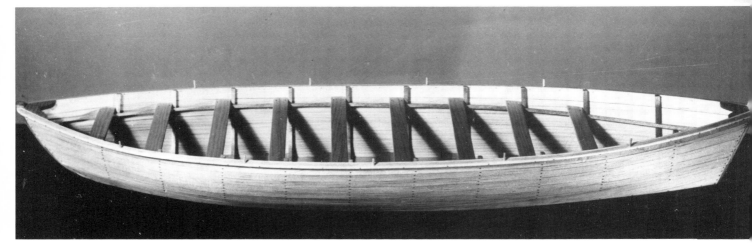

Top: Model of a colonial bateau. (—*National Archives of Canada.*)

Middle and Below: Reconstruction of a colonial bateau, built by Ian Morgan at the Marine Museum of the Upper Lakes. Morgan, a lecturer in industrial technology at the Ontario College of Art, used colonial tools such as broadax and adze, and followed an old British Admiralty plan. Views of the reconstructed bateau show the interior of the boat and its flat bottom. (—Both. *Ontario Historical Sites Branch*)

The *Oswego*, first British vessel on the Great Lakes. She was launched as a schooner but was soon converted to the sloop rig shown. A sister vessel launched slightly later, the *Ontario*, was rigged as a sloop from the beginning. (—*Canada Steamship Lines Collection of Canadiana*)

ing the winter and, as soon as weather permitted, work was begun on three vessels. In summer they were launched. The first was the *Oswego*, which in this way became the first British vessel on the Lakes; at the time of her launching she was rigged as a schooner. On August 24 came her sister vessel, the *Ontario,* rigged as a sloop. Then a second, smaller, schooner followed. The *Oswego* and *Ontario* each were about forty-three feet

in length over all and of about one hundred gross tons. In the common practice of the day they were painted in black and yellow bands. Each carried ten small cannon. The sloop rig of the *Ontario* quickly proved so much better than the schooner rig of the *Oswego* that before the end of the summer the latter vessel was rerigged as a sloop. Thereafter the two were identical in appearance.

The first naval encounter of the Lakes—it can scarcely be called a battle—took place in June 1756 on Lake Ontario. Captain Broadley of the *Oswego* was commodore of the tiny British squadron of three vessels (more were building at Oswego but had not yet been launched) which had been on patrol for several days. Broadley gave the story in his report:

> June the 27th being about Twenty two Leagues WNW from Oswego, the Ontario and one of the Small Schooners in Company, the wind westerly, we Stearing [*sic*] SE, at 2 past 3 in the Morning saw two Sail in the SW Quarter, upon which I wore and stood towards them, they at the same time coming down large upon us, at 4 Saw two more sail likewise bearing down, at 2 past 4 the two headmost being about two thirds of a Mile upon my weather bow, hall'd [*sic*] their Wind Tack'd, clew'd their Main Tops'ls up and laid them aback, one of them Hoisted a white Flag at his Fore Topmast head & fir'd two guns, the other two still coming down to them, at this time we plainly discover'd one of them to have Seven guns of a side, the other appeared to be about the same Size, we saw plainly she had Eight guns mounted with Ports for more but could not distinguish if there was [*sic*] guns mounted in them, they both appeared to be quite new. . . .

French fleet on Lake Ontario, 1757. The schooner *La Marquise de Vaudreuil* is at the left of the picture. (—*Metropolitan Toronto Library Board*)

The larger French vessel was undoubtedly *La Marquise de Vaudreuil.*

Captain Broadley signaled Captain Laforey of the *Ontario* to come aboard for a conference. After a brief consultation they decided that the British force was both outgunned and outmanned, facing two larger and more strongly crewed armed French vessels and with two others approaching. There seemed only one thing to do. The Britons turned and headed back toward Oswego with all possible sail, while the Frenchmen gave chase.

It soon became evident that the British sloops were fast enough to stay ahead, but the small schooner began to lag. Captain Broadley signalled her master to turn away more to the southwest, hoping that the Frenchmen would continue southeastward after the more desirable prizes, the sloops, and the schooner could escape. The French continued to chase the sloops, firing occasionally at such long range that the shots went wild. But the British schooner was still having trouble getting out of the way, and so she turned northwestward, her captain apparently thinking that she could move more quickly on that course. The second two French vessels observed the move and turned to follow her.

At about the same time it became obvious that the sloops were going to escape. The leading French ship trimmed her sails, wore round, and discharged her entire broadside at the *Ontario.* Not a shot struck the target. The two big French schooners then turned and sailed away to the northeast. The two British sloops went home; the one British schooner was in time overtaken and captured. Thus ended the first naval action on the Great Lakes.

OUTAOUAISE

As the Seven Years War progressed, events on the Great Lakes favored one side, then the other. The French took Oswego in August 1756 and with it six or seven British vessels of assorted sizes; the British for a time were swept from the Lakes. Then in 1758 Colonel Bradstreet came up the Mohawk with a brigade of whaleboats and bateaux manned by some three thousand New England sailors and provincial soldiers. They destroyed Fort Frontenac

and seized nine French ships, destroying all but two. In 1759 a British force under General Pridaux laid siege to Fort Niagara, at the mouth of the Niagara River. Upon the death of Pridaux, Sir William Johnson, the great Irish-born leader of the Iroquois five nations, continued the siege and took the fort. Also in 1759 New France launched two vessels on the upper St. Lawrence near present-day Maitland, Ontario. During the winter of 1759-60 the British constructed two slightly larger vessels at Niagara. There were then two French vessels and two British vessels in commission on the lake, a third vessel nearing completion on each side, and a variety of small craft.

On Isle Royale (now Chimney Island, near Ogdensburg. N. Y.) in the St. Lawrence, about one hundred miles above Montreal, the French built a defensive position intended to keep the British from passing down the river. This was Fort Lévis. Four miles upstream, at a place called La Presentation, the French ships were stationed to intercept any British forces moving from Lake Ontario toward the fort. Meanwhile General Amherst, commanding all British forces in North America, was assembling 10,000 soldiers and 822 boats which were to move from Oswego down to Montreal. The two French ships cruised off Oswego and observed the preparations there. On one occasion the British tried to cut them off so they could not return to the river, but the wind failed and after a long and frustrating chase, in which all four vessels were towed by their boats under oars, a fog came down and the Frenchmen disappeared.

In mid-August of 1760 the British force in its vast fleet of boats started down the St. Lawrence. As it progressed, the two navies blundered about among the islands. The British ships got into a dead-end channel and had to be painfully warped up against the current to get them out, while the French ran one of their vessels onto a sand bar and damaged her so badly that she was useless. This left the 10-gun *Outaouaise* on the French side against the 18-gun *Onondaga* and the 16-gun *Mohawk* on the British side.

The *Outaouaise* was a brig, a vessel with two square-rigged masts. In addition to her main battery of 12-pounders she probably carried a few smaller cannon. She was perhaps sixty feet long.

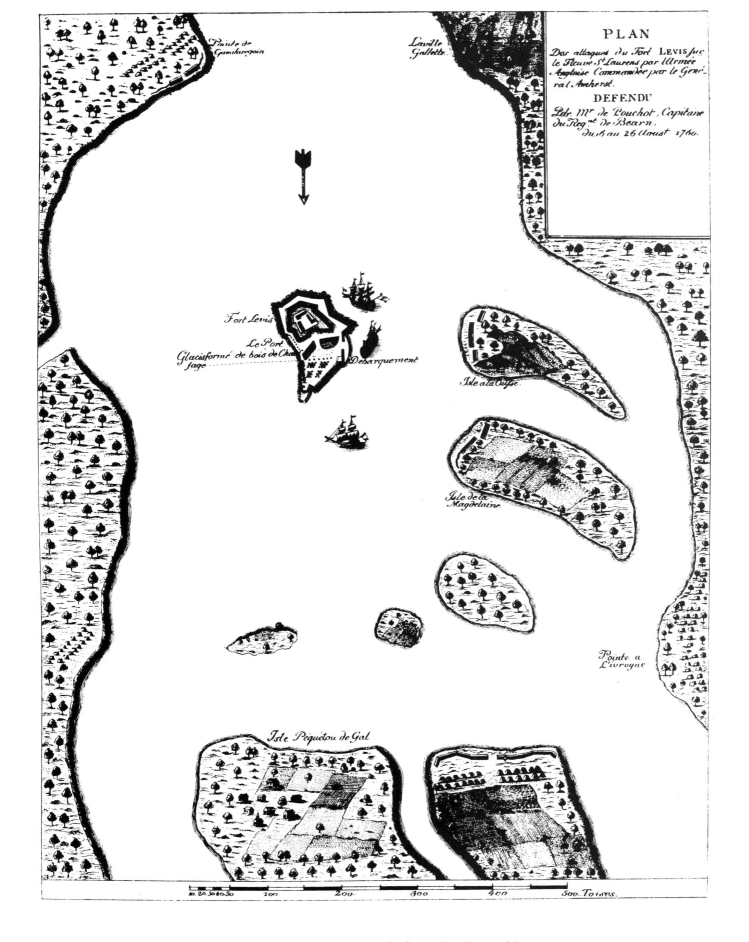

Plan of the St. Lawrence River around Fort Lévis. (*—Ohio Historical Society*)

The French brig *Outaouaise* being attacked by British gunboats on the St. Lawrence. (—*National Gallery of Canada 6271*)

Shortly after dawn on August 17, the *Outaouaise* moved away from La Presentation, heading upstream toward the oncoming swarm of closely packed unarmed boats; among them her cannon should do tremendous damage. Captain Labrocquerie tacked slowly up against the current. But while his vessel was moving sluggishly upstream in the narrow waters, she encountered five small British gunboats under Colonel Williamson of the Royal Artillery. These little boats, each of which mounted a single cannon, were propelled by oars and so could maneuver easily on the river. The oarsmen were colonial soldiers, the cannoneers were artillerymen. In the battle that followed, the *Outaouaise* was a lioness beset by hornets. She fired broadside after broadside at her vicious little opponents but had difficulty in hitting any of them. Despite her thunder she killed only one Briton and injured another. The gunboats, directed by Williamson moving among them in a small boat, exposed but unharmed, had a large, slow-moving target that was hard to miss. They killed three, wounded twelve, and did considerable damage aboard the French ship until, after two hours, she struck her colors.

General Amherst decided to lay siege to Fort Lévis. On several of the nearby islands and on the mainland he emplaced cannon aimed at it. He now had three naval vessels—the *Onondaga*, the *Mohawk*, and the old *Outaouaise* patched up and renamed *Williamson*—and he planned to have them move in close to the fort and by fire drive the Frenchmen from their batteries. Then the bateaux carrying British grenadiers and light infantry would make an assault landing and capture the fort.

On the 23rd at 7:00 in the morning the British opened fire. At 11:00, after a prolonged cannonade, Amherst ordered his vessels to close in on the fort. Either his captains did not clearly understand or the difficulties of river navigation were too much for them; in either event, they did not follow his plan. Instead of coming down on the fort all together they moved one at a time, and far from driving the Frenchmen from their guns, the vessels themselves came under a violent fire as the garrison concentrated every weapon on each one in turn.

First came the *Mohawk*. She anchored off the fort and opened fire. Her decks and rigging were crowded with sharpshooters, but the Frenchmen could look down on her from the walls of their fort and they produced such a fire that her captain, to avoid having her sunk, cut her anchor cable. She was carried out of range by the current.

Next came the *Williamson*, which was caught up by the current and carried briskly past the fort at seven or eight knots with only a passing exchange of shots, running aground a mile or so downriver.

Finally the *Onondaga*, the flagship, ran down on the fort, anchored within pistol shot, and blasted away. The garrison returned shot for shot. After some three hours of constant fire and counterfire the ship's ammunition was expended, eight of her guns were dismounted, and she was terribly battered. Captain Loring got his anchor up and attempted to set a few sails, but the strong current swept the vessel in to shore and there she stuck, a little way downstream, where the guns of the fort continued to smash at her.

Loring ordered his men into the hold, where they remained for two hours while the French cannon battered holes in the side of the vessel and wounded the men inside. Finally they mutinied. Some of them rushed on deck and pulled down her flag; others poured out onto shore, and several climbed into one of her boats. The captain seized a musket and ordered them back on board. Most obeyed, but a lieutenant of marines and two men remained in the boat. The French held their fire while all this was going on, but then as two boats loaded with British grenadiers started toward the *Onondaga* they began to shoot again. Meanwhile the British guns on shore began to fire at the boat carrying the mutineers as they pulled toward the fort; one man was shot.

When the French again opened fire on the stranded vessel, a cannon ball struck Captain Loring in the leg and disabled him. The two boatloads of reinforcements—forty grenadiers and twenty-six light infantrymen—braved the fire, reached the ship, and came aboard to run the flag up again and then tumble into the hold, where they might gain some protection against the furious concentration of French shot. After dark the British wounded were taken off by boat and at two o'clock the next morning the remainder of her original crew was taken off. The soldiers remained on her during the rest of the battle, but they made no move against the fort and it used no more valuable ammunition to fire at them.

These were the last victories for New France—anywhere. The British poured a constant fire from their land batteries upon the wooden fort, gradually splintering and destroying it. At 8:00 p.m. on August 25 the French garrison surrendered. The British were surprised to discover that the defenders numbered only about three hundred.

Amherst's force continued on down the St. Lawrence, which did them more damage than had the French. Sixty-four of the boats were swamped or stove in during the passage of the rapids and eighty-eight men drowned. The British army proceeded to Montreal, there to join other British armies arriving from Quebec and Lake Champlain. In the meantime the last French defenses were crumbling; militia were deserting and Indian allies deciding to be neutral. On September 8, 1760, Canada surrendered to the British.

MICHEGON AND *HURON*

The British conquered New France, but the far-flung Indian nations remained uncertain of the outcome. They were encouraged in their attitude by some of the Frenchmen who still travelled among them, and they were confirmed in it by the blundering British administrators. The whole Indian problem boiled over in the spring of 1763, in what became known as Pontiac's War, when the enraged tribesmen descended on the British posts and massacred the defenders of all except Fort Pitt, Niagara, and Detroit, which they placed under siege.

By 1762 the British had two vessels on Lake Erie. One, the *Michegon*, was an old sloop "sufficient for two years" which evidently had been inherited from the French. The other, the *Huron*, was a schooner "new & well found with all sorts of stores." The sloop was larger than the schooner; she was able to carry the basic armament of ten 6-pounder cannon while the schooner could carry four 4-pounders. (In actuality, however, the sloop was armed only with six 6-pounders and eight swivels, while the schooner was fully armed with the four 4-pounders and six swivels.)

These vessels carried men and supplies from the head of the Niagara portage to Presque Isle, Sandusky, and Detroit. After Pontiac's warriors had eliminated Presque Isle and Sandusky, the two little ships concentrated on getting to Detroit through the Indian blockade.

In May 1763 the *Huron*, under command of Nicolas Newman, left Detroit en route to Niagara, under orders to wait at the mouth of the Detroit River for two weeks in hopes of meeting and assisting an expedition under Lieutenant Cuyler that was coming along the northern shore in small boats. (But the Indians in fact attacked that expedition at a midway point and destroyed it.) Encountering a head wind part way down the river, Newman anchored; about an hour later he saw six canoes approaching and he weighed anchor and set sail, moving away. The breeze was so light, however, that the canoes were able to approach quickly and when they were within musket range the Indians in them began to shoot at the schooner. Newman fired his two stern swivels, "but the stocks breaking they were immediately dismounted." He had several of his men fire at the canoes with small arms and put others to work cutting gun ports in the stern and shifting other cannon to fire through them. When the Indians saw what was being done they quickly paddled away.

Newman anchored his schooner overnight, then dropped on down the river next morning, coming to anchor again at the river mouth where he intended to wait for Cuyler's expedition. Soon afterward he saw nine canoes which also came down the river and then drew abreast of him at a distance of over a mile. In the late afternoon one of the canoes approached; in it he could see through his spyglass someone in the regimental uniform of the Royal Americans, as well as the Indian paddlers. The uniformed man hailed him by name and said that he was Captain Campbell of the Detroit garrison, "who to save his life was obliged to demand the vessel and if he would give her up to the Indians, they would spare his life and all their lives; but that he knew his orders best." Newman refused and Campbell (who had been captured by the Indians at the beginning of the siege) advised him to move farther offshore, because there were forty canoes full of warriors near by. As soon as darkness fell, Newman moved the schooner some distance out into open water, but next morning stood inshore again to wait for Cuyler. When fourteen days had passed without a sign

of him, Newman sailed on down the lake to the Niagara River.

Later that season, Newman was transferred to command of the *Michegon* and a Mr. Hossey became master of the *Huron*. On August 28 Newman's sloop was caught in a storm off Point Abino on the north shore. According to one officer aboard, Lieutenant Montresor, the wind

> blew with such violence that obliged us . . . to come to an anchor under the windward shore, in which position she almost pitched under, which occasioned the Capt. to put again to sea. She sprung a leak, we kept two pumps going, at last labouring in such Tempestuous Sea, she started a plank abaft, & filled & drove up hatches & became water logg'd, we expected every moment either to go down or oversit. . . .

In an attempt to save her they threw overboard cargo and cannon:

> this done together with pumping and bailing & putting almost right before it, we struck within 155 yards of the shore. Her mast and rudder is [*sic*] carried away her decks are open & tis imagined her back is broke. . .

Newman sent his mate off to the commanding officer at Niagara to report the disaster; then while he did his best to salvage what he could of the sloop and her equipment, Montresor built an earthwork at a commanding point on the shore to protect the operation. On September 2d a force of some eighty men under Capt. Gavin Cochrane arrived from Niagara to help out. It was lucky that they arrived when they did; next morning a band of Indians attacked, killing three of the defenders, but were driven off. On the 14th another detachment of soldiers arrived from Niagara, bringing with them a number of boats to help in the salvage work, but for the next several days the wind blew so hard that the boats could not be used and considerably more damage was done to what remained of the sloop.

The schooner *Huron* arrived on the 15th, and the people on her reported that her master, Mr. Hossey, had been killed on the Detroit River when the vessel was attacked by Indians on her way upstream. Mr. Newman was promptly put in command of her again, and soon she set off once more for Detroit. Whatever discouragements a shipmaster may have faced on Lake Erie at that time, boredom was not among them.

ONONDAGA

Late in the 1760s the naval vessels and establishments of the Great Lakes, Lake Champlain, and parts of the St. Lawrence were pulled together into what was then called the Provincial Marine. The officers and men were drawn from the Royal Navy, plus those provincials who met the requirements for service. Among the latter were a number of French Canadians, of whom the most distinguished was René La Force, the last French senior naval officer on Lake Ontario, who was appointed to the same post by the British from 1780 to 1786.

The Provincial Marine was a transport and patrol service. At first it had a monopoly on Great Lakes shipping; no privately owned merchant vessels were permitted until 1785. During its heyday there was no fighting on the Lakes. True, the force was strengthened at the time of the American Revolution, but events of the Revolutionary War avoided the Lakes and the vessels never saw battle. Simply by being on the Great Lakes the Provincial Marine held them for the British.

One result of the Revolution was a sizable number of British sympathizers—Tories to the Americans, Loyalists to the British—who left or were expelled from their homes in the rebellious colonies and settled on the British lands around Lake Ontario, concentrating on Niagara and Kingston. The majority of these refugees seem to have come from the state of New York. The bulk of the migration took place about 1780, and many of the settlers sailed to their new holdings in vessels of the Provincial Marine.

His Majesty's armed schooner *Onondaga*, second British vessel of that name on Lake Ontario, was flagship of the Provincial Marine from the time of her launching near Kingston in 1790 until she was retired at the end of navigation in 1797. She measured sixty-nine feet on deck and some one hundred tons, and was rigged as a topsail schooner, with two

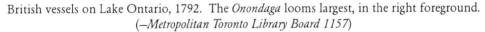

British vessels on Lake Ontario, 1792. The *Onondaga* looms largest, in the right foreground.
(*—Metropolitan Toronto Library Board 1157*)

square sails on each mast above her fore-and-aft sails. Her normal complement was twenty officers and seamen. The schooner was pierced for six guns on each side, but she actually carried only six altogether.

The English-speaking settlers north of the Great Lakes—most of them refugees from the new United States—were soon given their own province, Upper Canada. The first lieutenant governor of the province, Col. John Graves Simcoe, arrived to take office in July 1792. (His title is perhaps misleading; his duties were those of governor.) There were no roads worth mentioning; water transport was the only kind available. The *Onondaga* took Simcoe and his family from Kingston to Niagara, where he established his headquarters at the town of Newark (today's Niagara-on-the-Lake). Soon afterward he summoned his executive council and parliament for their first meetings, and many of the members travelled to it on board the schooner. Thereafter she frequently carried Simcoe on voyages about Lake Ontario. The following summer, when he established the town of York at present-day Toronto, several vessels of the Provincial Marine, including the *Onondaga*, took men and equipment there.

From time to time the schooner carried distinguished passengers, but most of her career was devoted to plodding between Kingston, Newark, and Toronto with occasional military detachments and such commodities as rum and wine, lumber, or salt and flour.

The last voyage of the *Onondaga* was her most eventful. Under command of Lt. P. M. Fortier she sailed from York on November 11, 1797, bound for Kingston. The wind was light and variable; the sky was dark and cloudy. As the day progressed the wind increased. By 11:00 that night there was a high sea running and some of her rigging was beginning to give way. At midnight the wind quickly and without warning changed to the west-northwest, blowing at hurricane strength. Fortier hove to under a double-reefed foresail. On the Lakes, however, vessels are almost always on a lee shore, and heaving-to is not as safe a procedure as it can be on the high seas. Fortier realized that his schooner was drifting eastward at considerable speed through the dark,

stormy night; he constantly took soundings, hoping against hope that he would not be able to reach bottom.

Suddenly his leadsman found bottom at twelve fathoms. At the same time the weather cleared enough that he could see land close on the lee side. Quickly he dropped anchor to avoid being driven on the shore. He paid out all of his anchor cable, finally making the end of it fast to the mainmast. There the *Onondaga* remained the rest of that night, driving her bowsprit under each wave and constantly threatening to break apart. At daylight Fortier scanned the shore and discovered a cove not far away. He cut her cable and, with the exercise of some clever seamanship, ran her into the little haven, thirty miles northeast of Oswego.

The *Onondaga* limped back to Kingston several days later. Capt. Jean-Baptiste Bouchette, then senior officer commanding Lake Ontario, reported that it would cost more to repair her than to build a new ship, so she was condemned. She had lasted eight years, which was about average for a vessel built of green wood, sailing on fresh water.

NANCY

Although the Treaty of Paris at the close of the American Revolution ceded the southern shores of the Great Lakes to the United States, Britain still held those shores firmly and permitted only British government vessels to sail the Lakes. British traders soon found these limited shipping facilities intolerable. The merchants at British Detroit, in particular, fumed because their goods were not coming through to them. In 1784 there was such congestion on the docks at Kingston and Niagara that half the goods destined that year for Detroit had to be held over to 1785, and the Detroiters suffered great losses.

The merchants protested bitterly to the governor general, who in turn forwarded the protest to higher authority. As a result he was granted permission to license building of private ships, though under stringent regulations, among them a requirement that naval personnel were to man them. The North West Company, the great Montreal trading combine, was among the first to respond; it sent men to the

The *Nancy*, one of the first privately owned vessels trading on the Great Lakes. Painting by George A. Cuthbertson. (—*Canada Steamship Lines Collection of Canadiana*)

head of the Sault Ste. Marie in 1785 and built a seventy-five-ton sloop, the *Otter*, on Lake Superior. In 1786 the same company launched a small sloop, the *Industry,* at Detroit. A few other vessels were also built under these provisions.

In April of 1788 the limitations were further relaxed and British merchant shipping in the normal sense was at last permitted. The first true commercial vessel appears to have been the tiny 15-ton sloop *Good Intent*, of Kingston, launched in 1788.

A Montreal firm of merchants and fur traders, Forsyth, Richardson & Co., decided to build a schooner at Detroit for use on Lakes Erie, Huron, and Michigan. To supervise her construction one of the partners, John Richardson, set out in May 1789 on the arduous journey west, with six workmen and a master carpenter. Richardson, a former New York Loyalist, had served as supercargo on the British privateer *Vengeance* during the Revolutionary War and was familiar with salt-water shipping; he was determined that the new schooner was to be "a perfect masterpiece of workmanship and beauty."

The master carpenter set to work building her to her owner's satisfaction, of oak and red cedar. Richardson sent off to New York, to the noted carver

Skelling, for her figurehead, "a lady dressed in the present fashion, and with a hat and feather." He knew that the vessel would be expensive to build, but she also would be durable—something that vessels like the *Onondaga* were not. (As it turned out, she lasted twenty-five years and still was serving well when she was destroyed on Georgian Bay by United States forces during the War of 1812.)

Richardson's schooner was christened *Nancy* and slid down the ways on November 24, 1789. She measured about 100 tons, was designed to carry 350 barrels, and mounted two 3-pounder cannon; even a merchantman carried some armament in those days. Next summer, when Richardson made another trip from Montreal to the Great Lakes he found that the *Nancy* was a great success: "She is spoken of here in such a high strain of encomium as to beauty, stowage, and sailing, that she almost exceeds my expectations."

The *Nancy* is remarkable in one other way. When she was destroyed in 1814 she was lying in the Nottawasaga River, at the southern end of Georgian Bay. She burned to the water line; then an island formed slowly around the remains of her hull. In 1928 those remains were dug from the island and now repose in a museum on it, where they may be seen today.

DETROIT

On May 19, 1793, a modest vessel was launched on the River Rouge, below Detroit. She was an eighty-ton sloop built for the Detroit firm of Meldrum and Park. There were a great many larger vessels sailing out of the port, the *Nancy* among them, and the small single-master though new was hardly impressive enough to justify naming her after that important place. Yet *Detroit* she was christened, and it turned out to be a suitable name. Just as the city was to become the first major port on the Lakes to fly the United States flag, so the sloop was to be the first vessel on the upper Lakes—and probably on any of the Great Lakes—to fly that flag.

At the time of her launching there lay between the Ohio River and the Great Lakes an area that belonged by treaty to the new United States but was controlled more by the British than by the Americans. The British maintained their garrison at Detroit and established another at Fort Miamis on Lake Erie, near present-day Toledo, Ohio. They intended to keep the area an Indian country, as a buffer zone and a source of pelts for the fur trade, and they encouraged the Indians in every way to resist incursions by the United States. The tribesmen, who saw what would happen to their lands if the flow of settlers reached them, needed little encouragement.

In the spring of 1795 a U.S. army under the Revolutionary War hero Anthony Wayne took the field in Ohio and moved steadily northward. On August 19 it approached Fort Miamis. There it was charged by a group of mounted Indians who drove back the militia cavalry that preceded it. Wayne's force threw off the attackers and buckled down to the real business at hand—dislodging a body of Indians and a few Canadian militiamen positioned in a tangled mass of fallen trees that had been uprooted in one of the violent windstorms that still sweep that corner of Lake Erie.

It was plain after General Wayne's victory at the Battle of Fallen Timbers that the United States had an effective military force and that Wayne could move on to Detroit if he wished. In London, Chief Justice John Jay had been trying to negotiate a settlement with the British, but until then had had a notable lack of success. After news of the battle reached London, Jay suddenly found British statesmen more interested in talking. The British already were beset with other problems and did not want to start a war in North America that could well end in the total loss of Canada. Soon they agreed to evacuate the western posts south of the Lakes and they accepted essentially the present boundary between Canada and the United States as far west as Lake of the Woods.

Capt. Henry DeButts, Aide-de-Camp to General Wayne, sailed from Fort Erie to Detroit in June 1796, on the same vessel that carried orders to the British commanders at Detroit and Mackinac that they were to turn over their posts to United States forces. Most of the British troops were to go immediately to Quebec; a few small detachments were to maintain order until the U.S. forces arrived. On

July 1 DeButts wrote to Wayne that he was procuring three vessels at Detroit and would send them to Fort Miamis. He hired two schooners and bought one sloop, the *Detroit.*

Colonel Hamtramck, commander of the first U.S. troops to move from Fort Miamis to the city of Detroit, used the sloop as his flagship. Then he dispatched the *Detroit* to Presque Isle (Erie) in Pennsylvania, to bring back a cargo of flour and whisky.

On August 7 Wayne officially received Fort Miamis from the British. On the 10th he sailed for Detroit in another vessel, arriving on the 13th. There he was welcomed by the Indian tribes and the remaining British and French population. On the 19th of August, Wayne sent off on the *Detroit* the U.S. garrison that would man the fort at Mackinac. He then proceeded with the business of turning over the administration of the newly acquired area to the civil authorities of the Northwest Territory, and toward the middle of November was ready to return to Pittsburgh, where he proposed to make his headquarters for the winter.

General Wayne boarded the *Detroit* on the 13th, bound for Presque Isle; from there he was to go overland to Pittsburgh. The sloop arrived at her destination on the 18th. Wayne was tired from the trip and planned to rest for a few days before continuing. At Presque Isle he was stricken with an agonizing pain that lasted for two weeks; contemporaries described it as "the Gout in his stomach." On December 15 he died.

The sloop *Detroit* remained in service until 1800, when she was reported to be rotten and unfit for service. That year the new U.S. brig *President Adams* was launched in the shipyard on the River Rouge; Capt. Peter Curry, who had commanded the *Detroit,* was master of the brig on her first voyage.

THE FUR-TRADE CANOE (I)

Montreal fur traders kept their grasp as long as possible on the country south of Lakes Erie and Huron, but they also pressed farther and farther westward. The quickest route to the West still followed the Ottawa River to Lake Nipissing and Georgian Bay, just as it had in the days of Étienne Brûlé; then

Voyageurs working a fur canoe up a rapid. The artist, W. H. Bartlett, observed a *canôt du maitre* on one of the Ottawa River rapids and was so impressed that he drew a picture in which until recently the very spot could be recognized. It was Portage Dufort, now inundated by a hydroelectric project.

Bartlett caught the general feeling admirably, but was not as successful in showing accurately the shapes of the ends of the canoe and of the men's hats. Below, a portage and a voyageur's grave appeared in a Bartlett engraving. (*—National Archives of Canada, top C 2390; bottom C 2336*)

ran along the North Channel, across the Sault Ste. Marie, and coasted the northern shore of Lake Superior to Grand Portage. Thence it went on to the Far North and West over the network of waterways that led all the way to the Arctic and Pacific Oceans. The only craft that could follow this route was the canoe.

After the conquest of Canada by the British the trade continued much as it had before. The canoes still were manned by French Canadian voyageurs and the canoe routes still rang with French songs or curses, as the occasion demanded. Over the years the Montreal traders gradually gathered together into a few combines, the largest of which was the North West Company. The small brigades of three or four canoes that companies had sent out in the earlier years were gradually replaced by larger brigades of canoes that all belonged to one firm, and the small canoes used by most of the Indians and the early explorers grew gradually into the big *canôts du maître*, some 35 feet long, that traveled between Montreal and the head of Lake Superior, or the smaller 25-foot *canôts du nord*, used from that point to the North and West. These craft were made of birch bark over a light frame. They were the only things that could navigate the rivers and be carried over the portages; the fur trade could scarcely have existed without them.

By 1800 the Montreal fur trade was nearing its peak. At the end of April that year a squadron of thirty North West Company canoes started westward from Montreal. Each canoe carried three and a half or four tons and was manned by eight or nine brightly dressed voyageurs. The squadron was divided into three brigades, each of ten canoes, and each brigade was commanded by a guide, who had much the same authority as the captain of a ship. He stood in the bow of the first canoe and chose the way.

As the heavily laden fur canoes moved along, they were passed by smaller, lighter canoes that carried dispatches or important people. On the trip up the Ottawa in 1800, for example, one young clerk, Daniel Harmon, noted in his journal, "Roderick McKenzie, Esq., agent for the North West Company, passed us, who with those that accompanied him, is on his way to the Grand Portage."

The brigades struggled up the Ottawa River. At smaller rapids the canoes were poled against the current, using long, steel-shod setting poles. Elsewhere they were drawn up by a tow line from shore or by men standing, perhaps waist deep, in the rushing water. When necessary, half the cargo would be taken out and the canoe paddled vigorously up the rapid to be unloaded and then return for the remainder. Portaging was a last resort. At a portage the voyageurs leaped into the water so that the frail outer shell of the canoe would not touch land, and unloaded the cargo which was made up into ninety-pound bundles. With two of these on his back, each voyageur moved across the portage at a trot. He made three such trips on each portage, carrying a total of about 540 pounds. Canoe brigades always travelled in a rush, so that they could get to their destination and back in the limited time between the spring thaw and the autumn freeze. "We push forward, with all the ardour and rashness of youth," Harmon commented.

At many portages and rapids men drowned, or died of heart attacks or strangulated hernias. Wherever a man died, whether or not his body was recovered, his companions erected a cross. At some of the more difficult rapids there were small forests of these crosses on the near-by shore.

From the Ottawa the brigades moved via smaller streams and portages to Lake Nipissing, across it to French River—at that point the voyageurs threw away the setting poles with a flourish to emphasize that now they would be travelling downhill—down French River to Georgian Bay, and on through the North Channel to Sault Ste. Marie.

At the Sault the North West Company had a small canal, with locks, to transport the laden canoes to Lake Superior. The squadron, that spring of 1800, picked up five more canoes that had preceded it to the Sault and on the first of June set off in four brigades along the shore of Lake Superior, but they soon encountered a heavy storm, with rain and snow, and spent the night of the third and fourth camped on shore. On the fifth, although the waves were high, they moved on again. The night of the 10th they discovered the entire countryside on fire and instead of camping were forced to anchor offshore in the shelter of a small island.

A modern picture shows Grand Portage, the fur-trade post at the western end of Lake Superior, at its height of activity c. 1780. Small sailing vessels were used on Lake Superior, but at this time canoes were much more useful in bringing trade goods from Montreal and carrying back furs. (*—Grand Portage National Monument*)

On the 13th the squadron arrived at Grand Portage, at the head of Lake Superior, near the mouth of the Pigeon River—today just inside the boundary of the State of Minnesota. Here each year the wintering partners who supervised the trade in the fur country met with agents and partners from Montreal who were responsible for the sales in Europe. Here they made every necessary decision from promotions of the personnel to amounts of the dividends. Harmon described the place:

> The Fort, which is twenty four rods by thirty, is built on the margin of a bay, at the foot of a hill or mountain, of considerable height. Within the fort, there is a considerable number of dwelling houses, shops and stores, all of which appear to be slight buildings, and designed only for present convenience. The houses are surrounded by palisades, which are about eighteen inches in diameter, and are sunk nearly three feet in the ground, and rise about fifteen feet above it. . . . There is also another fort, which stands about two hundred rods from this, belonging to the X. Y. Company, under which firm, a number of merchants of Montreal and Quebec, &c. now carry on a trade into this part of the country. . . .
>
> This is the Head Quarters or General Rendezvous, for all who trade in this part of the world; and therefore, every summer, the greater part of the Proprietors and Clerks, who have spent the winter in the Interiour, come here with the furs which they have been able to collect, during the preceding season. . . .

During the scant month in which the men of the East and those of the North and West came together at Grand Portage, there was little rest. Harmon noted:

> The people here pass the sabbath, much in the same manner as they do, the other days of the week. The labouring people have been employed, during the day, in making and pressing packs of fur, to be sent to Canada. . . .

These bales of fur each weighed about ninety pounds, so that they could be carried over the portages on the return trip just as trade goods were carried when the big canoes were outward bound.

Not all was work, however. One evening the clerks and partners dressed for a "famous ball" at which they danced to the music of bagpipe, violin, and flute. Harmon, by now over two months away from Montreal, found the Indian ladies who attended quite attractive. "I was surprised to find that they could conduct with so much propriety, and dance so well."

At Grand Portage Harmon left behind the big *canôts du maître.* Soon he was traveling westward in a *canôt du nord* that carried about two tons of cargo. Over devious waterways he finally reached Fort Alexandria, a trading post west of Lake Winnipeg on the upper reaches of the Assiniboine River. The big canoes turned around at Grand Portage and dashed

Harbor and military post at Sackets Harbor, N.Y., just after the War of 1812, showing the U.S. fleet laid up in the background. At the dock in the right foreground, the center of activity is a large bateau. (*—Library of Congress*)

back over the Great Lakes and the Ottawa to Montreal, carrying the furs.

Because of the boundary provisions of the Jay Treaty, the North West Company in 1803 abandoned Grand Portage and moved its rendezvous north to the mouth of the Kaministiquia River, at what later became Fort William. In 1804 the X. Y. Company followed. This new location forced canoes to follow a more difficult route inland and as a result they carried smaller loads.

THE BATEAU (II)

"'Tis a sad waste of life to ascend the St. Lawrence in a bateau," wrote Lt. Francis Hall. Despite the tedium of the voyage, however, bateaux were the primary means of carrying passengers and cargoes between Montreal and Lake Ontario for nearly two centuries. From the military expedition of Denonville in 1687 until the mid-1800s, well after the development of steamers, bateaux remained the work horses of the St. Lawrence. During the same period their use extended throughout the Great Lakes.

The French Canadian boatmen who manned them on the St. Lawrence were voyageurs, much like those who manned the big canoes of the fur trade. The work was nearly as arduous as that of the canoemen, rowing or poling or pulling their heavy flat-bottomed boats up the rapids, sometimes shoulder deep in the water; and it was nearly as danger-

ous, shooting the bateaux down the rapids again. But in contrast to the long, bleak canoe trip to the West, it took only seven days to go up the river and three to come back down, and as times passed settlements, farms, and inns grew up along the way, providing oases in the wilderness. One traveler reported:

> We slept at a poor village, the name of which I forget. Our boatmen, who had all day been pulling at the oars, like true Canadians, instead of going to bed, got up a dance with the village girls, and the ball was only stopped by the re-embarkation of the party on the following morning. The whole crew were drunk, with the exception of the conductor, but the appearance of the first rapid sobered them in an instant.

A bateau of normal size was about forty feet long and of six foot beam. The boats each carried from three to five tons of cargo. They were made of pine boards and were flat on the bottom and pointed at bow and stern. Each was equipped with a mast and sail, oars, setting poles, the necessary lines, and a grappling iron; and each was manned by four or five men and a master, who was variously styled guide, conductor, or pilot. By the early 1800s there were seventy or eighty bateaux in use and some 350 men regularly occupied in handling them. The men were paid from $8 to $11 each for the round trip up the river and back again; the guides or pilots $12 or $14. They were also given rations of rum or brandy and provisions of salt pork, biscuits, and dried peas.

At times the men might work for twenty-four hours at a stretch; while they were awake they ate every four hours.

Bateaux, like the big canoes of the fur trade, often travelled in brigades of from four to ten boats, so that the crews could help each other where necessary. At the Cedars rapids, for example, the bateaux would be unloaded and eight or ten men, walking on shore and hauling on lines, would pull each boat in turn up to the village of the Cedars, just above the rapids. The same procedure was followed at other bad places. The cargoes would be carried past the rapids by wagon, and passengers usually walked, but they might sometimes ride on the wagons, in carriages, or on horseback.

The boatmen slept on shore. Isaac Weld, who saw them in the 1790s, commented:

> ... when the weather is fair, they sleep on the grass at night, without any other covering than a short blanket, scarcely reaching down to their knees; during wet weather a sail or a blanket to the weather side, spread on poles stuck into the ground in an inclined direction, is all the shelter they deem necessary.

Most passengers felt the need for more comfort. Those who were well-prepared carried tents and bedding. At a few places there were accomodations for travelers. Weld found "a remarkably neat and excellent tavern, kept by an Englishwoman," at the village of the Cedars, and farther up the river, near the boundary between Upper and Lower Canada, "there was one solitary house ... which proved to be a tavern, and afforded us a well-drest supper of venison, and decent accommodation for the night." Not all inns were so pleasant; when Governor and Mrs. Simcoe travelled up the river in 1792 they found Carey's Inn, near the Gananoque River, so dirty that even though the weather was bad they preferred to sleep in a tent.

Travellers were sometimes taken in for the night by settlers along the way, and if no bed was available were permitted to sleep on the floor or on the hay in the barn. By the early 1800s, however, travel on the river had increased rapidly and people living on the shores had so often been plundered or mistreated by strangers that they frequently refused to have anything to do with them and even drove them from their barns.

By the 1880s bateaux were in use in lumbering operations throughout the Great Lakes region. Here is an 1888 "Bateau Crew" on Muskegon River in Michigan during the spring log drive. Although the boat shown is much smaller than those used earlier on the Lakes and the St. Lawrence, it is recognizably of the same type. The responsive qualities that made large bateaux useful in the St. Lawrence rapids made smaller ones useful for working in the often fast-moving tributary rivers. The canvas-covered scows in the background provided sleeping and eating quarters. (—*Great Lakes Historical Society*)

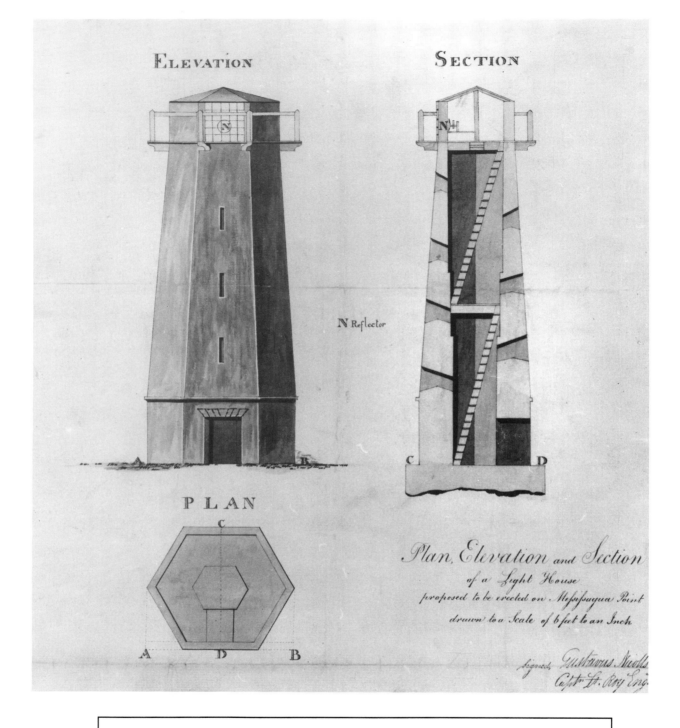

ELEVATION

SECTION

N Reflector

PLAN

Plan, Elevation and Section
of a Light House
proposed to be erected on Mississauga Point
drawn to a Scale of 6 feet to an Inch

signed, Gustavus Nicolls
Captn Lt. Roy Engs

The first lighthouse on the Great Lakes. Mariners on the Lakes had few aids to navigation as the 18th century moved into the 19th. But the legislature of Upper Canada, the most heavily populated area on the Great Lakes at that time, during its session of 1802-03 authorized erection of three lighthouses on Lake Ontario. Arrangements were made to bring from England "one of those reflecting lamps on a small Scale, which are now in general use at Home for similar purposes."

The new lamp arrived in Canada during the summer of 1803, and it and a supply of spermaceti oil for fuel were sent on to Fort George, the nearest government establishment to one of the proposed sites, that at Mississauga Point, at the mouth of the Niagara River.

Work went forward the following spring on a tower of stone, 45 feet high. Colonel Isaac Brock, commander at Fort George, was asked to lend help with the construction and to designate one soldier from the garrison to tend the light. The lightkeeper's dwelling, a log house, was built nearby. Dominic Henry, of the 4th Battalion, Royal Artillery, was appointed keeper. In June 1804 the light—the first one on the Great Lakes—began to function. It operated for the next ten years, all through the War of 1812, with Dominic Henry tending it. (—*National Archives of Canada C 27667*)

The voyageurs needed diverse skills to manage their craft. Weld described some of them:

They ascend the stream by means of poles, oars, and sails. When the current is very strong, they make use of the former, keeping as close as possible to the shore, in order to avoid the current, and to have the advantage of shallow water to pole in. The men set their poles together at the same moment, and all work at the same side of the bateau; the steersman, however, shifts his pole occasionally from side to side, in order to keep the vessel in an even direction. The poles commonly used are about eight feet in length, extremely light, and headed with iron. On coming to a deep bay or inlet, the men abandon the poles, take to their oars, and strike if possible directly across the mouth of the bay; but in many places the current proves so strong that it is absolutely impossible to stem it by means of oars, and they are obliged to pole entirely around the bays. Whenever the wind is favorable they set their sail; but it is only at the upper end of the river, beyond the rapids, or in the lakes or broad parts of it, where the current is not swift, that the sail itself is sufficient to impel them forward.

The trip downstream was quite different. When they were not actually shooting the rapids the men sang and laughed, but in dangerous places they were silent and attentive to business. When Governor and Mrs. Simcoe went down the river in 1796, she described the descent of one of the rapids, the Long Sault, "in an hour without sailing, and seldom rowing, though near particular currents they rowed with great exertion." The boats "appeared to fly" as they rushed through the white water. "The velocity was extreme; sometimes the whirlpool turned them around; at others the head of one and the stern of another appeared buried under the waves."

Cargoes carried down the river were wheat, flour, potash , and peltry. Those taken up were the merchandise in demand in the expanding settlements, and the military and naval supplies that the British needed in the Great Lakes region. The boatmen at times helped themselves to things that they liked. Patrick Campbell, who travelled upriver in 1791, made the error of leaving his own provisions on the boat while he walked along the shore. When he rejoined the bateau he found that "the Canadians had made free with a bag of biscuit Mr. John Fisher merchant in Montreal gave me and a fine roasted Goose a Mr. John M'Arthur had sent with me, so I had to provide myself in provisions as I went along for the future."

NIAGARA

Rivalry between Americans and British along the Great Lakes was a major factor leading to the War of 1812. The United States declared war in June of that year; in August the British once more seized Detroit. On Lake Erie a year-long shipbuilding race between the competing powers ensued.

It culminated in a naval battle between the opposing squadrons on September 10, 1813. By 2:30 p.m. that day the United States flagship, the brig *Lawrence*, under Master Commandant Oliver Hazard Perry (Commodore Perry by courtesy title, for he commanded the whole squadron) was battered beyond endurance. Her sails were in shreds, her rigging was frazzled and burning, and her cannon were silent as the opposing British ships concentrated their fire on her.

British shot smashed through the shallow hull, even killing wounded men being treated in the cockpit below decks. Her sister, the U.S. Brig *Niagara*, hung back out of battle. The commander of the *Niagara*, Lt. Jessie Elliot, had been senior on Lake Erie before Perry's arrival there; now he stood aside and watched as the enemy pummeled the flagship. It was evident that the *Lawrence* soon must strike her flag. Suddenly Elliot brought the *Niagara* freshly up into close action; now perhaps he could win the day and be its hero.

The 28-year-old Perry, who had been sick and was still recovering from a bout of fever, saw the *Niagara* come up. Quickly he ordered a boat put over the side. Manned by four seamen, it was just pushing off to carry him to the other ship when a soldier aboard dropped Perry's battle flag into his arms; this was the banner he had had made bearing the dying words of Perry's friend, Captain John Lawrence, for whom the flagship was named: "Don't give up the ship." The small boat pulled quickly across the open water amidst British fire. It reached the *Niagara* safely; Perry climbed aboard. Elliot quickly volunteered to go and bring up some of the smaller American vessels that were lagging behind and Perry curtly told him to do that.

The U.S. Brig *Niagara*, as she breaks through the British line during the Battle of Lake Erie. This mural was painted by Charles R. Patterson and Howard B. French for the United States Naval Academy. (*–U.S. Naval Academy Museum*)

Perry quickly ordered all sail made on the *Niagara*. He headed her directly for the British line. She broke through, firing both broadsides and raking the length of three British ships on each side. Then the *Niagara* luffed, spilling the wind from her sails, and remained in position; the small U.S. vessels, brought up by Elliot, added their fire. The British squadron, which a short time before had been in sight of victory, capitulated. The commander and second-in-command of every British ship had either been killed or wounded. Perry and the *Niagara* had won the day for the United States. Perry dispatched his famous message to General William Henry Harrison:

> U.S. Brig Niagara, off Western Sister,
> head of Lake Erie
> Sept 10, 1813, 4 p.m.
> Dear General
> We have met the enemy and they are ours. Two ships, two brigs, one schooner and one sloop.
> Yours, with great respect and esteem.
> O.H. Perry

This battle gave the United States control of Lake Erie. Soon after it, General Harrison with an army of 4,500 men crossed Lake Erie in Perry's vessels and a fleet of bateaux, pursued the retreating British land forces, and won a decisive land victory—one of the few for the Americans during the War of 1812—at the Battle of the Thames. Thereafter the United States held the strategic western end of Upper Canada, preventing British attack on Ohio or Michigan.

The *Niagara*, the *Lawrence*, and several of the smaller U.S. vessels had been built at Presque Isle in Pennsylvania during the preceding year. The two large brigs were sister ships, duplicates as nearly as possible in an age before mass production. Each was about 110 feet long, of 260 tons, and mounted two long 12-pounder guns and eighteen 32-pound carronades.

PRINCE REGENT

On Lake Ontario, which was considerably nearer the seats of power than Erie and the Lakes to the west, both Great Britain and the United States during the War of 1812 constructed powerful fleets. The warfare there was less dramatic and less decisive than that on Lake Erie, but the vessels involved were more impressive. Ontario was a basic link in the British chain of communications, and both sides realized its importance.

H.M.S. *Prince Regent*, a two-decked frigate, was launched by the British at Kingston on April 14, 1814. She was 155 feet long on deck, about 42 feet in beam, and carried sixty guns. This was considerable heavier armament than was normal for a salt-water vessel of the same size; war vessels on the Lakes did not have to carry fresh water or provisions for long voyages and so could mount more guns. The hulls of these British Lake ships were also slimmer, with less displacement than ocean-going vessels, thus making them faster and more able to beat to windward, qualities needed on the narrow waters of Lake Ontario.

That spring the British launched an attack against Oswego, where the Americans had a considerable store of supplies. On the 4th of May seven British vessels and eleven gunboats, all under Sir James Yeo, set sail from Kingston, carrying a land force of nearly a thousand troops. The *Prince Regent* was Yeo's flagship. Winds were light and variable; the squadron did not come in sight of Oswego until late next morning. The garrison there had had warning and the old fort on the right bank of the river was manned by nearly four hundred men. Four guns had been mounted on the walls to command the harbor entrance and there was another at the water's edge. The U.S. schooner *Growler*, of three guns, lay in the harbor with three merchant schooners and a number of small craft.

At 3:00 that afternoon the British squadron lay to and the gunboats, under oars, went in close to shore to draw American fire and in this way determine the location and number of guns in the defenses. They located the guns on the walls of the fort and noted the absence of any on the other side of the river, where the town and wharves were located. The gunboats withdrew about 5:30.

In the early evening the British troops prepared for an assault landing, but just as they were beginning to get into the small boats a wind squall swept

H.M.S. *Prince Regent*, in left foreground, and other British ships of the Lake Ontario fleet in action off Oswego. The hero of the battle, J. Hewett, a Lieutenant of Royal Marines, was also a competent artist; this print was taken from one of his pictures. Understandably, the flag above the fort flies from a very high pole. (—*National Archives of Canada C 794*)

Another painting by Lieutenant Hewett shows the storming of Fort Oswego by the 2nd Battalion of Royal Marines and a party of seamen. (—*National Archives of Canada C 793*)

in from the lake. Everyone hastily reboarded the ships; and they, finding themselves too close for comfort to a lee shore, started the long beat out toward open water. A gale blew during the night. Early next morning the wind fell, becoming light and uncertain. Not until 10:00 a.m. did a steady breeze come up in the east and not until 11:00 was the squadron able once more to approach the harbor.

Prince Regent, controlling the entire operation, stood a little way offshore. Three ships moved in to engage the fort. A fourth took position to sweep the streets of the village with fire, thus preventing a group of militia who had assembled there from crossing the river. Two brigs towed in toward shore a number of boats filled with troops and then covered the landings by fire. Other troops came in in a large flatboat and in one of the gunboats. The plan was effective; the British suffered some casualties, but soon landed. They formed in two columns and proceeded up toward the fort.

The garrison answered with brisk musketry that killed or wounded a number of the attackers but did not slow the attack. The British troops clambered over the walls in two places and the American de-

fenders fell back, first to the far side of the fort and then to a position outside the walls, from which they continued to fire. The United States flag had been nailed to the top of the flagpole. Two marines who tried to climb up to it were shot down by the Americans, one after the other. Then Lt. John Hewett of the Royal Marines succeeded in climbing to the top and pulling down the flag, receiving three wounds in the process.

The invaders, working all night, loaded the captured military supplies and provisions, raising the American schooners that had been sunk in the harbor and using them as transports. The fort was dismantled and what could not be taken away was destroyed. Meanwhile the American force retreated to Oswego Falls, but the British did not pursue, evidently thinking it more important to remove the valuable captured stores as quickly as possible. Soon after daybreak on May 7 the squadron sailed for Kingston.

By the end of 1814 both the Americans and the British were tired of war. American naval action had won battles on the high seas and thanks to Perry and Harrison the United States occupied the western part of Upper Canada, although the British held the rest of Canada firmly, from Quebec to Mackinac, and had extended their hold in the West as far south as Prairie du Chien on the upper Mississippi. Britain after a long period had finally toppled Napoleon and wanted an end to warfare generally, but Britain also had almost unlimited troops to commit in North America if necessary and almost unlimited naval power to place them there. At the Treaty of Paris a tired and weak United States faced a tired but strong Britain.

When the war began the United States coveted the western areas of Canada; the forces of settlement looked hungrily over the northern border. The British in Canada, on the other hand, finding themselves at war felt that they still had the opportunity to keep the area north and west of the Ohio River as an Indian country. At the final bargaining table Britain pressed this demand, which would continue the fur trade in that area and block westward settlement by the Americans. The United States opposed it strongly. They pointed to an accomplished fact; they now held part of Upper Canada. To expect them to give up what they considered their own territory when they also held a useful portion of their opponent's territory was a good deal less than reasonable. The British representatives did not personally know much about North America, but they did know that their government wanted peace. They agreed to a settlement that restored the international boundary just as it had been before the war,

The Montreal fur traders were weakened by the war, in which they had actively supported the British, and by the peace, which cut them off from the great western expanses south of the United States border. Soon they were forced to merge with the Hudson's Bay Company. Thereafter most of the traffic for the Canadian Northwest came in from Hudson Bay rather than across the Ottawa River-Great Lakes route.

Fur trade in the Great Lakes region itself diminished and finally disappeared. The forces of settlement had won.

Two of the earliest lake steamers. The *Frontenac*, above, was the first steamer on the Great Lakes. Painting by George A. Cuthbertson. Below, the *Walk-in-the-Water* was the first steamboat above Niagara Falls. The painting of the latter by Father Edward J. Dowling, S.J., noted marine historian, hangs in the (Episcopal) Mariners' Church, the oldest church building in Detroit. (—Above, *Canada Steamship Lines Collection of Canadiana*; below, *Dossin Great Lakes Museum*)

2
Steam and Settlement

After the War of 1812 there was a time of peaceful development. On the Great Lakes it brought an expansion in shipping, the most dramatic part of which was the appearance of vessels driven by steam. Steamers had run on the St. Lawrence, between Montreal and Quebec, just before the war; during it they increased in size and numbers. After the war a group of businessmen at Kingston, the Canadian city located on the shore of Lake Ontario near the entrance to the St. Lawrence, decided that they would build a steamboat. These men called their vessel a boat rather than a ship, and steamers on the Lakes have frequently been called boats ever since.

FRONTENAC

The *Frontenac*, as she was named, was quite worthy of the title of ship. She was 171 feet long and of 740 tons burden. Work began on her in October 1815 at Finkle's Point (later Ernesttown) near Kingston, under the supervision of two shipwrights who during the war had worked in the American naval shipyard at Sackets Harbor under the noted builder Henry Eckford. The engines which would drive her paddle wheels were meanwhile being made by the English firm of Boulton and Watt, at Birmingham. On Saturday, September 7, 1816, she slid down the ways while many people watched. She was fitted out that winter and the next spring she began her regular service. As the Kingston *Gazette* commented, "Steam navigation having succeeded to admiration in various rivers, the application of it to the waters of the lakes is an interesting experiment."

She was a handsome vessel with a clipper bow, a three-masted schooner rig (it would be many years before steamers ventured forth without rigging and sails for emergency and auxiliary use) and a single tall funnel. With a favorable wind she travelled at nine knots. She had a high-pressure engine, which made a great deal of noise, something like that of a steam locomo-

tive. One elderly man, who had built many ships but had never seen one propelled by machinery, heard her approaching and leaped to his feet, asking what made the noise. As she rounded the point and came into harbor he raised his hands to his head and declared that the world was coming to an end when a ship ran without sails. He may have been overemphatic, but in fact it was the beginning of the end for commercial sail.

Throughout her career the *Frontenac*'s captain was James McKenzie, formerly a master in the Royal Navy, who had served on Lake Ontario during the War of 1812. He appears to have run a tight ship. Among the rules enforced on board, a bell was rung as soon as the vessel left port to signal that the passengers were to choose their berths and pay for their passages, and no smoking was allowed in the cabin, "nor any gentleman allowed to visit the Ladies' Cabin without special permission." The steamer made three trips a month between Kingston, York (Toronto), and Niagara. One enthusiastic traveler who took passage from Kingston to York called her "a delightful mode of conveyance," and went on to say that "it required some recollections to perceive I was not in the Kingston Hotel."

Work on another steamer began in August 1816 on the American side of the lake, at Sackets Harbor, under license from the Robert Fulton Company of New York. She was smaller than the *Frontenac*, measuring 110 feet over all and 240 tons gross. In March 1817 she was launched, christened the *Ontario*, and placed on the run between Oswego, York, and Niagara, thus competing in part with the Canadian steamer. The owners of the latter in the spring of 1818 launched another steamboat, the *Charlotte*, which ran from the head of the Bay of Quinte, on the northern shore of Lake Ontario, to Prescott, on the upper St. Lawrence, with calls at intervening ports. The age of steam was well launched on the Lakes.

WALK-IN-THE-WATER

In 1818 a number of businessmen from Buffalo and New York City, who had formed the Lake Erie Steamboat Company, launched the first steamer on the upper Lakes at Black Rock, near Buffalo. She was launched sideways, a novel method at that time which later became customary on the Great Lakes. She was 135 feet over all and of 338 tons gross, and was rigged as a two-masted schooner. This vessel, perhaps the best known of the early Great Lakes steamers, was named *Walk-in-the-Water* after a Wyandot chief who lived on the Detroit River. It was both an appropriate name for the steamer and a compliment to the chief, whose Indian name *Mier*, thus translated literally, actually meant turtle.

Under Capt. Job Fish, who was imported from the East Coast to command her, the *Walk-in-the-Water* first left Black Rock on August 23. That port was on the Niagara River and the steamer, which was unable to move up against the current under power alone, was conveyed by the same "horned breeze" used to move sailing vessels from the harbor to the lake; she was towed by sixteen yoke of oxen plodding along the river bank. This big team pulled a hawser some three hundred fathoms long, which was supported by about a dozen boats placed fifty feet apart to buoy up the line between the ship and the shore.

Among the distinguished passengers on this first voyage were the Earl of Selkirk—the major holder in the Hudson's Bay Company—with his countess; Colonel Dixon, British Indian Agent in the Northwest; Colonel John Anderson of the U.S. Army, with his wife and sister-in-law; and Colonel Leavenworth, the explorer of the American West, with his wife and daughter.

In good weather the vessel moved at six or seven miles an hour. As she approached each port she fired the small cannon at the bow—steam was too precious to waste on a whistle—and as she came into port Captain Fish would stand on one of the paddle boxes and give commands to the engineer in a stentorian voice through a speaking trumpet. Between times he would greet the people who came out in boats to meet the steamer, and would carefully assist over the side any ladies who were going into the boats to be taken ashore.

Like sailing vessels, and like all early steamers, the *Walk-in-the-Water* steered from the stern. She also followed the pattern of sailing vessels in having a raised quarterdeck aft that stood about five feet above the main deck; below it, one came first to the gentlemen's cabin, then aft of that to the ladies' cabin, which could be partitioned off by folding doors. The ladies' cabin had the stern windows for illumination, plus a skylight that also extended over the gentlemen's cabin.

Captain Fish, despite his assiduous care of the ladies, was not well liked. For two years he commanded the vessel as she travelled from Buffalo to Detroit, with stops at Erie and Cleveland, and occasional trips as far as Mackinac. Sometime during the second year he departed. A Cleveland paper commented that "a thing of public utility may often become a public curse under the management of disagreeable or designing men," and noted that Capt. John Davis, pilot and mate of the ship who had succeeded to her command, was more accommodating than Captain Fish. In 1820 Capt. Jebediah Rogers, of New York, became her master; he was described as being "in the broadest sense a gentleman," and under his hand the steamer became popular with travelers.

On October 31, 1821, the *Walk-in-the-Water* left Buffalo at 4:00 p.m. As she proceeded, a gale began to blow and rain fell in torrents. Captain Rogers tried to reach shelter at Point Abino, but the head wind was too strong. About 8:00 p.m. the captain decided to turn back and run for Buffalo. When he thought he was near the Buffalo pier he let go three anchors; this was at about 10:00. The ship rounded up and lay there, plunging over the waves. A leak that had begun earlier now increased. The full power of the engine was applied to the pumps, but the water inside her gained steadily.

At 4:30 in the morning the captain called all the passengers on deck. He had decided to allow the steamer to go ashore. He ordered the chain of one anchor slipped and the hawsers of the other two cut; the gale carried her toward the beach. Time passed slowly. Finally, after half an hour, her keel grated on the bottom. A swell then lifted her up and dropped her with a great crash of glass and crockery, and the next wave carried her farther up the beach, where she lodged firmly in the sand, never to float again. Following waves broke over her, drenching the passengers huddled on the deck, many of whom were in night clothes. There they remained until daylight, when a sailor in a small boat managed to carry ashore the end of a hawser, which he tied to a tree. Using this, all aboard were ferried ashore. They found themselves on the beach about a mile from the Buffalo lighthouse, which they had not been able to see through the storm. The ship's engineer, a Mr. Calhoun, and one of the lady passengers ran the mile to the lighthouse. The others came along more soberly. The lighthouse keeper, who had anticipated that survivors of the storm might find their way to his light, had a fire roaring in his huge fireplace.

THE CANOE OF GOVERNOR CASS

When the *Walk-in-the-Water* left Buffalo for Detroit on May 6, 1820, she carried among her passengers several members of an expedition that was being organized by Governor Lewis Cass of Michigan Territory to explore the southern shore of Lake Superior and the upper reaches of the Mississippi. The one of those passengers whose name is most familiar today was Henry R. Schoolcraft, later to become an Indian agent and a famous student of Indians.

Cass, a large man who seems to have been liked by most of the Indians with whom he dealt and to whom he was affectionately known as Big Belly, governed what today makes up Michigan, Wisconsin, and part of Minnesota. Among his numerous duties was control of the Indian Agencies at Chicago, Mackinac, Green Bay, and Prairie du Chien. One of the most important things these agencies did was to lay the groundwork for cession of their lands by the Indians so that white settlers could move in. Cass himself was perhaps the most enthusiastic promoter of Michigan settlement; one of his moves to make the territory more livable was the establishment of a group of public statutes that came to be known as the Cass Code.

Lewis Cass was honest and forthright in his dealings with Indians. He was a typical American of his

This daugerreotype of Lewis Cass about 1850, thirty years after his first expedition in Michigan Territory, still shows the character of the man. (*—Chicago Historical Society*)

day in his attitude toward them, however, and later was to write:

> . . . what ignorance, or folly, or morbid jealousy of our national progress does it not argue, to expect that our civilized border would become stationary, and some of the fairest portions of the globe be abandoned to hopeless sterility. That a few naked wandering barbarians should stay the march of cultivation and improvement, and hold in a state of perpetual unproductiveness, immense regions formed by Providence to support millions of human beings?

Although the forces of settlement, as represented by Cass, were moving toward the development of Michigan Territory, not all of the Indians who lived there were enthusiastic about losing their hunting grounds. Many of the tribes had fought on the British side during the War of 1812 in an alliance that had as one of its aims the maintenance of an Indian country in Ohio and Michigan. They still had close ties with the British, whom they visited at Fort Malden, across from Detroit, and at Drummond Island, near Sault Ste. Marie, and from whom they received gifts. Then the Indians returned to Michigan Territory to harass the settlers and shoot at American soldiers.

Cass's party included friendly Indians, voyageurs, and soldiers (mostly of French descent), plus a few

The canoe of Governor Cass, from an 1827 volume, *Sketches of a Tour to the Lakes*, by Thomas L. McKenny (of the Indian Department and Joint Commissioner with his Excellency Gov. Cass). (—*Western Reserve Historical Society*)

officers, engineers, and scientists. The expedition had a number of aims: to permit Cass to visit personally the Indian tribes throughout the extensive area; to arrange for the extinction of Indian titles to lands in various strategic places; to assess the copper mines on Lake Superior; to learn what local Indians near Chicago thought of a proposed scheme to transport the Six Nations to that area; to estimate the extent of the British fur trade in the country that Cass traversed; and to discourage the Indians there from associating with the British.

The expedition set out on May 24, 1820, in three birch-bark canoes that had been especially made to the Governor's order by the Saginaw Indians. These were bigger than most Indian canoes and were midway between the *canôts du nord* and the *canôts du maître* of the Canadian fur traders. Each was about thirty feet long and paddled by nine men; at the stern of each flew an American flag. At 5:00 p.m. on the 27th they reached Fort Gratiot, at the entrance to Lake Huron, where the small garrison welcomed them with an artillery salute. They pushed along Huron's shore, which in that stretch was low and heavily timbered, and on the 29th encountered a violent storm. As Charles G. Trowbridge, a young man who had volunteered to accompany the expedition (and who later became a Detroit banker and businessman), noted in his journal:

. . . we were obliged very much against our wish to put ashore on a very rocky point, where with the greatest difficulty we succeeded in getting our canoes ashore uninjured; in fact the construction of these vessels, so frail yet so generally and so wisely used for the purpose of navigation on the Rivers of this Country, is such, that without the most extreme caution, the traveller is every hour in danger of losing his canoe, baggage, and perhaps his life; for the Bark of which they are constructed is not more than 1/16 of an inch in thickness, and this is stretched over and then sewn to Beams or knees which are not more than 3/8 to 1/2 inch thick; between these knees (which are placed very close to each other) and the bark, are thin pieces of cedar wood, of the thickness of a quarter of an inch and length of ten to twelve feet, and arranged in such a manner as to join the edges, whereby the bark on the outside is prevented from yielding to trifling pressures.

But the greatest strength of a canoe of this kind is the gunwale (which is made of strong tough wood and well bound with watape) and the stiffening poles which are laid in the bottom of the vessel to support the lading, and prevent it from breaking in the waves. So that a canoe is equally strong and safe, whether laden or empty, provided it is not too heavily laden. . . .

On June 6 they arrived at Mackinac and on the 13th they departed. Having left behind one canoe that proved too weak for safety and having acquired two others, they now had a total of four. These were laden with supplies that had been sent on ahead to Mackinac by schooner. The expedition also had twenty-five more soldiers, from the garrison at Mackinac. On the 14th, at 6:00 in the evening, they finally landed at the Sault. There they spent the next day seeing the sights, being entertained by the trader George Johnston and his wife, the daughter of an influential chief, and preparing for a council with the Indians.

Chiefs representing some two hundred Chippewas gathered on Friday the 16th at the tent of the Governor, who asked them to express their sentiments as to ceding the land. The younger chiefs spoke vehemently against giving it up. Cass attempted to explain that the Treaty of Greeneville (concluded with the Indians of Ohio by Anthony Wayne a quarter-century earlier) confirmed the right of the United States to land at the Sault, and he produced a copy of the treaty to show them. The Indians at the Sault were not greatly impressed. Governor Cass went on to say that the United States in any case was going to build a fort on the land at the Sault that legally belonged to it, and if the Indians wished to agree they would then be given compensation. If they did not agree, the only difference would be that they would receive no pay.

This reasoning did not make a favorable impression and the council broke up. The chiefs returned to their camp. Shortly afterward the governor saw the British flag flying in the middle of that camp. Telling his party to stay where they were, Cass strode alone into the camp and threw the flag to the ground. The astounded Indians stood by dumbly. He called up his interpreter and through him informed them that if they attempted to raise that flag again he would order his soldiers to fire on them. He had one of his men take the flag back to his own camp and then turned and walked away.

Within ten minutes the women and children of the Indian band, with all of the luggage, were crossing the river to the British side. The warriors who remained prepared for an attack. The members of the expedition, for their part, expected the Indians to attack them; they loaded their weapons and doubled their guards. The trader, Johnston, and his Indian wife quickly interceded, Mrs. Johnston warning the Indians, to whom bravery was the ultimate virtue, that Cass had the air of a great man and

would carry his flag through the whole country. Later in the day another council was held in the Johnston house. The young chiefs who were so opposed to the treaty were excluded and the remaining chiefs, in return for trade goods handed over on the spot, ceded to the United States sixteen square miles, the area on which the construction of Fort Brady was begun two years later.

The troops from Mackinac returned to that post. The rest of the expedition started out on Lake Superior on June 18, skirted the southern shore of the lake, portaged at Keweenaw, and on July 5 reached the American Fur Company's post on the St. Louis River. There they exchanged the big canoes for smaller river craft.

MICHIGAN

A Buffalo merchant named Oliver Newberry until 1820 had a ramshackle house in which he operated a grocery store on the west corner of Seneca and Main streets. He dealt with the Indians, exchanging groceries for furs, and with the local farmers. A tall, sturdy man with a large head, Mr. Newberry wore an Indian blanket coat in cold weather and was considered something of an eccentric by the other citizens of Buffalo, but it was generally acknowledged that he was extremely honest in all of his dealings and had a keen business mind. Newberry, a New Englander who had come to the Great Lakes region as a soldier during the War of 1812, had opened his store soon after the end of the war.

In 1820 he moved to Detroit and enlarged his operations in the fur and fish trades. Because his cargoes had to be moved down Lake Erie he became interested in shipping, first as a stockholder in vessels owned by groups of businessmen, later as the builder-owner of his own vessels. He had a great admiration for Napoleon and gave his schooners such names as *Marengo, Napoleon, Marshal Ney, Austerlitz,* and *Lodi.* This peculiarity annoyed a staunch Briton who lived on the Canadian side of the Detroit River, one Angus MacIntosh, agent of the Hudson's Bay Company at the town of Malden, who in retaliation named the big, handsome brig he had built for that company the *Wellington.*

Buffalo harbor, 1835, showing a steamer of the type then developing. Note also the ladies and gentlemen on a harbor tour in the boat in the right foreground. (—*I.N. Phelps Stokes Colleciton. New York Public Library*)

Detroit harbor in 1837, showing the steamer *Michigan* in the left foreground. (—*Burton Historical Collection*)

Perhaps this gave pause to the Napoleonic fancies of Oliver Newberry. In any event, when he decided to build the first of his own steamers he changed his naming system and christened her the *Michigan.* This 156-foot, 472-ton vessel, launched at Detroit in 1833, introduced a type of hull that in time became the accepted thing for sidewheelers and that continued to be used until paddle wheels disappeared from the Lakes. It was known as the longitudinal sponson hull.

Until the construction of the *Michigan*, the hulls of Great Lakes steamers followed the pattern of the *Frontenac* or the *Walk-in-the-Water.* They were much like the hulls of sailing vessels, to which were added on either side the paddle boxes that jutted out to cover and protect the paddle wheels. On the *Michigan*, however, the entire main deck was carried out over the paddle wheels; forward and aft of the paddles the sides of the deck curved in, gradually converging at the bow and stern. This provided a great deal of extra deck space. The new ship made use of the additional space by having a cabin built on the main deck. It only ran part of the length of the deck, but it was the first step toward what became another typical feature of Lakes steamers, the upper-deck cabin. Until the advent of the *Michigan*, steamers had followed what was then the ocean practice of having most cabins below the main deck, within the hull.

The *Michigan* had yet another innovation which proved considerably less desirable, though other vessels copied it from time to time during the years that followed. She had two engines, each coupled to one of the paddle wheels. In smooth water this gave her a good turn of speed—fifteen miles per hour maximum—but in rough water, as she rolled, the paddle wheel that was raised momentarily out of the water would race while the one that was submerged would labor. When she rolled the other way the process would be reversed. As a result she yawed from side to side, giving somewhat the effect of waddling through the water, and was hard to steer.

Following the opening of the Erie Canal in 1825, the passengers that traveled westward on the Lake Erie steamers were a vastly assorted group. Most of them were bound for settlement in the newly opened areas. A writer who made an October voyage in another vessel the year after the *Michigan* was launched gave a description that probably fitted all of the vessels on the Buffalo-Detroit run at that time.

> Should the Peace Society push its prospect for a "Congress of Nations," I would suggest a Lake Erie steam-boat, on a late passage, as the most feasible point of meeting. Each trip scarcely fails of furnishing an adequate representation, both of nationality and of professional interest. The hardy, country-loving Swiss; the drawling, drudging Dutchman; the persevering, opinionated Scotchman; and the reckless, roistering Irishman, as well as the shrewd and penetrating Yankee, were tumbled in admirable confusion, person and effects, upon the narrow area of an upper deck....
>
> But go to the foredeck, appropriated to horses, mules, and oxen—wagons, carts, and coaches; go to the forecabin, the resort of the vulgar and the vicious, the intemperate and the profane, with a gaping crowd of wonderers, just out of the center of confusion; go to the deck-cabin, the prison-house of the "women and children," and to the dining cabin, the sitting-room of the men, to discuss politics, religion, literature, and the wonders of steam; . . . [to the] throats of men and brutes . . . add the roaring of steam and fire, and the rattling of machinery; the trumpeted orders of the captain, and the witness of it all must acknowledge a steam-boat on Lake Erie to be a floating Babel.

The movement of such passengers and their belongings westward and the transport of cargoes eastward was a good business; it was largely the immigrant trade that enabled the steamers to run profitably. In addition to his sailing vessels Newberry launched a number of other steamers and became a personage of considerable importance in the shipping of the Great Lakes, known widely as "The Admiral of the Lakes." The one-time Buffalo grocer was soon the first millionaire of Detroit.

RAMSEY CROOKS

Mackinac and Sault Ste. Marie were the western outposts of the United States on the Lakes. At each there was a military garrison and fur traders, especially the representatives of the American Fur Company.

John Jacob Astor, the German immigrant whose skill at English never matched his finely honed cunning, had visualized a chain of trading posts along the Great Lakes, down the Mississippi, westward along the Missouri, and over the mountains to the Pacific. Settlement now was destroying the fur country as

Brigantine *Ramsey Crooks*, owned by the American Fur Company, from a painting by George A. Cuthbertson. (—*Burton Historical Collection*)

far west as Michigan, but beyond that the vision still was valid and the furs were there for the harvesting. On the Lakes, Astor's headquarters were at Mackinac, and from there his business looked westward and southward over the continent.

The peace treaty that followed the War of 1812 shut off the Montreal fur traders from the area south of the Great Lakes. It left there a group of U.S. government trading posts and the posts of Astor's American Fur Company, but in 1822 Congress closed the government posts. Astor was left alone to take the furs and crush any small competitors.

Fur traders never were bothered by undue scruples, but the American Fur Company had fewer than most. Colonel Snelling, who commanded the U.S. military post at Detroit, reported in 1825 that 3,300 gallons of whisky and 2,500 gallons of high wines (nearly pure alcohol which was diluted to make trade firewater) had been shipped by the American Fur Company to Mackinac during the past year, and he pointed out that the manner in which the company dealt with the Indians had a great deal to do with the behavior of the tribesmen in their drunken forays along the frontier.

The notorious operations of the company brought public reaction and in time some government control. Then too, the fur market was declining. The vogue for beaver hats was passing in Europe, and Astor himself was growing old. In 1834 Astor withdrew; the American Fur Company split into four smaller companies, but the one operating on the Great Lakes retained its original name. Its president was Ramsey Crooks, who had been Astor's right-hand man.

In 1836 that company built at Detroit the 100-foot-long brigantine *Ramsey Crooks*. Her construction was delayed by one of the fiercest winters the builders could remember, but she was in service by late spring, a handsome vessel of 247 tons. For the next ten years she carried supplies and cargo to Mackinac and Sault Ste. Marie, and with a few other sailing vessels linked these northern outposts to Detroit and the Lake Erie ports.

During this time the fur trade steadily declined. As early as 1837 Crooks, looking for other ways to make a profit, decided that there would be more income from fish than from fur, but the markets for fish proved smaller than he had hoped. He also tried to encourage the use of company vessels for general passenger and freight carriage. Despite these various efforts the American Fur Company lost money steadily until by 1845 its main object was simply to concentrate its business and pay off its liabilities. It was even unable to build new vessels.

In addition, a new element came into the picture: discovery of the massive copper and iron deposits along the southern shore of Lake Superior. The ores quickly drew prospectors, then miners, thus speeding the process of settlement. The remaining fur country south of the Lakes was doomed. The *Ramsey Crooks* was the last large vessel built for the fur trade on the Great Lakes.

UNITED STATES

In the 1830s Upper Canada—today the Province of Ontario—was governed by a conservative and well-entrenched group of business and professional men who ran affairs largely to suit themselves. In opposition to them was a reformist group that had as one of its leaders the editor-politician William Lyon Mackenzie. The conservatives were heavy-handed and inflexible, while Mackenzie was a firebrand who may not always have been rational and who overreacted to conservative stupidities. The classic ingredients were there; in December 1837 rebellion flared.

The government had troops, arms, and, as it developed, the support of most of the people. The rebels had a hastily assembled militia, makeshift weapons, and less general support. In short order the rebels were defeated; some of their leaders were imprisoned—later to be hanged—and Mackenzie escaped to the United States where he set about raising an army with which to invade Canada.

In the United States there was general sympathy for Mackenzie, and the authorities tended to ignore if not abet him. His activities along the northern border meshed neatly with the urge to take new territory that soon caused Americans along the southern border to pluck Texas from Mexico. Mackenzie himself was soon relegated to a minor role, while Americans who coveted land north of the border termed themselves Canadian "patriots," and organized for war.

The steamer *United States*, as painted by her commander, Capt. James Van Cleve, in his primitive style. During later years the captain wrote and illustrated a book of Great Lakes history, all done by hand, and as far as is known he made only four copies. Today they are prizes in various historical libraries. Van Cleve included his former command in the book. (—*Chicago Historical Society*)

Late in December of 1837 the American steamer *Caroline*, ferrying supplies from the U.S. to Mackenzie's headquarters on Navy Island, on the Canadian side of the Niagara River, was followed into American waters by Canadian troops and sailors, burned, and set adrift—to the violent indignation of some Americans, but to the general embarrassment of the U.S. government. The steamer quickly sank, yet artists from that time on have found it more dramatic to show her plunging in flames over Niagara Falls, sometimes even with bodies spilling overboard.

In May 1838 the Canadian steamer *Robert Peel*, operating on the St. Lawrence River, was boarded by a group of Mackenzie sympathizers dressed as Indians and commanded by Bill Johnston, a freebooter who had led a piratical existence along the St. Lawrence since fleeing Canada to avoid charges of smuggling and desertion from the militia. The band relieved the passengers and crew of all their money,

watches, and jewelry, and put them ashore, mostly in their night clothes. The raiders took a Canadian army pay chest with £20,000 of bullion, set fire to the steamer, and disappeared.

On Lake Ontario and the upper St. Lawrence the handsome 142-foot steamer *United States* had been operating for several years. She had two stacks abreast, two engines, and two walking beams, each driving a separate paddle wheel. The steering position had moved forward to a "steering room," or pilot house and she had a complete main-deck cabin. Her captain was James Van Cleve, whose nautical career had started as clerk on the steamer *Ontario* in 1826 (in those days the title of purser was seldom used on the Lakes).

Captain Van Cleve commanded the *United States* during the 1838 season while anti-Canadian activities flared along the borders. On November 11 the steamer left Oswego on the last trip of the season, bound for Ogdensburg. As she stopped at such intervening ports as Sackets Harbor and Cape Vincent, a large number of men came aboard. Soon after she left Cape Vincent a passenger approached Van Cleve, pointed out two schooners that were sailing nearby, said that he owned the cargoes they were carrying and that they were also bound for Ogdensburg, and asked that Van Cleve take them in tow.

It was a normal thing for steamers to tow schooners in narrow waters, and so Van Cleve struck a bargain and agreed. Both of the schooners were brought alongside and made fast. Then a great many men boiled out of their cargo hatches and poured over onto the steamer's deck. Although Van Cleve did not know it, he was host to a body of American irregulars under "General" von Schoultz, and the captain of one of the schooners was Bill Johnston himself, "Admiral of the Eastern Navy" by "patriot" appointment. The captain did realize, however, that something strange was going on, and he proposed to two of the owners of the steamer who were on board that he run her aground until the authorities could be called to investigate. The owners vetoed this idea, and so the *United States* and the schooners continued as far as Morristown, N.Y., where the schooners, carrying most of the men, cast off—later to attack Prescott, Ontario. This took place about 11:00 p.m. The steamer continued, with intervening calls, to Ogdensburg, arriving there at four in the morning. Before daybreak the pirates who had remained aboard seized her and ran her down to Windmill Point, just below Prescott, where more of the men landed.

The *United States*, still under control of her captors, started back up the river. As she passed Prescott, the British steam gunboat *Experiment* fired on her; one shot entered the steering room and killed the steersman. The pirates immediately abandoned her and her regular crew took her back to Ogdensburg. Meanwhile the invaders mounted what came to be known the Battle of the Windmill, held on for some time, but in due course were defeated by Canadian and British forces.

Next evening there arrived at Ogdensburg a U.S. Marshal, a small detachment of U.S. troops, and a few army and navy officers, who, now that the attackers had reached Canadian soil, seized the steamer and the two schooners, which had returned to that port. They also arrested Captain Van Cleve. The owners, in order to save their ship from being taken by the government, made the captain the scapegoat, blamed him for everything, and promptly fired him. This misfortune did not greatly hinder his career, however, and he went on to further achievements on the Lakes.

The steamer was returned to her owners and continued in service for a number of years, but she called only at American ports. Her name had become anathema in Canada because of her part in the invasion, and the owners feared what might happen to her in Canadian waters.

OSCEOLA

As the immigrants flowed into what now is the midwestern United States, Oliver Newberry, "Admiral of the Lakes," soon realized the growing importance of Chicago. Newberry, whose office was at Detroit, cast about for someone to represent him in Chicago and decided upon an energetic young man, George W. Dole. First he made Dole his agent, then his partner in Chicago, and the firm became Newberry and Dole.

The rapid influx of settlers and of soldiers to fight the abortive Black Hawk War with the local Indians in 1832 quickly used up the Chicago food supplies. Dole established a slaughterhouse and scoured the surrounding countryside for cattle and hogs. Before long he was producing more meat than was needed locally, and so in the spring of 1833 he sent a number of barrels of beef and tallow from Chicago to Detroit in Newberry's vessel, *Napoleon*. This was the first export of any manufactured product from the city.

Newberry had long been noted for his high business ethics; in Dole he found a kindred spirit. Immigrants poured into Chicago, and in the fall of 1835 the city found itself nearly out of flour. Only twenty or thirty barrels remained to sustain the growing city through the winter, and those barrels were owned by a merchant who asked $20.00 each for them, although the normal price was $8.50. It was late in the season and no more shipments of flour were likely to arrive. But then a shipment did arrive—in a Newberry vessel.

At that time ships had to anchor outside the bar at Chicago while their cargoes were lightered in.

First shipment of grain from Chicago's first dock, loaded aboard the brigantine *Osceola*. (—*Chicago Historical Society*)

There was some risk involved in that process, especially in the stormy autumn season. The merchant who was trying to corner the flour market arrived at Dole's office to offer $15.00 for each barrel on the ship, and he would take the risk of unloading it. Dole refused. He had the flour lightered ashore in bateaux and then sold it to private families, boarding houses, and hotels at $8.50 a barrel.

By 1839 the settlers around Chicago had begun to produce their own wheat and even had enough surplus to ship a little of it elsewhere. Many of them were too poor to own bags in which to carry grain; they laid sheets or blankets in their wagons, piled the grain on them and brought it, sometimes from 150 miles away, to the Newberry and Dole warehouse on the Chicago waterfront. The warehouse provided bags that were filled from the wagons, hoisted to the up-per floor, and carried back to be emptied into bins. In September of that year Newberry and Dole shipped the first cargo of grain to go out of Chicago. By then the harbor was sufficiently improved that the brigantine *Osceola* could be brought in to the Newberry and Dole wharf, the first one in Chicago. Grain was loaded by the most primitive means. Men filled the top of the loading chute in the warehouse and others carried boxes of grain from the bottom of the chute to the vessel's hatches.

The *Osceola*, commanded by Captain Billings, loaded about 2,900 bushels which were consigned to Black Rock, N.Y., near Buffalo. She could have taken 5,000, but they were not to be had. Nevertheless, the first trickle of wheat had started westward from the newly settled lands in Illinois. It was a trickle that soon would grow into a golden flood.

ERIE

Immigrants continued to reach Buffalo through the Erie Canal. There were no railroads as yet to the opening lands in Michigan and Illinois; the most common method of travel was by steamer. One of these immigrant ships was the steamer *Erie*, 176 feet long and of 497 tons. She was owned by the Reed line of Erie, Pennsylvania, and was on the Buffalo-Detroit run. Cabin passengers paid $8.00 for the trip; steerage passengers, the majority of them immigrants, paid $3.00.

The *Erie* left Buffalo at 4:00 on the afternoon of August 9, 1841. She had recently been overhauled and varnished. Passenger lists were none too accurate in those days; we know only that there were between 200 and 250 people on board, including the crew. Some 120 of the passengers were German-speaking Swiss immigrants. Among the other passengers were half-a-dozen painters, going to Erie to repaint a steamer there. They carried demijohns of turpentine and varnish, which were placed on deck immediately above the boilers. One of the *Erie*'s firemen, going on deck, was shocked to find the inflammables stowed there and quickly moved them away. Later someone else— it never was discovered who—moved them back.

A strong wind was blowing and there was some sea running when the *Erie* was off Silver Creek, about nine o'clock in the evening. At that time there was a slight explosion and then suddenly the whole ship was enveloped in flames. Captain Titus went quickly to the ladies' cabin, where about a hundred life preservers were stowed, but the heat was so great he could not get in. He returned to the upper deck, ordered the steersman to head for shore, eight miles away, and had three boats lowered. (The steersman, Luther Fuller, remained at his post and was burned to death there.) Chaos ensued. One of the survivors described the scene:

> The air was filled with shrieks of agony and despair. The boldest turned pale. I shall never forget the wail of terror that went up from the poor German emigrants, who were huddled together on the forward deck. Wives clung to their husbands, mothers frantically pressed their babes to their bosoms, and lovers clung madly to each other. One venerable old man, his gray hairs streaming in the wind, stood on the bow, and, stretching out his bony hands, prayed to God in the language of his fatherland.

> But if the scene forward was terrible, that aft was appalling, for there the flames were raging in their greatest fury. Some madly rushed into the fire; others, with a yell like a demon, maddened with the flames, which were all around them, sprang headlong into the waves. The officers of the boat, and the crew, were generally cool, and sprang to lower the boats, but these were every one successively swamped by those who threw themselves into them, regardless of the execrations of the sailors, and of everything but their own safety.

> I tried to act coolly—I kept near the captain, who seemed to take courage from despair, and whose bearing was above all praise. The boat was veering toward the shore, but the maddened flames now enveloped the wheel-house, and in a moment the machinery stopped. The last hope had left us—a wilder shriek rose upon the air. At this moment the second engineer, the one at the time on duty, who had stood by his machinery as long as it would work, was seen climbing the gallows head, a black mass, with the flames curling all around him. On either side he could not go, for it was now one mass of fire. He sprang upward, came to the top, one moment felt madly around him, and then fell into the flames. There was no more remaining on board, for the boat now broached around and rolled upon the swelling waves, a mass of fire. I seized upon a settee near me, and gave one spring, just as the flames were bursting through the deck where I stood— one moment more and I should have been in the flames. In another instant I found myself tossed on a wave, grasping my frail support with a desperate energy.

The steamer *DeWitt Clinton* had left Dunkirk and was proceeding westward, when just at dusk her people sighted the fire about twenty miles astern. She immediately turned and headed for it. By the time she reached the burning hulk of the *Erie* the upper works had burned away and the hull was swathed in subdued flames, but the engine was still upright in the hull. The *Clinton* was able to pick up twenty-seven people who were clinging either to the paddle wheels or rudder chains of the burning ship or to various floating objects. Other vessels arrived on the scene later and picked up a few more survivors. (Several people rescued from the water died later of their burns.) By 1:00 a.m. it appeared that all who had escaped had been found, and the *Clinton*, aided by another vessel, tried to tow the burning hull to shore, but it sank about four miles out.

The combination of a freshly varnished wooden steamer, insufficient life preservers, insufficient boats, and a large number of passengers was no doubt com-

The burning of the immigrant steamer *Erie*, as shown in a contemporary print. (*—Great Lakes Historical Society*)

mon enough. What seem to be outrageous safety hazards were accepted as normal. The one uncommon factor, which caused remark even then, was the turpentine and varnish stowed above the boilers. Almost certainly that was what caused the explosion and set the ship afire.

VANDALIA

Capt. James Van Cleve, after losing command of the *United States*, became master of another steamer the next season and remained in that position for several years. In December 1840 on a visit to New York City he was introduced to Capt. John Ericsson, the Swedish inventor of the screw propeller. Ericsson at that time was trying to interest builders of Erie Canal boats in his invention; at one of the New York shipyards he had a propeller mounted on a shaft. There Van Cleve looked at it and immediately decided that the propeller would revolutionize ship propulsion.

At Ericsson's New York hotel, Van Cleve described at length the shipping of the Great Lakes. The inventor paced back and forth as he listened; then he turned. "Van Cleve, if you will put a vessel in operation with my propeller, and do it within the year, I will assign to you one-half interest in my patent for all the North American Lakes."

Van Cleve agreed, and returned to Oswego to form a company. He took a quarter interest in the new vessel; the builder, Sylvester Doolittle, took a quarter, and friends of Van Cleve took the remainder. (Before her completion, however, Van Cleve for some reason sold his interest to the builder.) The engine was constructed in Auburn, N.Y., to Ericsson's design. By the summer of 1841 the *Vandalia*, as she was named, was launched. She made her first trip in November and was an unqualified success.

The *Vandalia* was 91 feet long on deck and of 138 tons burden, rigged as a sloop, with a shortened boom and the stack coming up at her stern. She was the first Great Lakes vessel to have her machinery all the way aft—an arrangement that later became commonplace on the Lakes. She was also the first commercial propeller-driven vessel in the world. The screw propeller first proved itself on the Lakes.

The *Vandalia*, first propeller-driven vessel on the Great Lakes and first commercial propeller-driven vessel in the world, as painted by Captain Van Cleve, who was one of the partners who built her. (*—Chicago Historical Society*)

By the early 1840s settlements were well established along the shores of every Great Lake except Superior. Settlers on the prairies of Illinois and southern Wisconsin were sending increasing amounts of grain eastward. Not only were numbers of steamers in service, but propeller-driven vessels had made their successful debut on the Lakes. (For some years to come, sailors on the Lakes would make a distinction between steamers and propellers, the former being driven by paddle wheels, the latter by the screw propeller.) Steamers had been able to thrive because of the immigrant trade; immigrants had been able to reach their new lands more easily and quickly because of the steamers.

Settlement had pushed farthest and fastest along the United States shores, but Canadian settlements had extended as far westward as Lake Huron. There was a small Canadian naval and military base on Georgian Bay, and a few people lived on the Canadian side of the Sault Ste. Marie. To the west of the Sault, on both shores of Lake Superior, the main outposts of civilization were still the trading forts. Probably the most important of these was Fort William, the Hudson's Bay Company establishment at the northwestern end of the Lake.

The first great pouring in of settlers was accomplished. Now those settlements would grow and develop, and soon the way would also be opened into Lake Superior.

At the time of Charles Dickens's visit to the Great Lakes, construction of the St. Lawrence canals was progressing. Here in an engraving by W.H. Bartlett we see the Cornwall Canal being built around the Long Sault rapids of the St. Lawrence. (*–National Archives of Canada C 2310*)

3
Opening the Way

The Great Lakes region drew tourists both from the Eastern Seaboard and from overseas. Among them was Charles Dickens, who came with his wife by land to Sandusky, Ohio, in April 1842.

Mr. and Mrs. Dickens were not impressed by the inhabitants. "Their demeanor in these country parts is invariably morose, sullen, clownish and repulsive. I should think there is not, on the face of the earth, a people so entirely destitute of humor, vivacity, or the capacity of enjoyment." At Sandusky the couple boarded ship for Buffalo. Dickens wrote to a friend that "She was a fine steamship, four hundred tons burden, name the *Constitution,* had very few passengers on board, and had bountiful and handsome accommodation."

That Charles Dickens, whose view of the western frontier was somewhat jaundiced, described a ship on Lake Erie as having handsome accommodation shows how well the transportation system was developing. Just at the time of Dickens's visit the Welland Canal, bypassing Niagara Falls on the Canadian side, was beginning to be important. Work was progressing on the St. Lawrence River canals. The portage to Lake Superior at Sault Ste. Marie was more and more active, and within three years the first Lake Superior steamer would be hauled on rollers over it. The year of Dickens's tour also saw the first steamer designed to break the ice in frozen harbors and it would not be long before there were clippers on the Lakes as well as on the Atlantic. In 1841 the gross amount of the Great Lakes trade was estimated at $65 million; by 1851 it would be over $300 million. In every way this was a period of development.

Dickens added to his comment on the *Constitution,* "It's all very fine talking about Lake Erie, but it won't do for persons who are liable to seasickness. We were all sick. It's almost as bad in that respect as the Atlantic. The waves are very short and horribly constant." The ship called at some "flat places" with low breakwaters and stumpy lighthouses, which reminded Dickens of scenes in Holland. Then about midnight they arrived at Cleveland.

> We lay all Sunday night at a town (and a beautiful town too) called Cleveland, on Lake Erie. The people poured on board, in crowds, by six on Monday morning, to see me; and a party of "gentlemen" actually planted themselves before our little cabin, and stared in at the door and windows *while I was washing and Kate lay in bed.* I was so incensed at this, and at a certain newspaper published in that town which I had accidentally seen in Sandusky (advocating war with England to the death, saying that Britain must be "whipped again," and promising all true Americans that within two years they should sing Yankee Doodle in Hyde Park and Hail Columbia in the courts of Westminster), that when the mayor came on board to present himself to me, according to custom, I refused to see him, and bade Mr. Q. [the Dickens's traveling companion] to tell him why and wherefore. His honor took it very coolly, and retired to the top of the wharf, with a big stick and a whittling knife, with which he worked so lustily (staring at the closed door of our cabin all the time) that long before the boat left, the big stick was no bigger than a cribbage-peg!

As the ship moved on toward Buffalo, Dickens heard through the partition between the staterooms some of the remarks of his next-door neighbor. "I appeared to run in his mind perpetually, and to dissatisfy him very much." The man in the next stateroom, unaware that the subject of his discussion could hear every word, confided to his wife that Boz—Dickens's pen name—was still on board, and finally concluded "I suppose Boz will be writing a book bye and bye, and putting all our names in it!" He then groaned and relapsed into silence.

Dickens did write the book, which was much politer about it all than his letters, but he omitted the names.

GREAT WESTERN

The longest single passenger run on the Lakes at this time was from Buffalo to Chicago, and the finest steamers travelled over it, carrying immigrants, tourists, and cargo. New developments often appeared first on these vessels, one of which was the *Great Western*.

When Margaret Fuller, the New England author, editor, and literary critic, went aboard a steamer at Buffalo in the summer of 1843, she summarized the picture in this way:

> SCENE: STEAMBOAT. — About to leave Buffalo. — Baggage coming on board. — Passengers bustling for their berths. — Little boys persecuting everybody with their newspapers and pamphlets. — J., S., and M [two of her friends and herself] huddled up in a forlorn corner, behind a large trunk. — A heavy rain falling.

That steamboat was probably the *Great Western*; much of Miss Fuller's trip was on the vessel and she probably started out aboard her. The *Great Western* had been launched at Huron, Ohio, five years previously, a steamer 183 feet long and of 781 tons. The large tonnage in proportion to her length indicates the feature that made her unusual: she had a complete upper-deck cabin.

Structures had been evolving on the decks of steamers since Newberry's *Michigan*, but before this vessel there was no upper-deck cabin so large or so long. While she was building, many wise heads were shaken and predictions were made that she would never last in a storm. She would be too top-heavy. As it developed she was both safe and comfortable.

When the ship was about to leave Buffalo, a bell rang, and one of Miss Fuller's friends went ashore. She and her remaining companion retired to their staterooms "to forget the wet, the chill, and steamboat smell, in their just-bought new world of novels." Next day she looked about at her fellow passengers.

> The people on the boat were almost all New-Englanders, seeking their fortunes. . . . It grieved me to hear these immigrants, who were to be the fathers of a new race, all, from the old man down to the little girl, talking, not of what they should do, but of what they should get in the new scene. It was to them a prospect, not of the unfolding nobler energies, but of more ease and larger accumulation.

The rain and fog accompanied the vessel as far as Mackinac, which was only visible through the mist, but as she pushed on into Lake Michigan, the skies cleared.

> . . . At night the moon was clear, and, for the first time, from the upper deck I saw one of the great steamboats come majestically up. It was glowing with lights, looking many-eyed and sagacious; in its heavy motion it seemed a dowager queen, and this motion, with its solemn pulse, and determined sweep, becomes these smooth waters, especially at night, as much as the dip of the sail-ship the long billows of the ocean.

Steamers at that time still burned wood and had to stop often to refuel. The one on which Miss Fuller rode put in at the Manitou Islands for that purpose and then steamed on toward Chicago. There and in the hinterland beyond, this author, just as Dickens before her, concluded that most of the people who lived near the shores of the Great Lakes were "thoughtless and slovenly."

> We passed a portion of one day with Mr. and Mrs. —, young, healthy, *gay* people. In the general dulness that broods over this land where so little genius flows, and care, business, and fashionable frivolity are equally dull, unspeakable is the relief of some flashes of vivacity, some sparkles of wit.

In Chicago the two favorite steamers were the *Great Western* and the *Illinois*. Whenever one of them was about to sail, the town filled with people from places farther south and west who were taking passage. Margaret Fuller noted, "These moonlight nights I would hear the French rippling and fluttering familiarly amid the rude ups and downs of the Hoosier dialect."

On her return trip she explored Mackinac, this time in fine weather, and waxed poetic.

> These evenings we were happy, looking over the old-fashioned garden, over the beach, over the waters and pretty island opposite, beneath the growing moon. We did not stay to see it full at Mackinaw; at two o'clock one night, or rather morning, the *Great Western* came snorting in, and we must go; and Mackinaw, and all the Northwest summer, is now to me no more than picture and dream.

The steamer had a high-pressure engine and therefore literally snorted—or at least chugged. After leaving Mackinac the vessel paused briefly at De-

Above: The *Great Western*, an early Great Lakes steamer with a complete upper-deck cabin, ran between Buffalo and Chicago. (—*Mariners Museum, Newport News, Va. LE-1922*)

Right: Margaret Fuller, author, editor, and philospher, whose 1843 account of her trip over the Lakes in the *Great Western* gives us one of the better records of steamer travel of that day. (—*New York Public Library*)

Below: View of Chicago of 1843, when Margaret Fuller visited it. (—*Chicago Public Library*)

troit, then pushed on into Lake Erie. The *Great Western* was a clipper-bowed steamer rigged with sails on each of her three masts. Thus she was equipped if necessary to work under sail as well as steam. Her cabin did give her rather a top-heavy appearance, however, and as a result of it she probably was not at all handy under sail. Her two tall smokestacks, belled slightly at the very tops, stood abreast, and on each side the big paddle box bore her name in large letters. Miss Fuller described the scene on board.

> In the boat many signs admonished that we were floating eastward. A shabbily-dressed phrenologist laid his hand on every head that would bend, with half-conceited, half-sheepish expression, to the trial of his skill. Knots of people gathered here and there to discuss points of theology. A bereaved lover was seeking religious consolation—Butler's Analogy, which he had purchased for that purpose. However, he did not turn over many pages before his attention was drawn aside by the gay glances of certain damsels that came on board at Detroit, and, though Butler might afterwards be seen sticking from his pocket, it had not weight to impede him from many a feat of lightness and liveliness.

The author left her readers there, as the *Great Western* approached Buffalo.

The ship continued in service for another twelve years, travelling usually between Buffalo and the Lake Michigan ports. In 1855 she was retired and soon afterward was scrapped. The normal life of a wooden steamer was about twenty years, but the departure from the scene by the *Great Western*, in her prime one of the finest ships afloat on the western Lakes, was hastened somewhat by the development of newer, larger ships.

U.S.S. *MICHIGAN*

Not all steamers on the Lakes were devoted to commerce. The Canadian rebellion of 1837 and the resultant attacks on Canada from the United States led the British Government to build two steam gunboats to defend the Canadian shores of the Great Lakes. Daniel Webster, then secretary of state, promptly sent a protest to the British Minister in Washington, and as promptly was informed, "It being unfortunately notorious that Her Majesty's Provinces are threatened by hostile incursions by combinations of armed men, unlawfully organized and prepared for war within the frontiers of the United States, and it being found by experience that the efforts of the United States Government . . . to

The U.S.S. *Michigan* in an early photo. (*—Mariners Museum, Newport News, Va. PN-1283*)

The U.S.S. *Michigan*, first iron ship in the U.S. Navy, launched at
Erie in 1843. (*—Mariners Museum, Newport News, Va. PA-3894*)

suppress those unlawful combinations are not attended with the wished-for success," the vessels were obviously necessary to protect Canada.

Thus goaded, in 1841 the United States appropriated one hundred thousand dollars for the construction of armed vessels on Lake Erie. The appropriation was accompanied by some ringing anti-British oratory by Senator William Allen of Ohio, but the real duty of the single vessel that eventually was launched was to maintain order in American waters. Government processes moved deliberately, and the new gunboat was to be built of iron, a new material for ship's hulls which required new methods, so construction proceeded slowly during 1842 and 1843. She was not the first iron ship on the Great Lakes—that was the British steam gunboat *Mohawk*, launched early in 1843 at Kingston—but she was the first iron ship in the U.S. Navy. Her designer and builders had to discover the solutions to many problems as they went along.

The U.S.S. *Michigan*, as the 163-foot vessel was named, was designed by Naval Constructor Samuel Hart and built in sections at Pittsburgh. These were sent via the Ohio canal system to Cleveland and thence by lake transport to Erie, Pennsylvania, for final assembly. The iron strakes that composed them averaged only eighteen inches in width and according to tradition were beaten into shape with wooden mauls in a bed of sand. Her frames were of wrought iron. The engines, also built at Pittsburgh, were far in advance of their time; they were long-stroke, slow-moving, low-pressure affairs that were highly efficient. The quality of the ship's design and construction is reflected in the fact that she remained in commission until 1923 and was not finally scrapped until 1949, 106 years after her launching.

She was rigged as a barkentine and was meant to be equally steamer and sailing vessel. Provision was made to lock her paddles whenever she was under sail. The engines could be reversed only by lifting the valves by hand—or rather, using a ten-foot crowbar. Even a strong man could do this no more than eight or nine times in succession, and so she did not back far or often.

On her launching day, December 5, 1843, many of the citizens of Erie gathered to see her go straight to the bottom, the inevitable result of building a ship of iron. To their disappointment and the embarrassment of Mr. Hart, the contractor, she stuck on the ways and could not be budged. The citizens retired and Mr. Hart went off to ponder ways and means. Next morning when they all arose, the U.S.S. *Michigan* was floating serenely, having launched herself.

She was a handsome vessel with a clipper bow, three tall, raking masts, and a tall smokestack. In her first years she was painted black to the top of her gun ports, with a white stripe along the bulwarks. Her draught was kept to nine feet so that she could enter most of the small harbors on the Lakes, and as a result of this and the limited knowledge of metal construction, her hull was flat-bottomed and somewhat boxlike in cross section. The combined flat bottom, shallow draft, and large upper works made her at times hard to handle. One old quartermaster, asked why he kept moving her helm from side to side while she was on a steady course, replied, "You have to keep her confused so that she won't take a sheer." The Iron Ship—her popular name—was at first armed with four 32-pound carronades and two 68-pound pivot guns, all of course smoothbore. No sooner was this fact reported in the press than the British Minister in Washington, with a certain lack of consistency, lodged a protest with the U.S. government that this armament far exceeded the provisions of the Rush-Bagot Convention, established after the War of 1812. As a result the *Michigan*, before she went on her maiden voyage, lost all of these weapons and was fitted instead with a single 18-pounder. That was all she carried for the next twenty years.

CHIEF JUSTICE ROBINSON

The builders of vessels constantly tried out new ideas. Because the Great Lakes are fresh water and therefore freeze easily in winter, the yearly period of navigation on them has always been limited. Lake sailors have made many attempts to break through the ice in harbors and river mouths during early winter and again in spring, and thus lengthen the navigational season. Perhaps the first vessel designed to do this—what today we would call an icebreaker—was the Canadian steam packet *Chief Justice Robinson* which operated on Lake Ontario between Toronto and Lewiston, N.Y., with Niagara as a port of call.

Built at Niagara, in Upper Canada, in 1842, she continued on the Lewiston-Toronto route for the next ten or twelve years. During most of this time she was owned by her master, Capt. Hugh Richardson. She had an unusual ram bow which enabled her to break through the ice on the lower Niagara River and in this way run earlier and later in the year than her icebound competitors.

Aside from her unique bow, the *Chief Justice Robinson* was representative of the best Canadian steamers that carried passengers and merchandise on Lake Ontario.

Chief Justice Robinson landing passengers on the ice of Toronto Bay. The illustration is from a drawing made by the artist and engineer William Armstrong soon after he came to Toronto from Ireland in the early 1850s. (—*Metropolitan Toronto Library Board JRR 517*)

The early icebreaker *Chief Justice Robinson* operated on Lake Ontario. She was painted by Captain Van Cleve and was included in his manuscript book mainly because of her unusual appearance. We have two views of her by competent technical men. (—*Chicago Historical Society*)

Normally she operated six days a week, running in opposite directions on alternate days. The luxury she offered her passengers was considerable. Sir Richard Bonnycastle, writing in 1846, commented:

> The comfort of some of these boats, as they call them, but which ought to be called ships, is very great. There is a regular drawing-room on board one called the Chief Justice, where I saw, just after the horticultural show in Toronto, pots of the most rare and beautiful flowers, arranged very tastefully, with a piano, highly-coloured nautical paintings and portraits, and a *tout ensemble*, which, when the lamps were lit, and a conversation going on between the ladies and gentlemen then and there assembled, made one quite forget we were at sea on Lake Ontario, the "Beautiful Lake," which, like other beautiful creations, can be very angry if vexed.

The Canadian steamers on Lake Ontario were probably the most comfortable and best run on the Lakes at this time. The expertness with which Britannia ruled the waves of the entire world and the comforts demanded by British travellers during this period could also be found on this most British of the Lakes. As Bonnycastle reported:

> You can have every convenience on board a Lake Ontario mail-packet, which is about as large as a small frigate, and has the usual sea equipment of masts, sails, and iron rigging. The fare is five dollars in the cabin, or about £1 sterling; and two dollars in the steerage. In the former you have tea and breakfast, in the latter nothing but what is bought at the bar. By paying a dollar extra you may have a stateroom on deck, or rather on the half-deck, where you find a good bed, a large looking-glass, washing-stand and towels, and a night-lamp, if required. The captains are generally part owners, are kind, obliging, and communicative, sitting at the head of their table, where places for females and families are always reserved. The stewards and waiters are coloured people, clean, neat, and active; and you may give sevenpence-halfpenny or a quarter dollar to the man who cleans your boots, or an attentive waiter, if you like; if not, you can keep it, as they are well paid.
>
> The ladies' cabin has generally a large cheval glass and a piano, with a white lady to wait, who is always decked out in flounces and furbelows, and usually good-looking....

The *Chief Justice Robinson* was 160 feet long. She had a vertical beam engine, the external mark of which was

Timber raft in a squall on Lake St. Pierre, drawn by W. H. Bartlett.
(—*National Archives of Canada C 2344*)

the walking beam, the constantly dipping elongated diamond that remained a feature of most side-wheelers until they disappeared from the Lakes.

THE TIMBER RAFT (I)

Lake Ontario not only floated British ships, but also was the base for the uniquely British timber trade. In the early 1800s Napoleon had cut off Britain from the Baltic, a major source of European timber. The British turned then to the timber exporters of Quebec, who drew on the great Canadian forests along the St. Lawrence and Ottawa Rivers and the shores of Lake Ontario. The cutting and exporting of timber there was a growing business.

A man whose name was to become synonymous with the timber trade moved in 1844 from the American side of the St. Lawrence at Clayton, N.Y., to Garden Island, in Canada at the point where Lake Ontario drains into the great river. He was Delano Dexter Calvin, a native of Vermont. The next year he became a British subject; this was clearly a matter of business for he always expected that some day he would go back to the United States. In fact, when he died one of his own steamers did carry his body back to Clayton, but Sir John A. Macdonald, Prime Minister of Canada, was one of the pallbearers, and D. D. Calvin's descendents continued with the Garden Island firm.

Garden Island was an ideal place for timbers—squared logs—to be unloaded after travelling across Lake Ontario by ship, and then to be made up into rafts to go down the St. Lawrence. The timbers were tightly assembled into drams, or raft sections about sixty feet wide and three hundred feet long, held together by a wooden framework to which the individual timbers were lashed and pegged. Oak timbers were assembled only one layer deep, mixed with enough pine to keep them afloat; more buoyant woods were assembled three layers deep. A wooden cabin was built on one dram to serve as a cookhouse and on another to be the crew's quarters. The drams were then lashed together into rafts, which might be 120 feet wide and 1,000 to 1,400 feet long. Each raft was provided with sweeps, masts and sails, anchors, and other marine equipment. There might also be cargo on board in boxes or barrels. As many as 800 barrels of pork, flour, or ashes would go on a single raft. The crew consisted of about a dozen men, usually French Canadian rivermen—who sang when the mood was right—and Iroquois Indians.

The raft, as it went down the river, had to run the rapids. At the more dangerous ones it was taken apart into its individual drams, each of which shot the rapids separately. Local pilots and extra crewmen were hired as needed along the river. Once the raft reached Montreal the rapids were left behind and travel was more serene, but still Lake St. Pierre had to be traversed. This was a shallow part of the river between Montreal and Quebec, twenty-three miles long and seven wide, celebrated in story and song for its sudden violent storms.

LAFAYETTE COOK

Not only did the timber trade use the St. Lawrence to carry rafts eastward, but it also was one of the first businesses to reach westward from Lake Ontario through the Welland Canal and the other Great Lakes. As the forests on Ontario's shores dwindled, timbermen had to look farther afield and the new canal gave them the opportunity.

The Welland Canal was the child of a Canadian merchant, William Hamilton Merritt of St. Catherines. As early as 1818 he had conceived the idea of a ship canal to bypass Niagara Falls and link Lakes Ontario and Erie. By 1824 he had gathered private and public money enough to begin construction; by 1829 the first two vessels went through. But there were further construction difficulties and it was not until 1832 that any real traffic used the canal and not until the 1840s that the traffic grew to a sizable volume.

Merritt's engineering problems were great, but his financial and political ones were if possible greater. He managed to attract private capital in both Canada and the United States and backing from the governments of both Upper and Lower Canada. His own political leanings were toward the Reform Party, but in order to win government support he had to make peace with the men in power; this brought him under violent attack from the extremist on the Reform side, William Lyon Mackenzie. Despite all these things he built the canal.

It is a paradox that Lower Canada—the present-day Province of Quebec—was probably more interested in the Welland Canal than was Upper Canada, where it was situated. The great commercial and financial center of Montreal had long dominated the Great Lakes. But in 1825 the Erie Canal was completed and suddenly the Great Lakes had a much easier route to the outside world, via New York. Montreal set to work canalizing the St. Lawrence and pushing construction

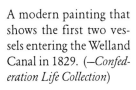

A modern painting that shows the first two vessels entering the Welland Canal in 1829. (—*Confederation Life Collection*)

Lafayette Cook, "canaller" brigantine with shallow, boxy hull to fit the locks of the early Welland Canal and with steeply canted bowsprit and jib boom to clear the lock gates. Her centerboard enabled her to sail properly in open water. Launched at St. Catherines, Ontario, in 1852, she was from the yard of the noted Maltese shipbuilder, Louis Shickluna. (—*Ohio Historical Society*)

on the Welland Canal, but she was never able to regain her dominant position toward the Lakes. Ironically, when Merritt's company finally collapsed under the financial burden, it was the government of Upper Canada that was forced in 1840 to take over ownership.

The timber trade was vitally linked to Montreal. Not only were there basic financial ties, but the St. Lawrence offered an effective way to raft timbers to a seaport while the Erie Canal did not. Thus the trade is perhaps the best example of the way the Welland Canal helped the Montreal financiers. A giant of the trade was D. D. Calvin, based on Garden Island; typical of the vessels he used was the brigantine *Lafayette Cook*.

Launched at St. Catherines in 1852, she was a vessel 113 feet long, 71 1/2 feet in breadth, and 11 feet in depth. At that time another timber merchant, Hiram Cook, was a partner of Calvin; he lived in Hamilton, not far from St. Catherines, and for a time controlled the western end of the business for the Calvin firm.

The *Lafayette Cook* was an example of what came to be known as "Welland Canallers," ships with boxy hulls and flat bottoms that would carry the maximum cargo through the small locks, which limited vessels to about 140 feet in length and 9 feet of draught. Such shallow vessels had to be fitted with centerboards if they were to sail properly, and their bowsprits and jib booms had to be canted up at a steep angle to clear the lock gates.

Timber droghers, as the vessels that carried timbers were called, usually had on board a team of horses, stabled on the deck. They provided the power for lifting timbers aboard and raising sails, and they helped to pull the vessels through the canal. The lowest-ranking member of the crew was the horseboy, who cared for and handled the animals. Going through the canal, the vessel's own team of horses was usually reinforced with other horses or mules. As C.H.J. Snider, the Toronto marine historian, has written, "The banks were lined with slippery, muddy towpaths, along which horses, mules, horseboys, and helpers and crews dragged lines, slipped, swore, fought, and disentangled themselves as best they could."

Vessels in the timber trade were heavily built. Their spars were thicker and their hulls sturdier than most. They might carry two-ton pieces of oak, either taken into the holds through ports in the stern or lifted onto the decks; the ships had to stand up to the wear and tear caused by such cargoes. The Calvin firm at first sent its vessels through the canal to the Ohio coast; the main place for loading oak was Toledo. Later they went into all of the other Lakes. The *Lafayette Cook* and others brought the squared timbers back to Garden Island where they were unloaded, sorted, and made into rafts for the trip downriver to Quebec.

The barkentine *Eureka*, which sailed from Cleveland around Cape Horn to the California gold fields. (—*Reproduced by courtesy of the artist, the late Rowley W. Murphy*)

EUREKA

The St. Lawrence was a highway for more than rafts. Various craft went down it to salt water. Perhaps the first direct clearance from the Great Lakes to Europe was made by the Canadian brigantine *Pacific* in 1844; she sailed from Toronto via the St. Lawrence with wheat for Liverpool.

Since 1832, when the Rideau Canal was completed between Kingston and the Ottawa River, there had been a roundabout way for small vessels to travel between Montreal and the Lakes. Regular lake vessels were too large for the canal, however, and could only go down the St. Lawrence, shooting the rapids. They could not come back up at all. But in 1848 a series of canals was completed around the rapids; after that vessels two hundred feet long and forty-five feet wide could move through them in either direction. The canals were meant for trade between Montreal and the Lakes, and several steamer lines sprang up to carry the trade. But the improvements in the St. Lawrence route made it even more the logical way to salt water.

A number of people on the Great Lakes were beginning to think that ships might go down to the sea. Odd-shaped vessels did sail occasionally across various parts of the Lakes and then go down the Erie Canal to New York or the Ohio Canal and River to New Orleans. In contrast, the St. Lawrence was a route that could be taken by normal lake- and sea-going vessels.

So when gold fever struck in 1849 and W. A. Adair and Company of Cleveland decided to send a ship carrying passengers around the Horn to San Francisco, it was through the St. Lawrence that she started out on her voyage.

She was the barkentine *Eureka*, built at what now is Lorain, Ohio, as a brig in 1847; she was 137 feet long on the keel and of 375 tons burden. Two years later, with the California trip in mind, her owner had her rerigged and fitted out for a long sea voyage. Late in September she sailed from Cleveland. Capt. William Monroe, her master, had already made several voyages around Cape Horn. Captain Barnett, who sailed as supercargo, had been in the Lakes service for many years and probably acted as pilot during the first part of the trip.

For the sum of three hundred dollars paid in advance, each of the thirty-eight passengers was entitled to cabin passage. He had to provide and care for his own bed and bedding; with him he could take a trunk and ten barrels of bulk freight. There were no steerage passengers. One passenger was a physician; his services later were needed.

The *Eureka* went through the Welland Canal—incurring some minor damage because of the tight fit—across Lake Ontario, and down the St. Lawrence. On October 18 she cleared customs at Montreal; on October 21 she arrived at Quebec, where she remained for about a month while being sheathed with copper and generally overhauled. She seems to have taken on more passengers there. She then headed away to Cape Horn.

Events of the voyage were not routine. On January 9 the vessel put into Rio de Janeiro because Captain Monroe was ill. There a Captain McQueen took command. A thief on board stole $270 from one man and a silver watch from another, but was never caught. A fight developed between an ex-steward named Beardsley and a drunken passenger who called him "a filthy name." The first mate waded in and helped the drunk beat up Beardsley, who as a result of his injuries had to go ashore to a surgeon. On board again, Beardsley contracted yellow fever and died, being buried at sea.

Rounding the Horn the weather was bad and no doubt the passengers were uncomfortable, but the *Eureka* came through it without difficulty, reaching Valparaiso fifty days after leaving Rio. At Valparaiso, where the ship spent fifteen days refitting, the passengers and crew waited upon the American Consul demanding the arrest of the mate for his treatment of Beardsley. The charges against the mate were dismissed after a hearing, but he did not continue the voyage.

W. A. Adair, the vessel's owner, reached San Francisco ahead of her by another route. On June 1, 1850, she arrived, 182 days out of Quebec, with 59 passengers of whom 7 were women. Adair presumably was on hand to welcome the *Eureka*, but by mid-August, according to report, he was "busted, blowed up, and gone to the devil," and had been forced to sell everything. The gold fever had evidently done its worst.

Eureka started back to Cleveland in October, but apparently was not well prepared for this voyage. She was becalmed, ran out of food and water, and after 72 days put into Acapulco with crew and passengers in deplorable physical condition and hating the sight of each other. Most of the passengers left her immediately and she was sold for $1,800 to pay for the rest of their journey.

CHALLENGE

The builders of Great Lakes ships not only were sending vessels to distant ports, but they were also improving the designs of their vessels. One such improved design was the clipper schooner *Challenge*, launched at Manitowoc, Wisconsin, in 1852.

In the 1840s a shipbuilding family of Nova Scotian origin lived and worked in Calais, Maine. The father, Stephen Bates, had a young and vigorous son, William, who by the time he was eighteen had designed and laid down a ship. William was restless. In 1845 he made a trip to the Great Lakes and spent the winter at shipyards in Huron and Sandusky; he went again in 1848, going as far as Lake Michigan, then swinging south to Louisville and New Orleans. All along the way he worked at building or repairing various kinds of vessels. From New Orleans he shipped to Boston as a seaman and went home to Maine.

In 1851 William Bates settled in Manitowoc, where there was a considerable demand for new vessels to carry the lumber from nearby forests to the Chicago market. His father either came with him or followed soon afterward, and they set up a shipyard there. This was the beginning of the clipper-ship period on the Atlantic, and both father and son knew saltwater shipping. In addition, William seems to have been a born engineer; he conducted experiments on buoyancy and water resistance and developed his own theories of ship design.

These theories were embodied in the small schooner *Challenge*. She was a shoal, centerboard vessel with sharp ends underwater; her bow was particularly fine and flaring. Her length on the load line was 80 feet and her "Custom-House tonnage" was 110. Because she often had to work in shallow water, her depth of hold was only 6 feet 5 inches. (She of course had a centerboard.) She was much criticized before her launching at the Bates yard but turned out to be a great success; a two-masted schooner, she could easily reach the speed of thirteen knots and was noted for the regularity of her voyages. She became so well known that a French naval constructor took her plan to France, where it was published in a work on naval architecture as an example of a fast clipper schooner.

While the *Challenge* was proving herself, mainly as a lumber carrier, the Bates shipyard turned out other clipper schooners from William's designs and soon Manitowoc became known as the clipper city. Bates himself may have inspired the title, for it was the *Clip-*

Sail and spar plan of the *Challenge*, first clipper schooner on the Great Lakes. (—*From the plans collection of the Wisconsin Maritime Museum, Manitowoc*)

per City that he named a fast lumber schooner launched in 1854. She was about one hundred feet long, and was reported on occasion to have sailed at twenty miles per hour. Larger Bates vessels followed and other builders began to adopt some of Bates's ideas.

Over the years it had become generally accepted that the fore-and-aft rig was better on Lakes vessels than the square rig. In narrow waters, where the vessel had to maneuver frequently and often had to beat against the wind, conditions were quite different than they were at sea, where square sails could be set and left alone for considerable periods of time, and where ships could follow one course, usually before the wind, for days on end. Thus it was that most of the Great Lakes clippers either were schooners or were brigantines and barkentines—vessels that had square sails only on the foremast. (Normally these rigs were called brigs and barks by lake sailors. Men of the Lakes at times went a step further and called all such vessels schooners; even Bates did this on occasion.)

William Bates had written quite widely about ship designing and building. In 1853 he and John W. Griffiths, a well-known naval architect of New York whom he may have consulted while designing the *Clipper City*, established *The U.S. Nautical Magazine and Marine Journal* and in 1854 Bates moved to New York to edit it, leaving his father to run the shipyard. The magazine became the technical voice of the clipper-ship era. The

era did not last long. It coincided with a business boom and the gold rushes and it ended soon after the depression of 1857, when the *Nautical Magazine* ceased publication. That journal, however, remains one of the best records of clippers on both fresh and salt water.

In less prosperous times, shippers were more interested in vessels with carrying capacity than in those with great speed. Soon afterward William Bates returned to the Lakes, where in time he designed and built other vessels, including steamers. In 1881 he and his son, Lindon W. Bates (who was to become an internationally known engineer) went to Oregon and built docks for the Northern Pacific Railroad. In 1889 he was appointed Commissioner of Navigation, a federal official, but resigned because of failing health and went to live in Denver with his daughter, a physician (at a time when women doctors were rare). His interest in ship design continued, however, and he wrote journal articles and two books on the subject.

SAM WARD

Indians mined copper on the Lake Superior shores in prehistoric times; French explorers later remarked its presence there. In the early 1770s an English company dug a mine to get ore and built a sloop to carry it, but the project was soon abandoned. Expeditions such as the one led by Governor Cass in 1820 noted the existence of copper, but there was

There is no known picture of the *Sam Ward*, but from written descriptions she was very like this steamer shown entering the upper end of the canal at Sault Ste. Marie after it was completed, and this picture may have been meant to represent her. (*—Great Lakes Historical Society*)

little public response. It remained for a young geologist, Dr. Douglas Houghton, to bring copper deposits to general notice. After nearly ten years of work in the area he published a report in 1841 that told of the great deposits along the southern shore of the lake. Growing interest followed and by 1884 the first modern copper mine on Lake Superior was established.

That same autumn a surveying party at work just southwest of what now is Marquette, Michigan, found the compass needle behaving strangely. Looking around, they discovered outcroppings of iron ore. The next spring a group of copper prospectors learned of the new discovery, found their way to the iron outcroppings, and established a claim. The first iron mine in the Lake Superior region soon was operating there.

All this brought such a flood of prospectors and miners that at the town of Sault Ste. Marie on the

American side of the St. Mary's River, through which most traffic channeled to Lake Superior, two hotels were opened in 1845. At first, all freight passing over the Sault portage was carried in a cart pulled by a gray horse belonging to one Sheldon McKnight, but as more people arrived and more vessels called at the lower end of the portage, McKnight expanded his business, finally in 1850 building a railway with a number of horse-drawn cars. These cars took supplies up to Lake Superior and ore down to Lake Huron.

The few small sailing vessels on Lake Superior could not meet the growing demands. In 1839 a schooner was hauled over the portage on rollers. In 1845 six more schooners were taken over the portage and another was built at the Sault. And that same year the propeller *Independence* was moved across the portage.

The moving of a sizable vessel on land was accomplished in much the same way that a house might have been moved. It took about seven weeks to transport the ship to Lake Superior; there she was launched again, the first steam-powered vessel on the lake. She had time for only one trip that fall. Some half-dozen more steamers were taken across the portage to Lake Superior in the following years, the last of them being the *Sam Ward*, which was hauled up to the lake in 1853.

Laurence Oliphant, an English traveller who in 1854 voyaged across Lake Superior in the *Sam Ward*, described what he found at the Sault before his departure.

> The most characteristic feature of the Sault Ste. Marie . . . is the tram-road which runs down the centre of the main street, and along which trucks, loaded with huge blocks of copper, are perpetually rumbling. The weight of each was generally marked upon it, and I observed that some of the masses exceeded 6000 lb. I was somewhat startled, upon the morning of our departure, to find, on coming to the door of the hotel, that our luggage had taken the place of the usual more valuable freight, and that, seated in picturesque attitudes upon piles of boxes and carpet-bags, about two hundred persons were waiting to be trundled away to the steamer, more than a mile distant. They were so thickly hived upon the long line of trucks, that I could scarcely find a spare corner in which to take up a position.

Oliphant was particularly impressed by the assortment of humanity crossing the portage on the little train.

Fragile, delicate-looking ladies, with pink and white complections, black ringlets, bright dresses, and thin satin shoes, reclined gracefully upon carpet-bags, and presided over pyramids of band-boxes. Square-built German fraus sat astride huge rolls of bedding, displaying stout legs, blue worsted stockings, and hob-nailed shoes. Sallow Yankees, with straw hats, swallow-tailed coats, and pumps, carried their little all in their pockets; and having nothing to lose and everything to gain in the western world to which they were bound, whittled, smoked, or chewed cheerfully. Hard-featured, bronzed miners, having spent their earnings in the bowling saloons at the Sault, were returning to the bowels of the earth gloomily. There were tourists in various costumes, doing the agreeable to the ladies; and hardy pioneers of the woods, in flannel shirts and trousers supported by leathern belts, and well supplied with bowies, were telling tough yarns, and astounding the weak minds of the emigrants, who represented half the countries of Europe.

These people all were taking passage on the vessel whose legally registered name, *Samuel Ward*, seldom was used in full. She was a wooden steamer 175 feet long, which had been built in Newport, Michigan, in 1847. Most of her crowded passengers intended to settle in some distant part of the Lake Superior country. Oliphant remarked that night, after she had begun her voyage, "Land was nowhere visible . . . it was difficult to realise the fact that this monster boat, with her living freight of near three

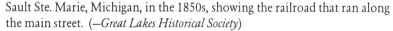

Sault Ste. Marie, Michigan, in the 1850s, showing the railroad that ran along the main street. (—*Great Lakes Historical Society*)

hundred souls, was already fifteen hundred miles from the ocean, and was bound upon a voyage of four hundred more."

Life on board was pleasant enough as they steamed along.

> I am afraid it was a dissipated, careless sort of existence—one to which the words of the old French song might very fairly be applied, "Le vin, le jeu, les belles, voila nos seuls plaisirs." As for the first, it was in the captain's cabin. He was the most hospitable and jovial of inland navigators; and as a mark of particular favour, we occupied the state room (as it is called) adjoining his. They both opened on a sort of balcony, and here at all hours was collected a noisy group, taking what they called "nips," smoking mahogany-tinted meerschaums or fragrant havannahs, with a standard rule that each member of the party should furnish a story, a song, or a bottle of wine.... As for *le jeu*, it was pretty well sustained all through the day. There was the game of Seven-up, accompanied by its incomprehensible exclamations of "hoss and hoss," and involving the mysteries of the "Sun-flower shuffle," and the "big greasy cut"; there was the Far West game of Old Sledge, and the fashionably down-east game of Euchre, and the universally popular game of Poker, and sundry others, with unrecollectable names, which were the means of causing considerable sums to change hands. Last, but not least, *les belles* were very well represented; but it required some little time to become acquainted with them, as they occupied the upper table at every meal, upon the sanctity of which we unprivileged bachelors were not allowed to intrude....

The best time to meet the ladies, Oliphant learned, was at the evening dances, where the Negro barbers acted also as the ship's band. His invitation to dance was accepted by "a lovely girl, with a noble, thoughtful brow, black hair and eyes, perfect features, and a most irresistible smile." The dance itself, however, proved vigorous and complicated, and as he struggled through it he became aware of the "glance of profound contempt with which my fair companion eyed my performance." At the end they both collapsed in exhaustion on a sofa. And the *Sam Ward* steamed steadily westward.

THE FUR TRADE CANOE (II)

Steamers such as the *Sam Ward* operated on Lake Superior, but so also did canoes. The fur trade was practically over on the American shores of the lake, but the Hudson's Bay Company still operated posts on the Canadian side; most of them had originally belonged to the North West Company before the merger of the two fur-trade giants in 1821. Those posts were still reached by canoe and schooner. The main supply route for the western posts of the company had long since been determined as Hudson Bay, but the posts along Lake Superior and some distance inland from it could be reached more easily by way of the Great Lakes.

In 1854 Henry John Moberly, a young man of nineteen, entered the service of the Hudson's Bay Company. His father had been a captain in the Royal Navy and young Moberly had been born at Penetanguishene, a remote spot on Georgian Bay, where his father commanded the naval base. The young fellow spent two

Sir George Simpson's canoe at Fort William, from the painting by William Armstrong. (*—Courtesy Mrs. P.C. Band*)

Governor Simpson, traveling in a north canoe in the waters northwest of the Great Lakes. He is accompanied by his personal bagpiper. (—*Courtesy Hudson's Bay Company*)

years in St. Petersburg, Russia, working for Lloyd's Bank. Finding this pretty boring, he returned to Canada, signed up with the HBC for five years, and in the spring of 1854 was at the post of Fort La Cloche, at the place where Georgian Bay joins the North Channel, waiting for a westward-bound canoe brigade.

The canoes came over the time-honored route up the Ottawa River, across Lake Nipissing, and down French River. After the canoemen rested a few hours at La Cloche, they moved on toward Sault Ste. Marie, taking Moberly with them. At the Sault they stopped for a day and a half. In contrast with the busy developments on the American side of the Sault, at this time there was little but a Hudson's Bay post on the Canadian side. There they awaited Sir George Simpson, Governor of the Hudson's Bay Company. Sir George, to save time and fatigue, travelled from Montreal to Chicago by train, thence to the Sault by steamer. He arrived on the scene with a chief factor who was on his way to take charge of Fort Garry, near Lake Winnipeg, and a judge who was bound to the same place to preside over the courts; the judge had with him his family. The HBC provided government and law in the territories it owned; Sir George's title of Governor was not intended to be quaint. The whole party arrived in the evening. At half-past one next morning the brigade left the Sault and started out on Lake Superior.

The brigade was composed of beautifully made birch-bark canoes, each manned by twelve middlemen, a bowsman, and a steersman. They were big Montreal canoes, about thirty-five feet long, carrying luggage and provisions but no freight. By this time the canoe in these waters was a fast means of passenger travel and freight was normally brought in by schooner. Sir George's canoe was manned by Iroquois, from a group that lived near Montreal. They wore the voyageur costume of red shirts, rough serge trousers, and red sashes. That first morning Sir George and his male secretary slept until seven as the canoes thrust westward. Occasionally Sir George, still apparently asleep, put his arm over the side and slipped his fingers in the water; then the canoemen suddenly increased the tempo from their normal steady stroke and the canoe leaped forward.

Exactly at seven they put ashore for breakfast; in half an hour, whether the meal was finished or not, they started out again. Sir George spent the morning dictating to his secretary while the canoemen from time to time broke into voyageur songs. At noon they put ashore again, this time for exactly one hour by the clock. Then they continued until after sunset, when they stopped and camped for the night. The crew was expert and quickly pitched tents and cooked supper; then everyone ate and turned in.

Four days later they arrived at Fort William, about ten o'clock in the morning. As they approached the mouth of the Kaministiquia River

Voyageurs at dawn, from the painting by Frances Hopkins. The members of a canoe brigade, which has camped overnight, are beginning to stir; soon they will embark again. (*—National Archives of Canada C 2773*)

where the fort was located, the HBC flag (a British red ensign with the white initials HBC in the fly) was run up, guns were fired, and a crowd of "gentlemen," Indians, and half-breeds gathered on the wharf to welcome Sir George, as well as officers from posts north of Lake Superior who had joined the brigade on its way. Sir George, stepping ashore, turned to his head canoeman and announced, "At ten minutes past six o'clock we start." Then to the chief factor who met him he said, "Council meets at one o'clock. Just two and a half hours for feasting and talking; then to business." Moberly described the banquet that followed:

> ... smoked and salted buffalo tongues and bosses, moose noses and tongues, beaver tails from the wooded country, the choicest venison, wild ducks and geese, fresh trout and whitefish, and a lavish spread of delicacies from the old world, brought by the Governor himself. Sherry and old port wine, with champagne, were all the beverages allowed, discipline being very strict in those days. Each person knew his place at table. The Governor sat at the head; next, ranging on each side, came the chief factors, then the clerks in order of their standing, the apprentice clerks from above and below the Sault, the post managers and the interpreters.

Sir George, with a straight face, introduced young Moberly as the new chief factor of Saskatchewan, seated him with the senior officers, and passed him the wine before anyone else. The reaction of the experienced men to a youngster who supposedly had been appointed to such an exalted position must have appealed to Sir George's Scots sense of humor, for he continued the joke at each post they visited during the remainder of the trip.

At one o'clock all the officers rose and went into the council room, leaving the junior men behind. This was the yearly conference between the governor and the chief factors and traders in charge of the posts within the area marked by the Sault and Fort William on the south, Moose Factory and Albany on the north. At this time and place they settled all important matters for the coming year. The governor and the others emerged from the council at five o'clock. There was general conversation until five minutes after six; then Sir George shouted "All aboard!" Those travelling with him filed down to the wharf where the canoemen were waiting with everything loaded in smaller north canoes for the journey to Lake Winnipeg. At exactly ten past six the brigade pushed away in the drizzling rain, much to the disgust of the judge.

COLUMBIA

Capt. Justus Wells, master of the little brigantine *Columbia*, did not have much in common with a 23-year-old Connecticut man who had a keen eye for the main chance, but because of the younger man, Captain Wells and his 91-foot command sailed into the history books.

The need for a canal to link Lake Superior with the other Lakes became more and more urgent, but over the years many false starts had accomplished little. Pressure continued; then in 1851 the few steam vessels on Superior had a series of accidents that put several out of service, and cargoes began to pile up at the Sault. With this added spur, the U.S. Congress finally granted 750,000 acres of land to the State of Michigan to pay for construction of a canal.

In the spring of 1852 Charles T. Harvey, the 23-year-old son of a Connecticut preacher, was employed as a salesman by E. & T. Fairbanks & Co. of St. Johnsbury, Vermont, manufacturers of scales. He was recovering from a prolonged attack of typhoid fever and his employers proposed to him that he spend the summer on Lake Superior, recovering his health and investigating mineral deposits in which they had an interest. He accepted the plan and set out for Sault Ste. Marie, where he made his base at the home of the Baptist missionary. During the summer he travelled in the Superior country, checking out its mineral resources and recovering his health. When he returned to the Sault to write his report he learned of the provision for a canal, and notified his employer, stressing the need for quick action to make this new investment.

Erastus Fairbanks, realizing that his company did not have the capital to build the canal while waiting for the state to grant the land to it and then, once it owned the land, waiting even longer to sell it, turned to the powerful financier Erastus Corning for help. To find out more, Fairbanks sent Harvey back to the Sault in October with an engineer who would prepare a cost estimate of building the canal. The esti-

The brigantine *Columbia*, which carried the first load of ore through the canal at Sault Ste. Marie. (*—Ohio Historical Society Library*)

mate was $403,500. That same fall an engineer for the state estimated that a canal would cost $557,739.

Through Corning, Fairbanks made contact with two Detroit men, John W. Brooks and James F. Joy, superintendent and counsel, respectively, of the Michigan Central Railroad. In January the Michigan legislature had to approve the plans; Harvey drafted a bill which, with some final amendments, was submitted and pushed by Joy. Among Harvey's provisions were that the locks would be 350 feet long and 70 feet wide, and that the canal be built within two years (the U.S. Congress had given a ten-year limit, but Harvey was a perennial optimist).

When the bill was reported, Capt. Eber B. Ward of Detroit, then the largest individual shipowner on the Lakes, took pen firmly in hand and wrote a letter to the members of the legislature, also sending copies to the newspapers:

> . . . The size proposed by the senate bill, 350 by 70 feet locks, is entirely too large for the locks. The crooked, narrow, shallow and rocky channel in the St. Mary's River will forever deter the largest class of steamers from navigating these waters.
>
> I do not believe there is the least necessity for making the locks over 260 feet in the clear and 60 feet wide, as no vessel of larger dimensions that could pass such locks can be used there with safety without an expenditure of a very large sum of money in excavating rock at various points along the river, a work that is not likely to be undertaken during the present century. . . .

The objection went unheeded, however, perhaps because the legislators knew that most of Ward's steamers were of the smaller size, and it would be useful to him if his boats had a near-monopoly on passage through the new canal. The bill passed as written and was signed on 5 February.

Joy then returned to his political stage-managing. On March 24, 1853, he wrote to Erastus Corning that he thought their group would get the contract no matter who the other bidders might be, and on April 5 his prediction came true. As a result, the St. Mary's Falls Ship Canal Company, a New York Corporation, was formed and Charles Harvey was made its general agent.

No one, least of all Harvey, seemed to realize the task ahead. He did not arrive at the Sault until June 6, thus losing at least a month's working time. With him he had only 232 men, including supervisors; by 22 Sep-

tember he had only 420. Then 350 more were rushed from Detroit, but the working season was almost over.

Harvey established a commissary department, built fifty-man shanties to house the workers, and constructed a hospital on an island in the river. To each shanty he assigned a couple as caretaker and cook; the hospital was put in charge of a salaried doctor. During the work Harvey travelled back and forth on horseback, usually at full gallop. His intense personality was not especially winning, and as he never cared if his galloping horse splashed mud on anyone within range his popularity did not improve with the local citizens, especially the women.

There was a shortage of tools. On 11 June a steamer brought in some wood for construction, some cattle, and some carts. Yet to come from Albany were wheelbarrows, picks, shovels, and crowbars. Harvey called for a bookkeeper, who arrived on August 1 and quickly reported that the records were in such disorder he could not be certain what had taken place before his arrival. At the work site, less important jobs were given priority over those that had to be completed before the entire project could go forward.

It was evident that the project was much bigger and more difficult than anyone had foreseen. In 1853 the stockholders were assessed an extra $5 a share in June, $10 in November, and $5 in December. (Before the canal was finished they would pay a total amount in assessments equal to their original investment and there would be an issue of bonds as well, but eventually they would realize a considerable profit.)

Harvey had become friends with the editor of the local *Lake Superior Journal*, had put him on the payroll as land agent for the canal company, but eventually discovered that during his company-paid land-hunting the editor had registered the limestone area on Drummond Island—which was intended to provide building material for the canal—in his own name. During the altercation that followed, Harvey refused to pay the editor for the stone and the editor used his paper to excoriate Harvey and the Canal Company, continuing to do so throughout the building period, at times stirring up major political

The lower end of the canal at Sault Ste. Marie soon after its completion.
(—*Institute for Great Lakes Research., Bowling Green State University*)

difficulties. (The Drummond Island limestone was never used).

Harvey was able to keep four hundred men who were willing to work through the winter, but sub-zero temperatures, snow, and ice greatly limited what they could do. Planning for construction materials was so poor that wood and stone were not available when they were needed. By spring the operation was falling apart in many ways.

The backers of the canal were having second thoughts about Harvey, who also had managed to quarrel with the experienced engineer appointed by the state. They decided that Brooks, who was Harvey's immediate superior, should temporarily leave his Detroit job and spend the summer superintending the canal work. Harvey was to do only what Brooks assigned him.

By this time there were 50 shanties and about 1700 laborers. They were worked 11 1/2 hours a day rather than the 10 that was then standard practice. Their only entertainment was in the primitive grogshops at the Sault. Morale was low and there were occasional attempts at strikes and riots, but they were soon quelled. Workers were recruited in the East wherever they could be found. Often they were poor physical specimens, scarcely fit for work. Some of them brought cholera with them: in the summer of 1854 epidemic struck. Ten percent of the work force died; the bodies were taken out quietly at night and buried in a remote place to avoid panic among the workmen. By contrast, the health of the soldiers at nearby Fort Brady remained normal throughout the year. Sanitation, the state of the men recruited, and working conditions almost certainly made the difference.

When Brooks took over, organization improved and work moved more quickly; he was described as a "perfect Napoleon." By December 1, however, Brooks had returned to Detroit (he would spend Christmas in Boston, sick in bed) and most of the men had been paid off. Harvey remained at the Sault with a hundred men. In January, the Canal Company asked the Michigan legislature to transfer to it the 750,000 acres that would eventually pay for the canal. Political opponents of the Canal Company, who coveted the land, put pressure on the legislature not to transfer it until the canal was completed, and not to grant any extension of time for completion. Brooks was back in Detroit recuperating, but now was having his teeth pulled. He telegraphed Joy to go immediately to Lansing; Joy did, but this time was unable to change the political situation.

Meanwhile Harvey plugged away at completing the canal. When Brooks sent instructions from Detroit, Harvey answered that he would not follow them and that he was too busy to explain why. Harvey later wrote his own account of those days, listing the astounding number of difficult things he accomplished; in fact he did work hard, but mainly in pinning down loose ends.

On May 11 Brooks and other directors of the company arrived at the Sault. Brooks took over the small tasks that remained to complete the canal. On May 21 the canal commissioners—the Michigan group whose main function was to approve the work—plus the governor and other dignitaries inspected the canal. On their way back down the St. Mary's River on the steamer *Illinois*, the commissioners and the governor gave Corning a written acceptance of the canal for the state.

But not all was well on the political front. Opponents, using whatever devices they could find, still were blocking the transfer of the 750,000 acres to the Canal Company. Corning wrote a letter to the appropriate politicians, appealing to the general interest of Michigan citizens in opening the canal, suggesting that he wanted to avoid litigation that would be costly to the state, and ending by saying that if the company did not get the land they would of course have to "hold the canal"—in other words, drain it and wait. The navigation season had opened, a multitude of business interests wanted ships and cargoes to pass through, and politicians who caused it to remain closed at this point would be monumentally unpopular. The land was quickly transferred to the company.

The cost of building the canal was approximately $913 thousand—roughly double the original estimates.

Michigan, once it owned the canal, had to pay maintenance costs; in 1859 the legislature authorized issuance of $100 thousand of canal bonds and the bonds were sold. (Half the money soon disappeared; the state treasurer was found guilty of embezzlement and jailed, but the $50 thousand remained missing.)

The man most responsible for building the canal was John W. Brooks, though his name has faded from history. Harvey, by outliving all the others involved, was able to publish an account saying that he had built the canal practically single-handedly, and for many years that was the accepted story. Harvey deserves credit for seeing a good opportunity and bringing it to the attention of his employer, but the basic honor must go to Brooks.

The brig *Columbia* was not the first vessel through the canal and certainly not the largest. But her significance was greater than either of these. She carried the first cargo of iron ore, leaving Marquette with it on August 14 and passing through the canal on August 17, bound for Cleveland. The total cargo was 132 tons. The *Columbia*, built in Sandusky, Ohio, in 1842, was 91 feet long and of 177 tons burden. The little vessel was actually a brigantine, with square sails on the foremast and fore-and-aft sails on the main, but Great Lakes sailors usually shortened the name to brig.

Justus Wells, her master, was a Vermonter born, who as a boy had run away from home to ship on one of the great clippers of the Atlantic. Later he came to Sandusky and sailed on various lake vessels. He retired from the nautical life in 1859, married, and settled on a Michigan farm where he raised five children and remained until his death, twenty-four years later. His life was fairly uneventful in its time, but thanks to the canal builders, Captain Wells and the *Columbia* became harbingers of the massive North American ore trade that was to follow.

MADIERA PET

Ships from the other Great Lakes could now go into the biggest and westernmost of the chain. It still remained for ships from the ocean to come into the Lakes themselves. The first salt-water vessel to do this was probably the British *Madeira Pet* in 1857.

Madeira Pet, an English brigantine, was the first ocean-going vessel to come into the Great Lakes. Here she is shown at her Chicago dock. (*—Chicago Historical Society*)

The preceding year a group of Chicago and Montreal men had sent the Cleveland-built schooner *Dean Richmond*, laden with Chicago and Milwaukee wheat, to Liverpool, where they sold both cargo and ship. This voyage attracted the attention of one W. J. Burch, a resident of St. John, New Brunswick, who also had interests in Chicago. He decided to bring a cargo in to Chicago from England. He had an agent charter a small British brigantine, the *Madeira Pet* of Guernsey, to make the voyage from Liverpool to Chicago and return. A neat-looking vessel with a beautiful figurehead of a lady, she was ninety-seven feet long. Her general cargo was made up of iron bars, earthenware, glass, hardware, and paint.

Capt. William Crang, "a fine noble specimen of a seaman," was her master. She sailed out of Liverpool on the morning of April 24, arrived at Montreal forty days later, ran aground briefly, then proceeded up the St. Lawrence river and canals to Kingston. There on June 3 she took a pilot on board for the trip up the Lakes. In the Welland Canal an American schooner ran afoul of her and damaged her rigging. Three days later she had the damage repaired and was on her way. At Detroit the cook jumped ship. The little vessel arrived in Chicago on July 14, eighty days after sailing from England.

A committee from the Board of Trade went by tug to the mouth of the river in order to escort the vessel to her berth. She was towed upriver between cheering crowds that packed the docks and bridges. On the evening of July 15 the city held a celebration in Dearborn Park with speeches, music, and a hundred-gun salute by the Chicago Light Artillery. The Great Western Band played "God Save the Queen," "Yankee Doodle," and other tunes. Next day the Chicago *Press* said:

> The Northwest can easily dispense with middlemen, and save herself annually millions of dollars which are now paid out in the shape of commissions and profits. She can import her own goods, and export her own surplus direct to European docks without breaking bulk or incurring any other cost than that of a reasonable freight.

It was a comment that has echoed and re-echoed through the years between.

Above: The *Western World.* This drawing is by Samuel Ward Stanton, the noted artist-historian who lost his life as a passenger on the *Titanic.* (*—From the American Steam Vessels Booklet Series by Samuel Ward Stanton*)

Below: A corner of Chicago harbor in 1857, showing the blockhouse of old Fort Dearborn at center. (*—I. N. Phelps Stokes Collection, New York Public Library*)

4
Tensions

The period of expansion during the 1840s and much of the 1850s was followed by one of tension and disaster. New developments continued and Great Lakes commerce still grew, but the atmosphere was different. Financial panic was followed by the Civil War. Britain favored the South during this struggle and Canada was British; feeling between the two countries that bordered the Lakes was not cordial. Confederate spies were based in Canada while Confederate raiders from Canada harassed the United States. After the war, the atmosphere was not improved when the Fenian Brotherhood, a militant Irish patriotic organization made up largely of former Union army soldiers, undertook to capture Canada from bases in the United States. Canada, expanding westward, was faced with rebellion in the Red River settlement it was taking over from the Hudson's Bay Company. Private interests in the United States, the Fenians, and the U.S. Government combined to encourage the rebels, while the United States did what it could to prevent Canada from sending over the Great Lakes the military expedition that finally quelled the rebellion.

WESTERN WORLD

By the mid-1850s Great Lakes steamers had become large and ornate. Sixteen first-class sidewheelers operated between Buffalo and Chicago; two of them sailed from each port every day. It took three or four days to make the voyage one way and it was not uncommon for a ship to carry four or five hundred passengers. Other glittering steamers connected Buffalo and Detroit.

These vessels competed with each other in such features as marble fountains in the lounges, leaded stained-glass domes over the ladies' parlors, nurseries, bathrooms with hot and cold running water, and of course bars. Their interiors were decorated with rare woods and gold moldings, and carpeted with the finest materials. The palace steamers were large, ornate, expensive vessels, and their days were numbered.

One of them was the *Western World*, owned by the New York Central Railroad and launched at Buffalo in 1854. Designed by a rising naval architect with the surprising name of Isaac Newton, she was 337 feet long. She and her sister *Plymouth Rock* were claimed to be the largest steamers afloat anywhere when they were launched at Buffalo. In their public areas they had crystal chandeliers, silk and damask curtains, murals, mirrors, and statuary. The cabin accommodations even included bridal suites. These two ships and the smaller *May Flower* provided daily service between Buffalo and Detroit, linking the western terminus of the New York Central with the eastern terminus of the Michigan Central. They all were commanded, according to the company, by "gentlemen and officers of great experience and ability."

Such long wooden vessels had to be strengthened in some manner. The device used was common at that time: two truss arches, one on each side, rose above decks and cabins for almost the length of the ship. Never before, however, had truss arches been so large or so long. The ship's engine provided 1500 hp; by contrast, the engine of the *Great Western*, one of the finest steamers on the Lakes less than twenty years earlier, had produced 300 hp. The *Western World* had a single tall mast forward on which a sail was set to be used in emergencies or to steady her in rough weather. She had a bowsprit, but unlike most bowsprits it was tipped with a gilded spearhead and seems to have flown a flag. The bowsprit-flagstaff was really an early example of a spar used to this day by many boats; now it is called a steering pole. On a Great Lakes vessel the pilothouse is often so far forward and so little of the hull extends ahead of it that the helmsman has difficulty in lining her up with navigational markers. The steering pole, slanting up and out like a bowsprit, gives him an extension of the ship to steer by.

Even as the palace steamers were running, railroads were being built along the shores of the Lakes. But the economy was soaring; transportation systems were expanding and at first it seemed that there would be enough traffic for both trains and ships. North America was riding an economic crest. The Crimean War in 1854-55 had provided large markets for America; gold discoveries in California had prompted a rapid expansion of banking; and the building of the railroads, the canals, and the steamers themselves had brought much money into circulation. Now this money was locked in these enterprises which were overexpanded and returning no profit. Late in August 1857, the Ohio Life Insurance and Trust Company failed. The tremors from this collapse brought down other financial institutions that had extended too much credit, and the Panic of 1857 was complete. Business came almost to a standstill. One after another the palace steamers were laid up; by mid-October not a single big sidewheeler was entering or clearing the port of Buffalo.

During 1858 few vessels moved on the Great Lakes and none of the big steamers was commissioned. In 1859 business improved somewhat and a few of them came back; but now the new railroads were drawing more passenger traffic and the more economical, compact propellers could carry freight over the Lakes much more cheaply. The big, almost new, side-wheelers were obsolete. The *Western World,* which had been laid up at Detroit in 1857, never sailed again. She remained out of commission until 1863; she then was towed to Buffalo and dismantled.

LADY ELGIN

Some of the elaborate sidewheelers did survive the Panic of 1857 and competition of the railroads. They were not the giants, but rather the fairly big ones that could fit into other trades. One of these was the *Lady Elgin,* 252 feet long, which weathered the economic troubles only to be lost a few years later in one of the greatest shipping disasters of Great Lakes history.

Launched in Buffalo in 1851 for the Buffalo-Chicago run she had a varied career, after which she

The *Lady Elgin,* engraved from a photograph taken at her Chicago dock the day before she was lost. (—*Chicago Historical Society*)

The *Lady Elgin* in harbor at Northport, Michigan, in the latter 1850s. This unusual perspective view gives a good idea of the way her complex upper works were arranged. (—*Institute for Great Lakes Research, Bowling Green State University*)

became part of the Lake Superior Line, on the U.S. side of the Lakes; she then travelled along the western shore of Lake Michigan and the southern shore of Lake Superior. Because of her luxurious appointments and speed she became known along her route as "Queen of the Lakes" and was a favorite among excursionists. It was carrying an excursion that she came to her end in 1860.

This one excursion was a peculiar development of the times. In the United States there were tensions between abolitionists and slaveholders and between proponents of federal control and those of States' rights. The governor of Wisconsin, Alexander Randall, was a strong abolitionist and a radical Republican. But he also was a violent states' rights man, and it was commonly rumored that he would take Wisconsin out of the Union unless the federal government abolished slavery. Feeling was so strong in Wisconsin that one assemblyman introduced a resolution directing the governor to declare war against the United States.

At this point the adjutant general of the state sent agents to all of the militia companies, asking where they stood if the state did secede. One of the four companies in Milwaukee, the Union Guards, was com-

manded by Capt. Garrett Barry, a prominent Democrat who had graduated from West Point, taught infantry tactics to such officers as Sherman and Grant, and distinguished himself in the Mexican War; after the war he had resigned from the Regular Army and settled in Milwaukee. He replied that he was as opposed to slavery as anyone, but his primary allegiance had to be with the federal government; any other stand was treason. The agent reported this and in due course the adjutant general revoked Barry's militia commission and directed that the Union Guards turn over all their weapons to another militia company.

Most of the seventy members of the Union Guards were Irish Americans. Their reaction to this order may be imagined. They were proud of their organization and determined not to disband; their first move, they decided, was to raise money to buy new arms, and one way was to sponsor an excursion. They arranged for the *Lady Elgin* to carry their excursion to Chicago. Between four and five hundred people were on board when the steamer left Milwaukee after midnight on the morning of Friday, September 7. Later that morning they arrived in Chicago. The Union Guards paraded; then the whole excursion went sightseeing, and finally in the evening there was a banquet and dancing.

The master of the steamer, Capt. Jack Wilson, a man with a full beard and mustache, was a competent seaman who in 1855 had commanded the first vessel to pass through the Sault Ste. Marie canal. He hesitated to leave Chicago in the face of probable bad weather, but his passengers were insistent and finally he agreed. The steamer headed away from Chicago harbor about 11:30 p.m. with a freshening northeast wind on her port bow. By 2:00 a.m. the wind had increased to a gale; a number of excursionists still were dancing but others had retired to their staterooms. At 2:30 a shudder ran through the whole ship and the *Lady Elgin* suddenly heeled over on her port side, shattering lamps and plunging much of her interior into darkness. As she righted herself slowly, chaos ensued among the passengers.

The two-masted schooner *Augusta*, under all sail but her gaff topsail, heavily laden with a cargo of lumber and without lights, had appeared suddenly out of the night and rammed the *Lady Elgin* just aft of the paddle wheel on the port side, slicing into the steamer's main saloon. There she hung for a moment, pulled along by the speed of the other ship, before dropping away and disappearing into the storm.

Captain Wilson attempted to calm the passengers. He ordered that some 150 cattle in the hold be thrown overboard and had as much freight as possible moved to the starboard side, opposite the hole left by the schooner, in the hope that he could raise that hole above the water. Captain Barry and other Union Guards worked with the crew to accomplish this. Wilson also directed the passengers to go to the starboard side, but most of them were too scared to follow orders.

At the same time Captain Wilson lowered two lifeboats in command of ship's officers to make repairs; they were laden with mattresses and sailcloth to plug the hole. One boat, as it developed, had only one oar and could not be controlled. The second boat filled with water, was bailed out, and then was so far away it was unable to reach the ship. Only one boat was left on the steamer.

The captain ordered the whistle tied down and the bell rung constantly, hoping to attract some passing vessel. They were about ten miles off Winnetka, Illinois, and he turned the ship toward shore, but the water soon reached her fires and put them out; as she ran

The collision between the *Lady Elgin* and the *Augusta*. (—*Chicago Historical Society*)

The sinking *Lady Elgin*. (*—Chicago Historical Society*)

out of steam she lost way slowly and began to settle. The 500 life preservers aboard were stowed in such a way that they could not be reached. Passengers and crew tore doors off hinges and pulled up pieces of deck to make life rafts, and anything that could float was thrown overboard to support the terrified passengers who leaped into the water.

As the ship reeled and took her final plunge, a sea struck her upper works and lifted away the hurricane deck, which became a huge raft. A number of people climbed onto it. One survivor described what followed.

> On this extempore raft not less than 300 persons were collected, the majority of whom clung to their places until nearly daylight. The raft was mostly under water from the weight of the living burden, and very few who clung to it but were above the waist in the turbulent sea. The captain was constantly on his feet, encouraging the crowd, and seems to have been the only man who dared to move from his recumbent position, which was necessary to keep a secure hold upon the precarious raft. He carried a child which he found in the arms of an exhausted and submerged woman, to an elevated portion of the raft, and left it in charge of a woman, when it soon was lost. He constantly exhorted the crowd to keep silent and not only to make no noise, but to refrain from moving, in order that the frail framework might last the longer.

Waves in time broke the hurricane deck into smaller pieces. Both Wilson and Barry were credited with many acts of bravery in attempting to save lives. As the floating debris and the people clinging to it neared shore, the situation became worse if that were possible. The shore at Winnetka consisted of forty-foot cliffs, against which the storm dashed the survivors. Wilson managed to save two women before he was thrown against the rocks and killed. Barry, exhausted from his efforts, was drowned a hundred feet from shore. Crowds lined the bluffs and looked down in horror, unable to help as some 120 people died there.

As was usual in those days, there was no record of the exact number of people on board the *Lady Elgin* and no one knew exactly how many were rescued. Estimates of the number dead range from 350 to 380; the Milwaukee newspapers said that nearly a thousand children were orphaned as a result. Travelling on the

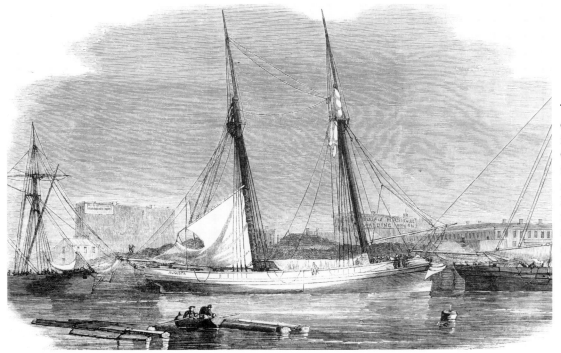

The schooner *Augusta*, which collided with the *Lady Elgin*, from a photograph taken in Chicago afer the disaster. At this time sailing vessels outnumbered steamers on the Lakes by nearly four to one; the *Augusta* was a typical schooner. This picture and the one on page 80 appeared in the *London Illustrated News*. (*—Chicago Historical Society*)

steamer but not part of the excursion were several distinguished people who were lost, among them Herbert Ingraham, a British Member of Parliament and owner of the *London Illustrated News*.

How much to blame was the master of the *Augusta*, Capt. Darius Malott? The question has never been finally settled. The second mate of the schooner had informed the captain ten minutes before the collision that he had seen the lights of an approaching steamer, yet Captain Malott took no action until just before his vessel rammed the other, and then it was too late. In those days the rules of the road were vague. The arrangement of lights on the steamer was said to be defective, but the schooner had none at all. Captain Malott claimed he had no idea of the damage he had caused and thought his vessel had merely knocked off some of the steamer's trimmings; for that reason he did not lie to and give assistance. In the formal investigation he was exonerated, but that ruling has been argued ever since.

Factors contributing to the disaster were much like those brought to light by other marine disasters of the period, and such things were probably also common on most ships that did not get into trouble. On the *Lady Elgin* there were too many people and not enough boats, at least one of the boats was not properly equipped, life preservers were not readily available, and the navigational lights were not correct.

Public reaction to the disaster was enormous. Newspapers of the day debated the pros and cons with high emotion, casting as villains Governor Randall and especially Captain Malott. Memory of the *Lady Elgin* did not fade quickly. Nearly forty years later a historian wrote, "One of the greatest marine horrors on record was the loss of the steamboat Lady Elgin." The collision has been the subject of paintings, plays, poems, and songs. Best known—and still performed by folk singers—is "Lost on the Lady Elgin," written by Henry C. Work, who also wrote "Marching Through Georgia" and "Grandfather's Clock."

COLLINGWOOD

While towns were springing up along the U.S. shore of Lake Superior and steamer lines such as the one to which the *Lady Elgin* belonged were growing there, the northern shore of the lake remained wild and was populated only by Indians and the staffs of occasional Hudson's Bay Company posts. Technically, Canadian territory extended past the end of the lake and contained those posts, including the major one, Fort William. But the Canadian land was only a fringe along the shore; north and west of it lay the areas belonging to the Hudson's Bay Company. Thus there was no reason for anyone to travel there unless it was on HBC or government business.

The first Canadian steamer to go to the head of Lake Superior, the *Collingwood*, ran aground near Michipicoten Island during the voyage, but was freed by the efforts of her crew and passengers. (*—National Archives of Canada C 29923*)

In 1857 the Canadian government sent an expedition to explore a part of the HBC territory, the Red River area—the country that lay south of Lake Winnipeg—where there was a colony of *métis*, people of mixed voyageur and Indian ancestry, centered about the HBC post of Fort Garry. Canada was beginning to look westward, and the Hudson's Bay Company was not unreceptive. The Canadian government chartered the steamer *Collingwood*, which was in the local service on Georgian Bay, to carry the expedition as far as Fort William. On July 24 the vessel headed out of Collingwood, bound north and west.

The *Collingwood*, 188 feet long and of 440 tons, had been launched at Buffalo in 1852 and christened *Kaloolah*. She came to Georgian Bay in the following year. In 1855 the harbor town of Collingwood sprang suddenly to life when the first railway north of Toronto made that point its terminus. The steamer was given the name of the new town, which became her base.

One member of the expedition was Henry Youle Hind, professor of chemistry and geology at Trinity College, Toronto, a vigorous man involved in several expeditions and explorations at this time. As the steamer crossed Georgian Bay he noted the pollen of pine trees floating over the surface of the water, and near St. Joseph Island and at the Sault he remarked "the odour of the balsam . . . perfuming the air with most delicious fragrance."

On the 27th the *Collingwood* passed through the Sault Ste. Marie Canal—probably the first Canadian steamer to do so—and entered Lake Superior. Immediately those on board saw a storm approaching; a dense black cloud about six miles long was coming toward them at considerable speed, "and as it approached masses seemed to detach themselves from the main body, and be whirled or driven in its van. . . . Its form changed rapidly and a white line of crested waves beneath it gave warning of an approaching squall, which soon came down with great force, and compelled us to seek shelter in Whisky Bay."

Next morning the vessel steamed out of her refuge and started on her way again. About 9:00 a.m. fog began to appear and continued throughout the day. Sunlight occasionally penetrated it, and the people on the steamer then saw "fogbows," and "on looking over the side of the vessel a double halo of very brilliant colours might be seen encircling the shadow of the observer's head projected on the dark coloured waters. Every man saw 'his own halo,' but not that of his neighbour."

The fog continued after dark, and Captain McLean, master of the steamer, knew that the mineral deposits in this area might make the compass unreliable. Two of the Indian canoemen who accompanied the expedition were stationed in the bow as lookouts in addition to the regular watch, and the captain, mate, and some of the passengers stayed awake and paced the deck.

An evident feeling of anxiety was common to both passengers and crew; several of the former went to their berths without taking off their clothes. The night was extremely foggy; it was impossible to see more than a few yards beyond the bow of the vessel. The lead was cast several times with no bottom at 288 feet. At a quarter to 12 P.M. no soundings were obtained within twenty fathoms; a few minutes afterwards the lead showed forty-five feet of water; the signal was given to stop her, and then to "back water," but it was too late, a harsh grating noise, a sudden uplifting of the bow of the steamer, and a very decided shock quivering through the vessel, told that she had struck. The alarm and anxiety inseparable from such an incident followed....

They lit torches and inspected the ship and the rock ledge on which the *Collingwood* was stuck. She did not appear to be damaged. Her bow rose five feet out of the water and the ledge sloped back so that there was 36 feet below her stern. On either side there were huge masses of rock just below the surface. The crew set to work moving anchors, chains, fuel, and cargo aft, hoping to change her balance and get her off, but this did not work.

Next morning the fog cleared somewhat and the men on the steamer found that she was firmly lodged on a small rocky island just south of Michipicoten Island and about two miles from Michipicoten Harbour, where there was an HBC post. They sent a boat to the post and in time it returned with enough timber to build a derrick. That afternoon they finally got her free "by the aid of derricks, steam, and a continued rolling from side to side by the united efforts of the passengers running with measured step from one side of the vessel to the other." She proceeded into Michipicoten Harbour so that the crew could inspect her more carefully for damage and move the cargo and fuel back to their normal places. Just inside the harbor she grounded once again, but this time they released her fairly easily.

At 4:00 p.m. on the 30th they steamed away and steered for Thunder Bay at the northwestern corner of the lake. The following morning they passed Isle Royale; at 2:00 p.m. they passed Thunder Cape and at 4:30 the chain rattled out as the *Collingwood*, the first steamer to reach the Canadian Lakehead, anchored off Fort William. Mr. McIntyre, the HBC officer in charge of the fort, greeted them warmly and gave some of the party

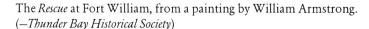

The *Rescue* at Fort William, from a painting by William Armstrong.
(*—Thunder Bay Historical Society*)

The *Merchant,* first iron propeller on the Great Lakes. (*—From American Steam Vessels Booklet Series, drawing by Samuel Ward Stanton*)

accommodations for the night. They unloaded the canoes they brought with them and made ready to leave the steamer and start up the Kaministiquia River on the route to Fort Garry.

RESCUE

In 1858, the year following the *Collingwood's* pioneer voyage to the Lakehead, another vessel began the first regular service along the Canadian shore of Lake Superior. She was the *Rescue,* a twin-screw steamer 121 feet long, owned by a group of Toronto men who had obtained a contract to carry the mail to the Red River. One of them was Capt. James Dick, master of the ship, which had been built at Buffalo in 1855. The mate, A. McNab, was from Collingwood.

At 10:30 on the morning of July 12 the Royal Mail Steamer *Rescue* left Collingwood. In charge of the mails was Capt. William Kennedy, an old Hudson's Bay Company man. In addition to Kennedy there were six other passengers including one lady, a Mrs. Abrahal, who accompanied her husband. They passed Cove Island light, at the entrance to Georgian Bay, that evening. The light was not officially opened by the Canadian government until the next year, so the lantern on top of the tower, visible only about two miles on a clear night, must have been temporary.

After a stop at the Bruce and the Wellington copper mines on the North Channel and another stop to take on wood at the Canadian Sault, they passed through the Sault Canal on the 14th. The Hudson's Bay Company put aboard a pilot at the Sault, the captain of the HBC schooner that sailed these waters; he took them as far as Pine Point, where they engaged his son-in-law to pilot them the rest of the way. They pushed on past Michipicoten as darkness fell, with a heavy wind on the beam; the ship was steady and comfortable and her twin 200 hp engines pushed her along at 10 1/2 mph all that night. Shortly after daybreak they encountered a heavy fog and lay to until it cleared at 1:00 p.m. Then they proceeded, and anchored at Fort William, outside the bar at the river mouth, at 7:00 p.m. on Thursday the 15th.

It was a bright night and the steamer soon was surrounded by a hundred canoes paddled by Indians who had come out to see the monster. Presently there appeared in the moonlight a "huge gondola rowed by twenty Indians, who sang their boating songs," carrying Mr. Loranen, who was in charge of the fort during the absence of the factor, Mr. McIntyre. The HBC officer and the passengers spent much of the evening in conversation, and next morning Loranen sent out boats loaded with wood to refuel the steamer.

Several of those aboard the *Rescue* took trips through the near-by area that day, visiting the Jesuit mission about three miles upriver or going fishing and discovering that the speckled trout were so large they broke the tackle the men were using. Other passengers looked over the large farm of the HBC at Fort William, where there were fifty cows as well as other animals, and where oats, barley, and vegetables were grown. They learned that Sir George Simpson, governor of the company, had returned from the Red River just before their arrival and had set off for the Sault with two nine-man canoes.

Next evening at 8:00 they left Fort William and headed for Grand Portage. They lay to outside the bay until daylight, then went on in. Captain Kennedy bought a small canoe and hired two Indian canoemen; after a handshake all around he was on his way with the first mail—three letters and two newspapers—over the old canoe route to the Red River.

This route followed the international boundary inland; along the lake shore on the United States side was a small village where surveyors were laying out town sites and a lighthouse was to be built that summer. American steamers called there twice a month and the *Illinois*—she had been the first vessel through the Sault Canal—was expected within the day. Steamer service now had encircled the Great Lakes.

MERCHANT

Most steamers at this time carried both passengers and freight, commonly described as merchandise or package freight to distinguish it from the bulk loads of grain, ore, or lumber that usually were moved in sailing vessels. A few had begun to carry only package freight. In the early 1860s it became evident that the package-freight business was growing, just as the passenger business was shrinking, and two Buffalo men, J. C. Evans and his son E. T. Evans, decided they needed a ship designed especially to carry this sort of cargo.

The 190-foot, 650 ton vessel they had built was unusual in several ways. She was the first iron ship to be built completely in the Great Lakes region, starting with the manufacture of her plates at Black Rock, near Buffalo, and ending with her launching by David Bell at Buffalo on July 12, 1862. She was christened *Merchant*.

Her owners were not yet ready to forsake the passenger business entirely, and so she was equipped with a single long deck that contained staterooms. In appearance, however, she contrasted strongly with steamers of the immediate past which had two or more passenger decks. On August 2 she was placed on the Buffalo-Chicago run. The Evans firm also operated several other vessels between these cities; their line prospered and they added still more. Ten years after the *Merchant* was launched, her owners took the next logical step. They removed most of her deck cabin and passenger accommodations and at the same time added thirty feet to her length, thus increasing her cargo capacity. She was then completely a package freighter.

PHILO PARSONS

The *Philo Parsons*, a wooden sidewheeler 136 feet long and of 220 tons, was a typical coastal steamer, plying between Detroit and Sandusky, Ohio, with stops at intervening points. On Monday, September 19, 1864, she started out from her Detroit dock on her regular run, carrying about forty passengers. Among them was Bennet G. Burley, a stocky, 25-year-old man of less than average height, who had a thin, fair beard. He wore English clothes and spoke with a British accent.

Burley reminded the ship's clerk (today we would call him purser), Walter O. Ashley, that he had arranged for the steamer to pause at Sandwich, on the Canadian side, to pick up several of his friends, one of whom was a cripple; they were going on an outing to Kelleys Island. Accordingly the *Parsons* stopped briefly at the Canadian town to pick up four men, one of whom limped as he came aboard. She then made her regularly scheduled call at Malden, also on the Canadian side; there about twenty roughly dressed men boarded her, carrying with them an old trunk. After that the steamer headed out of the Detroit River, into Lake Erie.

The gentlemen from Sandwich mingled sociably with the passengers, the cripple no longer noticeably lame. There seemed to be no connection between Burley's party and the other group, whom the crew assumed to be some of the "skedaddlers"—Civil War draft dodgers and bounty jumpers—who frequently travelled back and forth across the border. As the steamer approached the Erie Islands off the Ohio shore, those on board could smell the aroma of the grapes in the vinyards there. She made regular calls at the various islands; at Middle Bass Island her master, Captain Atwood, went ashore to spend the night with

The *Philo Parsons*, a typical coasting steamer of medium size, was seized by Confederate raiders on Lake Erie. From the painting by the Rev. Edward J. Dowling, S.J. (-*Dossin Great Lakes Museum*)

his family, and his son-in-law, First Mate D. C. Nichols, assumed command.

The next call was at Kelleys Island. There four men came aboard to talk to Burley and his friends; then they all told Clerk Ashley that they had decided to go on to Sandusky together. At 4:00 p.m. the steamer left Kelleys Island; about 4:20 one of the group, a man about thirty years old, clean shaven except for a small beard, approached the mate and asked "Are you the captain of this boat?"

"No sir, I am the mate," responded Nichols.

"You have charge of her at present, have you not?"

"Yes sir."

The passenger then asked Nichols to step aft for a minute; they walked along the hurricane deck and stopped near the base of the tall smokestack. There the man produced a revolver, announced that he was a Confederate officer, and ordered the mate to run down and lie off Sandusky harbor.

Meanwhile the rough customers who had brought the old trunk aboard opened it and equipped themselves with the pistols, hatchets, and other weapons it contained. At the same time four men with drawn pistols took over Clerk Ashley's office and placed him

under guard. The Confederates then rounded up passengers and crew, herding most of them into the cabin and the hold. Deck hands were ordered to throw overboard the cargo of pig iron, which otherwise would become cannon or equipment for the Northern armies. The fireman and engineer were kept in the engine room and the mate and wheelsman were kept in the wheelhouse, all under guard. With Capt. John Yates Beall of the Confederate States Navy, the thirty-year-old man, in charge, the vessel steamed toward Sandusky Bay.

At one of the better Sandusky hotels, the West House, was registered Charles H. Cole and his attractive wife—who seems not to have been his wife at all but a Cleveland prostitute named Annie Brown. The West House had an excellent view of Sandusky Bay, of the camp for Confederate prisoners of war on Johnson's Island in the bay, and of the U.S.S. *Michigan*, which usually lay at anchor off the island.

Cole, who claimed to be secretary of a Harrisburg, Pennsylvania, company, had spent a good deal of money and made a number of acquaintances in Sandusky. Actually he was an adventurer who apparently had lived for a time in Pennsylvania, had then become a lieutenant in the Confederate army and after earning a thoroughly bad reputation in his regiment had finally been cashiered. After that he went to Canada and approached the Confederate Commissioners there, representing himself as a lieutenant in the Confederate navy and a captain in the Confederate army, who as a member of Morgan's Raiders had been captured by U.S. forces, had escaped, and then made his way to Canada. He must have had high talents as a confidence man, for he convinced the honorable gentlemen. One of them, Jacob Thompson, thereupon appointed him to capture the U.S.S. *Michigan* so that she could be used as a commerce raider on the Lakes and to free the Confederate prisoners on Johnson's Island. Cole moved on to Sandusky.

One of those whom Cole made it his business to meet in Sandusky was Capt. J. C. Carter of the *Michigan*. He decided quickly that there was no possibility of tampering with this crusty sea dog, and so he went on to make friends with some of the crew members. Meanwhile, to keep the flow of Confederate gold coming, he reported to Jacob Thompson that he had had great success in bribing the gunboat's crew. The highly exaggerated reports were evidently so convincing that as a result of them Thompson dispatched the raiders who took over the *Philo Parsons.* Cole himself must have realized that the raid could not succeed, for when he was arrested at the West House on the 19th he and his lady had their bags packed, had paid their bill, and were about to leave.

Unfortunately for the Confederates they not only had put their faith in a complete rascal, Cole, but a member of their organization in Canada had passed a warning to U.S. authorities in Detroit. As a result the U.S.S. *Michigan* was prepared for action, the garrison on Johnson's Island was alerted, and a detachment was sent to bring in Cole.

The *Philo Parsons,* with the Confederates in control, went far enough that those aboard could see into Sandusky Bay and observe both the *Michigan* and Johnson's Island. At that point, however, her captors learned that the *Parsons* did not carry fuel for the seven- or eight-hour operation planned by Captain Beall; she had only enough to take her to Sandusky and return her to Middle Bass, where she normally refueled for the next voyage to Detroit.

Before the raid could continue, back she must go to Middle Bass for more wood.

Her arrival there about 7:30 that evening, completely off her normal schedule, caused a sensation. When the owner and some of the workmen at the woodyard refused to load her up for a crew of strangers, the Confederates fired several shots. All of this brought Captain Atwood, her master, from his home down to the dock, where he was promptly ordered aboard the vessel at gunpoint and taken into the cabin. At that moment the whistle of another steamer sounded and the 121-foot *Island Queen*, an open-deck boat of 179 tons that traded between the islands and Sandusky, came unsuspectingly alongside. A number of the Confederates leaped aboard her.

The *Queen's* passengers and most of her crew were soon locked up on the *Parsons;* some of her deck hands were put to work loading wood. Captain Beall then talked to Captain Atwood for a time and it was arranged that most of the passengers, a number of whom were women, and some of the crewmen would be put ashore under Atwood's care. There was no telegraph on the island and the raiders had the only two steamers that called there regularly, so this was safe enough.

A little after 8:00 p.m. the *Philo Parsons* once more left Middle Bass Island, this time towing the *Island Queen*. The Confederates smashed open a valve in the side of the latter and set her adrift to sink; instead she lodged on a reef in shallow water. The captive officers and crew of both vessels were put in the hold of the *Parsons* except for the wheelsman and the engineer who were kept at their posts under guard. When the ship reached Marblehead Light at the entrance to Sandusky Bay, the wheelsman demurred at making the dangerous trip into the harbor at night, pointing out that they probably would run aground, and as a result the vessel halted there momentarily.

The Confederates stared toward the U.S.S. *Michigan*, perhaps expecting a signal from her that did not appear. Captain Beall still was determined to run into the bay and capture her, and Burley, a Scot who had been a blockade runner before accepting a commission in the Confederate navy, backed his superior. The others feared that something had gone wrong. A kind of polite mutiny ensued, with most of the others vot-

Above: The *Island Queen*, a small local steamer, was also seized by the Confederate raiders and was then scuttled. From a painting by Father Dowling. (*—Dossin Great Lakes Museum*)

Below: The camp for Confederate prisoners of war on Johnson's Island in Sandusky Bay. In an attempt to free the men on the island and disrupt Great Lakes shipping, Confederate raiders captured the steamers *Philo Parsons* and *Island Queen*. From a lithograph published in 1865. (*—Ohio Historical Society OHS-3*)

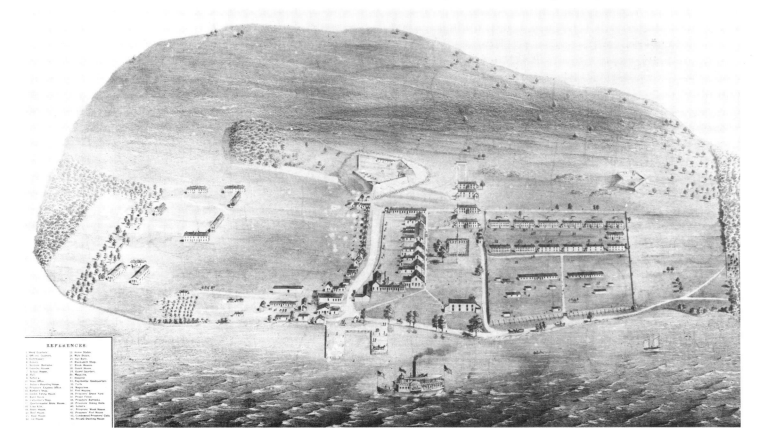

ing against their dashing captain. The helmsman was told to turn the ship around and head for Malden, and the engineer was ordered to run her at full speed. Observers on Middle Bass Island peering through the moonlit night saw her pass about 1:00 a.m.

Between 4:00 and 5:00 a.m. the *Philo Parsons* came into the British channel at Malden, flying the Confederate flag. The raiders marooned most of her crew and the few remaining passengers on a small island from which they were soon rescued and then ran into the dock at Sandwich, where they stripped the ship of her valuables, even her piano, and carried them ashore. After some discussion as to whether they should burn or sink her, they cut her injector pipes and let her sink at the dock.

The key men involved in the raid met various fates. Cole remained in prison until the end of the war. He changed his story every time he spoke and no one was ever certain what crime to charge him with, so he never was tried and eventually was freed. Burley was in time extradited from Canada to the United States on a charge that he had robbed Clerk Ashley of his personal money, as distinguished from that belonging to the ship. At this there were protest demonstrations in the streets of Canadian cities and cries that Canada had given up her sovereignty. Burley was tried and the jury disagreed; while awaiting retrial he escaped from prison, returned to Canada, and then went back to Scotland.

John Y. Beall, former member of the Virginia House of Delegates, came onto U.S. territory again that September in an attempt to derail an express train near Dunkirk, N.Y. He was arrested before he could get back to Canada and was tried by a military commission on charges based on both the *Philo Parsons* affair and on the express train attempt. He was found guilty on nine counts, was sentenced to death, and was hanged at New York on February 24, 1865.

What of the *Philo Parsons* and the *Island Queen*? Within a week after the raid they both had been raised, repaired, and put back on their former runs.

IRONSIDES

The development of iron and copper mines on Lake Superior and the opening of the canal at Sault Ste. Marie ensured that the Civil War would bring a boom to the Great Lakes—and perhaps even ensured a Union victory.

Ore deposits were on the westernmost and northernmost Great Lake. Coal deposits providing fuel for smelting the ore lay south of Lake Erie in the Appala-

Ironsides, wooden passenger and freight steamer, built in Cleveland in 1864 for the Lake Superior Line. (*—From American Steam Vessels Booklet Series, drawing by Samuel Ward Stanton*)

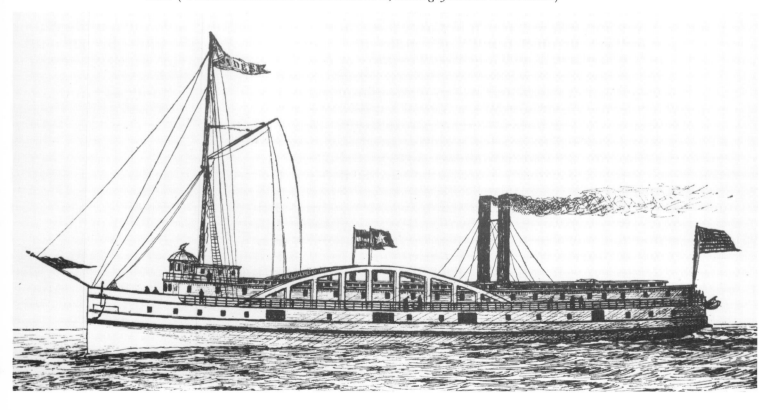

chians. Ore travelled south and east by water; coal travelled north by rail. They came together in Chicago, Detroit, Cleveland, Buffalo, and some of the smaller lake cities. Commercial iron, steel, and copper plus manufactured guns and machinery poured out of these cities for the use of Northern industry and the Union armies. No wonder the Confederacy would seriously consider even such a wild scheme as the one proposed by Charles H. Cole to capture the U.S.S. *Michigan*, if it provided a chance to disrupt Northern shipping on the Lakes. They also tried to outfit a privateer, the propeller *Georgian*, at Collingwood on Georgian Bay, but the Canadian government stepped in and seized her.

Smelters sprang up. Capt. Eber B. Ward, deciding that the days of passenger steamers were about ended, put his money into steel mills at Detroit. Other shipowners built vessels to carry ore. Most of these were still propelled by sails, but some of the steamers moved cautiously into the new trade. One of them, built of wood despite her name, was the propeller *Ironsides*, 218 feet long. She was launched at Cleveland in 1864 to run between that city and the Lake Superior ports.

Second mate of the *Ironsides* was a 19-year-old Scot destined to become famous on the Great Lakes. Alexander McDougall had come out to Canada with his family at the age of 10, settled near Collingwood, and shipped as a deck hand when he was 16. That he gained an officer's ticket in three years, and that such a youthful second mate was appointed to one of the finest new ships on the Lakes, tells much about his abilities.

The *Ironsides* carried iron ore from the Lake Superior mines to Cleveland and copper ore to Detroit. The ore was brought aboard in wheelbarrows and unloaded the same way, a hugely inefficient method but the only one that would work on a vessel of this type. Crew members acted as longshoremen and the mate supervised the work. Bound from Cleveland or Detroit back to Lake Superior, the ship carried merchandise and mining machinery; once again, the crew and the mates had to load the cargo, stow it, and unload it at the many small ports. Under wartime pressures the ship never paused during the navigational season and as a result the crew seldom slept; when not standing watch they were working all night to load and unload. Young

McDougall worked seven months that year without one good night's sleep. Perhaps this was another reason the Lake Superior Line hired such a young mate.

It may have been just as well that the crews kept so busy. The Cleveland waterfront in those days was a place where a seaman visiting a brothel might later wake up with a drugged hangover, outward-bound on a ship other than his own and minus all of his money. It was also a place where skill at no-holds-barred fighting was a useful talent. At the other end of the run, the ore towns were not quite as well known for uninhibited amusement and uninhibited fighting as the lumber towns later became, but they were good places to find trouble.

The *Ironsides* carried passengers as well as ore and merchandise. During those boom times people were travelling in both directions. Many explorers and prospectors were pushing into the Lake Superior region and the ship had to carry them into numerous out-of-the-way little harbors. Steamers on Lake Superior, like sailing vessels on all of the Lakes, commonly had a yawl boat hung on davits at the stern. It was the duty of Second Mate McDougall to go ahead in the yawl and take soundings as the ship felt her way into these strange places. No charts of the Lakes were generally available then, and this sort of training taught a young sailor his profession.

The frantic Lake Superior trade ended abruptly when the Civil War ended and the ore prices plummeted. In 1866 people poured out of the Lake Superior region and many of the vessels were laid up. Others ran sporadically and some failed to pay their crews. For a time, settlement of the area around Lake Superior was nearly halted. As for the *Ironsides*, she survived, in 1869 was sold to a Milwaukee company, and continued in general Great Lakes service, finally being wrecked on the bar off Grand Haven, Lake Michigan, in 1873.

JAMES F. JOY

In July 1866 there was launched at Detroit a fine big sailing vessel, the *James F. Joy*, 175 feet long, 35 feet in beam, and of 582 gross tons. James F. Joy was the Detroit lawyer who had played a key part in building the Sault Ste. Marie canal. A graduate of Harvard Law School, he eventually became president of several

The *James F. Joy*, a 175-foot barkentine launched in 1866 at Detroit, was representative of the largest bulk-freight carriers on the Lakes at the time. Vessels rigged as barkentines were usually called "barks" by Lakes sailors. From a painting by Charles R. Patterson, Barkhausen Collection. (—*Institute for Great Lakes Research, Bowling Green State University*)

midwestern railroads, including the Michigan Central. The vessel named for him, like most of the largest cargo carriers of her day, was rigged as a barkentine, with square sails on the foremast and fore-and-aft sails on the remaining two masts, a rig that probably originated on the Lakes. Soon she gained the reputation of being very fast.

Bulk freight carriers were almost entirely sailing vessels. Ore was loaded at Marquette and other iron ports from tall docks that were similar in principle to some of the remaining gravity loading docks today. Rail cars ran out onto the docks carrying the ore; it was dumped into pockets underneath and from there fed by chutes into the holds of ships. Gravity did most of the work.

Vessels could be loaded much faster than they were unloaded; the method of unloading was strikingly inefficient. At Cleveland about forty horses were at work on the receiving docks. A block with a manila line was fastened in the rigging of the ship; a bucket tied to the end of the line was dropped into the hold. The other end of the line was led through a second block to one of the horses. Men with shovels working in the hold filled the bucket; the horse was then walked forward to hoist bucket and ore out of the hold to the level of a temporary staging built on the deck, where a man dumped the ore into a waiting wheelbarrow. The wheelbarrow was walked ashore on a plank gangway to a scaffolding built over the ore pile and was dumped there.

In the spring of 1867 J. D. Bothwell, a member of the firm that operated the Cleveland ore dock, stood watching a small steam engine being used to lift wooden piles through the air before they were driven into the riverbed. It occurred to him that a similar engine could hoist ore buckets from the holds of vessels. He asked an engineer, Robert Wallace, to design and build a portable steam engine that could be moved around the dock.

Left: Winter navigation demanded especially hardy seamen in the days of sail. Here is the *Parana*, a barkentine similar to the *James F. Joy*, in port at Milwaukee after a December passage in 1871. (—*Marine Historical Collection, Milwaukee Public Library*)

Below: A section of a panoramic view of Marquette harbor in 1863, showing part of the fleet of sailing vessels in harbor and two of the earliest ore docks. The docks operated on the same principle as some ore docks still in use today; ore was dumped from rail cars into pockets under the dock and from them was loaded through chutes into vessels. The barkentine at the more distant dock is similar to the *James F. Joy*. (—*Marquette County Historical Society*)

Above: Dart's elevator at Buffalo about 1846; detail from a lithograph of Buffalo harbor. Note the two schooners being unloaded directly behind the steamer *Oregon*. The long arms that were let down into the holds carried grain up into the elevator. (*—Buffalo Historical Society*)

Left: Unloading a sailing vessel at Cleveland. Note steam donkey engine at lower left. (*—Courtesy McDowell Wellman Engineering Co., Cleveland*)

The engine cost $1,200. Bothwell and Wallace set it up on the dock; the master of the next vessel to come in, one Capt. Smith Moore, looked over the rail and asked what that thing might be. When he learned it was going to unload his cargo he strode about his deck in a rage, saying with fiery eloquence that he wanted to get unloaded and go on his way, not sit there all week while that profane object tried to lift cargo out of the hold. He demanded horses! Bothwell persisted, however; the steam engine went to work lifting three buckets at a time; the shovelers, dumpers, and wheelbarrow men continued as before, though presumably they had to work faster. The vessel, the *Massilon*, also a large barkentine, was unloaded by evening. After that there was no question about the steam donkey engine. The dock operators, the firm of Bothwell and Ferris, soon became rich. The builders of the donkey engine, Wallace, Pankhurst & Co., immediately received orders for nine more from people along the Cleveland waterfront and were on their way to prosperity.

Like other big freighters, the *James F. Joy* carried cargoes of grain as well as ore. The methods of unloading grain had advanced far beyond those for ore and coal; of course grain was a lighter and finer substance and therefore easier to handle. As early as 1843 Joseph Dart of Buffalo had built a grain elevator with steam-driven machinery; by this time there were more than twenty-five such elevators in Buffalo, the major grain-receiving port of the Lakes. The large elevators were much improved over the earlier ones, but all followed the same general principle. A movable wooden arm was put down from the top of the elevator into the hold of the vessel. The arm was hollow and contained an endless chain of buckets that lifted the grain, which laborers in the hold shoveled toward its lower end. At the top of the building the buckets emptied into a chute which ran the grain through a scale or measure watched by a tallyman. From there it was transferred through other chutes and pipes by the force of gravity to a waiting canal boat or to storage areas within the building. The efficiency of unloading grain was striking as compared with the considerable inefficiency of unloading the heavier cargoes.

Anthony Trollope in 1860 saw a Buffalo elevator at work. Like many other Englishmen he felt recurring pangs of disgust at various aspects of American life.

It will be understood, then, that this big movable trunk, the head of which, when it is at rest, is thrust up into the box on the roof, is made to slant down in an oblique direction from the building to the river. For the elevator is an amphibious institution, and flourishes only on the banks of navigable waters. When its head is ensconced within its box, and the beast of prey is thus nearly hidden within the building, the unsuspicious vessel is brought up within reach of the creature's trunk, and down it comes, like a mosquito's proboscis, right through the deck, in at the open aperture of the hole, and so into the very vitals and bowels of the ship. When there, it goes to work upon its food with a greed and an avidity that is disgusting to a beholder of any taste or imagination.

This particular beholder obviously had more taste and considerably more imagination than appreciation for efficient machinery.

But the big freighters continued to come down the Lakes with cargoes of grain or ore and to return with coal. Large barkentines such as the *Joy* used their square sails to advantage in running before the prevailing westerlies and their fore-and-aft sails in tacking back up the Lakes. In 1870 one listing showed 214 barks, 159 brigs, and 1737 schooners on the Lakes (most, if not all, of the "barks" and "brigs" were actually barkentines and brigantines, with square sail only on the foremast). The largest three-masters in the lake trade at this period were almost invariably barkentines, a few even bigger than the *Joy* though evidently none faster. Such vessels were sometimes able to repay their cost to their owners in two seasons; the faster they were, the more cargoes they could carry.

The *James F. Joy* continued in service for a number of years. One of the most famous of Great Lakes pictures, that of the tug *Champion* towing sailing vessels through the straits at Detroit in 1880, shows the *Joy* as the fourth ship behind the tug. At this time she used the services of a tug only in narrow waters, but eventually, like many old sailing vessels, she was given a simpler schooner rig and was towed wherever she went.

Her end came in 1887. The Ashtabula *Telegraph* on Friday, October 28 of that year, reported:

> The schooner J. F. Joy, laden with 996 tons of ore from Escanaba for Erie, while attempting to enter this port during the gale of last Sunday night, went ashore 500 feet east of the piers and sunk [*sic*] in twenty feet of water.... The tug Winslow was chartered to tow her to Erie, but during the gale of Sunday let go her line above Fairport and ran back to Cleveland, leaving the schooner to look after herself. She drifted down off this port and let go both anchors at 4 o'clock that morning. The tugs Gordon and Red Cloud made every effort to get her inside, but her lines parted and before she again could be taken in tow sank as above stated. The crew, thirteen in number, barely escaped with their lives, being taken from the rigging in a small boat, manned by the crew of the M. R. Warner.

The small boat was from a schooner that was loading in Ashtabula harbor. William Packer, the *Warner's* mate, organized a group of volunteers to row their yawl boat out to the wreck. It took them two hours to get there through the storm; among those they rescued was the woman cook of the *Joy*. Fourteen years later Packer was awarded a gold life-saving medal for his bravery on this occasion.

BRITOMART

At the end of the Civil War the vast Union armies were demobilized and the soldiers went home. Men who were used to travel and fighting were not always eager to bury themselves in quiet labor. Many of those who returned to the industrial cities were Irish, and Irishmen who were bored with civilian life had a happy alternative: they could join the Fenian movement.

The Fenian Brotherhood was an Irish patriotic organization whose supposed aim was to liberate Ireland from the British; the means by which it set about doing this were sometimes peculiar. One faction of the organization decided to annex Canada. It held a convention in Chicago in 1863 at which it wrote the constitution of a Canadian republic and appointed the cabinet to govern it. Another convention in February 1866 approved a Canadian invasion. Money poured in from Irish Americans who had been touched by sentimental appeals or more vigorous approaches; surplus U.S. Army weapons and supplies were bought up and stored along the Canadian border.

"General" Sweeney, Fenian Secretary of War, prepared the invasion plan. Lakes Huron, Erie, and Ontario were to be held by the Fenian navy while the Fenian army seized Canada West, as Ontario was then known, and descended on Montreal. A fleet from San Francisco would take Vancouver Island. When it was all over, the United States would recognize occupied Canada as "New Ireland."

United States authorities were aware of Irish-American political power and at first were not unsympathetic. The American attitude toward the group was much as it had been toward William Lyon Mackenzie and his adherents thirty years earlier; U.S. officialdom indulgently looked the other way. The gathering invasion force was no secret, however, as large bodies of Fenians began to appear openly in American lake cities. The alarmed Canadians began to mobilize their militia.

Not long after midnight on June 1, 1866, several hundred Fenians under John O'Neill, a former Union army captain of some combat experience, now termed "Colonel" and "General" interchangeably, set out from Black Rock, near Buffalo, in two barges towed by a tug. They crossed the Niagara River and landed in Canada at the town of Fort Erie without opposition. By the end of the day they had brought some 1,500 men and nine wagonloads of supplies across the river and had begun to move inland. The next two days saw battles between Fenians and ill-trained and badly led Canadian militia. Generally, O'Neill's motley army won. But he was plagued by desertions and was baffled that the Canadians did not greet him as a liberator and join his forces. More and possibly better Canadian forces were gathering and Fenian reinforcements from Buffalo were not arriving. O'Neill, who never seems to have been certain what his exact mission was, fell back again to Fort Erie. By then desertion had reduced his force to about 800 men. There, after dark, he decided to withdraw across the river to Buffalo.

Belatedly the American authorities had armed two Buffalo tugs and set them patrolling the Niagara River and nearby Lake Erie, thus cutting off O'Neill's

H.M.S. *Britomart*, one of three similar British gunboats sent into the Great Lakes during the Fenian disturbances. (*—Imperial War Museum, London*)

reinforcements. That old standby, the U.S.S. *Michigan,* arrived at Black Rock and anchored in the harbor in time to capture some boats of the retreating Fenian army.

After this invasion the United States took a somewhat sterner view of Fenian shenanigans, and U.S. revenue cutters began to investigate the numerous minor alarms in U.S. waters along the Lakes, where vessels were seen flying the Fenian flag—green with a gold harp. The Canadian government chartered several steamers and converted them to gunboats. And the Royal Navy dispatched three of its gunboats, the *Heron, Cherub,* and *Britomart*, to the Great Lakes. All three were approximately 105 feet long on the keel and of 270 tons, propeller-driven vessels with barkentine rigs, having smokestacks mounted on hinges so that they could be lowered when they would interfere with the sails.

The gunboats arrived on the Great Lakes in August 1866 and after some minor repairs were stationed in various places. The *Heron* was based at the eastern end of the Welland Canal, to guard the canal and Lake Ontario. The *Cherub* went to Goderich, on Lake Huron, to protect the Canadian shores of the upper Lakes. The *Britomart* patrolled the northern shore of Lake Erie, with Port Dover as the center of her activities.

The Fenians continued to swagger and occasionally launched an attack elsewhere along the border, but now that both the United States and British forces were on the alert along the Lakes, there were only small episodes there. The British gunboat crews had rather pleasant duty. People of Port Dover and surrounding towns gathered to see the *Britomart*, commanded by Lt. Arthur M. Arlington, when she first came to that port, and the city fathers gave a dinner for the captain. Next spring she arrived back at Port Dover just in time for her officers and crew to carry the furniture from a burning house.

One result of the Fenian raids that the Fenians did not expect was the Confederation of Canada. There had been many moves over the past years to join the provinces of British North America into one country with one government, but sectional differences had always interfered. The jolt administered by the Fenian attacks and the surge of anti-American feeling that followed caused the provinces suddenly to come together. In 1867 the British North America Act passed Commons in London. The only argument was between those who wanted the new country to be the Kingdom of Canada and those who feared the word "kingdom" would be an incitement to the United States. Faint hearts won out, and it was decided that on July 1, 1867, the Dominion of Canada would be born.

Britomart was in Canada for that first Dominion Day (a holiday whose name changed to Canada Day in 1982). The ship was dressed with flags and her complement paraded through the streets with two of the local militia companies. This was followed by practice with the vessel's two Armstrong guns, firing at a target fixed to an offshore reef. Then crew members climbed a greased pole attached to the pier and amused bystanders by falling into the water until one man reached the top and won the pig in a basket that was attached there. Later that day the sailors demonstrated fencing.

Throughout the summer there were parties on board the *Britomart* and picnic excursions on her for the local people. Late in August on one such trip she anchored for the day, but by evening when it was time to return, she was aground. The lake, in one of its unexpected shifts of water, had placed her firmly and quietly on the bottom. A midshipman with four oarsmen was sent off in a gig to get a tug, while the party continued with games and singing until midnight. No tug having arrived, the gentlemen slung hammocks on deck, turning over the cabins and the quarterdeck to the ladies. Next morning the gunboat was afloat again—the water level had risen. All sail and steam were made back to Port Dover.

Not all of the ship's duties were social, however. She spent most of her time patrolling the coast. On one occasion, in November 1867, the U.S.S. *Michi-gan* appeared off Port Dover and signalled that her captain wished to confer with Lieutenant Arlington; H.M.S. *Britomart* went out and the two captains discussed matters that history does not record. By the end of the navigational season of 1867 the Fenian alarms had died down sufficiently that the Royal Navy decided Canada could handle the situation by herself; the *Britomart* and her two sister gunboats departed. Arlington and one of the other gunboat commanders eventually became admirals—probably the only senior officers of the Royal Navy in their generation to have seen service on the Great Lakes.

CHICORA

The new Dominion of Canada soon began negotiations with the Hudson's Bay Company for its great expanses in the North and West, and eventually agreed to buy the lands for £300,000.

The HBC post of Fort Garry lay on the Red River, which runs north from St. Paul to Winnipeg. Along the river near the fort were settlements made up largely of *métis;* the white ancestry of most of them was greater than the Indian and for most of them it was French. They were products of the fur trade, for which this place had long been a central depot, and their white forefathers had been voyageurs and adventurers in that trade. Most of the *métis* families were based on farms, narrow strips that ran back from the river in the manner of Quebec farms along the St. Lawrence. The men of these families were mostly frontiersmen and workers for the HBC; they were buffalo hunters, teamsters, and on occasion still canoemen.

The *métis* awaited the westward thrust of civilization with foreboding. It certainly would change their country and it might destroy them. The statesmen in Ottawa and merchants in London saw no reason to tell the people who lived in the area what they planned to do with them; not even William Mactavish, chief officer of the company at Fort Garry, was informed of the plans. They all lived in an atmosphere of rumors and twisted news reports. There was also a small but assertive group of Anglo-Canadian Protestants who scorned the *métis* and made it known that when Canadian government

Above: The *Chicora* at Collingwood. A former Confederate block-ade runner, she was probably the first steel-hulled vessel on the Lakes. Almost all structures above the line of the hull were added after her war service. This engraving appeared in the *Canadian Illustrated News,* June 25, 1870. (–*National Archives of Canada C 30169*)

Below: Men and matériel of the Wolseley Expedition landing at Sault Ste. Marie. The United States finally, under diplomatic pressure, al-lowed the ships of the expedition to pass through the Sault Canal, but required that all troops and supplies be unloaded and carried across the portage on the Canadian side. This drawing is by William Armstrong, who was appointed an army captain and made chief engineer of the expedition. (–*Metropolitan Toronto Library Board JRR 2423*)

came they would be the chosen ones. Add to that the presence of several clever Americans, representatives of the merchants and politicians of Minnesota who coveted the British Northwest. It was an explosive mixture.

Before the land purchase was complete or final plans even announced, Canadian surveyors arrived in the Red River country. One day a survey party, which spoke no French, started to run a line across the established farm of a man who spoke no English. The excited farmer ran for help and returned with a number of friends led by a stocky, curly-haired, 25-year-old who had been educated in Quebec, Louis Riel. Riel calmly put his moccasined foot on the surveyors' chain and announced in English, "You go no farther."

Thus began the explosion. Quickly Riel and his followers took over Fort Garry and established their own government. The St. Paul Chamber of Commerce demanded U.S. annexation of the British Northwest and Minnesota legislators took up the cry. An American Fenian, W. B. O'Donoghue, arrived at Red River and became treasurer of Riel's government. The Protestant Canadian group there resisted the *métis*; there were plots and skirmishes, and some of the Anglo-Canadians landed in jail. One of them, Thomas Scott, a young fellow described by a contemporary as "a rash and thoughtless man," persisted in cursing and insulting his *métis* captors. After a while they tired of him, tried him briefly, put him before a firing squad, and executed him.

The newly formed Canada almost came apart at the seams. Protestant, English-speaking Ontario seethed and cried for revenge. Catholic, French-speaking Quebec reacted against the Ontario reaction. During all of this it was evident that the United States might take over the Red River country at any moment. Beset on all sides, the Canadian government quickly passed the Manitoba Act, establishing the new province with its own legislature and representation in the Dominion Parliament; but it also sent to the Red River a military expedition. To reach its goal that expedition had to cross the Great Lakes from Collingwood to Thunder Bay at the head of Lake Superior; from there it had to find its way westward over forest roads and waterways.

An established Canadian steamer line ran from Collingwood to Thunder Bay. It had two vessels, the *Algoma*, an old and rather slab-sided boat, and the *Chicora*, a fast, neat ship that had been a Civil War blockade runner. Her hull was constructed of exceptionally thin steel plates, and she probably was the first steel vessel on the Lakes. She had been launched at Birkenhead, England, as *B, Letter B,* or *Let Her B*—references vary, though most prefer the last, most colorful name—and having been owned by the Chicora Export and Import Company, she in time was called *Chicora*. During the war she was based at Nassau, in the Bahamas, and at Charleston, S.C. To bring her to the Lakes she was cut in two and the pieces towed by tug through the canals to Buffalo, where they were again spliced together. She arrived at Collingwood in 1868 with gun mounts still on her decks; there she was converted to passenger service and put in the Lake Superior trade in 1869. She was 221 feet long, of 26 feet beam and 539 tons, a long, lean ship with big paddle wheels and two tall, raking smokestacks.

On May 3, 1870, on the first trip of the year, the *Algoma* set out from Collingwood carrying 140 workmen and voyageurs to build the roads and man the boats that were necessary to move an expedition from the northwestern corner of Lake Superior to the Red River. She passed through the Sault Ste. Marie canal, which belonged to the State of Michigan, and went on to the head of the lake. On May 7 the *Chicora* left Collingwood with a similar group of 120 voyageurs and workmen, and with supplies for their use. On the 10th she was stopped by the Michigan authorities and not allowed to go through the canal. Hamilton Fish, Secretary of State to President Grant, had written to the governor of Michigan telling him that it was the president's wish that neither a Canadian military expedition nor its boats be permitted to use the canal. The canal authorities decided that that included the *Chicora*.

The Governor General of Canada sent off an outraged telegram to the British Minister in Washington, who represented Canadian interests there.

The Michigan state locks at Sault Ste. Marie, about 1870. These are the locks that were at first closed to the *Chicora* and through which she and oth[er] vessels of the Wolseley Expedition were later allowed to pass. The locks were first opened in 1855. (—*National Archives of Canada C29404*)

The *Algoma* ran opposite the *Chicora* but was completely different in construction, being an old wooden vessel of typical Great Lakes design. Here she is shown passing Thunder Cape near the head of Lake Superior, carrying members of the Wolseley Expedition. From a drawing by William Armstrong reproduced in the *Canadian Illustrated News*. (—*Metropolitan Toronto Library Board*)

Collingwood harbor in 1871 or 1872, just after the Wolseley Expedition embarked there. The steamer is the *Cumberland*, which replaced the *Algoma* in service to Lake Superior. Note also the barkentine at the harbor entrance. The lumber boom was getting under way on Georgian Bay at this time and Collingwood harbor, like others on the Bay, was cluttered with logs.

. . . great surprise . . . Canadian steamer *Chicora* stopped from passing the Sault Ste. Marie Canal. . . Canadians at all times have allowed free use of Welland and other canals to American vessels . . . Present action considered very unfriendly. . .

Edward Thornton, the Minister, conferred with Hamilton Fish and noted politely that if Canada shut the Welland Canal to American vessels it would be most inconvenient for them. President Grant held a cabinet meeting on May 16 to discuss the matter; he began by commenting that he regarded the refusal to let the *Chicora* pass as unfriendly to England, and added "I guess we all feel so too." The cabinet laughed heartily. But when they got down to the real discussion they finally decided to reopen the Sault canal to British vessels with commercial cargoes only, mainly because of the Canadian threat to close the Welland. That meant that vessels of the expedition could go through, but all troops and military supplies had to be unloaded at the foot of the canal, taken over the Canadian portage road, and reloaded on Lake Superior.

The commander of the expedition was a rising British officer, Col. G. J. Wolseley, who in time be-

came the model for Gilbert and Sullivan's "Modern Major General," and later was Commander-in-Chief of the British army. He commanded a brigade made up of a British Regular infantry battalion, an enthusiastic and sanguine Ontario militia battalion, and a considerably less enthusiastc and smaller Quebec militia battalion, plus detachments of artillery and other elements.

On May 14 Wolseley sent two companies of the 1st Ontario Rifles on the *Chicora* to Sault Ste. Marie. There were reports of Fenians gathering at Chicago to launch an attack against the Canadian portage road, and he wanted to get a military force there as quickly as possible. Other vessels soon brought more troops there. Two Canadian gunboats also patrolled the southern approach to the Sault. They were the converted vessels the government had used during earlier Fenian episodes on the Lakes; by coincidence one of them was the steamer *Rescue* which had carried the first mail from Collingwood to the lakehead for the Red River.

On the 21st Wolseley himself sailed out of Collingwood on the *Chicora* with his staff, a company of British infantry from the 60th Rifles, and voyageurs, teamsters, and horses. The steamer also carried fifteen boats to be used on the waterways west of Lake Superior. She arrived at the canal on the morning of the 23d. There the local Member of Parliament came on board and assured Wolseley that the U.S. commander at Fort Brady, just across the river, had very cordial feelings toward the Canadians; Wolseley evidently need not fear an attack from that particular quarter. After going through the laborious business of unloading the *Chicora*, marching the troops and hauling the equipment over the road, and reloading her again, they sailed away for the lakehead. At the same time other vessels of the expedition were following the same procedure. Those arriving at the Sault with only supplies and no troops had troops put aboard there, for warnings had been received that Fenians among the Irish laborers in the iron mines at Marquette were chartering a steamer to attack the expedition on Lake Superior.

Four days later the *Chicora*, carrying Wolseley and his men, arrived at Thunder Bay and anchored off a shore where there had been a forest fire; the landscape now consisted only of tall burned trunks and black smoking rock. A few shanties had been erected there by the advance party of workmen. Wolseley christened the spot Prince Arthur's Landing; thus began the city of Port Arthur, later to be merged with Fort William into the present city of Thunder Bay.

Vessels plied between Collingwood, the Sault, and Prince Arthur's Landing for nearly two months, carrying troops and supplies, all of which were unloaded, taken over the portage road, and reloaded again. Five Canadian steamers, four chartered American steamers, and four schooners were used. Among them was the *Chicora*, which speeded regularly between Collingwood and the lakehead.

From the head of Lake Superior the expedition struck inland, clearing roads and portages as it went. A hospital and supply base were left behind at Prince Arthur's landing, and a company of the Quebec militia with two cannon was stationed there to guard against Fenian attack. Such an attack never came, perhaps because the expedition was ready for it. The *Chicora* and *Algoma* provided regular communication with Collingwood, carrying messages and non-military supplies. On August 24 the expedition arrived at Fort Garry; Riel and his immediate supporters fled as it arrived. Manitoba was finally and definitely Canadian.

There was an abortive Fenian attack in Manitoba in October of the following year, 1871, after most of the troops had gone home, but it failed completely. After that the tensions gradually faded between Canada and the U.S. True, Louis Riel did return from the U.S. to the Canadian West fourteen years later to lead another revolt of *métis* and Indians against progress directed by an insensitive government, was captured, and was hanged—many said in revenge for Scott's execution. Much of the world pled for mercy and Canada herself went through another spasm of sectional and religious hatred. But this time the United States was not actively involved. By then Canada and the U.S. were going forward together through an era of expansion and development.

View of Chicago harbor from the Rush Street Bridge about 1869. Sailing vessels were the primary cargo carriers. (—*Chicago Historical Society*)

5
Transformation

The two decades that began about 1870 brought unprecedented changes. This period was what the skeptical Mark Twain called the Gilded Age and the vastly successful Andrew Carnegie saw as the Triumph of Democracy. It was a time of ruthless industrial expansion and intense worship of the dollar, but it was also the time that mass education and health services developed. It was an era of growing complication to provide increased efficiency, when the individual shoemaker gave way to machine operators who, by sixty-four different operations, made one shoe.

Ships did not lend themselves to factory production, but they were affected in other ways. They were needed to carry all those shoes and other products to market, and more important on the Great Lakes, they had to carry raw materials to the mills and factories as well as carrying the increased flow of grain from more efficient farms. As a result of all this, they grew in size and became more efficient in design. New methods were devised to handle cargo. Sail lost the race to steam; before the end of the period the last true schooner had been launched. Iron and steel began to supplant wooden construction and the lake freighter appeared in much the form it would have for the next century. The period transformed the look of shipping on the Lakes.

R. J. HACKETT AND FOREST CITY

In 1869 the first of a new kind of vessel was launched at Cleveland. The builder, Eli Peck, had constructed many lake ships. This time he put his mind to devising a steamer that could easily handle bulk cargoes of ore, and the new one, a 211-footer christened *R. J. Hackett* after one of her owners, was the result.

Until this event sailing vessels had almost a monopoly on bulk cargoes. The complex upper works of steamers made it difficult to load and unload cargo in bulk, and so most steamers carried only package freight and passengers. Their occasional attempts to carry ore or bulk grain were not too satisfactory.

Peck, however, designed a ship that had clear, unbroken decks like those of a sailing vessel. He gave her three masts and built the same boxy hull as a sailing vessel that was designed to carry as much cargo as possible into shallow harbors and through narrow passages. Then he put a steam engine all the way aft, driving a single propeller under a steamer stern, and he gave her a straight, steamer bow, above which rose a deck cabin and pilothouse. Thus was born the first lake freighter, in general appearance

Reproduced here in its original size, a sketch of the *R. J. Hackett* by the noted marine artist Samuel Ward Stanton. As the inscription shows, it was made at Detroit in 1893. (—*Mariners Museum, Newport News, Va.*)

Above: *Forest City*, a sister of the *R. J. Hackett* with pilot-house forward and machinery aft. To keep her decks clear like those of a sailing vessel, the big truss arches that rose above the decks of early steamers have been eliminated, but two smaller ones have been built into each side of the wooden hull. (—*H.C. Inches Collection, Great Lakes Historical Society*)

Below: Steam barge entering Cleveland harbor in the early 1890s. After the success of the *R. J. Hackett*, many similar vessels followed. (—*Cleveland Picture Collection, Cleveland Public Library*)

much more like many of the freighters we still see today than like anything that preceded it.

This sort of vessel, which used big sails in a fair wind and for steadying, might accurately have been called a steam schooner, but instead it became known as a steam barge. (The term had first been applied, more accurately, to steam-driven lumber barges with pilot houses aft which began to appear about 1867, but now it was broadened to include the new steam freighters.) The *R. J. Hackett* did so well that the following year Peck launched the *Forest City,* almost a twin sister except that she had no engine. (Forest City was a nickname for Cleveland that then had some meaning.) The *R. J. Hackett* towed the *Forest City.* Just as the powered ship was called a steam barge, the one without power was called a tow barge; the first name disappeared over the years, but an unpowered freighter still is known on the Lakes as a tow barge. Other vessels soon followed the *Hackett* pattern and by the time the *Forest City* was given her own engine in 1871 the forward pilothouse was becoming common.

Hatches on these boats were spaced so that their centers were twenty-four feet apart. The pockets in the loading docks at Marquette and other ore ports ended in chutes just twelve feet apart; with this spacing of hatches the crew need only move the ship under the chutes, empty one set of dock pockets, move up twelve feet, empty the other set, and then take her on her way.

THE FUR TRADE CANOE (III)

But in any age, no matter what its technology, simple and good designs have a way of lasting indefinitely. In a day of complex electronics one still can easily buy a spade or a candle. Thus it was with the birch-bark canoe. Invented by the Indians, refined slightly by the fur traders, it was ideal for its purpose, and despite the industrial revolution it went on wherever travellers had to navigate difficult rivers and lakes. It lasted, in fact, into the twentieth century.

Probably the best artist to depict fur-trade canoes was Frances Ann (Beechey) Hopkins, wife of Edward M. Hopkins; he was secretary to the noted governor of

A *canôt du maitre*, one of the big fur-trade canoes, painted by Mrs. F. A. Hopkins. She is one of the two passengers shown; her husband is the other. The resin-covered seams and gores, where pieces of the bark covering were fastened or shaped, are clearly shown. Typically, the stern rides a shade lower than the bow. (—*National Archives of Canada C 2771*)

Mending a canoe by the light of a campfire, from a painting by Frances Hopkins. (—*National Archives of Canada C 2772*)

the Hudson's Bay Company, Sir George Simpson. The collection of Mrs. Hopkins's canoe paintings in the National Archives of Canada is a basic source for any student of the craft.

She came from one of those many-talented English families that seem to have been normal in the Victorian era. Her father was a rear admiral and explorer who also was president of the Royal Geographic Society; her grandfather was a noted portrait painter, Sir William Beechey. She had little formal training in art, but she became a continuous exhibitor in the Royal Academy and is said to have had more paintings accepted by it than any other woman of her day. She married Hopkins about 1858; she was then twenty, he a widower and considerably older. She spent much of her early married life caring for her three stepchildren in their home near Montreal, but she interrupted her domestic routine by making frequent trips over the continent with her husband. On these trips canoes and voyageurs began to fascinate her.

Some of her best pictures show canoes on Lake Superior and on the route to the Red River. Several date from the Wolseley Expedition of 1870; she accompanied that expedition, sharing her husband's canoe all the way. Some of these pictures were handed down through the Wolseley family in England before they were presented to the Canadian government.

Although the Hudson's Bay Company sold its lands to Canada, it remained very much in business there, just as any other company might be. In 1870 it used canoes as a rapid means of passenger travel on the major waterways and as freight carriers in some of the more remote areas. Frances Ann Hopkins painted the travel scenes and camp life that she saw.

Some time after the Wolseley expedition, but still probably in the year 1870, Hopkins retired and he and his wife returned to England. From there she made frequent trips to France and many of her later paintings are of French scenes and people.

Birch-bark canoes remained in use until the early part of the twentieth century. . By that time, however, they were not often seen on the Great Lakes but were employed mainly in the fur trade on the rivers and lakes of the North. Gradually they were replaced by canvas canoes, which kept the basic form while changing the outer material.

JAPAN

Jay Cooke, the Philadelphia banker who got rich during the Civil War by selling many government bonds at a very small profit per bond but a very large total profit (and who owned a magnificent castle of a summer home on Gibralter Island in Lake Erie), in 1868 set out to build the Northern Pacific Railway. It started at St. Paul and headed both northward to Duluth and westward, through the expanding farmland of the northern prairies. It began operation in 1871. Cooke and some of his Philadelphia associates decided also to organize a steamer line that would connect the terminus of the Pennsylvania Railroad at Buffalo to that of the Northern Pacific at Duluth. The bankers and railroaders brought in two shipping experts, E. T. and J. C. Evans who had built the first iron propeller on the Lakes, the *Merchant,* and the Erie and Western Transportation Company was born.

That company, which soon became known as the Anchor Line, started out in 1870 with one steamer, commanded by young Capt. Alexander McDougall. During the winter of 1870-71, however, three passenger and package freight ships were built for the line at Buffalo, and Captain McDougall was retained to be the company's representative at the shipyard that winter. In the spring the three steamers were launched; they were christened *China, India,* and *Japan.* Soon they became known as the triplets.

They were iron propellers unlike anything else that had sailed the Lakes, although it was obvious that the *Merchant* was their close ancestor. The hands of the Evanses, father and son, were clearly seen in their design. It may also be that the Evanses' recollection of what happened to the palace steamers of the 1850s brought some restraint in the size and magnificence of these new ships, which were beautifully efficient and continued in service for the next thirty years. (They then were sold to other owners and eventually lasted into the 1920s.)

Each of them was 210 feet long and of 932 tons. Each had a low green iron hull topped by a brown and red stripe, above which rose spotless wooden upper works that were carefully washed at the end of every trip. Above all stood a single stack and two masts, a short one a little distance forward of the stack and a taller

The *Japan,* an iron-hulled passenger and package-freight steamer launched in 1871, was of a highly efficient design for her time. She and her two sister ships, *China* and *India,* looked so much alike that they could not be told apart at any distance. (—*Great Lakes Historical Society*)

Above: The *India*, sister ship and close duplicate of the *Japan*, at dock in Marquette. Painters touch up her company monogram. (*—Dossin Great Lakes Museum*)

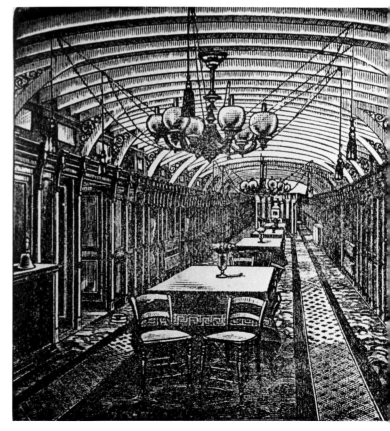

Right: The cabin interior of the *India*, as shown in a book published in 1881. (*—Institute for Great Lakes Research, Bowling Green State University*)

one, rigged for a sail, just aft of the pilothouse. (In later years the foremast was replaced by a shorter one without the rigging.) On top of each pilothouse stood a two-thirds life-size carved wooden figure of a native of the namesake country. These vessels were powered by single cylinder, double acting steam engines, at that time the best way to drive their propellers.

Captain McDougall, at 26 one of the youngest masters on the Lakes, took command of the *Japan*, the last of the triplets launched. She sailed before daylight on Friday, September 29, without a trial voyage and without having her compasses adjusted. It was a boom time; rates for carrying freight were higher than ever before, and the owners wanted to get in as many trips as possible before navigation closed. Factory products were moving to the new farms of Minnesota, which in turn produced great quantities of wheat that flowed into the new port of Duluth for shipment eastward. The Anchor Line worked to full capacity.

The unadjusted compasses on the *Japan* were useless and the Lakes were covered with smoke. It had been a long, dry summer and forest fires burned everywhere; that also was the autumn that Chicago burned. Because of the high freight rates there were many vessels on the Lakes and unless the *Japan* knew where she was at all times, she was in some danger. The inventive McDougall figured out his compass variation as he went along by observing the sun and stars and dropping empty boxes and barrels overboard in a line and then turning around and running back along the line—an approximation of what the compass adjusters do when they "swing ship." In this way he adjusted the compasses as he traveled. On Lake Superior, after leaving Marquette, he encountered an October storm and had to wait out the blow in the shelter of the Apostle Islands, but soon the storm was over and the ship was on her way again. That year the *Japan* made four trips and had a highly profitable season.

The boom reached its peak in 1871, however, and was followed by the depression of 1872. That depression actually started late in '71 and even the Chicago Fire has been blamed for some part of its beginning. Fundamentally, however, the country had invested in land, railroads, and factories to a degree far beyond its current need. There was no immediate way to use these things productively. Wheat from the western lands now gutted the market; the owners of the one completed transcontinental railroad, the Union Pacific, split into warring groups; the factories were silent. European investors, faced with the Franco-Prussian War at home, did their best to rid themselves of what now seemed to be dubious American securities, throwing them back on U.S. bankers.

Anchor Line's ships barely subsisted. In 1872 McDougall even carried a cargo of iron ore in his beautiful new *Japan*. The next year the triplets sailed only between July 1 and September 1. It was a bad year everywhere; throughout 1873 borrowers were called by banks; on September 18 Jay Cooke failed and the Northern Pacific collapsed. But the Pennsylvania Railroad owned a major part of the three iron steamers and they managed to struggle along. The Evanses had conceived them well.

For their time the vessels had good accommodations. Each of them could carry about 150 passengers. The staterooms all had running (cold) water. The long main cabin of each ship was finished in black walnut and maple paneling with carved trim. At the forward end of the main cabin was the barbershop and smoking room; at the after end was the ladies' cabin, complete with piano. Meals were eaten at tables arranged the length of the cabin, the food being sent up from the galley below on a dumb-waiter to a pantry on the port side forward. Lighting was by oil lamps, described in one contemporary account as "tasty chandeliers."

In 1875 the Russian Grand Duke Alexis, accompanied by a Russian admiral, made a tour of the Great Lakes to observe the shipping and methods of handling grain. When they visited Buffalo they went over Captain McDougall's *Japan*. E. T. Evans, general manager of the Anchor Line, discussed mutual problems with them, and after they went home he decided to send Captain McDougall to Russia that winter to see if the Russians would let an American company build elevators and ships for their grain trade. McDougall was also to learn how well Russia might compete with the U.S. in European markets.

The captain spent the winter in Russia gathering information. He also pointed out to the Russians that the mouth of the Neva River on the Gulf of Finland

The *Alaska*, a package freight steamer built with the same hull and machinery as the triplets, was less elaborately finished than her passenger-carrying sisters. (—*Institute for Great Lakes Research, Bowling Green State University*)

was similar to the mouth of the Saginaw River in Michigan; that at one time the products of the Saginaw Valley were lightered out to where the vessels anchored or to an island, in the manner that the Russians lightered grain out to the island of Kronstadt for transshipping to deepwater vessels; and that the U.S. government had then improved the mouth of the Saginaw so that larger ships could come in to the main docks there. The Russians were sufficiently interested that they obtained more information on the project from Washington and in time made a port out of the Neva as McDougall suggested.

By 1876 the depression eased. The *Japan* and her two sisters remained on the Buffalo-Duluth run, becoming popular as passenger vessels and proving their efficiency as package freighters. They soon became fixtures on the Lakes and remained so until the early 1900s.

THE MACKINAW BOAT

In 1876 Captain McDougall decided to try something different. He knew a place near the middle of Lake Superior, at Stannard Rock, where he had seen great shoals of trout, so he entered the fishing business,

going into partnership with Alex Clark, a well-known fisherman of Collingwood.

McDougall rented a dock at Marquette and put up 2,000 tons of ice in a Marquette icehouse. He had the tug *Siskiwit* built at Buffalo; E. T. Evans lent him the necessary money. He bought salt and fish boxes. Clark provided four big Mackinaw fishing boats, twenty miles of gill netting, and crews of fishermen.

Why the boats were called Mackinaws is uncertain. The name was applied at different times to various small craft on the Lakes, but it finally came to mean these particular boats. They originated at Collingwood about 1858 when a boat-builder named William Watts began to turn out fishing skiffs there. Over a period of time the Collingwood skiffs, as they first were known, became larger and more heavily rigged, and went farther afield into the other Lakes. By 1876 the larger boats were about thirty-five feet long; the forward ten feet or so were decked over, and bunks and a stove were installed under the deck. They were shallow boats equipped with big centerboards and rigged as gaff ketches, with two unstayed masts and a jib set on an extremely long bowsprit. All of the Collingwood boats

114

had pointed sterns, and most were of lapstrake construction. Builders and fishermen on the other Lakes began to copy them, adapting the design to their own ideas, and the general class of Mackinaw fishing boats came into existence. They were the best known, and probably the most seaworthy, of the small Great Lakes sailing craft.

Captain McDougall arranged to sell his fish in Buffalo, Erie, and Chicago; steamers could land at the Marquette dock to load the fish and carry it to market. In May 1876 McDougall and Clark arrived at Marquette with one of the best fishing outfits on the Lakes. While part of the crew got the gill nets ready, McDougall and some of the others went out to Stannard Rock and set lines, with a total of 2,000 hooks baited with herring. The next day they set another 2,000 baited hooks. The following day it was foggy, and as it was dangerous to approach the rock in a fog with the steamer, two of the sailing boats went with her to lead the way. McDougall stayed behind on this trip and when the tug and boats did not return in a reasonable time he began to think they all had run on the reef. But the following day tug and boats returned, over-

flowing with fish. "Every bait was gone or every hook had a trout on it; a few had a small trout and a monster trout had him partly swallowed, thus we had two trout on one hook."

As the season progressed, they continued to bait hooks and set nets for whitefish. The usual procedure with the Mackinaws was to lay nets or lines over the stern as they sailed along. Then when the time came to raise them again, the rudder of the boat was unshipped, the after boom and gaff swung forward out of the way, and the nets or lines were taken in over the sharp stern, working up against wind and waves. The absence of any stays on the masts let the spars be moved easily in this way and also permitted freer handling of nets and lines.

The partnership packed fish in ice in the fish cars—wheeled wooden boxes holding 1,200 pounds which then were rolled aboard the steamers. They also salted fish and packed them in hundred-pound half-barrels for the regular salt-fish trade. But just as things were moving well, the bottom fell out of the fish market; that year there were big catches everywhere. McDougall took the tug *Siskiwit* off towing

Part of the Collingwood fishing fleet about 1885. Boats of this type spread through all of the upper Great Lakes and in time came to be known as Mackinaw boats, the most famous of all Lakes fishing boats. When Captain McDougall, who later was to invent the whaleback, tried his hand at the fishing business on the U.S. side of Lake Superior, he turned to these Collingwood fishermen and fishing boats.

Mackinaw boats were used for pleasure as well as for work. Here is a typical boat of the Collingwood model, out for a sail in Midland harbor about 1904. This close-up gives a good view of the characteristic doubled-ended, clinker-built, gaff ketch rig, and long, curved bowsprit.

logs to make some money on the side. Clark and his men got disgusted and went home, shooting the Sault rapids en route. The partners had lost their total investment.

Captain McDougall took the tug back to E. T. Evans, who sold her, and as McDougall said, "I paid all our debts and had a great fishy experience out of it." That was not quite the end of his fishy experience, however; several years later when he was more prosperous he sent Clark a check for all that Clark had lost, with accrued interest.

This event at least displayed the Georgian Bay boats to observers at Marquette, who may then have begun to pattern some local boats after them. The reputation for seaworthiness of the Mackinaws is witnessed by the feat of Alex Clark's boats in running the Sault rapids; such boats were also sometimes used as lifeboats and with experienced crews were known to perform rescues when regular lifeboats could not go out. They continued in use in the fisheries until World War I and also served as car and truck for many families who lived in isolated places. An occasional one may still be found as a pleasure boat.

MOONLIGHT

When the schooner *Moonlight* first splashed into Milwaukee harbor at the shipyard of Wolf and Davidson in the year 1874, she was one of the finest cargo vessels on the Lakes. After a few seasons under command of the hard-driving Capt. Dennis Sullivan,

who liked to carry lots of sail, she became known as one of the fastest. Her fame seems to have been the result of a happy combination: Captain Sullivan and his driving ways plus a well-built ship of good design.

The speedy *Moonlight*, 206 feet long, was primarily a grain carrier. Such big schooners would of course take any available cargo, but those based on Lake Michigan most frequently carried grain or lumber. The schooners loaded grain at Lake Michigan ports and carried it either to Collingwood or Buffalo. From Collingwood it went by rail to eastern Canada or New England; from Buffalo it went by canal or rail to the eastern states.

Lumber came from the mills that sprang up at Lake Michigan ports; big and little schooners came to load the lumber and take it to Chicago, whence it was sent out to settlements of the present Middle West, or to Tonawanda, N.Y., for reshipment to New York. Other establishments also sprang up at the lumber ports. Enterprising businessmen and women quickly built places of recreation for sailors and for the loggers who were bottled up all winter in the woods and came to town in a body in the spring after driving their logs down the rivers. At Muskegon, Michigan, a fairly large port, there were reputed to be three hundred girls working in the dives erected on the sawdust fill along the harbor front, not to mention those in the somewhat more elegant places uptown. The most notorious resort of all the lumber coasts was at Muskegon; it was known as the Canterbury.

Right: The *Moonlight*, fast bulk-freight carrier launched in 1874. Her rig, with its big square sail and triangular raffee topsail on the foremast, was a Great Lakes development that simplified the earlier barkentine rig. Like the barkentines, vessels with the rig shown here were often referred to as "barks" on the Lakes. (*—Marine Historical Collection, Milwaukee Public Library*)

Below: *Moonlight* in dry dock at Cleveland, about 1894. This picture shows the schooner's big anchors at her bow as well as details of her construction. It also shows the flat sides and relatively flat bottom of Great Lakes schooners, which were designed to go through canal locks and into restricted harbors. Such vessels were fitted with centerboards, however, that enabled them to sail well; *Moonlight* was a notably fast and handy vessel. (*—Great Lakes Historical Society*)

Grain schooners, many of them with the same rig as the *Moonlight* (note the cocked yards on the foremasts), at the Collingwood elevator in the 1880s. The arm let down from the elevator to unload grain is not much different from those in Dart's first Buffalo elevator.

Cockfights, dogfights, and prizefights were standard attractions to draw customers to the Canterbury's booze and women. On special occasions the proprietor staged "circuses," which included displays of most of the popular types of perversion as well as some of the more exotic forms. John Williams, who owned the Canterbury, also owned the Redlight Saloon, celebrated in a loggers' ballad:

Got left in Muskegon and this was my doom;
To pay a short visit to the Redlight saloon.
I boldly walked in, I stepped up to the bar;
And a dashing young beauty says, "Have a cigar."

The grain trade was perhaps not as colorful as the lumber trade, but it had its moments of excitement. The big schooners would race each other into harbor, each trying to reach the elevators first. Particularly at Collingwood, where there was only one elevator to transfer cargo from ships to trains, incoming schooners would keep on all sail until the last possible moment. It paid to be first. The first one unloaded might gain a day, or if the elevator was full and the trains not moving quickly she might gain a week.

Not all of the racing was into Collingwood or Buffalo, however. It was on a voyage from Buffalo back up the Lakes to Milwaukee that Captain Sullivan of the *Moonlight* challenged Capt. Orv Green of the schooner *Porter* to a race. As the two vessels sped along the 800-mile course they remained fairly close together. Word flashed ahead by telegraph, and wherever their paths brought them close to shore, people came out to watch. Then they passed through the Straits of Mackinac and headed westward into Lake Michigan. Not long afterward a sudden violent windstorm struck both of them. Capt. Green kept sail on and never changed his course. Capt. Sullivan, on this occasion showing that while he might be a driver he also could use discretion, took in sail and ran into shelter of the high bluffs near Port Washington; then when the worst of the blow had passed he went on into Milwaukee.

There he found the *Porter* at dock, but without any of her masts, spars, sails, or rigging—she was only a bare hull, blown clean by the storm. The harbor tugs at Milwaukee, alert for the arrival of the racers, had found her after the storm and brought her in. Which schooner won the race? The two captains apparently considered it a tie, for they adjourned to a convenient bar for a joint celebration.

Aside from her notably fast voyages, the *Moonlight* was typical of the larger bulk-freight carriers of her day. By the 1870s Great Lakes schooners had achieved a distinctive form. They had shoal, flat-sided hulls fitted with centerboards to help them sail to windward. Such a schooner would probably be slightly longer and narrower than an ocean-going schooner of similar tonnage, because of the narrow harbor entrances, rivers, and canals she had to navigate. The bigger lake schooners were usually three-masted, and when one of them was running before the wind she would set on her foremast a large square sail as well as a triangular topsail that was known as a raffee and that had originated on the Lakes. Both it and the square sail could be set and furled from the deck, a useful feature in bad weather when it was hard and sometimes dangerous for sailors to work aloft.

The rig was a compromise between the pure schooner with only fore-and-aft sails and the barkentine with its traditional square sails on the foremast. The rig used by lake schooners was nearly as efficient before the wind as that of the barkentine, but it was easier to handle and less expensive to build than the heavy square rig with all of its yards, its complex foremast, and its equally complex rigging. The mast lengths of these Lakers followed a distinctive pattern; the mainmast was tallest, the foremast slightly shorter than the main, and the mizzenmast shortest of all. These masts had the same relationship as the masts on square-riggers, another indication of the close relationship between lake schooner and barkentine. (As true barkentines disappeared, the term "bark," which commonly had been applied

Lettie May, 47-foot schooner built at Fort Howard (Green Bay) in 1874. Many little schooners of this type carried all sorts of small cargoes on the Lakes. The photograph shows her about 1880 at one of the harbors in Door County, Wisconsin. (—*Marine Historical Collection, Milwaukee Public Library*)

to them on the Lakes, was often used for big schooners with some square sails.) Three-masted schooners of the Atlantic Coast, by comparison, were rigged with masts all of the same length.

LETTIE MAY

In contrast with the bigger vessels such as the *Moonlight* were the many little schooners on the Great Lakes. Roads were poor and there were no motor trucks; small vessels provided much the service that trucks do today. They could enter almost any sort of harbor and carry in or out whatever was necessary. There were hundreds of them, and lists of their cargoes included most rural products and most of the things that were needed by little communities along the lake shores: salted fish, grain, rope, fence posts, pork, coal, shingles, salt, bricks, butter, and livestock. Little schooners were fitted out as travelling stores that called at isolated villages to sell housewives the necessities and a few of the luxuries, and might accept in return produce or furs instead of money. Vessels in these trades normally were something under a hundred feet in length and a few were little more than large fishing boats decked over.

A true schooner, but a small one, was the *Lettie May,* launched in 1874, the same year as the big *Moonlight.* The *Lettie May* was built at Fort Howard, Wisconsin, which later became Green Bay. She was forty-seven feet long, but for her size she carried a number of sails; in a good breeze she undoubtedly could keep her crew of three quite busy. The size of the crews on small schooners varied considerably. At least one little vessel that was a floating store on Georgian Bay was sailed by her captain-owner singlehandedly, but no doubt she had fewer sails than the *Lettie May.* Others were sailed by a man and a boy, although four or five men were about average.

Schooners of this kind often were owned and sailed by a single family. The captain's sons would be the crew and his wife or daughter might be cook. Such women were frequently called upon to do other jobs on board. The story of Minerva Ann McCrimmon, the captain's daughter who steered the schooner *David Andrews* when she drove ashore on Lake Ontario during a wild storm in 1880, was prob-

ably not too unusual. Some unknown person composed a decidedly lumpy ballad about the event, however, and so the story has come down to posterity how,

> Above the roar of the water,
> And the reefing's [*sic*] thundering din,
> I heard her call to her brother
> "Bill, please get mother's grey shawl from the cabin,
> And pin it under my chin."

The girl steered while the men fought the sails, and she brought the vessel onto the beach so neatly that no lives were lost.

Also on Lake Ontario, the cook on the small schooner *Pioneer,* Mrs. Mary Pement, saved all aboard by realizing that something was badly amiss when the vessel heeled over before a good breeze. She had just rung the dinner bell and Captain John Allen, his mate, and four sailors were heading for the cabin table. "Don't come to the table till you've been to the pumps, captain," Mrs. Pement called. "That puff brought water up on the corner of the cabin floor." The captain quickly discovered seven feet of water in the hold and knew the hold was only seven feet deep. Hastily he ordered the schooner headed into the wind and the yawl boat launched from its place at the stern. First into the boat went the cook and a twelve-year-old girl making the trip as a guest; the men followed. Captain Allen jumped off the rail into the boat just before the schooner disappeared. The cook's warning had saved them from being trapped in the cabin at the dinner table. Mrs. Pement was a widow, Captain Allen a widower. Perhaps the captain decided that a cook who kept such a cool head should be signed on permanently; in any case, they were married soon afterward.

One variety of sailing vessel less handsome than the normal ones such as the *Lettie May* was the scow schooner. Scows were rigged like other schooners, but as the name indicates, their hulls were usually squared-ended and slab-sided. There were different kinds of scows, however; some had normal bows grafted on the scow hull and some were round-bottomed but squared-ended. They did much the same small bulk haulage as other schooners of their size but seem to have been used most frequently in carrying lumber. Often their captains would buy odd lots of lumber from a mill, carry them to market, and resell them at a profit.

The steamer *V. H. Ketcham*, from the painting by the late Carl Gaertner that hangs in the board room of the Interlake Steamship Company. Her builders started to make her a schooner, but changed her to a steamer before she was launched in 1874. She was then the largest ship on the Great Lakes. (*—Courtesy Interlake Steamship Company*)

Little ships of this kind were constantly at work. *Lettie May* had a long and useful life. In 1892 she was rebuilt, lengthened to sixty-nine feet, and given three masts; she must then have been one of the smallest three-masters afloat. She and similar vessels continued to carry small bulk cargoes. But gradually small steamers took over, and when finally the motor truck arrived on the scene after World War I, the last tired little schooners were finished.

V. H. KETCHAM

The evolution of the steam freighter from the schooner is shown most clearly in a vessel that was launched at Marine City, Michigan, in 1874. This boat, first intended to be a big schooner 233 feet long, was changed to a steamer while she was building. We do not know how much her builders were inspired by the design of the *R. J. Hackett* and to what extent they reached their decisions independently, but when she was finished she was truly a steam schooner, although the term seems never to

have been used on the Lakes. She had the schooner hull—even to the clipper bow and schooner stern—four tall masts with sails, and the long, unbroken deck. She also had a small deck cabin and pilot-house at her bow and another deck cabin and her machinery all the way aft.

This steamer, the *V. H. Ketcham*, was so large that at first she could not enter many of the ports. Docking facilities were growing as quickly as the size of vessels, however, and before long she was returning an excellent profit. When in 1883 the Marquette hardware merchant James Pickands joined the Cleveland iron broker Samuel Mather and the mining expert Jay Morse to form Pickands Mather & Co., the new firm soon bought shares in the *Ketcham*, which became the first of a long series of vessels to fly the Pickands Mather flag.

But there were problems other than the size of docks and channels. In ports where ore was unloaded the work was painfully slow. It still required single buckets to be loaded by shovel in the hold, pulled up on ropes to the deck by donkey engines, and dumped

121

Unloading coal from a schooner in Milwaukee harbor about 1880. This unusual photograph shows how, before mechanical unloaders were invented, barrels or buckets full of coal, loaded by hand in the hold were pulled up and emptied into wheelbarrows on a gangway above the ship's deck. (—*Great Lakes Historical Society*)

into wheelbarrows which then were taken ashore over gangplanks. More and bigger ore boats came down the Lakes, but the unloading was nearly as slow as ever.

In 1880 Alexander E. Brown, son of iron-ore magnate Fayette Brown, devised what came to be known as the Brown hoist and set up the first one at Erie. It still used the hand-filled buckets, but they were lifted from the hold and carried either to rail cars or storage piles by a network of cables, controlled from a central point. The machines were movable and could be grouped to unload ore from all the hatches of one vessel at the same time. In 1882 a battery of permanent unloaders of another design were installed at Chicago. They too used hand-filled buckets which were then lifted up and dumped into a series of chutes that carried the ore to waiting railroad cars. These unloaders were spaced so that each of them stood above one of the hatches of an incoming freighter.

GEORGE M. CASE

In 1871 the Canadian government began a plan to enlarge the locks of the Welland and St. Lawrence canals, but it was not until 1887 that the improvements on the Welland were completed, and until 1884 vessels still were limited to a length of 140 feet, a beam of 26 1/2 feet, and a draught of 10 feet. (Completion of the St. Lawrence improvements lagged until 1901.)

As a result, the class of vessels known as "canallers" which had first developed in the late 1840s and 50s continued to flourish. Any shipowner who wanted to carry cargoes into or out of Lake Ontario from the other Lakes had to have vessels that conformed to the dimensions of the locks. Probably most canallers were built on Lake Ontario, but some came from other places as well. The *George M. Case* was built at Saugatuck, Michigan, in 1874.

For good reason was the old Welland Canal nicknamed the "raging canal." As the locks were too small to admit both vessels and tugs, canallers were still pulled through by teams of six horses or mules. When a strong

The *George M. Case*, a big canal-type schooner, unloading coal at Racine, Wisconsin, in 1880. No machine hoists had yet reached that port, not even a donkey engine. The single horse beyond her bowsprit lifts hand-filled buckets to the men on the scaffolding. (—*Racine County Museum*)

wind blew the length of the canal the situation could be reversed and a vessel, gaining momentum, could tow the animals and horseboys off the muddy towpath into the water. Then while beasts and boys clambered out of the canal the vessel would be moored to the bank until the wind changed. Even when the wind did not blow, vessels moving slowly at the end of towlines were hard to control; they wandered from side to side, sometimes grounding and blocking traffic both ways until they could be pulled loose by horse and manpower. Sometimes a vessel had to be partly unloaded to get it over a lock sill, then loaded again. It took at least forty-eight hours for a ship to get through the canal, and sometimes it took a week.

The canal also levied its toll of limbs and lives. Men became tangled in towlines or fell from the rigging when vessels grounded with a jolt. Legend has it that one captain who had built a new schooner got her hopelessly jammed in a lock on her first passage. She was just a little too big. No amount of adzing would trim her down so that she could move either way. Finally he walked into a nearby woods, carrying his razor with him, and cut his throat from ear to ear.

The *Case* never seems to have had such a disastrous problem, although she was about as big as the canallers came—137 feet over all. Like most of the bigger ones she had a plumb bow, so as to get the maximum carrying space within her length, and like all of them she was relatively narrow for her length, having a beam of 26 feet. She was typically flat-sided, carrying her full beam as far forward and aft as possible, to add to her capacity.

CHAMPION

The easiest way to apply steam power to sailing vessels was by towing them. At Great Lakes ports of any size there developed towing companies with steam tugs that brought ships in and out of harbor. They would meet incoming sailing vessels and tow them to their docks, or tow outward-bound vessels clear of harbor complexities and traffic and then release them to begin their voyages. Tugs also towed ships through canals and narrow passages, wherever it was difficult to maneuver under sail.

Of all the places where tugs operated, the Detroit and St. Clair Rivers were the busiest. Almost any vessel making a long lake voyage went through the straits. Sailing vessels bound down could sometimes get through unaided by making clever use of wind and current, but it was nearly impossible to make the ninety-mile upstream passage from Lake Erie to Lake Huron without help.

As a result, some of the biggest and finest tugs on the Lakes worked out of Detroit. When the wind was such that sailing vessels would be arriving at ei-

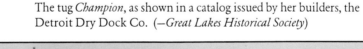

The tug *Champion*, as shown in a catalog issued by her builders, the Detroit Dry Dock Co. (*—Great Lakes Historical Society*)

The tug *Champion*, towing sailing vessels through the straits at Detroit. This lithograph was made from a painting by Seth Arca Whipple, a noted ship portaitist of his day, and on the back of one copy the artist wrote the names of the vessels from front to rear: *Wells Burt, Michigan, Elizabeth A. Nicholson, James F. Joy, Francis Palms, Sweetheart, Sunnyside,* and *Emma L. Coyne.* (—*Inches Collection, Great Lakes Historical Society*)

ther end of the straits, the tugs would go out and cruise, waiting for ships to come along. Competition was acute and as soon as one tug captain scented a change in the sailing breeze and started away from his Detroit dock, all the others would be racing after him. Each tug hoped to pick up several vessels and tow them through the river in a long train; if the wind was right, the ships would set their sails to help them along.

One old-timer, Lauchlen P. Morrison, who grew up on the straits, remembered how the tows would pass, moving at no more than seven or eight miles per hour, fastened together by towlines of three or four-inch diameter manila rope. The heavy towlines sagged down so that their centers dragged in the water. Small boys, out swimming on nice summer days, liked to straddle the lines or even to walk on the rope. If a ship carried a woman cook, as many did, the boys, who never had heard of bathing suits, were quickly chased away by the sailors; the ladies were probably fairly unshockable, but the amenities had to be observed

Of all the tugs at Detroit, the *Champion* was most famous. Described by her builders, the Detroit Dry Dock Company which launched her in 1868, as a lake and river tug, she was 146 feet over all—a sizable vessel. She belonged to the Grummond Tug Line, which operated a number of similar boats. The picture of her in 1880 hauling eight sailing vessels has been partly responsible for the *Champion's* fame; it was tremendously popular and was often copied. In some of the copies the appearance of the vessels was changed and various names were given them.

Such lengthy tows were rare but not completely unknown. Lauchlen P. Morrison remembered when the *Champion* and her champion tow passed. According to his recollections, the *Champion* on that occasion happened to pick up eight ships, probably because her competitors were not on their toes, and brought them along the St. Clair and Detroit rivers.

Tugs replaced horses and mules in moving vessels through the Welland Canal as soon as the locks were made big enough. In this picture of the Mountain Locks about 1885, an unidentified tug is taking a full-sized three-master through the canal. (—*National Archives ovf Canada C 18670*)

The word was passed along the rivers ahead of the convoy and the people from some distance away congregated along the banks to view the marine parade. There was plenty of time to take it all in as it took nearly an hour for it to pass. It was within viewing distance for nearly two hours from our point, much longer in the straighter stretches of the river.

By 1880 sailing vessels were at the height of their development and most of them were much handsomer than the crude steamers of the day. But the dependability of the steamers and their ability to maneuver in narrow waters was fast giving them an advantage over sail. The big tugs, however, enabled sailing vessels to compete for a while longer.

ASIA

The Welland Canal produced not only a special kind of sailing vessel, but also a special class of steamer, designed to fit the limited space within the locks. All of these steamers were propellers, for sidewheels would take up too much room, and all had boxy hulls. The sailing vessels could not be built with large cabin structures, but no such limitation affected the steamers. As a re-

sult they had extensive upper works. On top of the relatively low and narrow hull rose a boxed-in main deck, above that a cabin ran the full length of the upper deck, and on top of the forward end of the cabin stood the pilothouse. Such vessels carried the maximum amount of cargo and the most passengers back and forth through the canal, but the features that made them useful for canal work made them particularly tricky to handle in open water. Steam canallers frequently got into trouble, but none other as spectacularly as the *Asia*.

She was a typical canaller, 136 feet long and of 26 feet beam, launched at St. Catherines, Ontario, in 1873. She had the usual high superstructure on a narrow, shallow hull. The upper works were of relatively light construction, and with cargo in her hold such a vessel could stand up well enough, but if she was unladen she could be hard to handle, and if she was loaded wrong she could be a deathtrap.

In 1882 the *Asia* was brought to Georgian Bay and put in the local service as a temporary replacement for the fine new *Manitoulin*, which had burned

126

Above: *Asia*, a steamer of the Welland Canal type, with narrow, shallow hull and high upper works, foundered in a storm on Georgian Bay with the loss of over 100 lives. (*—Courtesy Mrs. Fred Landon*)

Below: The *Asia* lying beside the larger *Ontario*, probably at Kincardine on Lake Huron. A comparison of the two steamers shows that the *Asia* was narrower than the other boat, but her upper works were about equally tall. The picture does not show what was undoubtedly also true, that the *Ontario* drew much more water. Schooners designed to fit the locks of the old Welland Canal managed also to be seaworthy, but the Welland Canal steamers had a record of disaster in open waters. (*—Institute for Great Lakes Research, Bowling Green State University*)

earlier in the year. On September 13 she left Collingwood on a normal run, stopped at Owen Sound to take on more cargo and passengers, and not long after midnight on the 14th steamed northward out of Owen Sound harbor.

The autumn movement to the lumber camps was beginning, and in addition to her normal cargo she carried a load of winter supplies and a number of horses. To avoid the extra labor of stowing the cargo in the hold and then unloading it again, most of the freight was carried on the main deck and there was even some on the hurricane deck. The exact number of people on board was not recorded, but it was over a hundred. The staterooms were filled and men slept on sofas and on the carpets in the cabin; on the main deck lumberjacks slept wherever they could find space.

As Capt. J. N. Savage took her out into Georgian Bay the weather became worse. The storm grew and by 7:30 a.m. a stiff gale was blowing. At that point he turned and headed straight across the Bay toward the lumber port of French River. The gale then struck directly against the high upper works of the top-heavy steamer at the same time that she found herself wallowing in the trough of the sea. Not only did she have too little weight in her hold, but most of her cargo was aft, so that her bow rode light and high. When the captain ordered the wheelsman to head her into the storm, the high, flat bow acted like a sail and the wind thrusting against it kept her from answering.

One of those aboard, a teen-age boy named Dunk Tinkiss, afterward described the scene:

> The storm was raging, the wind blowing a perfect hurricane and the waves appeared to be rolling mountains high . . . nearly all the passengers by this time had come on deck. . . . Those not on their knees rushed frantically about, thus adding to the general confusion. I did not see the captain or crew, and in fact I do not think they could have been of any service what ever; but I heard a single order to throw the cargo overboard. Being on the upper deck, I could not see what was going on below, but from the noise which I heard I am under the impression that the order was obeyed. . . . The steamer had got into the trough of the sea, and though her engines worked hard the vessel refused to obey her helm. Wave after wave swept over us, each of which threatened to engulf us, until one larger than the rest struck us and the boat careened over. . . . I cannot attempt to describe the feelings of those people when they felt the boat sinking under their feet without the slightest hope of safety. . . . Her stern went foremost and she was swallowed up by the angry waves.

Tinkiss and the other eventual survivor, a young woman named Christy Morrison, in company with several others including the captain, mate, and purser, finally got into the one lifeboat that still was floating. The waves constantly turned the boat over and over, striking and injuring many of those in it, who were then carried away by the storm. The two young people finally remained in the water, one at each end of the boat, holding on to it but avoiding injury.

As the storm subsided the boat floated right side up, partly filled with water. There were no oars in it, only a single useless paddle, and they were twenty miles from shore. Through the afternoon two of the men died of shock and exposure. About 5:00 p.m. they saw land but had no way of reaching it. One by one the others died, the last one being the captain. At daybreak next morning the boat drifted ashore. The two survivors spent that day and night trying, in their exhausted state, to move along the shore. Late the following morning they were discovered by an Indian in a sailboat. In return for Tinkiss's gold watch he took them to the town of Parry Sound.

DAVID DOWS

Builders and owners of sailing vessels responded to the competition of steam freighters by producing larger and larger schooners. In April of 1881 the largest schooner in the world, the *David Dows*, was launched at Toledo. This mammoth had five masts and was 278 feet long over all. She was named for David Dows, Esq., a New York commission merchant who was a friend and business associate of her owner. To give some idea of the massive construction required for a wooden ship of this size, her planking up to the turn of the bilge was half a foot thick. The Toledo *Blade*, in the journalistic fashion of the day unable to keep political commentary out of even the marine news, reported, "Her sails will require over 70,000 yards of canvas, or enough to furnish clean shirts for a large portion of the Democratic party in Ohio."

The above painting of the *David Dows*, by Father Edward J. Dowling, S.J., admirably catches her impressive power as she snores along before a fair wind with all sails set. The builder's sail plan of the *Dows*, below, shows that she set her square sails on a schooner foremast similar to her other masts, rather than on a stepped square-rigger foremast as the painting shows. But some contemporary paintings also show the stepped foremast, so she may have been built with it despite the plan, or she may have been fitted with it after one of the accidents that plagued her. (—*Above, Marine Historical Collection, University of Detroit Mercy; below, from* Great Lakes Wooden Shipbuilding Era *by H.C. Inches, reproduced by courtesy of the late Captain Inches*)

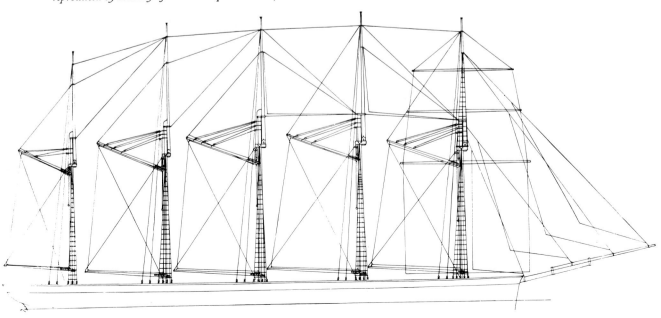

But was the *Dows* a schooner? Sailors have argued the point ever since she first appeared. She had square rig on the foremast, which should make her a barkentine according to the dictionary or a bark according to Great Lakes usage. She also, however, had a large fore-and-aft sail on the foremast, and this should make her a schooner. Further, the mast itself was a schooner mast. A single tall foremast, some ninety feet high, carried a single topmast, sixty-five feet high; a true square-rigged foremast would be made up of several shorter masts stepped one above the other. In any event, her builders, Bailey Brothers, and her owner, M. D. Carrington, seem to have considered her a schooner, and probably that should suffice.

Never before had five masts been seen on the Lakes on one vessel. Her two centerboards provided another novelty; this was not as unusual as the five masts, but most Lakes schooners had only one board. She was designed to carry 140,000 bushels of grain, and to be handled by a relatively small crew—twelve men, a captain, two mates, a cook, and a cook's helper—with the aid of a steam donkey engine to hoist sails and anchors and a steam pump to empty her bilges. The donkey engine made life bearable for the crew, but scarcely easy. It took nearly eight hours of steady work by all hands to take in the towline when a harbor tug cast off, to set the sails, and to coil down all the gear. After that the crew settled down to their normal four-hour watches with half the men on duty and half below.

It took rough, tough men to do the work. Sailors of the time often returned from an evening ashore in highly stimulated condition. The usual climax to such a night, once they had reached the fo'c'sle, was for someone to douse the light and call, "Every man for himself for fifteen minutes." A no-holds-barred fight in the dark followed until the mate, who had the job of keeping order on board, arrived on the scene. According to story, the *Dows* had a particularly big mate who was a champion rough-and-tumble man himself, and on one occasion he waded into a fight in the dark fo'c'sle, grabbed the first man he reached, threw him bodily out onto the deck, moved on to the next, and in short order had the entire crew piled up in a bruised heap in the sobering fresh air. The mate hitched up his trousers and went about his duties while the crew untangled themselves and limped quietly back to their beds.

Even with that kind of crew and officers, and with the help of the donkey engine, she was hard to handle. A news report from Buffalo in May 1881, not long after she was launched, said:

> The monster *David Dows* was lying at Central Wharf on Saturday afternoon, her ten boat-loads of wheat having been discharged. A plank was laid from the platform in front of the Board of Trade rooms to the vessel's rail between the first and second masts, and many visitors passed over this bridge to inspect the huge craft. The figurehead and stern ornament of the *Dows* was carved by G. E. Buck, of this city. The former represents a dragon, and the head of the animal is a very fine specimen of work. Capt. Skeldon made an arrangement with the Captain of the propeller *St. Paul* to tow the *Dows* to Erie on Saturday evening, but as it looked squally outside the *St. Paul* left without the five-master, taking only her consort, the *Owasco*. The tug *Mollie Spencer*, Capt. James Hannett, started out with the *Dows* yesterday, a little before noon. Capt. Skeldon says he will take about 3,000 tons of coal from Erie to Chicago.

Apparently Captain Skeldon would rather take a tow from Buffalo to Erie than go through the hours of work necessary to get her under way and the nearly equal time to get ready again for port.

On September 10 of that same year, the *David Dows* was sailing down Lake Erie near Pelee Island in company with two other schooners. The *Dows* was in the lead, about a half mile behind her was the three-masted schooner *Charles K. Nims*, and an equal distance behind the *Nims* was a third schooner. A heavy westerly squall struck all of the vessels suddenly from astern, and the masters of at least the *Dows* and the *Nims* momentarily lost control of their ships. "The night was smoky and there was some rain, but it was not very dark," an admiralty court later stated. "Lights could be seen on the island and mainland, but vessels could not be distinguished over half a mile distant."

The *Dows* and *Nims*, which had been heading generally eastward, suddenly found themselves heading south. Their captains and crews struggled to regain control; those on the smaller vessel managed first to bring her back on her original course, but in doing so unfortunately sailed her directly in front of the *Dows*, which rammed and sank her.

The owners of the *Nims* sued the owners of the *Dows,* contending that the latter vessel was improperly constructed, being an "experiment"; that she was undermanned, having on board only seven men, a master, and two mates; and that she was "negligently and unskillfully maneuvered." The court decided that nothing about her design or construction contributed to the accident, that she had a sufficiently large crew to handle her under the circumstances, but that both her captain and the captain of the *Nims* exercised poor judgement in maneuvering their vessels and each was partly at fault.

Court findings notwithstanding, it was already becoming plain in the course of one navigational season that on the Great Lakes, where maneuver room was limited and voyages often short, a sailing vessel as large as the *Dows* with as complex a rig did not fit in well. (On the Atlantic Coast, even larger schooners were successful and one seven-master was eventually built.) She continued in service, however, until sometime later she had another collision, this time with the schooner *Richard Mott.* Four men were furling sail on her upper topsail yard when she hit the other vessel; her fore-topmast snapped off and all four were thrown overboard and lost.

After that her topmasts were taken down, her rig was simplified, and she was converted to a barge, travelling at the end of a towline behind a tug. Even in this role she lasted a relatively short time; on November 30, 1889, she foundered near Chicago. The *David Dows* was the largest sailing vessel ever built on the Great Lakes and the only five-master. Her main achievement was to prove that such vessels were not well suited to these waters.

IRON DUKE

More and more steam barges were launched. In 1881 the Detroit Dry Dock Company launched the *Iron Duke,* a wooden freighter 212 feet long, of 1,152 gross tons, and with an engine of 700 hp. She had four tall masts on which sails could be set.

In March of 1883 a young man named Loren W. Burch joined the crew of the *Iron Duke* while she was fitting out at Detroit. He sailed on her as a lookout all that season, until she was laid up in Octo-

Steam barge *Iron Duke,* painted by Loren W. Burch who sailed on her for a season as lookout. She is towing her consort, the *Iron Cliff.* (*—State Historical Society of Wisconsin*)

ber at Chicago, and later he wrote an account of it. This was a typical season on a Great Lakes freighter except that the turnover in the crew, and particularly in first mates, was perhaps a little high. By the time she was laid up, Burch, a fireman, and the second mate were the only members of the original crew left.

On her first trip up the Lakes that year the *Iron Duke,* with her consort, the tow barge *Iron Cliff,* headed for Duluth to load grain for Buffalo. Already these freighters, conceived first as ore carriers, were taking other cargoes. About twenty miles past Whitefish Point, as the steamer and tow were moving into Lake Superior, they ran into an ice field and were icebound for two days. They then saw a break in the ice and "all hands and the cook were called upon to help 'break out' from the grip of the ice by swaying the main boom as far as possible from one side to the other and going ahead, then backing on the engine." This procedure soon got them loose and they were on their way to Duluth.

There young Burch was given the extra job—and pay—of tallyman. He climbed to the top of the grain

By the mid-1880s steamers were appearing at the ore docks amidst the sailing vessels. The loading dock shown is at Marquette, Michigan. (—*Marine Historical Collection, Milwaukee Public Libraary*)

elevator and tallied the weight of each hopper before it was dumped into the chute; it was dirty, dusty work. At Buffalo he did the job in reverse. But then the *Duke* moved over to the coal dock and loaded coal for Duluth, so he was done tallying for the time.

The *Iron Duke* went out into the harbor and lay behind the breakwater until the *Iron Cliff* was loaded and brought out by tugs. The chief engineer of the *Duke* had been out on the town while she was at the coal dock and had not yet quite sobered up. As a result, five or six miles out of Buffalo he let the water get so low in the boiler that a "soft plug"—a safety device—blew out, and the ship was left without steam and with a hot boiler. As there was no steam to run the donkey engine, the crew "sweated up" the sails by hand, no doubt at the same time remarking on the ancestry and habits of the engineer. Because a barge, with its high bow and cabin and with no centerboard, could not tack into a breeze, the two vessels turned around and headed back to Buffalo. (Tow barges sometimes were called schooners; they had no power and did have a schooner rig, so the descrip-

tion was technically accurate, but they were never meant to be sailing vessels.)

As morning came the *Duke* rounded the end of the breakwater again, and headed up to anchor in its lee. At that moment the engineer, who evidently had revived and done some work on the boiler, started his engines ahead. The captain, who was standing on the wheelhouse, signaled him to stop, but he did not respond. The captain danced a little dance and breathed fire. In a moment the engine stopped, the captain rang for her to go astern, and the *Iron Duke*, about to ram into the breakwater, slowly came to a stop and backed away. A short time later the *Duke* and *Cliff* were again on their way up Lake Erie. At Detroit the engineer became the first of the crew to leave the ship—by request.

A little later the captain was transferred to a newly launched ship, the first mate became captain, and a former schooner captain named Paddy Ryan became first mate. One day Burch started to make a salvage strap, a device of plank and rope to support an anchor; it was a difficult little job that he

A typical wooden passenger steamer of the 1880s (except for internal reinforcement of bow and hull permitting her to operate in ice), the *Depere* of the Goodrich Line is shown unloading cargo on the ice off Manitowoc, Wisconsin, in March of 1885. Vessels of this sort carried package freight and passengers while steam barges such as the *Iron Duke* carried bulk cargoes. (—*Marine Historical Collection, Milwaukee Public Library*)

had learned to do from an officer of another steamer on which he had sailed. Mr. Ryan watched for a time, then asked what he was doing. Burch told him.

"Say." Ryan looked at him more closely. "What salt water have you sailed on?"

Burch said he never had been on salt water.

"Don't tell me that," said the mate. Thereafter he was convinced that Burch was a salt-water seaman and refused to have him do any of the dirty work such as polishing and scrubbing; that wasn't a true sailor's job.

A trip or two afterward the *Iron Duke*, towing the *Iron Cliff*, was heading toward the Sault Canal from Lake Huron, against the current, through the Detour passage. She was navigating the Neebish Rapids, where the water twisted and whirled over the rocks off her starboard side. Just then about a mile ahead another big barge and tow came toward them; they were the *W. L. Whitmore* and her consort *Brunette*. (*Whitmore* is Burch's spelling; she was probably the *W. L. Wetmore*.) Burch was helping the wheelsman bring the *Duke* through these tricky waters, and the two men immediately saw that there

was a question whether the ships could pass in the narrow channel.

Captain Beyer was on the pilot house giving orders to us at the wheel. On came the *Whitmore* looking big and menacing, and, as we could see, taking up all the road. We heard our captain talking and muttering to himself. I ventured to look up the speaking ventilator and could see his face. There were tears in his eyes and I heard him say, "We can never pass—no we can't pass."

I jumped back, took a fresh grip at the wheel and said, "Mack, the old man has lost his nerve. We must take her through."

The *W. L. Whitmore* and *Brunette*, carried along by the current, bore down on the *Iron Duke*. The two men at the *Duke's* wheel held her steady; it was all they could do.

The *Whitmore* came on with a rush. When our bows were opposite, it looked like we had room. "Steady there; don't let her swing." Our pilot houses were opposite each other. I heard the voice of the captain of the *Whitmore* as he sang out, "I couldn't hold her back captain, I had to keep on coming." We were glad to hear a good strong voice in our captain reply, "I know it captain. I guess there is room."

The *Duke* and *Whitmore* eased by each other without touching, although a man could readily have jumped from one deck to the other as they passed. But the two consorts, without any power of their own, were a different problem.

> Both steamships had their consorts on shortened tow lines, but they were both apt to swing out of line. Every man was on his toes, and as we watched the two schooners pass each other we thought it was a miracle. Look out there, they are coming together! Sure enough, just as they were about to clear each other, they came together just as they were opposite the jigger mast of the *Iron Cliff*. Bang! Up in the air went their after fenders, torn from their lashings and the consorts were by.

A couple of trips later the *Iron Duke* had finished loading ore at Marquette and had moved out to the breakwater waiting for the *Iron Cliff*. Mr. Ryan, the mate, had a hangover from his celebrations ashore and was in a bad mood. Both the mate and the captain were on the forward deck, talking, when suddenly Ryan let out a roar and sprang for the captain, who made no effort to call for help or stop the mate, even though he was being forced backward over the bulwarks. Then Burch and the wheelsman came to his aid, persuading the angry mate to back off. Word of this contretemps flashed to the owners by telegram; when the *Duke* arrived at Erie with her load of ore, a new captain and mate were waiting to take over.

This new mate did not last long either, but the new captain, William Rolls, a six-footer with a long curly mustache, was a quiet but forceful master who commanded the ship the rest of that season. On their last trip down from Duluth with grain for Buffalo, a gale came up. By that time the *Iron Duke* had acquired still another in her series of new mates. This one did not like the storm.

> Along in the middle of the afternoon the new mate, an ex-captain, came to Captain Rolls and advised him to let go of the *Iron Cliff* or we would founder. It was impossible to tow her any longer he said. Did you ever see a mild mannered man get mad? Oh, how the captain went for that mate. In the gale of wind you could hear his voice above the roar and tumult. "Let go of the *Cliff*?" he said. "When I let go, we'll all let go and not until then."

Both ships made shelter in Waiska Bay sometime after four o'clock that afternoon. They lay there two days while the storm blew itself out, then moved to the Sault to go through the canal. They came in to the government dock to wait overnight before locking through. Burch and a deckhand were standing by the headlines when the order was passed for them to look after the towline to see that it did not foul the propeller. The two of them went aft. While they were there the mate came running around the end of the cabin, shouting that they had not been ordered there and were to go forward and attend to the headlines. "Aye, aye, sir," and forward they went.

The two men got a headline to the dock and made it fast, when the mate appeared again and began to rake them over the coals for going aft to the towline. Burch tried to explain; the mate simply got madder. Finally he hit Burch. Burch knocked him down and sat on him, telling him that he was not going to let him up until he promised to act like a gentleman. The captain was up in the wheelhouse and it was too dark for him to see what was going on, but he called out, "What's the matter down there?" Burch let the mate get up and he promptly ran up the ladder to the pilothouse. They could hear him complaining loudly to the captain. Burch felt that he was really in trouble, but then they heard the captain say, "You had no business to hit him."

When the *Iron Duke* came to Detroit, a new mate came aboard by boat and the old one was sent ashore. The captain had Burch, who also took care of the ship's paperwork, pay off the discharged mate before he left.

The ship sailed on to Buffalo. "The *Iron Duke*, covered with ice, looked like a spirit coming out of the North. But as we approached Lake Erie, we lost our coating of ice rapidly and sailed into Buffalo as on a summer day." There they unloaded their grain and took on a cargo of hard coal for Chicago.

Heading back up the Lakes they met some fog and then ran into a snowstorm on Lake Huron. By the time they passed the Straits of Mackinac the ship again was covered with ice. In Lake Michigan they not only had snow, but also a head wind. The cap-

LIFESAVING

The Lakes early gained a reputation for danger. The sudden storms and shores near at hand combined to wreck many ships and take uncounted lives. In 1874 the U.S. Congress established a Life-Saving Service with a number of stations on both the sea and the Great Lakes, to be manned by trained, full-time crews. By 1876 there were 29 stations completed along the U.S. shores of the Lakes.

Lifesaving stations made many rescues, but they were not always successful. In September of 1879 the crew of the Pointe aux Barques station, on Lake Huron, went seven miles along the beach, their boat drawn by a "pair of strong and spirited horses," launched the boat and made a number of trips out through a heavy sea to take 44 people off a wrecked steamer. But a crew from this same station on a later occasion put out in a storm to a wreck farther off shore. The men tired; their boat capsized and was righted several times, eventually drowning all but the coxswain. He washed ashore with the boat and was found wandering in a daze, muttering, "Poor boys! Poor boys! They are all gone—all gone!"

The first superintendent of the stations on Lakes Ontario and Erie was Captain David P. Dobbins. He had grown up on the Lakes, captained Lake vessels, and found time for several ocean voyages; as early as 1853 he had organized his own lifesaving crew at Buffalo. After his appointment he set out to find the ideal lifeboat and in time designed a self-bailing, self-righting boat. The picture shows the launching of a Dobbins boat.

During the 1880s it began to replace other types in U.S. lifesaving stations and to be adopted as a ship's lifeboat on both fresh and salt water; lifeboats in use today have features originated by Dobbins. When the Canadian Government established its first organized lifesaving station on the Lakes, at Cobourg in 1882, that too was equipped with a boat of the Dobbins type that had been built at Goderich. (*—Sketch courtesy Ohio Historical Society Library*)

The *Onoko*, the first steam barge with an iron hull, was the forerunner of the steel freighters of today. (*—Courtesy Lake Carriers' Association*)

tain "decided that he could make more money by conserving the coal pile" and went into shelter behind Beaver Island for two days. When the sun came out they went on to Chicago, first drying her sails, then stripping her of sails and running rigging and tagging it all for winter storage in one of the Chicago sail lofts.

ONOKO

This was a time of many new developments. Not only had the steam barge been devised as a new means of carrying bulk cargoes, but new kinds of ship construction were being used for the freighters. In 1882 the Globe Iron Works of Cleveland launched the first iron steam barge, the *Onoko*, 282 feet long and of 2,164 tons burden. For the next few years she had the greatest carrying capacity of any vessel on the Lakes. Aside from her size and construction she looked like most of the other steam barges, complete with masts and sails.

But insurance underwriters did not like iron hulls. They claimed that after five years an iron vessel was a poor insurance risk, but they agreed that if her bottom was sheathed in wood, her life expectancy would be much greater. The prejudice against iron seems to have been unjustified, but certainly wooden sheathing helped protect the bottom of a vessel if she ever grounded. Because of this skeptical attitude toward iron hulls, vessels with composite hulls were developed; they had closely spaced iron frames, oak planking, and iron plates sheathing the wood from the water line to the main deck or above. The Detroit Dry Dock Company was a major builder of these ships, beginning in 1878 with the construction of an otherwise typical sidewheeler. In 1887, five years after the first iron freighter, the Detroit Dry Dock Company launched the first composite freighter, the *Fayette Brown* (one of a number of vessels that have borne this famous name); she was 252 feet long and of 1,740 gross tons. The *Brown* was described as a "coarse freight propeller"; the term "steam barge" was beginning to lose favor. Within the next three years five more coarse freight propellers and one package-freight propeller of this construction were built by the Detroit company.

Meanwhile, in 1886, the Globe Iron Works of Cleveland produced another development, the first steel freighter. She was the *Spokane*, a vessel of 310

The *Spokane*, first steel-hulled Great Lakes freighter, on the ways just before her launching at Cleveland in 1886. (—*Institute for Great Lakes Research, Bowling Green State University*)

feet and 3,400 gross tons. Quickly steel became the usual material for the construction of Great Lakes freighters; iron and composite construction soon disappeared although wooden construction lasted a little longer. It is interesting, though, that as late as 1894 one steel freighter had her bottom sheathed with wood, and in this way obtained a lower insurance rate.

ALGOMA

In 1884 the Canadian Pacific Railway put its new fleet of steamers into operation on the upper Lakes. The CPR line was the creation of Henry Beatty, a Scots-Canadian who withdrew from his own family shipping company in 1882 to become general manager of the Canadian Pacific's newly founded marine operation. He was one of the few people with experience in shipping on the Canadian waters of Lakes Huron and Superior. A well-favored man whose flowing mustaches and shaggy eyebrows only slightly masked his firm jaw and piercing eyes, Beatty gave the line a personality that lasted to its end. It was composed equally of Canadian knowledge of the cold northern waters and Scottish engineering, operating together in almost naval efficiency.

Beatty turned to the finest shipbuilders in the world, those in Scotland. There he placed orders for three steel passenger-and-freight liners, each 263 feet long, with 130 first-class cabins and bunks for 200 steerage passengers. Into the design of these vessels went Beatty's own knowledge of the Great Lakes and the expert builders' most advanced seagoing practices. The ships were as nearly the perfect Great Lakes steamers as the Victorian era could provide. They were given distinctive Canadian names, *Algoma*, *Alberta*, and *Athabaska* (the spelling almost immediately altered to *Athabasca*), and in 1883 they sailed from the River Clyde, across the Atlantic to Montreal. There each was cut in two in order to pass through the small locks of the St. Lawrence River canals and the Welland Canal. The half-ships then were towed to Buffalo, where they were again put together; at Port Colbourne, on the Canadian shore not far from Buffalo, their cabins were completed over the winter. They arrived at Owen Sound, on Georgian Bay, in the spring of 1884.

The CPR steamer line ran from Owen Sound to Port Arthur, at the head of Lake Superior. On May 11, 1884, Capt. John Moore stood on the bridge of the *Algoma* as she pulled out of Owen Sound carrying 1,100 passengers, most of them immigrants from the British Isles and Sweden who travelled steerage, and a large quantity of freight. The immigrants were

The *Algoma*, as featured in an advertising poster of her day. (—*Marine Museum of the Upper Lakes*)

Above: The end of the *Algoma*, showing wreckage washed ashore.

Right: The wreck of the *Algoma*. Note the snow on the deck and on the rocks. (*—Both, Thunder Bay Historical Society*)

bound for the newly opened prairie provinces of Canada. This was the first voyage for the new line; the *Alberta* and *Athabasca* followed on their initial voyages at two-day intervals, each carrying full loads.

All that season the line prospered. The ships were laid up during the winter and began operation again in April 1885, soon after the ice had broken up in the Lakes. During this second season the CPR liners were as successful as they had been during the first— until on Thursday, November 5, the *Algoma*, under command of Captain Moore, steamed away from Owen Sound and headed north and west.

Because it was late in the season she had on board only five cabin passengers and six steerage passengers. She also carried 540 tons of merchandise. Early Friday she left the Sault Canal and entered Lake Superior. Crossing that lake Captain Moore had the sails set on her two masts and she sped along driven both by her engines and a strong breeze. At 4:00 a.m. Saturday the wind reached gale velocity. Rain,

sleet, and snow were cutting down visibility. The captain ordered sail taken in and decided to turn back into the lake until the weather cleared. At 4:30 all sail was in except the fore trysail, and that was partly in. The wheel was put hard starboard; as she swung about, now sideways to the seas, the *Algoma* rolled wildly. She continued to swing around toward her new course.

Suddenly there was a great crash of steel on rock; her rudder had struck. It was hopelessly crumpled and as a result the ship was entirely out of control. She began to pound on the rocks as each of the seas raised her and then dropped her again with a shattering jolt. Seas also broke over her, smashing most of her lifeboats. The *Algoma* had struck on Greenstone Island, just off Isle Royale.

The captain ran through the ship, calling passengers and crew on deck and ordering the steam valves opened to prevent an explosion. He then had a life line rigged from the mainmast aft, and as the

Dining saloon of the *Athabasca*, sister ship of the *Algoma*, about 1884. Note the stateroom doors opening on the saloon. (*—Notman Photographic Archives No. 1405, McCord Museum, McGill University*)

Painting of the *Algoma* in the St. Mary's River, artist unknown. (*—National Archives of Canada C 3824*)

passengers gathered on the deck he told them to hold to it. The constant hammering on the rocks brought down one of the cabins, which fell on Captain Moore and injured him; First Mate Joseph Hastings took over. At the same time that the captain was injured one of the seamen was washed overboard and lost. Captain Moore was carried to the afterdeck with the passengers.

It still was dark at 6:00 a.m. Suddenly then the *Algoma* broke in two and everything forward of the boilers plunged into deep water. Only fourteen survivors were left on the canted afterdeck, clinging to the life line. As daylight came, some of the crew put on life preservers and tried to reach shore, about sixty feet away. Only three reached it. The remaining survivors huddled on the storm-broken stern section all of Saturday and Saturday night as rollers crashed on the rocks, carrying with them some of the dead bodies.

By Sunday morning the gale had passed and the group left aboard made their way ashore on a small raft. Altogether there were fourteen survivors. Some local fishermen discovered them and took them to their nearby shanties to wait for rescue. There was no wireless telegraphy yet and the company agents at Port Arthur would expect the ship to be delayed by the storm.

At the captain's request the fishermen went out in their steam tug to intercept the *Athabasca*, the *Algoma's* sister ship, which had left Owen Sound on Saturday, and was due to pass Monday morning. Officers of the *Athabasca* came to the island on the tug and took the survivors back with them to the ship.

When the *Athabasca* reached Port Arthur with the news, another tug was sent out to what remained of the *Algoma* with a number of people aboard.

Cora A., one of the last true schooners built on the Lakes, launched at Manitowoc, Wisconsin, in 1889. She is shown passing Welcome Island, near Fort William (now Thunder Bay), Ontario. (—*Marine Historical Collection, Milwaukee Public Library*)

Among them was J. F. Cooke, a photographer who took several pictures of the wreck. They also recovered two of the bodies. Despite the wreck, with its loss of forty-five lives, the CPR line continued for many years. The *Athabasca* and *Alberta* later were joined by other vessels, among them the *Manitoba*, built at Owen Sound in 1889 and powered with the Scottish engines salvaged from that battered stern section of the *Algoma*.

CORA A.

The year 1889 also saw the launching of the last true schooners. One of them was the *Cora A.* of Manitowoc, a typical three-master 149 feet long and of 381 tons. She represented the final development of the Great Lakes schooner and had all of the usual features; she was a ship with rather flat sides and a typical Lakes rig. Vessels that were called schooners were built in later years, but they were intended mainly as tow barges and spent most of their working lives at the ends of cables. One of these was the four-masted *Minnedosa*, the largest Canadian schooner ever built, launched at Kingston in 1890. She was capable of sailing by herself, but she seldom did. For practical purposes, the end of sailing vessel construction was the end of the season of 1889.

Many factors worked against sail. Bulk carriers were getting larger and larger, and there were correspondingly fewer ways in which a small freighter could earn her way; yet large sailing vessels such as the *David Dows* had proved too unhandy in the narrow waters of the Lakes. At that time there were no internal-com-

Bulk-freight carriers unloading ore at Cleveland, about 1889; note Brown Hoist unloaders in left distance. By this time the construction of sailing vessels was almost at an end. (—*Cleveland Picture Collection, Cleveland Public Library*)

bustion engines to provide compact auxiliary power. Anything much larger than the *Cora A.* would need a tug to help her maneuver in a great many places on the Lakes, and so the tug might as well go along permanently and the other vessel become a barge. There also was increasing pressure for reliable speed; shippers wanted to be certain that their cargoes would move quickly from one port to another. On occasion a sailing vessel could be marvelously fast, but on the next she might be damnably slow. Time had acquired value, as witnessed by the various efforts to speed the unloading of bulk cargo. The more grain, ore, or timbers that a merchant could move during a season of navigation, the more money he could make. Then too, the growing mechanization of the past two decades had had its psychological effect on sailors. A seaman on a barge or steamer had an easier job than one on a vessel that carried much sail, and so in the 1880s when a seamen's union was formed, one of its first moves was to require higher pay for men who shipped on sailing vessels rigged with topmasts and the full number of sails.

Conditions had so changed in the period from 1870 to 1890 that there was not much place left for schooners. Those already built did continue to work for some years; the *Cora A.* finally went to salt water during World War I, foundering off Cape Hatteras in 1916; others lasted on the Lakes in small numbers into the 1920s. But after 1890 no one wanted to build them any more. Few things better illustrate the changes during this period than the fact that sailing vessels, at its beginning the primary bulk carriers on the Lakes, by the end of it were obsolescent.

Western Reserve, steel freighter built in 1890 and lost in 1892 when her hull cracked open during a storm on Lake Superior. (—*From American Steam Vessels Booklet Series, drawing by Samuel Ward Stanton*)

"Whirlies," self-propelled cranes that ran on tracks and were able to spin around on their bases, were a common unloading means. Here several of them unload ore at Erie, Pennsylvania, during the late 1890s. (—*Library of Congress LC D4 12895*)

6
Bigger and Better

During the quarter-century from 1890 to 1914, financial giants such as Morgan and Rockefeller strode across the economic scene. Edward VII ascended his throne in 1901, thus beginning the Edwardian age in a world still largely dominated by Britain. He died in 1910, but the qualities of the era named for him persisted until the First World War. Generally it was a period of development and growth when, as has been said, the sun always shone. The depression of 1908, like that of 1893, did not leave deep scars and the total period was one of steady economic development. People knew that many things were wrong, but they felt that the faults were being corrected; probably more than at any time since, they were confident of the future.

Throughout this period, the United States gradually expanded investments outside its own boundaries. Along the Great Lakes, American firms crossed over into Canada, in order to manufacture goods for sale without paying the high Dominion tariffs and to reach Canadian supplies of raw materials. Among the most obvious signs of expansion were the giant rafts of logs that moved across the upper Lakes from Canadian forests to U.S. sawmills in the late '90s. Between 1900 and the start of World War I, Canada saw one of its greatest periods of economic development, based on a huge influx of both immigrants and foreign capital. But even by 1914, American investments in Canada amounted to less than half those of Britain.

The Great Lakes saw the rise and decline of a truly new ship, the whaleback, designed by a man who came from Scotland, spent his boyhood in Canada, and worked most of his adult years in the U.S. Wooden shipbuilding practically ceased. Both freight and passenger vessels grew ever larger and more elaborate. Transportation on the Lakes was relatively cheap. In 1900, for example, it cost 4.42 cents to move a bushel of wheat from Chicago to New York by lake and canal, as opposed to 9.98 by rail. Under these conditions Great Lakes shipping prospered. By 1910 the U.S. Lakes fleet was bigger than the ocean fleet of any country other than Britain and Germany.

WESTERN RESERVE

The 300-foot-long and 45-foot wide steel freighter *Western Reserve* was launched in 1890 at Cleveland. Steel was the coming thing for Great Lakes vessels, although the more conservative mariners still preferred wood. Capt. Peter G. Minch, who had commanded ships before he became a shipowner, was not a conservative: the Minch Transit Company must have the most modern kind of freighter.

The new boat was given the same name as the 5,000-square-mile area of northern Ohio centering about Cleveland, an area that at one time belonged to the state of Connecticut and was first settled by Connecticut people. In Captain Minch's day the Western Reserve had no more political significance than it has in our day, but the people who lived within this detached bit of New England, where town squares and frame churches were normal things, were proud of its traditions. And so the freighter *Western Reserve* went into service on the Lakes, loading ore at Lake Superior ports and unloading it as such cities as Cleveland or Erie.

This unloading might be done by the big Brown hoists or by a device that was less efficient than the hoists, but also was considerably less expensive and more flexible. It was a steam derrick, mounted on railroad wheels; the cab of the derrick and its attached arm could pivot and the whole thing was self-propelled. It rode on a track—of much wider gauge than a normal railroad track—which was laid along the edge of the unloading dock. Usually a regular track

Ports along the southern shore of Lake Erie flourished because of the interchange there between rail and water transport. This picture of the docks at Erie in the 1890s shows part of the rail complex that served the port. (—*Library of Congress LC D4 12893*)

to carry gondola cars ran beside the wider track. The crane would move into position beside the open hatch of a laden ship, lower a bucket on a cable into the hold, pull out a bite of ore or coal, then spin around and dump the bite into a waiting rail car. Before long everyone called such cranes "whirlies."

On August 28, 1892, two seasons after she was launched, the *Western Reserve* sailed light out of Cleveland, with only enough water ballast to keep her propeller under the surface. She was bound for Two Harbors to load ore. On board for a summer holiday were her owner Captain Minch, his wife, their two children, and his wife's sister and her young daughter. They went up Erie and Huron, through the Sault Canal, and headed into Lake Superior. Storm warnings were flying as they moved out of the canal and a storm broke even before they reached Whitefish Point. Furniture was sliding about the cabin and dishes were crashing to the floor. Captain Meyer, the master of the ship, wanted to run in to shelter; Captain Minch felt that his big new vessel could weather any August storm and so they went on.

About 9:00 p.m. they were well out in Lake Superior, still pushing into the storm. At that time there

was a great crash; the ship quivered; the mainmast fell and the deck amidships started to buckle. Rivets in the hull began to crack off with a noise like rapid gunfire.

Harry W. Stewart, a wheelsman, was in his bunk. He grabbed coat, cap, and boots and ran aft. It was dark and he almost ran into a break in the deck that he later estimated was four feet across. He jumped and got over it. Quickly the crew lowered the two boats. On the port side, upwind, the metal boat was swamped and everyone it was thrown into the water. The wooden boat, launched on the lee side, was able to pick up only Captain Meyer's son and the steward; the others from the metal boat drowned. The wooden boat now held nineteen people. They headed into the wind and pulled away just in time; they were no sooner clear than the *Western Reserve* sank.

The boat contained the women and children, Captain Meyer and his son, Captain Minch, and some of the crew. They went all night in constant danger of swamping; half of them bailed and half rowed. At one time they saw the lights of a ship and called frantically, but could not make themselves heard in the storm. At daybreak they saw land and headed toward it, but when it still was a mile away, about seven o'clock, a large wave rose over the boat. Some of those in it stood up in panic, and it swamped.

Wheelsman Stewart saw Mrs. Minch trying to swim while holding one of her children. He managed to get a floating life belt and put it on. By then only he and Carl Meyer, the captain's son, were still visible. They started toward the shore. Young Meyer soon tired and sank; Stewart swam on alone. Then as he came close to shore he found himself alternately thrown forward by the waves and drawn back by the undertow. Finally he shrugged off his life belt, swam as hard as he could under water, riding a wave in, then dug his hands into the sand and held on. As the wave dropped back he staggered up onto the shore and collapsed.

After a time he made his way along the beach to the Deer Park lifesaving station and reported the wreck. An immediate search by the lifesavers found the boat tossed up on the shore. Then the bodies of Captain Minch and his sister-in-law were found; no others were ever recovered. Stewart was the only survivor; thirty-one people were drowned.

The fate of the *Western Reserve* stunned the owners and builders of steel ships. Stewart's narrative was the only record available and they studied it carefully. They decided that she should have carried enough ballast forward so that her bow rode deeper in the water. But their main conclusion was that the steel used in her construction was too brittle and thus cracked under the twisting and pounding given it in a heavy sea. Thereafter ships were built of tempered steel, flexible enough so that when necessary it could give and spring back. The tragedy became one more step in the development of modern freighters.

CHARLES H. BRADLEY AND TOW

Wooden freighters still were built. In 1890 the steamer *Charles H. Bradley* was constructed for the Bradleys of Bay City, Michigan, a prosperous family of lumbermen. She was launched at the yard of F. W. Wheeler and Co., of West Bay City, a firm that produced many wooden ships. Of 200-foot length, 37-foot beam, and 13 1/2-foot depth, she was a typical lumber steamer—what frequently was called a "lumber hooker." Her planking was of four-inch

The *Charles H. Bradley* and tow. This wooden vessel was representative of the many lumber steamers, most of which towed two or three barges. The barges might be old schooners cut down or they might be vessels built specifically for the purpose. (*—Marine Historical Collection, Milwaukee Public Library*)

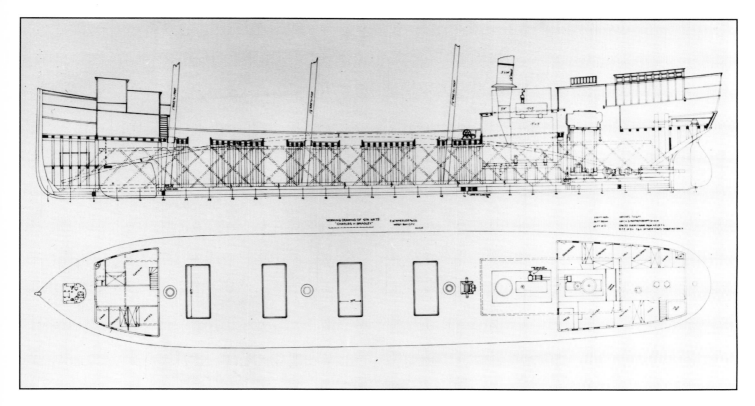

Longitudinal section and deck plan of the lumber steamer *Charles H. Bradley.* Note the centerboard (in its raised position) under the forward deckhouse. Few other lumber carriers had this feature, which gave the vessel increased stability when towing barges in open water. (*From* Great Lakes Wooden Shipbuilding *by H.C. Inches, reproduced by courtesy of the late Capt. Inches*)

oak and inside her hull there was an arch truss on either side to brace her stoutly.

Bay City stood at the mouth of the Saginaw River; Saginaw itself was twelve miles upstream. There were over 100 sawmills along the river and some people said that a man could walk from one city to the other on top of the lumber piles. Bay City was neither as big nor as lively as Saginaw, but it had 39 sawmills at its zenith, and at least 80 dives. The toughest one, with the worst reputation along the whole river, was a place called the catacombs, located at the center of town near the Third Street Bridge. There the clients were robbed, and when necessary the bodies dropped through a trap door into the water. At the other end of the entertainment scale, Cassie Hawkins, a young woman who resembled Lillian Russell, dispensed costly pleasure as proprietor of the one elegant five-dollar house in town.

The Michigan lumber boom was deflating by 1890; The Bay City mills were cutting less than they had before, and mill owners were having to bring in logs from farther and farther away to keep the saws whining. Thus the *Bradley* arrived late on the Bay City lumber scene, but apparently her owners had no problem in keeping

her busy. They not only filled her hold with lumber, but also piled it on her decks as was usual with these boats. Also typically they provided three barges for her to tow.

Many schooners ended their days as barges towed behind steamers; even such a proud vessel as the *Moonlight* in time suffered this fate. Not all schooner-barges were in the lumber trade by any means. Whatever bulk cargoes there might be, steamers and barges stood ready to carry them, but the steamer towing a string of cut-down schooners was a particularly common sight along the lumber coasts. During the '90s a number of so-called schooners were also built specifically to be towed, sometimes with modifications to make them useful as barges. One of the commonest changes was a straight steamer bow on what otherwise was a schooner hull; the stays from the foremast led directly to the bow, with no bowsprit to get in the way. Most schooner-barges set no topsails; if they did set them, the seamen's union required an extra 25 cents a day in wages. (At this time a sailor's pay might average $30 a month.) Thus initially schooner-barges could set their sails to help the towing steamer or even in an emergency to get themselves into port; but as time passed, masts rotted and sails wore out, and usually neither was replaced.

Lumber steamers were a distinct Great Lakes type. Most were built of wood, which was only natural. All were relatively small; the *Bradley* was among the largest. Most of them had the typical Great Lakes freighter profile, with living quarters and machinery concentrated in the ends and an open deck between. In these boats, however, that profile was somehow exaggerated: the ends seemed higher and the deck lower. Normally they carried deckloads of lumber and the high raised structures at bow and stern undoubtedly helped to secure and protect those loads. On the *Bradley* the space beneath the wheelhouse on the starboard side was the captain's cabin; across from it to port was a cabin for the two mates and another for the lookout. An unusual feature of the *Bradley* that was found in few other lumber steamers was a centerboard under her bow structure; it was useful in keeping the steamer on course when she was towing a string of barges in open water. In the after structure on the starboard side lived engineers, firemen, and wheelsmen. To port was the room for the cook (usually a woman), the galley, and the mess area.

Almost all of these lumbermen had a depth of hold of about thirteen feet. They were loaded and unloaded by hand, a board at a time; the standard length of board was twelve feet, and the thirteen-foot depth provided for the easiest and quickest handling of the cargo. If a ship were deeper, more handling was required, and that cost more money.

As Bay City and Saginaw ran out of logs and the mills began to close, the loggers moved on to the upper peninsula of Michigan, then to Wisconsin and northern Minnesota. By 1901 the lumber town of Hibbing, north of Duluth, which had been established for some eight years, was a thriving center. It boasted 60 saloons, 200 prostitutes, a race track, a professional baseball team, and some excellent prize fights. Lumber hookers (the boats as well as the girls) followed the trade as it expanded along the shores of Lake Superior. The steamers and their tows carried lumber from the head of Superior back to Chicago or Tonawanda, when necessary braving the autumn storms.

One of these steamers, the *C. F. Curtis*, about the same size as the *Bradley*, but built eight years earlier,

pulled out of the little harbor of Baraga on Keweenaw Bay on November 18, 1914, towing two barges. All were laden with lumber. It was nearly the end of the lumber era on the Lakes, but some was still moving; the cargoes of the three vessels were consigned to Tonawanda. The three of them sailed out into Lake Superior carrying twenty-six men and two women, the latter the cook and stewardess of the *Curtis*. That night a northwesterly blizzard struck. All through the long day of November 19, the helpless lifesavers at Grand Marais could hear the ship whistling for the harbor, but apparently the answering sound of the Grand Marais fog horn was blotted out by the noise of the wind. Finally, the steamer and her barges, unable to locate the harbor, were forced into shallow water by the driving wind and there broke up. The following day the bodies of six men and two women, all frozen stiff, washed ashore with wreckage from the *Curtis* and one of the two barges. Bodies continued to wash ashore. Only two men were able to make land; one was frozen to death and the other drowned at the harbor's edge as they tried to make their way to shelter. Wreckage from the third vessel blew ashore some distance away, but there were no bodies. Lumber was strewn along the shore.

Lumber continued to move over the Lakes in small amounts, although the boom days were gone forever. The best life of a wooden ship on the Lakes was over after fifteen years and she normally was completely useless by the time she reached twenty-five. But somehow the *Charles H. Bradley* survived until 1931, when she burned on the Keweenaw Waterway, not far from where the *C. F. Curtis* loaded her last cargo.

THE TIMBER RAFT (II)

As the lumber business spread through the Lakes, the timber business dwindled. It was a September evening in 1880 when D. D. Calvin, founder and major partner of the great timber-forwarding concern based on Garden Island at the foot of Lake Ontario, turned to his son and commented, "Hiram, we've no raft on the river tonight," something that could not have been said at that time of year during the preceding quarter-century.

But throughout the 1890s the timber trade, which brought squared timbers across the Lakes to Garden

A dram, or section, of a timber raft enters the Lachine Rapids of the St. Lawrence, about 1890. The men at the oars are at the bow of the dram and are swinging it so that it will pass to the right of Ile au Heron, seen in the distance. (—*Ontario Department of Lands and Forests*)

Island to be made into rafts and sent down the St. Lawrence for eventual shipment to England, remained fairly prosperous. Partly this was because Garden Island was a good location, partly because the Calvins were good businessmen. They were among the first to tow their schooners with steamers in order to make more trips over the Lakes and thus carry more cargoes during the navigational season, beginning the practice in the early 1870s. And as the forests were cut and the timber trade faded, they stopped buying and selling timbers and concentrated instead on handling them for others. By the 1890s they had only one competitor sending rafts down the St. Lawrence and soon they had none.

The last of the line of Garden Island raft foremen was Aimé Guerin. During half the year he lived on his farm near Laprairie, across the river from Montreal; during the other half he took the rafts down the river. Guerin, known as *Le Vieux Aimé*—Old Man Aimeé— was a fierce commander whose skillful French invec-

tive blistered erring raftsmen or blundering river pilots. When he first was put in charge of the Calvins' rafts the theft of timbers from them suddenly ended. He was a broad-shouldered man with aquiline features who for thirty-four years supervised Garden Island rafting. But he was also a man of Gallic urbanity; when an Anglo-Saxon of comparable station might have been reduced to hat-in-hand stammering, Guerin could associate easily with his employer and his employer's friends.

By the 1890s each raft that went down the river was shepherded by a shallow-draft paddle steamer which towed it where that was possible. Leaving Garden Island in the late afternoon, the steamer and raft continued on as darkness fell and the men placed white navigational lights on the corners of the raft. All that night and the next day they went on, reaching Prescott late the next evening. There they tied up overnight, for the first rapids were near and they could not be run safely in the darkness.

The raft ran the first two rapids with the steamer towing it. Here the water was fast but smooth. Men stationed at long sweeps at the stern of the raft steered it. Then for the next ninety miles the steamer and raft moved along easily, helped by the current. As they approached the Long Sault, local pilots and their men came aboard. The senior pilot here, Richard Dafoe, spoke no French and needed an interpreter to talk to Aimé Guerin; the interpreter also needed to be a diplomat who could screen out some of Aimé's more pointed comments when things went wrong. Above the Long Sault the raft was broken down into its drams. As the steamer towed the raft along, the drams would break away, one after the other, forming a long line with considerable space between each dram. Each was then taken through by its own pilot, with oarsmen at bow and stern to steer it around the turns. The dram carrying the foreman's cabin went first. The steamer preceded them all and collected them at the foot of the rapids. Pilots and extra oarsmen were paid off and went ashore. The steamer went on with the raft to the head of the Coteau Rapids, usually arriving in late afternoon and again tying up overnight.

Sometime before sunrise another group of pilots and raftsmen, this time French Canadians, came aboard. Once more the drams were strung out and run separately through the series of four rapids that began with the Coteau. They were then reassembled and the raft towed down to Lachine. There a group of Caughnawaga Indians came aboard to act as pilots and oarsmen; the senior pilot, who wore his long black hair plaited and coiled about his head, was known as Michel. Once again the drams were separated and the steamer went first. As they approached these most dangerous of rapids, Aimé knelt to tell the beads of his rosary.

D. D. Calvin, grandson of the original D. D. Calvin, described what it was like shooting the Lachine rapids on a dram:

> The towing steamer went on ahead: through field-glasses one could see her rolling and twisting in the main "pitch" a mile or more ahead of our leading dram. From time to time old Michel signalled silently for a few strokes of the long steering-oars at bow and stern. A glance at the shore showed that we were gaining speed—great eddies and swirls appeared on the water. Straight ahead, and ever nearer, the long line of the white, leaping, menacing crests of the great waves of the rapids glinted in the sun. Far beyond was smooth water again—but at a much lower level, for we saw only the towing steamer's smoke—she was hidden under the "hill" down which we were to follow her.
>
> Presently the long dram undulated over the first smooth rounded waves of the rapids, a moment more and we had fairly entered. As the dram hit the first big waves of the sharper descent the steersmen hauled in their oars and ran back to escape the water as it boiled over the bow of the dram, whose whole fabric bent and strained to conform to the long waves of the rapids—we dashed down the main "pitch" in what seemed no more than a few seconds. There was a curious illusion that the great barely submerged rocks were rushing upstream as we passed them; the heavy timber bumped and thudded underfoot, the water spurted up in great jets as the sides of two pieces of it struck flat together . . . .

Once again the steamer reassembled the raft, and the pilots and their men were paid off. Then Aimé sat down where he could watch what was happening while the cook lathered his face and shaved him. This procedure was subject to interruption; if the steamer did anything that Aimé thought wrong he jumped up, ran to the bow of the raft, and shouted orders to the captain. He never used a megaphone but he always made himself heard above the splash of the paddle wheels and the sound of the machinery.

Then as the raft moved more slowly in the widening stretches of the river Aimé had himself rowed on ahead into Montreal. The raft itself would continue down to Quebec under the supervision of a lesser man; Aimé only took it through the most dangerous part of the voyage. Landing at Montreal near Bonsecours Market, he paused at Bonsecours Church to give thanks for a safe passage, then proceeded to a little hotel where he telegraphed his employers to say that he had arrived and to ask for instructions. These might require him to return to Garden Island, or if the rafts were moving swiftly, he might join one at Prescott or Brockville. During a busy season he saw as many as thirty rafts through the rapids.

Gradually the trade diminished. In 1906, the last year of consequence, eighteen rafts were sent down to Quebec. The sources of the timbers for that year show how far afield the Calvin firm had to go to obtain them. True, some of the timbers were delivered by rail at Toronto from the timbered areas of central Ontario. But those brought from the traditional Ohio timber port of Toledo had been cut along the Ohio River and in Kentucky; there were timbers that the Algoma Central Railway had brought to Sault Ste. Marie from northwestern Ontario and others loaded at Green Bay from the thinning Wisconsin forests; there were also timbers loaded at Duluth that had come by rail from as far away as the foothills of the Rockies.

Human factors were changing also. The Caughnawaga Indians, who formerly made up not only the crews for the Lachine run but also a large part of the men who took the rafts through the whole voyage, began to drift away into structural steel work. High steel men had an even more hazardous job than raftsmen, but they also received more pay. Other men preferred to sail on comfortable lake freighters rather than on wet and dangerous rafts. The remaining raftsmen were true experts, but they also were growing old.

Aimé Guerin died at his Laprairie home in the summer of 1909, soon after bringing his last raft safely to Montreal.

CHARLES W. WETMORE

In the spring of 1891 a vessel was launched at West Superior, Wisconsin, that was the twelfth of her kind ever built. It was a good time for Capt. Alexander McDougall; his great invention, the whaleback, was becoming popular. The twelfth one was the 265-foot by 38-foot steamer *Charles W. Wetmore*, a vessel of particular interest because she was built especially for saltwater service.

From 1878 to 1881, McDougall had been master of the wooden bulk freighter *Hiawatha* for the Wilson Transit Company, towing one and sometimes two wooden barges up and down the Lakes and through the connecting waterways. (Capt. Thomas Wilson, owner of the line, had once commanded a steamer on which McDougall had served as mate, and the men were close friends.) While Captain McDougall travelled back and forth he studied the ships with which he worked and developed the plans for an iron vessel that would be light and strong and would also be extremely

The *Charles W. Wetmore*, a whaleback freighter. She is seen here in the Sault Ste. Marie locks. This particular ship was built for ocean service. She shot the St. Lawrence rapids, crossed the Atlantic to England, returned to the U.S., rounded Cape Horn, and operated for a time on the Pacific Coast, finally grounding off the coast of Oregon. This picture shows the rounded deck, the snoutlike bow, and the turrets. Her wheelhouse, cabin, and machinery were at the stern, a typical whaleback arrangement. (—*The Mariners Museum, Newport News, Va. PB 26691*)

Two whalebacks at Cleveland about 1900; a tow barge is in the foreground, a steamer lies farther back. Brown Hoist unloaders, the ultimate form of bucket and cable unloading devices, range the dock. When larger and heavier unloading machinery was adopted, it could not go through the relatively small whaleback hatches, and whalebacks soon became obsolete. (—*Courtesy McDowell Wellman Engineering Co., Cleveland*)

stable. In 1881 he moved with his family from Cleveland to Duluth and became involved in the shore end of the shipping business, soliciting charters, insuring vessels and cargoes, and organizing stevedoring crews. Meanwhile he continued to refine his ship designs, build models, and attempt to sell his ideas.

The whaleback design was that of a vessel with a flat bottom that gave it stability, a rounded top that gave it strength and would not permit water to stay on the deck, a snoutlike bow to move easily into the water, and turrets rather than cabins. A later generation might have called it streamlined. McDougall's contemporaries had never seen anything like it and they reacted with derision: "You call that damn thing a boat—why it looks more like a pig."

Finally Captain McDougall, with the help of his friend Captain Wilson, scraped together all the money he could raise and with it built a whaleback tow barge at Duluth, launching her in June of 1888. She was built of steel and had no frills; neither did her name—he called her *No. 101*. At the launching ceremony, as this odd-looking object slid into the water, Mrs. McDougall turned to her sister-in-law and said, "There goes our last dollar!"

McDougall had the *No. 101* towed to Two Harbors by tug, filled with ore, and then towed to Cleveland. He rode on her and heard all the jokes that

sailors made as they saw her pass. In Cleveland everyone made fun of her, but she went into service, towed usually by a freighter of the Wilson Transit Company. Nothing daunted by the skeptics, McDougall made a model of a larger barge; unable to sell the idea to anyone on the Lakes he took it to New York to Colgate Hoyt, an associate of John D. Rockefeller. Wilson arranged the introduction. Hoyt agreed to form a company to build and operate whalebacks, and the American Steel Barge Company was the result. Whalebacks began to pour from McDougall's shipyard and he could afford to smile at those who called his brain children hogs and referred to one of the steamers towing two of the barges as a sow and pigs.

Mariners' qualified admiration for the design of these vessels was prompted by more than their looks; comfort aboard them was limited. One contemporary wrote:

> ... they are mercilessly hot iron boxes in summer, slippery and cold in winter, and noisy to the point of sleeplessness all the year round.... It is said that the first trip on a whaleback is always a memorable experience, especially if a storm comes up. Six feet of blue water rushing down the length of the deck from where the bow was a moment ago is an impressive sight; and when it strikes the turret and bounds up under the decking of the elevated cabin it makes an impressive noise.

The *James B. Colgate*, a typical whaleback steamer launched in 1892.

The *John Ericsson*, last whaleback steamer built, though one or two unpowered barges were launched after her. In this vessel McDougall varied his usual deck arrangement by using a forward wheelhouse and bridge similar to those of normal Great Lakes freighters. The *Ericsson* came out in 1896. From a picture by the noted marine photographer Pesha. (—*Both Great Lakes Historical Society*)

Capt. Alexander McDougall, inventor and builder of the whalebacks. (—*Collingwood Museum*)

The *Turret Court*, like the other turret vessels, was built in Sunderland, England, by William Doxford and Sons. She combined some whaleback features with the normal characteristics of the ocean freighters of the day. Over 180 turret ships were produced by the Doxfords for world-wide service between 1894 and 1911. A few of them, including *Turret Court*, were brought to the Great Lakes by Canadian owners. A Pesha photograph. (—*Institute for Great Lakes Research, Bowling Green State University*)

The *Charles W. Wetmore* was named for a major stockholder in the American Steel Barge Company. After she was launched and fitted out, McDougall took her to Kingston, Ontario, at the head of the St. Lawrence. Two more whalebacks followed her. Captain McDougall left her there for some minor repairs and proceeded to investigate the St. Lawrence; the ship was too large for the canals and if she was to reach salt water she would have to shoot the rapids. For three days McDougall went down the rapids by day and came back to Kingston by rail at night, studying the possibility of running the rapids with what then was a large steamer. After the first trip he telegraphed his backers in New York:

> All river pilots and our captain say it is not safe or possible to run the rapids. Am still of opinion it can be done and will proceed to do so unless I hear from you to the contrary.

He received no answer. After each trip he sent the same message; none was answered. It was up to him. The pilots refused to take her downriver, so he decided to do it himself. McDougall found an old riverman who said he didn't much care if he drowned then or died a little later and agreed to take her through the smooth parts if the captain took her through the rough ones.

> We ran her through without a scratch. There were places where it was like going over the side of the house and there were whirlpools where the least deviation would have meant shipwreck. But we came through without even marking the paint. The second whaleback was equally fortunate. The third bumped once and dented a plate and started a few rivets, but without material harm.

The *Wetmore's* first ocean voyage took her to England with a cargo of grain. There British shipowners William Johnston and Company were sufficiently impressed to place an order in 1892 for a whaleback cargo ship to be built by the well-known Newcastle-on-Tyne builders, W. Doxford and Sons, under license from McDougall. Meanwhile the *Wetmore* returned to the U.S., loaded an assorted cargo, and set out from Wilmington, Delaware, around Cape Horn to Everett, Washington, a city established by McDougall and his associates. The ship carried two knocked-down saw-mills; machinery for a paper mill, a nail factory, and several other small factories; and shipyard machinery and fabricated steel. The latter was used to construct another whaleback, the *City of Everett*, which is said to have been the first American steamer to circle the globe and to pass through the Suez canal.

The *Wetmore* was put in the Pacific Coast coal trade; early in 1892 she stranded off the Oregon coast and became a total loss. In the meantime whalebacks were turned out back at West Superior in a steady stream. By the end of 1896, eight years after *No. 101's* appearance, thirty-nine of them had been built on the Great Lakes and four on salt water. But the three boats launched in 1896, two barges and a steamer, were the last ones ever built. The design had become obsolete.

How had this happened in such a short time? After all, the whalebacks did have major advantages. They were cheap and strong. Their rounded tops and round turrets enabled them to work in heavy weather when normal flat-sided vessels were so pounded by the water that they could not operate. The rounded upper corners of the hulls made them self-trimming; that is, the bulk cargo automatically balanced itself. But they had one great weakness: their hatches were small. The ever-developing tools for quick unloading could not move

in and out. The open clamshell of a Hulett unloader had a 24-foot spread, far more than the 8 x 10-foot hatch openings possible with the basketlike steel framework inside a whaleback hull.

Various Great Lakes builders modified the whaleback design. Some of these vessels were known as monitors; they had somewhat rounded decks but conventional steamer bows. They appeared during about the same years that whalebacks were launched. A similar vessel was built by McDougall himself in 1898 and called the *Alexander McDougall*. Another variant was the "turtleback," a type that had a rounded forward deck.

The Doxford yards in England also modified the design, producing what were known as "turret ships," essentially typical ocean freighters except that they had rounded whaleback decks. They were built in England in some numbers (Doxford built 176; other builders under license built six) through the year 1911 and were used all over the world. Several of them were brought to the Great Lakes by Canadian owners and operated there, in at least one instance until after World War II. English competitors of the Doxfords built similar self-trimming ships and some of them came to the Lakes. So although the basic whaleback design became obsolete very quickly, many of McDougall's ideas went on and on.

The whaleback *Christopher Columbus*, designed to carry passengers from downtown Chicago to the Columbian Exposition of 1893. She later had an additional deck added and was put into regular passenger service, during which she carried more passengers than any other American ship. From a painting by Howard Sprague. (—*The Mariners Museum, Newport News, Va. QO 454*)

Christopher Columbus maneuvering in harbor with the help of the tug at left. This photograph shows her with the three passenger decks she had during most of her career, operating on a day run between Chicago and Milwaukee. (*—Marine Historical Collection, Milwaukee Public Library*)

CHRISTOPHER COLUMBUS

On May 1, 1893, there opened in Chicago the extravaganza of the century, the World's Columbian Exposition, honoring the 400th anniversary of Columbus's discovery of America. This World's Fair, like most others, provoked some violent discussion about its architecture, but it is remembered best for three things: Little Egypt, an attractively undulating dancing girl; the Ferris wheel, the first in North America and the biggest in the world, 265 feet high; and the only whaleback passenger steamer ever built, the *Christopher Columbus.*

Alexander McDougall built the vessel the preceding autumn; work began on September 7 and she was launched on December 3, a considerable feat in construction of a steel passenger steamer 362 feet long and of 42 feet beam. Her hull was painted white and her stack pink. She arrived in Chicago on May 18, 1893, to be greeted by the welcoming whistles of all the ships in harbor and the cheers of the crowds on shore. She was put in service carrying World's Fair visitors between the city proper and the Exposition Grounds at Jackson Park, and was able to carry 5,000 people at one time.

The *Columbus* had the typical whaleback hull. From it rose a line of seven steel turrets, which acted as supports for an upper deck running from the forward turret to the after one. On this deck was open space for passengers and a long enclosed cabin bridging the turrets below. The cabin housed the grand saloon, which was furnished with velvet Wilton carpet and chairs and lounges of russet Turkish leather. The murals were predominantly mauve in color and there was paneling and wainscoting of carved oak. Aquariums, statues, and paintings were all part of the décor.

Above the saloon deck was a promenade deck 287 feet long, with a skylight 151 feet long running down its center and illuminating the cabin below. At the forward end of the promenade deck were the wheelhouse, captain's cabin, and quarters of the other officers. As befitted the most modern vessel, she was equipped with incandescent lights and a 2,400-candlepower searchlight.

Left: Bridge of the *Christopher Columbus.* Capt. Charles Moody, who commanded her for 36 years, stands at right.

Below: *Christopher Columbus* immediately after her only serious accident, which brought a Milwaukee dockside water tower down on top of her. (—*Both, Marine Marine Historical Collection, Milwaukee Public Library*)

The whaleback carried some two million people between the Randolph Street dock in Chicago and Jackson Park. The great fair came to its close in October, and that month, as if to put a final period to the celebrations, a disappointed office seeker assassinated Mayor Carter Harrison (the elder) in the doorway of his home. Harrison had been eager to be mayor during the exposition, had run again for that purpose, and had won.

The winter that followed was a grim one amidst the depression of 1893; Jane Addams and her associates at Hull House worked twenty hours a day helping the hungry poor; the City Hall corridors were left open each night to shelter some 2,000 people who crowded in. The following spring employees housed in the nearby company town of Pullman went on strike because their wages were cut but their rents were not. When Pullman refused to arbitrate, Eugene Debs's American Railway Union struck across the United States. Federal Troops were called in, Debs was sent to jail, and organized labor suffered a major blow.

With the joyous aura of the fair quickly dissipated by all this, the *Christopher Columbus* was placed in utilitarian service on the Chicago-Milwaukee route as a passenger vessel. This brought her into direct competition with the venerable Goodrich Line, which had run local steamers on Lake Michigan since 1857; among its early captains was Frederick Pabst, who finally left the nautical life for the brewing industry, where the name is still known. The big whaleback proved a difficult vessel to compete against; A. W. Goodrich, who then ran the company, solved the problem five years later by buying the *Columbus*. Thereafter she departed Chicago each morning at 9:00 and left Milwaukee each afternoon at 4:00. Soon after buying her, Goodrich added a third passenger deck. She was tremendously popular and is said to have carried more passengers during her career than any other American ship has ever done.

Economic conditions improved again and Chicago regained its reputation as an incredible and a festive city, a suitable home port for the most incredible passenger ship in the world. After all, the port handled the fourth largest tonnage in the world, being exceeded only by London, New York, and Hamburg. The section of the city known as the Levee was probably the most fes-

tive part of it; the most expensive retreat in this section was the Everleigh Club, operated by two pretty sisters from Kentucky, Ada and Minna Everleigh. The sisters were well dressed and much bejeweled; one old photo shows them in a tallyho with a number of their girls, on their way to the Washington Park Races. This presumably was legitimate advertising, but when they dared in 1911 to publish an advertising booklet, complete with pictures of the Japanese Throne Room and other chambers in their bordello, Mayor Carter Harrison (the younger) was affronted and insisted that the place be closed.

The delights offered by the *Christopher Columbus* were of a different sort, but they did attract a great number of people. Usually there was a dance orchestra aboard, deck games were provided, and when movies became available they were shown to the passengers. Motorcars in any number and highways in any degree of smoothness were still in the future; people travelled by water both for business and for pleasure. The powerful, fast steamer (2,600 hp and 20 mph) attracted them by the hundreds. She maintained her reputation for modernity, too; in 1910 she had a wireless system installed to communicate with stations on shore.

Only once in her entire career did she have a serious accident. It was on June 30, 1917, as she was leaving Milwaukee on the return trip to Chicago. The Milwaukee River was high and running fast. At the juncture of the Menominee River, the tugs that were handling her started to turn her around so that she would go out into Lake Michigan bow-first. The forward tug cast off the port line and moved to pick up the starboard bow line. But the current then carried the ship quickly away from the tug and toward the far side of the river where a large water tower stood more than 100 feet high on steel supports above a dock. Captain Moody's best efforts failed to avert catastrophe. The long overhanging bow swept along the dock; it struck two of the supports holding the water tank, snapped them, and the whole supporting framework buckled.

The steel tank, heavy with tons of water, crashed down on the ship just forward of the pilot house, demolishing the structure and tearing a twelve-foot hole in the deck above the restaurant. People were crushed in the impact, knocked overboard by the shock, and washed overboard by the flood released from the tank. Altogether sixteen were killed and twenty seriously hurt.

The ship went into drydock and was out of service until the next season, when she was put back on her former run. Year after year she carried more passengers than any other vessel under the American flag and made more money than any other vessel in the Goodrich fleet. But in 1932, at the depth of the Great Depression, she was laid up. By 1937 the Depression and old age were too much for her and she was scrapped. One old timer spoke for many when he said, "I cry every time I think about her—a lost sweetheart." The steel from her hull was sold to Japan.

THE LOG RAFT

Log rafts were perhaps the greatest man-made obstacles to navigation that ever were seen on the Lakes. They ranged from eight to over twenty-five acres in area and were towed by as many as three tugs. They traveled at one mile per hour. In storms they pulled the tugs off their courses and sometimes broke away entirely. They were not well lighted at night and in rainy or foggy weather became nearly invisible. One dark night in August 1890 the propeller *Jewett* ran into an unlighted raft on Lake Huron and broke all the blades of her wheel; at the same time a steam barge ran between the raft and its tug and became entangled in the towline, finally having to be towed to port herself for repairs. Rafts could also be dangerous in clear daylight. That same month the steel steamer *Joliet* met a raft at the entrance to the St. Mary's River, was forced out of the channel, and was badly damaged on the rocks. Another steamer following her escaped only by steering straight through the raft, cutting it apart in the process.

The log rafts of the upper Lakes were quite different from the timber rafts of the St. Lawrence, and were a much later development. The squared timbers in a St. Lawrence raft were lashed and wedged together to form solid drams that made up the raft itself. The logs in a raft of the upper Lakes floated freely without any fastening or restraint except a boom of chained logs that formed the perimeter of the raft.

By the mid-1880s the hungry mills at Saginaw and other eastern Michigan towns were running out of logs and their owners were casting farther afield. Many of them bought timber rights along the northeastern shore of Georgian Bay and on the North Channel. Canadian mills had been established on Georgian Bay for a

A log raft passing among the Georgian Bay Islands about 1895. In order to keep the raft long and narrow so it would fit the channels, it was tied together at intervals. (*—Parry Sound Public Library*)

Until recent times rafts of pulpwood logs have been moved across the Great Lakes in the same manner as the saw logs of the late 1800s and early 1900s. Small log rafts may still be found. This picture, taken in the 1940s on the northern shore of Lake Superior, shows a raft being assembled by the process of floating logs down a river into a bag boom. (—*Green Lakes Historical Society*)

number of years, producing lumber that for the most part was exported to the United States. Now the Michigan lumbermen decided to cut and export the logs themselves and saw them in Michigan.

In the autumn of 1886 the first Georgian Bay raft destined for the United States was formed at the mouth of the French River, to be towed across the Bay and Lake Huron to mills at East Tawas, Michigan. The tug *Mocking Bird* started out with three million board feet of logs. But a storm broke out at the same time and after pulling diligently at the raft for eight days without going anywhere, the tug gave up and went off to do other chores. Returning in the middle of October, the tug successfully moved the raft out of Georgian Bay into Lake Huron, but then another storm came up and tug and raft were forced back into the Bay. Finally the tug abandoned the raft in a Georgian Bay cove; the logs were sold the next year to a Canadian mill.

Despite the frustrating result of this attempt, the log raft by this time had reached an advanced stage of development. The most practical system of rafting was devised by Capt. Benjamin Boutell of Bay City. He made up a boom of relatively short logs—about sixteen feet long—of relatively large diameter—three to four feet. The logs were chained together end-to-end, the boom that resulted was formed into a vast circle or "bag" on the water, and the bag was filled with logs floating loose. The bag boom was towed by a tug and the logs inside it were drawn along willy-nilly. Because the logs making up the boom were short they adjusted readily to the surface as they moved over the waves; because they were thick the free logs inside were not able to ride over or slide under them.

Captain Boutell's invention had already been tested by taking a raft from the southern shore of Lake Superior to Bay City during the summer of 1885, and it was workable. As the mills in Michigan found themselves in greater and greater need, their owners tried again with rafts; by 1890 some 25 million board feet annually were being rafted from Georgian Bay to Michigan ports. By 1894 the amount had increased to over 300 million. Several minor and two major companies were engaged in rafting; Captain Boutell was a partner in one of the largest. The two big companies together operated fourteen tugs.

Rafting was the best way to get logs across Lake Huron to the mills, even if it continued to wreck steamers. But rafts were not always pure joy even to their owners, as one raftsman described:

> The latter part of May in most years is pleasant on the lakes, but on Decoration Day, 1889, a terrific storm swept over the lake region.... No less than six large rafts went ashore. Gathering up the scattered logs was attended to by the hardy river drivers, who, with their peavies, rolled the logs into the water so that they would float, when they were pushed into deep water with large pike poles. Long strings of booms were used to gather in the floating logs, the shore end being handled by teams, and the other end, reaching far out into the lake, by tugs. At night the ends of the string of booms were brought together and towed into sheltered water, where they were tied up until enough were got together to make up a raft.

Because of the not infrequent casualties to rafts and because some logs always escaped from the booms, there came in time to be a regular patrol on Georgian Bay by men known as "log-pickers" who followed along the shores in small boats, collecting stray logs, sorting them by the marks stamped into their ends, and making them up into rafts which then were towed back to their owners.

As a result of the many accidents caused by the rafts, the Lake Carriers' Association protested to Congress. In 1893 Congress appointed a board of engineers to investigate. The board recommended stringent regulation of rafting, including a provision that in many of the narrow passages and harbors no bag rafts be permitted. Instead, the engineers said, crib rafts of limited size should be used; crib rafts were essentially rafts like those used on the St. Lawrence, built as solid structures. The vessel owners pressed to have the restrictions made law and the next year the House of Representatives passed them, but the powerful lumbermen carried the fight to the Senate and there defeated the measure.

The people of the Georgian Bay region watched in growing despair as their forests went floating away to mills in Michigan, and even sometimes as far away as the southern shore of Lake Erie. The production of lumber and lumber products was almost the only industry on the Bay; logs taken elsewhere represented money taken from the pockets of everyone from laborer to mill owner. From 1890 through 1896 the Canadian and American lumbermen, each working through their own governments, made a number of moves and countermoves, but without great result. Then in 1896 William McKinley was elected President of the United States.

McKinley was a fervent advocate of high tariffs. By August of the next year the Dingley Bill, named for its sponsor, Representative Nelson Dingley, Jr., a Maine Republican, had been drawn up and passed into law. The bill enacted the highest tariffs in United States history up to that time, tariffs that affected a wide range of items from wool and linen to lead and hides. Most important, so far as the Great Lakes were concerned, it also affected lumber. While it was being drafted, the U.S. lumber barons had a clause inserted providing a duty of $2.00 per thousand board feet of sawn lumber, and another clause providing that if any country charged an export duty on raw materials sent into the United States an equal amount would be added to the U.S. import duty on finished products made from those same materials. As a result, Canadian lumber with its new U.S. duty couldn't compete in U.S. markets, and if the Canadian government attempted to put an export duty on those logs that were being carried away, that would simply make the U.S. tariff on Canadian lumber that much higher. Because of the Dingley tariff, most of the Canadian mills closed down and many of the mill towns were reduced to poverty. The logs continued to raft away to the States.

Rafts were still unwieldy and sometimes dangerous. Late in July 1897 a raft broke away from its tug in a storm and drifted south in Lake Huron. The Canadian sidewheeler *Cambria* with 150 passengers aboard, in the middle of the summer gale, at 1:00 a.m. ran into the unlighted raft. She cut through the boom and quickly was surrounded by tossing logs that battered at her. Her paddle wheels were smashed and as a result her engine was disabled. Unable to maneuver, she drifted toward shore, surrounded by logs that continued to hammer at her sides. Before daylight she grounded 200 yards off the beach a mile or two north of Point Edward, heeling over at an angle as she lodged on the bottom. The steam line to the electric generator

North West, steel luxury liner built at Cleveland in 1894. The drawing at top shows her in her original glory. Below it is a photograph taken immediately after the *North West* (on the right) was launched and before fitting out was completed. At left the steam barge *V. Swain* undergoes repairs to her forward bulwarks. The Pesha photograph at bottom shows the external results of the rebuilding of the *North West* and her sister *North Land* during the winter of 1902-03: two stacks instead of three, additional cabins on the upper deck forward, and the wheelhouse and bridge moved nearer the bow. At least equally important were the changes in the engine room. The 28 Belleville boilers on each ship had become so notorious for their numerous minor explosions, which scalded or burned members of the engine room crew, that few men would sign on as fireman or coal passers. According to some accounts, men regularly had to be shanghaied from waterfront saloons to maintain the full number of hands in the fireholds. These boilers were replaced by ten Scotch boilers on each vessel, permitting elimination of the forward stack and making it possible to obtain an engine room crew in more orthodox ways. (—*Top, from American Steam Vessels Booklet Series, drawing by Samuel Ward Stanton; middle and bottom, Great Lakes Historical Society*)

broke, plunging the ship into darkness. But the captain managed to avert panic among the passengers, waited until daylight came, and then lowered boats and ferried everyone safely ashore.

The blight caused by the Dingley Bill on the Canadian lumber industry was finally removed by the Ontario provincial legislature. The timber rights sold by Ontario were licenses to cut timber on Crown lands; the lands themselves remained property of the province. In April 1898 the legislature passed an act requiring that all logs cut on government land be manufactured within the province. This was not a duty, but the regulation of a landowner in respect to its own property, and the retaliatory clause of the Dingley Bill did not apply. The Michigan holders of Ontario timber limits promptly claimed breach of contract; the Province of Ontario replied that the licenses were for one year only and if they were renewed the holders must agree to the new rule.

This move practically killed the American log rafting business. A few rafts still came down from the U.S. shore of Lake Superior and rafts continued to move over Georgian Bay itself, bringing logs from local forests to local mills, but no more of them moved across Lake Huron. Deprived of the supply of Canadian logs, many of the Michigan companies closed their mills at home and set up new ones on the Bay. Large rafts continued to move between points on Georgian Bay until the late 1920s. Even today rafts of pulpwood logs which are essentially the same as Captain Boutell's invention can sometimes be found around the shores of the upper Lakes. There are not many, however, and they are tiny compared to the big rafts of the 1890s.

NORTH WEST

James J. Hill, the St. Paul, Minnesota, business giant, was born in a log cabin near Guelph, Ontario, and rose to be the builder and operator of the Great Northern Railway. While he was consolidating his rail holdings he also entered the Great Lakes shipping business, in 1888 forming the Northern Steamship Company, which operated six lake freighters. Hill put his mind to improving the efficiency of Great Lakes freight movement and established his steamer line on an economical basis; when the owners of Buffalo grain elevators ventured to fix their charges higher than he thought necessary, he built his own big elevator in Buffalo and undercut them all.

In 1893 and 1894 he had two fine passenger liners built on the Lakes, the *North West* the first year and the *North Land* the second. The sisters were considered the most beautiful lake ships of their day, and it can be argued that they were the most beautiful of any day. They were not, however, money-makers. The writer of Hill's authorized biography, Joseph Gilpin Pyle, took modest pride in his subject's ruthlessness but did not dwell on his few examples of bad commercial judgement; in this Pyle no doubt reflected Hill's own feelings. Pyle tells of the freight operation on the Lakes and how Hill "broke the elevator pool" in Buffalo, but he does not even mention the *North West* and the *North Land*.

The original vessel plans, however, show that on the lower decks there were layers of bunks in dormitory style intended to carry steerage-class immigrants. Carrying immigrants would have supported the vessels nicely, but competing railroads prevailed on Congress to block such carriage. All that remained were the much advertised but little profitable luxury accomodations.

The two ships were built by the Globe Iron Works of Cleveland and were put into service between Buffalo and Duluth. Each was 384 feet long, with twin engines providing 7,000 hp, and each was able to cruise at 20 mph; reports of their top speed vary from 22 to 27 mph. They carried nothing but passengers. In their interiors, according to one contemporary description, there was "a rich mahogany finish, spirited carving, soft coloring, and a judicious use of gold, producing a symphony of brown, bronze-green and gold with the delicate carving and relief work repeated through an imposing length of space." The exteriors of the vessels were painted white, the stacks cream, and there was a red star on the center stack that was floodlighted at night.

The impending arrival of these two marine wonders sent chills along the spines of the owners and operators of boats that would have to compete with them. When the general passenger agent of the Northern Steamship Company called upon David Carter of the Detroit and Cleveland Navigation Company and proposed that the new steamers call at Mackinac Island, thus competing with one segment of the D & Cs operation, Mr. Carter was scarcely cheered. He reported

City of Erie, sidewheel steamer that normally ran between Cleveland and Buffalo, shown here on excursion with all flags flying and many passengers. *(The Mariners Museum, Newport News, Va. PB 2350)*

to his board of directors that the Northern would probably take thirty percent of the D & C's Mackinac business, and soon afterward wrote to the general passenger agent of the Northern, saying, "It would be utterly impossible for two such lines to run to common points like these without clashing which would be bad for us both." The Northern Steamship Company, a true Jim Hill organization, went ahead anyway. It did, however, fix its rates to Mackinac at a dollar higher than those charged by the D & C, and Mr. Carter and his directors had to be satisfied with that. As it turned out, the D & C did not lose the thirty percent of its business, but seems instead to have profited more than the newcomers.

In 1895 Mark Twain, on a speaking tour of the Great Lakes cities—the last speaking tour he ever made—took the *North West* from Mackinac to Duluth, where he had an engagement. Fog and stormy weather delayed the ship. Her famous passenger was becoming noted for his withering outbursts when frustrated, and on this occasion his companions were pleasantly surprised that he remained calm and in good humor. But Twain did, after all, have some experience with steamboating in other waters, and he probably understood quite well that a temper tantrum could not propel the *North West* any faster. The ship arrived at Duluth eight hours late; Twain went ashore clothed in evening dress and went directly to the church in which he was to speak, where 1,200 people still waited for him. They received him with enthusiasm and he was a great success.

Jim Hill's white elephants, as the big passenger liners were soon known, were the height of contemporary luxury travel. As one account said:

> Besides the ordinary staterooms, which are light and airy, the North West has several suites of apartments which boast of luxury and comfort. They are situated forward on the hurricane deck, and are finished in white mahogany and furnished with full-sized brass bedsteads in special designs. Rich rugs, beautiful lace spreads, tables, and lastly, elegant private bathrooms, secure a luxurious comfort. The staterooms are lighted by 16-candle-power lamps, enclosed in ground-glass globes; these lamps are lighted and extinguished by a switch placed adjacent to the berth.

For a five-day round trip of one of these ships the average food order included 3,000 pounds of beef, 5 1/2 barrels of flour, 450 pounds of butter, 350 pounds of sugar, 500 gallons of milk, 40 gallons of cream, and 430 dozen eggs. One story has it that Hill specially imported a famous chef from the East Coast just to be able to serve his onion soup on board.

The *City of Erie* moving briskly out of harbor, in a photograph by Pesha. (*—Great Lakes Historical Society*)

The vessels were in reality medium-sized ocean liners. A contemporary description says proudly, "Nearly 26 miles of electric wire are used, conducting fluid for 1200 16-candle-power lights. The lamps exceed by 300 the number on the largest ocean steamship." Reportedly some of the crew members of these vessels were sent to train aboard ocean ships before serving on the Northern's steamers.

In 1902 the ships were rebuilt, being given two stacks instead of three and an extra deck forward. They continued in service through the season of 1910. In the spring of 1911, while the ships were at their Buffalo docks being fitted out for the season about to begin, the *North West* was gutted by a fire and sank. She was raised and lay at her pier until 1918; during this time her engines and boilers were taken out and shipped to salt water for installation in wartime vessels. Then her hull was stripped and cut in two, in order to be taken through the canals to the Atlantic, reassembled, and made into an ocean ship. But in November 1918, as the forward half was being towed across Lake Ontario, a sudden squall descended and it foundered. The after section reached the lower St. Lawrence, was given a new forward section, and was turned into a freighter named *Maplecourt*.

The burning of the *North West* presaged the end of the Northern Steamship Company's passenger service. The *North Land* ran only a little longer; in 1919 she was sold

and cut in two for removal to Quebec and reassembly for ocean service. But the wartime demand for ships was over, and instead she was dismantled at Quebec in 1921. Under the flag of Canada Steamship Lines *Maplecourt* eventually returned to the Lakes, then went back to the ocean during World War II after being rebuilt again at Montreal. She was torpedoed in the Atlantic in 1941.

CITY OF ERIE.

Although Jim Hill brought ocean liners to the Lakes, the traditional sidewheelers still flourished. One of the firms that operated such vessels was the Cleveland and Buffalo Transit Company, which was organized in 1892 as a child of the long-established Detroit and Cleveland Navigation Company. The general manager of the D & C, T. F. Newman, moved to Cleveland and became general manager of the C & B, which was underwritten by a group of Cleveland businessmen. It started out using two of the D & C's steamers which it first chartered for a year, then took over permanently. Service began in 1893. By 1895 the line was prospering enough that it ordered the *City of Buffalo* to be built; she was then the largest sidewheeler on the Lakes. In 1898 the company took delivery of an even larger new steamer, the *City of Erie*.

She was 324 feet long, 77 feet 2 inches wide, and of 2498 gross tons. The two new boats then ran opposite each other in night service between Cleveland and Buffalo. The *City of Erie* was a steel passenger and package-freight steamer with 163 staterooms, a permit to carry 600 passengers normally and 2,700 on excursions, and the ability to carry 600 tons of freight. Her officers and crew totaled 108.

In those days steamboats were a common subject for discussion in Great Lakes ports. Everyone knew them, rode on them, and took a personal interest in them. Thus when A. A. Parker, president of the White Star Line of Detroit, which owned the new sidewheel excursion steamer *Tashmoo,* in October of 1900 casually told a newspaper man that he'd be willing to bet a thousand dollars his fine new steamer could beat either the *City of Buffalo* or the *City of Erie* in a race, "in still weather and still water," the remark was news and was duly reported in the Detroit *Free Press.*

T. F. Newman of the C & B read the story and wrote to the newsman, J. W. Wescott:

> My attention was attracted yesterday to a Detroit newspaper article having the heading, "Will Wager $1000." Upon reading the article I was much surprised to see that it was my old friend A.A. Parker, who seemingly has been so prosperous during the past season that he is willing to give away $1000, for upon such a wager as he proposes, the making is equivalent to a gift to the person taking it up.
>
> My surprise increased as I read the wager he desired to make was that the *Tashmoo* in still water and still weather can beat the *City of Erie* or *City of Buffalo.* This statement is so extraordinary that I cannot believe it was made seriously for publication.... Indeed the only still water in which I can conceive the *Tashmoo* would be on even terms with either vessel would be in a dry dock.

There was considerably more in the same vein; with the letter went a check for $1,000 to cover the challenge. Mr. Parker quickly accepted, also depositing a $1,000 check with Wescott.

Conditions for the race were agreed on. They included the course—100 miles along the southern shore of Lake Erie—selection of judges and timekeepers, and the starting time: 9:30 a.m., Tuesday, June 4, 1901. The boats were to be abreast and at a standstill and were to start upon the signal of one gun fired from the stake boat that marked the beginning of the course. Newman selected the *City of Erie* to oppose the *Tashmoo.*

The two vessels were designed for entirely different kinds of service. The *Erie* was a night boat intended to carry passengers and freight in the open Lakes in most kinds of weather. The *Tashmoo* was an excursion boat designed to carry only passengers on short trips and to operate in smooth water. The *Erie* was just sixteen feet longer than her opponent, but she was almost twice as heavy. The *Tashmoo* was generally regarded as the faster boat. Even Mr. Newman had his doubts. When Jim Rendall, engineer of the *Erie,* came into Newman's office and asked him to place a $1,000 bet for him on the *Erie,* Newman tried to dissuade him. Rendall would not back down; so Newman let him go but cautiously refrained from actually placing the bet.

Tashmoo was put in dry dock for scraping and repainting, and then she was run through a series of trials to determine the conditions under which she would be fastest. She arrived in Cleveland the afternoon before the race, carrying a number of rich Detroiters who used one of the hotels as their Cleveland base and made large bets with anyone who would cover them. The *City of Erie* returned from Buffalo on her regular run with passengers and freight on the morning of the race, unloaded, and hastily made what preparations she could. Capt. Hugh McAlpine had the crew stow the lifeboats and flagpoles on the lower deck to eliminate the resistance they would offer to the wind. The engine room

The end of the race between the *Tashmoo* and the *City of Erie.* The *Erie* is at far right, the *Tashmoo* at far left. The other vessels carry spectators. (—*Great Lakes Historical Society*)

crew had installed new piston rings during the lay-over in Buffalo and built a wooden bulkhead around the steam condenser, forming a box about ten feet square and six feet deep. Just before the race they filled the box with cracked ice. This of course lowered the temperature of the condenser and increased the power of the engine. They also slacked off all the bearings to avoid friction.

Choice of position was determined by lot. The *Tashmoo* won and Capt. B. S. Baker wisely chose the outer position where the water was deeper. At 9:30 a.m. the two ships were abreast and waiting. Because of safety regulations passengers were not permitted aboard them during the race, but to match the contingent of rich Detroit men aboard the *Tashmoo* a number of distinguished Clevelanders signed on as additional members of the *Erie's* crew for this voyage and were known ever after as the millionaire deck hands. Shortly after 9:30 a small gun was fired from the stake boat at the start of the course. Both steamers were off to a good start, the *Erie* a little ahead of the *Tashmoo*. Before long the lighter vessel caught up and the two of them continued side by side for about an hour, with smoke billowing and paddle wheels foaming.

Engineers on the *Tashmoo* had also tried to increase the power of their engine by installing a bypass to carry more high-pressure steam into the low-pressure receiver. This, however, actually caused back pressure and some loss of power. Meanwhile on the *City of Erie* the engineer decided that one of the steam inlet valves was closing too sluggishly; he looked around for a weight to put on it and grabbed one of the seamen, John Eaton. For the rest of the race Eaton sat on the top of the rising and descending valve rod. Early in the race the starboard engine blower of the *Erie* failed; it was eventually repaired but full steam pressure was never fully recovered.

As the two steamers passed Fairport, the value of the *Tashmoo's* outer position became evident. At that place the inner course led through shoal water. Sidewheel mariners had long contended that shoal water slowed their vessels and the race seemed to prove the point: the *City of Erie* lost speed and dropped behind. Then as she came into deep water again she picked up speed. Gradually she pulled up on the *Tashmoo* and by the time they were opposite Ashtabula they again were even.

Newspaper reporters aboard each vessel sent off their stories, some by carrier pigeon, others by sealing the papers in tin cans which they tossed overboard at prearranged places where small boats waited to pick them up. In the *Erie's* engine room John Eaton rode up and down on the head of the valve rod. And as the ships passed Conneaut the *City of Erie* moved ahead.

Twenty miles from the finish line the *Erie* was three lengths ahead. The *Tashmoo* thrust along, trying to close the gap without success. The two vessels maintained the same distance as they bore down on the small craft that marked the end of the course off Erie. First across the finish line was the *City of Erie*; as the judges' and timekeepers' boats tossed in the swells, they clocked the *Tashmoo* across the line just forty-five seconds later. The

The *United Empire*, shown on the first trip of the season in 1901. The arch truss, a necessity in large wooden steamers, can be seen here only amidships, where it is worked into the superstructure. (—*Courtesy Mrs. Fred Landon*)

The *United Empire* in her earliest days, when she still carried a sail on her foremast. (*—Metropolitan Toronto Library Board*)

average speed of each vessel was nearly twenty-two miles per hour, or nineteen knots.

Other steamers at the finish line burst out with a great noise of whistles as the two racers sped past and then slowed and turned back. The judges' boat signaled the result to the waiting public on shore by a prearranged message, three kites sent aloft. The *Tashmoo*, learning officially that she had lost, saluted the victor.

T. F. Newman was probably sufficiently delighted with the result, which brought an immense amount of advertising to the C & B Line, that he did not even mind his failure to place the bet for the chief engineer, Jim Rendall. Newman and the millionaire deck hands all dug down and contributed to a fund that would cover the engineer's bet. He never learned that it had not really been placed at all, and he saw to it that his supposed winnings were distributed among the whole crew.

UNITED EMPIRE

At one time Canada issued a four-dollar bill. On that bill appeared one of the finest Canadian steamers of the day, the *United Empire*, which plied regularly between Sarnia, Ontario, and Fort William at the head of Lake Superior. This vessel was one of the last big wooden passenger ships on the Lakes, and she lasted well after some of the more elaborate steel ships appeared.

She was an arch-trussed vessel, the development of a type that originated a half-century earlier, when wooden steamers became so large that they had to have extra bracing to keep them stiff and solid. But the builders of the *United Empire* had learned how to work such arch trusses neatly into her upper works so that she had an integrated appearance, quite different from that of some of the earlier ships. She was launched in 1882 and was 253 feet long, 36 feet in beam, and of 1,961 gross tons.

A description of the interior of the big steamer was given by Fred Landon, who sailed on her as a young man in 1901.

> She was first of all a passenger boat, but she always had a full cargo of freight for Western Canada's needs. We occasionally had horses aboard but they had to be tied cross-wise, not longitudinally, to prevent them swaying with the vessel. From the engine deck to the saloons above there was a broad stairway. The forward half was the dining room with about eight tables each seating eight people. The staterooms in this forward portion of the vessel opened directly on the tables but these were only set up for meals and were often used by groups for card playing, or for writing letters.
>
> In the after saloon there was a piano and comfortable couches. The hurricane deck aft of the pilot house was the popular place with passengers unless there was too much wind. In the evening they gathered in the after saloon, though if there was someone aboard who could play the piano we might have some music....
>
> I do not recall a real bathroom on the *United Empire* at all, though there was running water in each room.

The Northwest Transportation Company brought out the *United Empire*, commonly known as "Old Betsey," and a slightly smaller but similar vessel, the

169

Monarch, launched eight years later. The oak they were made of was cut in the extensive forests that still existed near Sarnia.

The Beatty family owned the Northwest Transportation Company, which was usually called the Beatty Line. In 1899 it merged with two Georgian Bay lines to form the Northern Navigation Company. When the young college student, Fred Landon, first saw the *United Empire* on April 30, 1901, shortly after the merger, she was ploughing through the ice in the St. Clair River. He went aboard and served as a "hasher"—a waiter—all that season.

She was then under the command of Capt. John McNabb, one of the many Scots-Canadian Great Lakes captains. He was known as the master who never lost a passenger or crew member. The chief engineer, Samuel Brisbin, delighted in telling lake stories and in leading curious passengers to the very bottom of the ship to show them the turning shaft that drove the propeller. He served as chief engineer on a number of vessels sailing out of Sarnia, the last of them being the *Noronic*.

During the 1901 season "Old Betsey" encountered only one real storm, late in September:

> The steamer lay in Port Arthur until four o'clock on the morning of the 23rd. Storm signals were up but Captain McNabb decided to make a start down the lake. . . . The boat was rolling about badly and as we neared Passage Island it became so severe that everything on the tables in the dining saloon was going on the floor and chairs were falling in every direction. . . .

The captain decided to take her into shelter at Rock Harbor, on Isle Royale.

> . . . Rock Harbor is created by a fringe of islands extending for miles parallel to the south shore of the main island. Once we were behind the first island the water was calm and we proceeded to steam westward for several miles . . . and finally anchored near an old lighthouse, apparently not in service. Nearby was a fishing camp with reels of nets drying in the wind and occasional sunshine. . . .

There they remained for five hours. This was before wireless telegraphy on the Lakes and there was no way of getting weather forecasts or information as to the weather conditions farther ahead. Finally the weather seemed to be improving.

> It was decided then to raise the anchors and move out. The *United Empire* was not equipped with steam winches on deck but we had on board 25 Italian laborers, deck passengers for the Sault. They took on the anchor raising task on promise of being given their supper and by three o'clock we were ready to leave Rock Harbor. . .

By 6:00 p.m. the wind had changed and the boat, now in the open lake, was again rolling badly. The captain followed the northern shore and pushed ahead.

> All night long there was a continual din, the creaking and groaning of the vessel, the noise of the engines as the propeller screw lifted out of the water or dashed into it again with the alternate heaving of the boat. Streams of water ran the length of the decks but fortunately it was not cold enough to form ice. Chief Brisbin and his men stood hour after hour by the engines, while deckhands were sent to the help of the firemen in keeping up steam. Many of the passenger cabins were flooded, to the discomfort of their occupants.

They followed the storm down the Lakes; after the ship passed through the Sault locks, Captain McNabb found that Lake Huron was raging. They remained a night and a half the next day in shelter at the head of Lake Huron before starting out. "The height of waves that afternoon on Lake Huron was the greatest I saw in four seasons on these boats." Eighty-three hours after leaving Port Arthur the *United Empire* reached Sarnia.

In 1904 she was rebuilt at Collingwood, coming out the next year with a new name, *Saronic*. In December 1906 her smaller sister *Monarch* was wrecked in a snowstorm on Isle Royale, not far from where the *United Empire* took shelter that day in 1901. In 1915 "Old Betsey" was damaged by fire at Sarnia during the winter. She was converted into a steam barge, then a tow barge, and a few years later was abandoned.

Her passing marked the end of the big wooden ships. By 1915, when she went out of passenger service, the Northern Navigation Company (which had just become part of the great Canada Steamship Lines) had acquired three fine steel passenger ships. They were much larger and more luxurious; the passengers found more to do and tended to have an extended party aboard. But the new ships had somehow lost a bit of the old character. As they became more like floating hotels the passengers became more insulated from the essential business of moving the ship across the water. The vessels were undoubtedly pleasanter to travel on, but they did not inspire quite the same affection. None of the *United Empire's* successors was ever selected to appear on a four-dollar bill—or any other currency.

BANNOCKBURN

During the first quarter of the twentieth century, sailors occasionally saw the small steel freighter *Bannockburn* on Lake Superior, passing through the mists common on that lake or disappearing into the early evening. Her profile was unmistakable, with three raking masts and a tall funnel. But the strange thing was that the *Bannockburn* had disappeared on Lake Superior in November of 1902, and had never again reached port.

By the early 1890s vessels approaching 250 feet in length could move through the St. Lawrence canals into Lake Ontario and then of course through the Welland and Sault Ste. Marie canals into all of the other Great Lakes. As a result, a class of steamers developed that came to be known as "canallers"—the same name once given to sailing vessels that fitted the Welland and other canals of an earlier day. Most of these later ships were Canadian. There were both bulk freighters and package freighters among them; as was also true of their larger sisters that navigated only the Lakes, the bulk freighters considerably outnumbered the package freighters. One of the companies that owned and operated canallers was the Montreal Transportation Company, and one of the bulk freighters belonging to that company was the *Bannockburn*.

The banking and shipping interests of Montreal were controlled largely by men of Scottish descent, and so it was only fitting that a Montreal ship be named for the battle in which Robert Bruce defeated a larger English army under Edward II. It perhaps gave an added fillip that it was in England that the ship was launched during 1893 for the Montreal firm. She was 244 feet long, of 40 feet beam, and of 1736 gross tons. Built by a well-known British shipyard, that of Sir. R. Dixon and Company, she was rated A-1 by Lloyds. She steamed across the Atlantic to Montreal and in due course was put in service through the canals and on the Lakes; in the latter trade she often towed one or two barges, her most frequent consort being the big four-masted *Minnedosa*, the largest Canadian schooner on the Lakes. The *Bannockburn* had the black hull, brown cabin, and black stack that were the colors of the Montreal Transportation Company; on each side of her stack were the white letters MTCo. Typically, such a vessel picked up grain at the head of Lake Superior and carried it by lake and canal to Montreal. She was based at Kingston, where she could equally well travel up the Lakes or down the St. Lawrence; as a result, many of her crew came from that city.

In the autumn of 1902 she was operating alone, probably because her owners did not want to saddle her with a tow during the stormy autumn weather and because they wanted her to move quickly, making as many trips as possible before the Lakes froze over. She took a cargo into the port of Midland, on Georgian Bay, then headed northward again into Lake Superior, to load grain at Port Arthur. There she took on 85,000 bushels of wheat consigned to an elevator at Midland, and she steamed out of Port Arthur at about 9:00 a.m. on November 21.

That afternoon the steamer *Algonquin* was pushing westward into a stormy head wind. About fifty miles southeast of Passage Island and northeast of Keweenaw Point, Capt. James McMaugh sighted another ship, travelling easily with the wind behind her. She was the *Bannockburn*. He went about his duties for a few minutes and when he looked again she was gone. The weather was misty and he assumed she had vanished into the haze, but he remarked to his first officer that she certainly had disappeared quickly.

As darkness fell, the big passenger steamer *Huronic* was also heading westward into the growing storm. Sometime during the night her pilot-house crew looked out over the waves and saw the *Bannockburn* passing. It was a casual matter and the officers mentioned it briefly next morning at breakfast, where they were overheard by young Fred Landon, who was working that season aboard the ship and serving the officers' table. All those on the *Huronic*, however, were much more interested that her engines had sustained some light damage in the storm than they were in the commonplace fact that they had passed another ship.

But the *Bannockburn* never reached port. As it became evident that she was overdue, there was a flurry of stories that she was lying in shelter behind Slate Island; that she was ashore on the northern shore of Lake Superior; or that she was ashore on Michipicoten Island. None of them was true. She had simply disappeared.

Searchers went out in tugs and found nothing. One American steamer reported that in passing Stannard Rock, near the middle of Lake Superior, she had seen con-

Left: The canal-size lake freighter *Bannockburn* was built in England in 1893 and disappeared on Lake Superior in November 1902. (—*Institute for Great Lakes Research, Bowling Green State University*)

Below: Elevators at the Georgian Bay port of Midland, Ontario, about 1903. It was here that the *Bannockburn* was bound when she was lost on Lake Superior. The grain-unloading arms were still much the same as those of Dart's early Buffalo elevator. Vessels shown here are typical of the turn-of-the-century navigation on the Great Lakes. The big three-masted schooner *James G. Blaine* represented the final development of sail; the tow barge at the near elevator and the steam freighter beyond were the modern thing. A J.W. Bald photo. (—*Huronia Museum*)

172

siderable floating wreckage; but other vessels had passed that way since the *Bannockburn* disappeared and had seen nothing. Did the wreckage drift in from somewhere else?

Theories as to the ship's fate were numerous. Captain McMaugh of the *Algonquin* decided in retrospect that the missing vessel's boilers had blown up between the time he sighted the *Bannockburn* and the time he saw that she had disappeared. It is barely conceivable that in the growing storm he had not heard such an explosion, but others pointed out that the boilers of a relatively new ship almost never blew up, and of course the *Huronic's* people saw her later. There had been a considerable row a short time previously because the Canadian government had shut down the Caribou Island lighthouse on the 15th even though navigation had not yet ended. Many people assumed that the steamer had smashed into that island at night, but what about the floating wreckage near Stannard Rock? Perhaps the most extreme theory was that in the storm her engines had somehow gone through her bottom and that she had sunk forthwith.

Whatever theory one prefers, the fact is that the *Bannockburn* has never entered harbor since she left Port Arthur. Some fifteen months later a life belt bearing her name washed ashore, and in 1927, a quarter-century later, an oar was found with the name *Bannockburn* still faintly readable on it. But meanwhile the ship herself continued to be reported from time to time, running through the Lake Superior mists or passing at night in a storm, one of the ghosts of the Great Lakes.

J. PIERPONT MORGAN

The first of what came to be known as "standard 600-footers" was launched in 1906. She was the freighter *J. Pierpont Morgan*, built at South Chicago for the Pittsburgh Steamship Company. The 600-foot length was approximate; in fact she was 605 feet over all and of 58 foot beam. She and eight sisters that were launched that year and the next were the largest vessels on the Lakes. For the next twenty years the 600-footers (some of which eventually ranged up to 612 feet) were the biggest things on the Lakes, and for the next 35 years they formed the backbone of the major Great Lakes fleets.

Ships of the Pittsburgh Company had red hulls, white cabins, and silver funnels. Because of the funnels they were known to lake sailors as the "Tin Stackers,"

The *J. Pierpont Morgan*, first of the "standard 600-footers," carried ore from Lake Superior to the receiving ports on Lake Erie. The length of the ship is evident in this picture. (*—Marine Historical Collection, Milwaukee Public Library*)

Left: Freighter *George W. Peavey*, built in 1901, loading at a Duluth ore dock in the early 1900s. The docks are higher and the rail cars bigger, but the principle is the same as that of the first docks. (—*Library of Congress LC lot 2964*)

Right: The original steam-driven Hulett unloader in the hold of a vessel about 1899, showing the operator's position. (—*Courtesy McDowell Wellman Engineering Co., Cleveland*)

Left: Several inventors designed improvements on the Brown Hoists. Among the designs were clamshell hoists, seen here unloading a freighter at Ashtabula about 1908. The inner ends of the arms were hinged, so that the devices could be raised clear of the ships. Of all such unloaders, the Huletts quickly proved their superiority, and other designs such as this one fell into oblivion. (—Trash and Treasure, *Ashtabula*)

Early steam-powered Hulett unloader at Conneaut, Ohio, about 1902. Note the freighter being unloaded at far left. (*—Institute for Great Lakes Research, Bowling Green State University*)

and because of their background they were known to businessmen and shipowners as the Steel Trust Fleet. This fleet, the largest on the Lakes, was the end of more than a decade of business conflict and development.

Following 1893, four years of depression had wiped out most of the small owners and operators of iron mines; the larger operators were able to gather in the holdings of the smaller ones and emerged stronger than ever. As the depression ended, the three biggest iron companies on the Lakes were the Consolidated Iron Mines owned by John D. Rockefeller, the Minnesota Iron Company in which the Cleveland partnership of Pickands Mather & Co. had a large interest, and the Oliver Mining Company in which Henry W. Oliver, Henry Clay Frick, and Andrew Carnegie were associated. Pickands Mather for a number of years had owned some vessels on the Lakes and had operated other vessels for other owners; among the latter was the whaleback fleet of the American Steel Barge Company. Neither Rockefeller nor Oliver had had experience in Great Lakes shipping.

It was evident, however, that the mine owners would be in a much better position if they owned their own ships, rather than depending on others to carry their ore from the head of the Lakes to Cleveland or Erie. Mr. Rockefeller took the first step, a characteristic one. In 1895 when Samuel Mather of Pickands Mather & Co. was visiting New York, a mutual friend persuaded him to call upon Rockefeller one evening before dinner. Mather was reluctant; he could stay only a few minutes. Rockefeller assured him that they could fin-

ish their business in ten. Then he announced that he intended to transport his ore in his own ships and he wanted Mather to take charge of their construction. Mather of course said that he was in the shipping business himself and had no desire to bring Rockefeller into it. John D. replied that someone was going to establish a fleet for him in any event and that Mather might as well have the profit. Samuel Mather thought this over briefly and then agreed.

He returned home to Cleveland and before long each of the major Great Lakes shipyards received a letter signed by H.G. Dalton, one of the Pickands Mather partners, asking them to bid on one or two ships, the plans of which were enclosed. Word soon got around that Pickands Mather was building a couple of ships. The economy still was depressed and each shipbuilder was eager to get the contract; each of them quoted as low a figure as he felt he possibly could, hoping to underbid the others.

The bidders were all invited by Samuel Mather to come to Cleveland the day before the contracts were to be awarded. Each was asked into Mather's private office for a special conference on all the details of his bid; each somehow thought he must be the lucky one. Next day the shipbuilders all returned to the Pickands Mather offices; one by one they were asked to go in and see Mr. Mather. Each of them came out with a signed contract. As they began to compare notes, their confusion grew; every one of the bids had been accepted without quibble and each builder apparently had bid only against himself. It was not until later that they realized

Samuel Mather had used this method to avoid the high prices that would have been certain if anyone had known in advance that a total of twelve ships was to be ordered—let alone the fact that Rockefeller was behind the orders.

The Rockefeller fleet was the Bessemer Steamship Company. During the next five years it acquired fifty-six boats. At this same time negotiations were going forward to join together the nine largest Great Lakes shipyards; in 1899 the American Ship Building Company was formed from this group. Rockefeller, through his interest in McDougall's shipyard in Duluth, became a stockholder in the new company.

Oliver and his partner Carnegie found themselves shipping ore in Rockefeller vessels. Oliver had had six ships built for his subsidiary, the Pittsburgh Steamship Company, but they were not enough. In 1900 he placed orders for more ships and made an offer to buy the whaleback fleet of the American Steel Barge Company. But at the same time Carnegie decided that the ships they owned gave him sufficient leverage to handle the situation in another way. He served an ultimatum on Rockefeller that he must halve his freight rates.

John D. Rockefeller was not a man to accept ultimatums and the extreme rate cuts demanded were obviously unfair. He refused. Carnegie persisted. Promptly Rockefeller wired his agents on the Lakes; soon every Rockefeller ship carrying a Carnegie and Oliver cargo lay at anchor without moving or unloading. At the same time the American Ship Building Company, of which Rockefeller was a stockholder, refused to bid on new ships for Oliver. And the whaleback fleet, in which Rockefeller had an interest, instead of going to Oliver was transferred into Rockefeller's Bessemer Steamship Company. Carnegie was left in Pittsburgh with panting steel mills and no ore. Before long he decided to pay Rockefeller the usual rates.

Meanwhile Judge E. H. Gary, backed by J. P. Morgan, had formed the Federal Steel Company, a growing young giant, which took over the Minnesota Iron Company and its subsidiary, the Minnesota Steamship Company operated by Pickands Mather. In 1901 Carnegie, who was growing old and perhaps did not want to compete with Morgan, decided to retire. He sold his steel business to Morgan for bonds and stock worth half a billion. The combined result was the United States Steel Company. One of the directors was Samuel Mather. U.S. Steel also wanted the Rockefeller holdings; Rockefeller sold them a month later for $90 million, a large part of it in U.S. Steel stock, and Rockefeller's Bessemer Steamship Company was part of the deal. The Carnegie holdings had included the Pittsburgh Steamship Company, which was already a part of the U.S. Steel organization; it therefore retained its name and the Rockefeller ships and others that were gathered into the huge fleet all came to fly the Pittsburgh flag. The Pittsburgh Steamship Company then had over a hundred ships and the Steel Trust Fleet had come to the Lakes.

The management of such a fleet required a strong and clever hand. Judge Gary asked one of the Pickands Mather partners, Harry Coulby, who had been born in England thirty-nine years previously and had arrived in Cleveland at the age of nineteen, if he would take over. It was agreed that he also could continue in his Pickands Mather partnership, and so Coulby in 1904 became president of the Pittsburgh Steamship Company. Pickands Mather had lost many of the vessels it had managed to the Steel Trust fleet; now it started again to build up its own shipping operation, eventually leading to the formation of the Interlake Steamship Company, second largest on the Lakes.

The concentration of so many ships under the Pittsburgh Steamship Company led some people to expect that company to control prices and squeeze out competition. Since its formation had ended competition between the separate lines that once owned its freighters, it was able to revamp its fleet to its own advantage. Powerful, fast steamers that had been built to outperform other steamers now in the same fleet were no longer economical, and so Pittsburgh had their engines replaced by smaller ones; the more powerful engines went into larger vessels that were soon to be built for the fleet. But despite all this the big company did not seek to restrict others. From 1901 through 1910 some 200 new steel bulk freighters were built for other owners who were changing over from wooden ships. The expansion of the American economy was so great that there was plenty of room for the others. In 1901 U.S. Steel had sixty-five percent of the national steel mar-

The *J. Pierpont Morgan* in Ashtabula habor at the electrically driven Hulett unloaders shortly after they were installed there. Compare these machines with the earlier steam-driven Huletts. (*—Marine Historical Collection, Milwaukee Public Library*)

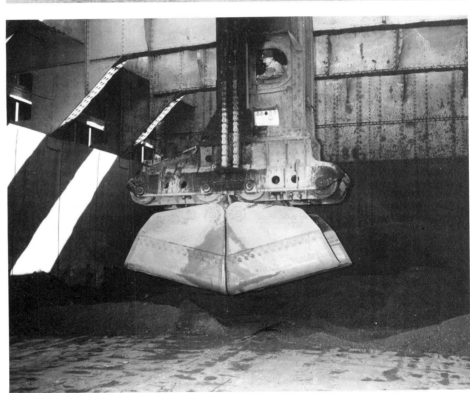

A later model Hulett with jaws closed, about to rise out of the hold of a freighter. It was this type of unloader that made a record of two hours and fifteen minutes in unloading the *J. Pierpont Morgan* in 1930. (*—Courtesy McDowell Wellman Engineering Co., Cleveland*)

Hull of a freighter in dry dock at Lorain, Ohio, in 1913, showing the boxy midsection of such a vessel, designed to carry maximum cargoes through canals and into restricted harbors. This view, looking forward from the stern, also shows clearly the plates of which the ship is constructed. (*—Ohio Historical Society*)

The *Wyandotte*, first ship built as a self-unloader, was launched in 1908. In 1910 she was lengthened to 346 feet, as she is seen here; her breadth was 45.2 and her depth 24. She contrasted with the 600-foot-long ore carriers then coming into use. She and other self-unloaders that gradually developed were specialized vessels designed to bring cargoes of coal or stone into small harbors that had little unloading equipment. The skeletonized self-unloading boom, to be swung out over the dockside receiving area, has marked most self-unloaders ever since. (—*Institute for Great Lakes Research, Bowling Green State University*)

ket; by 1927, although it had grown steadily, its share of the total market was only thirty-three percent.

In 1905 the Pittsburgh Company had the first four ships built especially for its fleet. They were 576 feet long and were briefly the largest ships on the Lakes. But the next year the *Morgan* and her sisters came out. They were big, carried large cargoes and, like the *Morgan,* most of them had efficiently uneventful lives. Their greatest adventures were carrying cargoes of record sizes and cargoes that were unloaded at record speeds.

The unloading process had taken another big step forward at about the same time that U.S. Steel was formed—a step that made larger and larger vessels feasible. An eccentric genius named George H. Hulett, who wore baggy clothing and chewed tobacco throughout high-level business conferences, designed a monster piece of machinery to unload freighters. He set up the first example on the docks at Conneaut in 1899. By 1900 three of them were in operation and in 1901 a fourth was added. They also appeared at Cleveland and Erie.

It took Hulett's genius, and probably his eccentricity as well, even to conceive of the machine named for him. The Hulett unloader consisted of an enormous vertical plunger so big that the operator stood in a space inside its lower end. On its bottom was mounted a clamshell; the early ones took ten tons of ore in one bite. The vertical plunger was attached at its top to a horizontal rocker arm, which in turn was pivoted at its center to a support rising from a steel bridge that spanned several railroad tracks and that itself moved on heavy rails. A second horizontal arm to steady and guide the vertical plunger was attached a little distance below the main one. The operator lowered the plunger into the hold of the vessel, riding down inside it, took a bite, and rode up again. As the plunger moved up it was carried toward the dock by the rising arms and by machinery in the bridge. At the top of its stroke it stood over a hopper; there the jaws opened and dumped the ore into the hopper which led to chutes inside the bridge and thus to waiting rail cars.

The first Huletts ran by steam; the pipes went through the operator's cubicle and as a result he was never cold and in summer he was exceedingly hot. Electrically operated Huletts were built later, starting about 1911. These were kinder to their operators, bigger, and more efficient. Each of their buckets held 17 tons. It was a battery of these machines in Conneaut that in

The *Imperial*, the first tanker on the Great Lakes, initially had an open bridge and no wheelhouse. In this early photo of her by Pesha, small auxiliary sails can be seen and she had ratlines on her shrouds in the manner of a sailing vessel. (—*Institute for Great Lakes Research, Bowling Green State University*)

1930 unloaded 11,369 tons of iron ore from the *J. Pierpont Morgan* in two hours and fifteen minutes, thus establishing one of those brief records that were the high points in the big ship's career.

IMPERIAL

At Wellington Quay on the Tyne, in England in the year 1897, a two-hundred-foot tanker was launched for the Black Sea trade. She belonged to the Minerals Oil Corporation and was intended to carry crude oil from the Baku field to a new refinery on the Thames. But when the company met reverses she was sold to Anglo American Oil Company Ltd., which chartered and then sold her to Imperial Oil. At that time she was renamed *Imperial*. In 1909 Imperial Oil, which had been operating on the Great Lakes with tank barges, brought the *Imperial* to the Lakes; she was the first self-propelled tank ship to be seen there. She was 200 feet long, of 32 feet beam, and 14 feet depth.

Imperial Oil, Ltd., was the Canadian arm of John D. Rockefeller's Standard Oil Company, although it began as a purely Canadian amalgamation of smaller companies and was at first intended to combat American penetration of the Canadian oil industry. That industry, from the late 1850s till the early 1870s, had been a leading producer (in the small scale of its day) of petroleum products. It had exported them to the United States, Britain, and Europe. But then Ontario oil supplies began to dwindle and Pennsylvania fields began to open. Rockefeller started buying up Canadian firms, building Canadian plants, and applying leverage to Canadian railways to obtain good freight rates.

Canadian oilmen lacked Rockefeller's capital, but more important, they lacked oil. By 1897 John D. had convinced the Canadian Parliament that it must lower duties on imported oil and in 1898 Standard Oil bought Imperial Oil. The result was not immediately happy for Canadians. Farmers from the prairie provinces sent delegations to Ottawa to protest rising kerosene prices. Seventeen large Canadian manufacturers who had changed previously from coal to oil jointly drafted a letter to the prime minister: "Since the Standard Oil Company secured the control of the product there has been a tendency to curtail the supply and reduce the quality, and in fact in some cases to cut it off altogether, as well as advance the price materially."

Within the next few years, however, Canadian businessmen had made connections with Rockefeller's competitors in the United States and "The Trust," as Imperial had come to be known in Canada, no longer had a monopoly. The Canadian oil business assumed a more normal shape. As competition went on it became evident that to meet it, Imperial Oil needed tankers on the Great Lakes. The first of them was the *Imperial*. She went into service on the Lakes, often towing *Barge No. 6*, a tank barge built in 1903. The tanker had a capacity of 5,500 barrels, the barge one of 7,000 barrels. Capt. F. C. Smith, Imperial Oil's port superintendent at Sarnia, has written of the *Imperial*, "She could tow *Barge No. 6* faster than some of our present ships can run." The *Imperial* was the first of several tankers that Imperial Oil brought to the Lakes in the next few years.

In time her open bridge was replaced by an enclosed pilothouse. Those who knew her began to call

The *Imperial*, showing her with an open bridge as she looked during her first years on the Lakes. (*–Great Lakes Historical Society*)

When nautical styles changed, the *Imperial* was given a wheelhouse on her bridge and lost her sails, as shown here. (*–Marine Historical Collection, Milwaukee Public Library*)

The second *Imperial*, launched at Collingwood in 1938, was an updated version of the first one. She operated on the Pacific Coast from 1939 until 1970, then under various owners and flags until 1987, when she was broken up in Spain. (*–Courtesy Imperial Oil Limited*)

her "the Yacht." She was not that much smaller than her newer sisters, which did not exceed 250 feet in length (most of them used the St. Lawrence canals at various times and had to be of limited size), but she was noticeably smaller, had a more graceful hull than most, and was always clean and shiny.

In 1922 Imperial Oil decided that it would distribute petroleum products in bulk along the British Columbia coast. Just as the small *Imperial* had been the right size for pioneer service on the Great Lakes, she was the right size for pioneer service on the Pacific Coast. And so in 1922 she left the Great Lakes under tow, travelled down the Atlantic Coast, through the Panama Canal, and up to Ioco, British Columbia, her new home base. There she served until 1938, when her name was changed to *Impoco* so that the name *Imperial* could be given to a new Great Lakes tanker launched that year in Collingwood. In 1939 the little "Yacht" was scrapped.

ANN ARBOR NO. 5

Late in 1910 the steel car ferry *Ann Arbor No. 5* was completed at the Toledo Shipbuilding Company; on January 1, 1911, she was turned over to her owners, the Ann Arbor Railroad. The vessel was 360 feet long, 56 feet in beam, and of 2,988 gross tons. She was the biggest car ferry on the Lakes and continued to be for the next sixteen years. Early in January she set out, cutting her way through the ice, until she reached the port of Frankfort, her base on Lake Michigan, where she was put in regular service.

The Ann Arbor Railroad, under its earlier name of Toledo, Ann Arbor & North Michigan Railway, was the first rail line to operate a ferry service that carried its cars across the open Lakes. Earlier car ferries had been limited to crossing rivers and the narrow waters of the Straits of Mackinac. But James M. Ashley, former governor of Montana and organizer of the railroad, was determined to thrust his service across Lake Michigan. Ashley, a pugnacious man, had been a member of congress from Toledo and had led the impeachment proceedings against Andrew Johnson. Later, appointed governor of Montana by President Grant, he had been so outspoken in his criticism of Grant's administration that the President had removed him from office after less than a year.

In pushing his tracks from Toledo to Lake Michigan, Ashley at one point when his funds were low confiscated thirty-two carloads of rails someone had routed over his line and used them to lay track on his own roadbed; as a result he went to jail for several days, but like most politicians he had friends and was soon released. Later he had an argument with another railroad that persisted in tearing up his tracks; this reached a point where both sides massed gangs of men and in a free-for-all Ashley's gang drove off the others.

Such a man as Ashley was not deterred by the ridicule that met his idea of an open-water car ferry. Neither investors nor shipbuilders reacted to the idea with notable enthusiasm. Eventually, however, he persuaded a Toledo company to build such a vessel and even persuaded the noted marine architect, F. E. Kirby of Detroit, to design it and supervise construction. Once this wooden vessel, *Ann Arbor No. 1,* arrived on Lake Michigan, Ashley had to find someone willing to ship traffic aboard her. Finally he pressured the coal company that sold him fuel for his locomotives into sending four cars of coal across Lake Michigan on his new ferry. There were problems getting the cars aboard and then, as the ferry approached the harbor of Kewaunee on the Wisconsin shore, feeling her way through a fog, she grounded. There she sat for two days until a tug pulled her off. In Kewaunee she discharged the four cars of coal, took aboard twenty-two cars (her maximum load was twenty-four) and headed eastward. Rail ferry service was in operation across Lake Michigan.

Ann Arbor No. 1 was followed by *No. 2, No. 3,* and *No. 4,* all wooden vessels. Meanwhile in 1897 the *Pere Marquette,* a steel car ferry, was put into service across Lake Michigan by the Flint & Pere Marquette Railroad. Numerous other Pere Marquette ferries followed. The numbering system used by both companies seems to have been derived from railroad practice; it suggests the marine custom of placing roman numerals after a name that repeats that of an older vessel, but in fact it is quite different. *Ann Arbors* and *Pere Marquettes* were all in service at the same time, and in at least one instance a number was repeated. When *Pere Marquette 18* foundered in 1910 she was replaced by a new *Pere Marquette 18.*

The Pere Marquette line had the most complicated numbering system and eventually the largest number

Left Top: *Ann Arbor No. 5* passing Marine City through two feet of ice. (—*Great Lakes Marine Historical Collection, Milwaukee Public Library*)

Left Middle: *Ann Arbor No. 5* in Lake Michigan ice. (—*Great Lakes Marine Historical Collection, Milwaukee Public Library*)

Below: *Ann Arbor No. 5* displays her speed and power. this is a comparatively late photograph; note the radar antenna. (—*Marine Historical Collection, Milwaukee Public Library*)

The car-ferry lines also ran some ordinary passenger-and-freight steamers. Here one of them, the *Pere Marquette 3*, is shown aground in a storm at Ludington, Michigan, January 1902. The people aboard were rescued by breeches buoy. (*–Great Lakes Historical Society*

of boats. It operated several passenger and package-freight steamers as well as the car ferries. In 1901 it sorted them all out and began numbering the passenger and package-freight vessels with numbers under 15. The original, unnumbered *Pere Marquette* was considered to be number 15 and the remaining car ferries were given numbers above 15. Thus the *Pere Marquette 18*, whose foundering shocked the owners of both lines and led to some changes in design of the vessels, was the fourth car ferry acquired by this company.

Pere Marquette 18, loaded with 29 cars of coal and general merchandise, sailed from Ludington for Milwaukee on September 8, 1910. In midlake, about 3:00 a.m., an oiler discovered seven feet of water in the after compartment. Despite efforts to pump it out, the jettisoning of several rail cars to lighten the stern, and the filling of the forward water compartments to balance the vessel, she continued to settle. She sent out a wireless signal of distress and about 6:30 a.m. the *Pere Marquette 17* arrived at her location. But by then the officers of *No. 18* felt that they had won the battle and were proceeding toward harbor; it seemed wise, however, for the other boat to come alongside and take off passengers and some of the crew. *No. 17* began to maneuver closer. Suddenly the stern of *No. 18* sank; her bow rose and then exploded from the air pressure inside, throwing debris through the air, and the ferry disappeared. *No. 17* picked up about 35 survivors; some 30 were lost. No one ever knew the exact cause of the disaster.

As a result the new *Ann Arbor No. 5*, designed by Kirby, became the first car ferry to be fitted with a sea gate, a new device that shortly was put on all Lake Michigan ferries, old and new. The stern of a car ferry, through which the cars were loaded and unloaded, was at the same level as the docks it used, had to be very low, and thus was the Achilles' heel of the vessel. It was this weak spot that the sea gate closed off; the gate on the new vessel was 5 1/2 feet high. The new boat was a steel vessel with twin screws and triple-expansion engines that provided 3,000 hp. She had an icebreaker bow. All the ferries had been icebreakers of a sort, for all of them operated throughout the winter. They had bows that permitted them to ride up on the ice and crush it with their weight (in contrast with the early *Chief Justice Robinson* on Lake Ontario that plowed the ice with a sort of ram bow, raising it from underneath). But the new *No. 5* was larger and more powerful than any of the others to that date, and was particularly effective in breaking her way through ice.

In the winter of 1912, an especially severe one, *Ann Arbor No. 3, No. 4*, and *No. 5* were sent out together to Manistique. Some five miles from that port *No. 3* and *No. 4* lodged in the ice. The powerful *Ann Arbor No. 5* made her way around them, unloaded at Manistique, reloaded for the return trip, returned to the stuck boats and cut them free. She waited for them to discharge and reload, then escorted them back across the lake, helping to free them when necessary. The trip took five days.

The *City of Milwaukee*, shown here at Muskegon, was built in 1931. Note the sea gate at the stern that closes off the opening through which rail cars are loaded, and the stern wheelhouse used to back the vessel accurately into dock; both were typical of car ferries. (—Photograph by the author)

On her car deck, *Ann Arbor No. 5* had four tracks and could take as many as thirty rail cars. On the ferries, cars were lifted off their trucks slightly by jacks and chained down tightly with turnbuckles to the deck, thus making them in effect part of the ship and eliminating any separate motion. The ferry had two deck cabins, the one forward of her twin stacks housing the officers and a few passengers. The stacks were placed one ahead of the other Her profile remained typical of car ferries throughout their heyday, although on later vessels the passenger cabins gradually expanded over the entire deck.

The period from 1910 until 1929, ushered in by *Ann Arbor No. 5,* was the great one for railroad car ferries. *No. 5* had a long career, eventually being retired in the mid-1960s. Car ferry service flourished on Lake Michigan and also appeared on Lakes Erie and Ontario, but on these other lakes it again disappeared in the late 50s. It then dwindled on Lake Michigan, finally dying in the 1980s. The railroads, which once thought it better to ferry rail cars across Lake Michigan than to take them around the lake through the congested Chicago area, now decided that the disadvantages outweighed the advantages. Community action by the ports involved, brought to bear through state and federal governments, kept the vessels in service for a time. But the railroads began the same sort of rear-guard action to get rid of the ferries as they used a few years earlier in getting rid

of passenger trains, and eventually they succeeded. One ferry, the *Badger,* built in 1953, is no longer owned by a railroad and has been converted to carry automobiles. So far she has been commercially successful, during the summer months carrying autos and passengers across Lake Michigan from her base at Ludington.

SEEANDBEE

The Cleveland and Buffalo Transit Company, which owned a number of Lake Erie passenger and package-freight steamers, in 1912 took stock of its position. What it saw was good. Between 1893, when it was founded, and 1911 its gross earnings had risen by over 400 percent. The C & B Line decided that the time was ripe for further expansion, and in April 1912 the stockholders approved construction of what would be the largest passenger steamer on inland waters anywhere in the world.

The new vessel was designed by Frank E. Kirby, the well-known marine architect whose sidewheelers were his most famous products. She was 500 feet long and 98 1/2 feet in beam, had six decks, 510 staterooms, and 24 parlors. Her engines provided 12,000 hp and she cruised at 18 1/2 mph. This crowning achievement of the prewar era was launched in November 1912 at Wyandotte, Michigan, completed and fitted out during the winter, and sailed from the yard in June 1913. She was launched without a name, but with a large

The *Seeandbee* operated in the days when smoke was only a symbol of power and air pollution had not been heard of. (*–The Mariners Museum, Newport News, Va. PB 309*)

question mark painted on either side of her bow. The company, as part of a vast advertising campaign, was holding a naming contest. The winning name, submitted by a schoolgirl, was *Seeandbee*, and it was as the *Seeandbee* that the great steamer first arrived in Cleveland on the afternoon of June 19, 1913.

The many people who lined the lake front to greet the new boat saw an enormous vessel, with four great smokestacks rising above her six decks. Those who went aboard found the ultimate in Edwardian opulence. Passengers first entered a lobby on the main deck, where there were the purser's and steward's offices, telephone switchboard, and check room. Aft of the lobby was the big dining room; forward was the freight deck (advertised as accommodating a full trainload of freight) and the engine room. Above the main deck were three decks of staterooms and parlors, in the center of which rose

the grand saloon, a room three decks high. The woodwork throughout the passenger areas was finished in mahogany and ivory. The most elaborate of the staterooms had brass beds. (The brass bed seems to have been the symbol of luxury afloat on passenger ships of this era; the psychological reasons are interesting to surmise.)

The same day, the Great Ship *Seeandbee*, as the company liked to call her, left Cleveland at 10:00 p.m. on her first trip to Buffalo. On board were members of the Wholesale and Manufacturers Board of the Chamber of Commerce. Thereafter she ran between Cleveland and Buffalo, normally running opposite the *City of Buffalo*, which had been lengthened to 340 feet in 1906 but still was dwarfed by the larger vessel. Usually the heaviest traffic out of Cleveland was the Friday evening exodus to Niagara Falls, the heaviest traffic out

Above: The *Seeandbee* as viewed from above. (*—Great Lakes Historical Society, Cleveland*)

Left: The grand saloon of the *Seeandbee* in all its Edwardian splendor. (*—Institute for Great Lakes Research, Bowling Green State University*)

Interior view of the wheelhouse of the *Seeandbee*. In this builder's photo, taken before the vessel went into service, the control station looks positively antiseptic. Note the spittoon seen through the wheel at bottom right. (*—Institute for Great Lakes Research, Bowling Green State University*)

of Buffalo the Sunday evening rush to get back to Cleveland. In order to handle this situation, the line normally ran the *Seeandbee* out of Cleveland on Friday evening, then brought her back on Saturday by day, so that she could carry the fairly large number departing on Saturday for Buffalo and then could bring all the week-enders back to Cleveland on Sunday night.

Owners of night boats were uneasily aware that not all travelling couples were married, at least to each other. About all they could ask was reasonable discretion on the part of such voyagers. They did, however, make considerable effort when assigning single passengers to staterooms (almost all of which were doubles) not to mix the sexes. But one day when the manager of the C & B Line started to read a letter he had received from a

clergyman who had taken recent passage he saw trouble ahead.

The reverend gentleman related that he had bought a lower berth and had been assured by the ticket seller that he would have the room to himself. He sat on deck until nearly midnight, went to his room, undressed, and went to bed. In the morning he rose early and discovered a woman in the upper berth. At this point in the letter the manager expected to be threatened with anything from a lawsuit to a religious crusade; but to his surprise the minister simply asked that if the subject ever arose with his family or his congregation the company would testify that it was no fault of his. Heaving a large sigh of relief, the manager immediately sent off a letter of apology, assuring the clergyman that if the certificate ever were needed it would be forthcoming. He never heard anything more of the incident.

World War I loomed on the horizon. A series of marine disasters on both the high seas and the Great Lakes from 1912 through 1915 dampened public enthusiasm for water travel. The LaFolette Seaman's Act of 1915 required such large crews that thereafter the big steamer could run profitably only between May 15 and September 15. The *Seeandbee* survived, operating on her limited schedule, but the company dropped any plans it may have had for a sister ship.

The *Seeandbee* continued in service until the depression year of 1932, when she was laid up. From 1933 onward she went on Lakes cruises during the summer months rather than running as a night boat. But the combination of spreading highways and improving cars, the still-unpaid part of the debt incurred in building the *Seeandbee*, and the expenses of improved fire protection for its entire fleet, caused the company to go bankrupt in the spring of 1937. It reorganized and decided to give up all activities except the big ship's summer cruises, but it was unable to raise even enough money to run the *Seandbee*. It leased her to another firm that ran her during the season of 1940 and bought her in 1941.

The next year she was sold to the U.S. Navy to be made into a training aircraft carrier for World War II. She became one of the two sidewheel carriers ever known. The *Seeandbee* was stripped of her upper decks and refitted with a 550-foot flight deck. Operating out of Chicago under the name U.S.S. *Wolverine*, she trained pilots seven days a week throughout the year; during the winter Coast Guard icebreakers escorted her. Altogether she trained some 18,000 aviators who made a total of 65,000 landings aboard her during the war. In 1945 she was retired and in 1947 she was scrapped.

————

The Great Ship *Seeandbee* was launched too late. She was a product of the Edwardian period, a time of comfort and stability for the middle class and the well-to-do. Being one of its finest developments, she came at its end. When a World War smashed its foundations abroad and workingmen challenged its assumptions at home, the era suddenly ended. The big steamer quickly became a relic from another day, although she continued on like a grand but threadbare lady wearing the fashionable clothing of her youth. Bigger sidewheelers would be built during the boom of the 1920s, but they would have short lives. After 1914 the world of the elaborate, multidecked sidewheel passenger boat was nearly as distant as the world of Cleopatra's barge.

7
Into the Present

*W*orld War I shattered the comfortable Edwardian pattern of life. It enlarged existing economic problems and brought a host of new ones, leading a decade afterward to the Great Depression. At the same time it brought enormous technical advances. The internal-combustion engine, for example, was perfected and mass-produced under wartime pressures and emerged in a form that revolutionized transport; radio was developed to a point where it was not only a practical means of communication but soon also a source of entertainment in every household. The first Great War ushered in the modern era, laying the groundwork for its problems and its achievements.

As the war progressed, the industries grouped about the Lakes turned to production of war supplies. Rural workers, among them many black people, were drawn to the booming factories of the Great Lakes cities. Shipyards there began to build vessels to carry wartime cargoes and new shipyards sprang up. After the war the economy, freed of its wartime burdens, raced ahead into the boom of the '20s; it was the period of flappers, petting parties, and speakeasies. Rumrunners in a variety of high-powered small craft scooted furtively across the Lakes, circumventing Prohibition. Both passenger and freight vessels became larger and larger. Wealth and income steadily increased.

The stock market crash of 1929 which followed was so dramatic that it normally is used to mark the beginning of the Depression, although there were earlier symptoms of trouble and the depths of the economic slough were not reached until later. From the early '30s till the Second World War, Lakes shipping followed the overall pattern of general retrenchment. Many of the largest vessels were laid up; few new ones, and none of any size, were built.

The war years again brought a great increase of activity much like that of 1914-18. In 1940 the big passenger boats were back in service and making money. By 1941 the shipyards were booming and in 1942 lake and ocean freighters were again sliding down the ways of Great Lakes yards. Warships of various sorts followed. The big new lake freighters broke carrying records as they moved larger and larger cargoes of ore to the roaring steel mills. Concentrated wartime technical advances once again brought new developments; perhaps the most important to shipping was radar.

Some historians believe that the changes since 1940 have been as great as those in all the preceding centuries of the human race. These years have brought revolutionary advances in many fields. In 1939 influenza and pneumonia still killed about as many people as cancer; in 1940 serious study of nuclear fission had just begun; in 1944 the first automatic, general-purpose, digital computer was unveiled. Scientific and technical progress has been coupled with a general economic prosperity. The real income of American workers doubled between 1939 and 1964. Many aspects of life have changed. Statistics can be quoted to show everything from a huge increase in the number of houses with baths to a great concentration of people in urban areas. Cars and highways multiplied fantastically. Jet aircraft appeared. Television became a universal presence.

The impact of all this on Great Lakes shipping is still hard to measure. Improved technology certainly helped to construct the St. Lawrence Seaway, which at last made the Great Lakes part of the world's oceans, but the increased wealth available in our society was probably what really did the job. The most obvious developments are part of long-term trends; autos and wages have dealt the final blow to passenger travel; the ever-growing value of time has increased the navigational season; every move of the economy has forced us toward larger and larger freighters.

EASTLAND

Before the days of mass-produced cars, excursions were a popular way of taking an outing. During 1914 and again in 1915, the passenger steamer *Eastland* carried many of them out of Chicago. Built at Port Huron, Michigan, in 1903, she was mainly an excursion boat, a handsome one very much in the style of her day. She was 269 feet long with a beam of 36 feet. In appearance she was the exact opposite of the broad sidewheelers; she gave somewhat the impression of a knife on edge, rising high above the lake, an impression borne out even more when her twin propellers drove her through the water at a speed of 22 mph.

The *Eastland* operated first out of Chicago, then between Cleveland and the amusement park and resort area of Cedar Point, and finally out of Chicago again. During the time she was based at Cleveland she was popularly called "Speed Queen of the Lakes." On at least one occasion she made the round trip to Cedar Point in a blow that kept her sidewheel competitors at their docks, and her crew was proud of her and her status. But her tendency to list suddenly and drastically when she turned under power scared a few timid Clevelanders, who refused to travel on her.

In 1914 she was back in Chicago. On Saturday, July 24, 1915, she and several other excursion steamers docked at the Chicago waterfront to take aboard the annual outing of Western Electric employees, most of them factory workers, who were to be carried to Michigan City, Indiana. The dock at which the *Eastland* tied up was somewhat higher than her passenger gangway, so she was lightened by pumping some 800 tons of water out of her ballast tanks. She then rose in the water sufficiently that the gangplank could be placed between ship and dock.

Passengers began to come aboard. When she was about half loaded, those aboard congregated along the dock sides of the upper decks to hear the bands and watch the throngs below. The ship listed toward the dock, once again causing problems at the gangway; this was reported to the officer on the bridge who notified the engineer to straighten ship. The engineer pumped 400 tons of water into the ballast tanks on the side away from the dock; those on the dock side still were empty. The ship straightened up; she would have listed strongly the other way except for the numerous mooring lines used to hold her to the dock because of the heavy current in the river at that point. (The current was out of the lake, up the river, in the direction of the Chicago Drainage Canal.)

In due course about 2,500 people were all on board. The captain arrived from his duties uptown, obtaining clearances and doing the routine administration before a voyage, and proceeded to the bridge. Knowing nothing of the water ballast he ordered the mooring lines cast off. The *Eastland* then took a decided list away from the dock. At about this same time a fireboat passed on the river, and the excursionists crowded to the outer rail to see it. Further, the pilings of an old wharf had been cut away underwater by the city to permit steamers to land there, but they had not been removed entirely as they should have been; the steamer's bottom on the dock side came to rest on them and they propped up that side of her hull as the other began to settle in the water. And a number of her lower deadlights, just above the normal water line, were open. The water rushed in.

A deck hand on one of the other steamers saw her going. "'My God,' I whispered to myself, 'The *Eastland* is lurching!'" He and two other deck hands ran to launch a boat. One little girl who was on board the *Eastland* recalled that as the ship tilted the passengers came tumbling down a passageway and the force of their bodies pinned her against the railing. Then she found herself under water. "I wanted to scream for mother as I kept going down but whenever I opened my mouth water would rush in and start to choke me." Finally she grabbed a man's foot and he hauled her to the surface.

An eighteen-year-old boy who was on one of the upper decks with a young friend recalled:

> All of a sudden, the boat lurched. Folding chairs started sliding to the river side. We heard loud crashing from below decks, and people started screaming.
>
> The ship slowly turned over, and Joe and I started scrambling for the railing near the shore side. We got there and crawled over the railing onto the hull as the boat settled in the water.

Above: The *Eastland* shortly before the disaster. **Below**: The result. (—*Both, Chicago Historical Society*)

Right behind us was a man who hooked a cane on the railing. We helped him over the side, and as we did, we could see people in the water. Men were holding women by the hair. The screaming was awful. People were calling out, looking for loved ones.

The deck hand from the nearby steamer *Theodore Roosevelt*, who had launched the lifeboat with two others, was named Jack J. Billow. He described what followed:

> The scene was horrible. People were leaping from the *Eastland*, screaming and crying, waving their arms. Acting quickly, we rowed to the capsized ship where we helped people from the water and saw them safely to shore. Then we decided we could give more help in the water. Donning lifejackets, we leaped in and formed a human chain from the starboard side of the *Eastland*, the decks of which were still above water, to the docks. We passed people down the line to safety.
>
> Warehouse employees of nearby warehouses, meanwhile, were throwing barrels, boxes, crates—anything that would float—to others standing nearer the shore to be thrown into the water for the victims to cling to. Police, fireboats, tugs, private yachts, Coast Guard boats, waterfront factory workers and passersby soon crowded the scene to help in the rescue operation.
>
> However, we were unable to help hundreds of victims. Many were trapped inside the *Eastland* and others in the water panicked. Their instincts for self-preservation overrode all other feelings. I saw many a drowning person push someone else under in his struggle to stay above water.
>
> Mothers and fathers ranged the shore, screaming the names of their children. The bodies of the dead floated past, ignored by the rescuers who were trying their best to save the living. . . .

By then there were so many boats at hand that Billow and his companions left the water and began to help with the job of bringing the dead up from inside the hull, "where picnic hampers, derby hats and vacuum bottles bobbed alongside the bodies."

The work continued for hours. Torches were used to cut through the hull so as to remove bodies that were then taken to morgues set up in warehouses and armories. For five or six days afterward, long lines of people filed through the morgues, trying to identify missing victims, some of whom were never found. Reports of the number lost vary; the best figure seems to be 835. In any event, it was the greatest disaster in all the history of Great Lakes shipping.

Immediately there was a great public outcry, led by the Chicago *Tribune*, which headlined, "Nation, State and City Join to Place Guilt." Everyone involved in the disaster was blamed by someone and also blamed someone else. All of the crew members were placed under arrest; the captain and chief engineer were accused of criminal negligence. The owners were accused of running an unseaworthy ship and the U.S. Steamboat Inspectors of permitting an unseaworthy vessel to operate. The City of Chicago was accused of having an unsafe shipping terminal.

Commissions, courts, and boards of inquiry were hurriedly appointed by various city, county, state, and federal agencies. These bodies with overlapping jurisdiction, all holding hearings, did little to clarify the charges and countercharges. The hearings dragged on and on; it was not until 1935 that the U.S. Court of Appeals threw out the last of the lawsuits, thereby bringing the matter to an inconclusive end. No one was ever found guilty of anything, although one court did state that the basic fault was that of the engineer who controlled the ballast tanks. The company was found blameless and liable only up to the salvage value of the ship.

One of the expert witnesses called during the early hearings was Capt. Merwin S. Thompson of Painesville, Ohio, her former master. Driving from his home in Painesville into Cleveland on the morning of the disaster, he was halted by police officers who were looking for him on all the roads between the two cities. He was hurried to Chicago to give testimony. There he maintained stoutly that nothing whatever was wrong with the ship and that any ship would have foundered under the same conditions. Her later career seems to prove that he was right.

The *Eastland* was raised, righted, and towed to a shipyard. The First World War was exploding in Europe and on the high seas; ships were at a premium and the United States Navy was among those who needed them. The Navy bought the ship and remodeled her into a training vessel, but the work moved slowly because of the growing shortages of materials. She was ready in 1918 and was renamed U.S.S. *Wilmette*. Between the wars she was given new

The launching of *War Fox*, an ocean freighter built on the Lakes for the Cunard Line during World War I, at Wyandotte, Michigan on November 3, 1917. Such vessels built for British owners all had the prefix *War* in their names. When the U.S. entered the war this vessel was taken over by the U.S. government and became a "Laker," the U.S.S. *Lake Forest*, carrying mines for the Navy. (*—Institute for Great Lakes Research, Bowling Green State University*)

engines and further remodeled, and she traveled over 150,000 miles on training cruises. After further training service during the Second World War she was finally scrapped in 1948. Never during her naval service did she cause any trouble.

WAR FOX.

With the outbreak of World War I there was a great shortage of ocean shipping, and European shipowners turned to builders wherever they were available, among them to those on the Great Lakes. Since the early 1890s Great Lakes shipyards had launched occasional steel ships for ocean service. If they were too long to fit the canals, they were cut in half and taken piecemeal through the locks. After 1901, when enlargement of the St. Lawrence canals was completed, a vessel 260 feet long and 43 1/2 feet wide could go through intact and several that approached those dimensions had been built on the Lakes for salt water use.

Scandinavian countries placed some of the first war orders. Naturally the orders were for vessels that could pass easily through the canals and equally natu-

rally they were for vessels of a type that had evolved on the Baltic and North Sea, medium-sized ships of what was known as the Frederickstad design. These were compact steamers with the typical ocean freighter profile: machinery, deckhouses, and bridge amidships and a small raised forecastle and poop deck. The vessels were well adapted for coastal use, and so they were also being built for other European nations and for the American coastal trade. The design was standardized, some prefabrication was used, and they were turned out at a number of Great Lakes ports.

As the pressure for wartime construction increased, new yards were established. One of these was erected at Rice's Point, Duluth, in 1916 by the McDougall-Duluth Corporation. Its moving spirits were Capt. Alexander McDougall and his son Miller. Captain McDougall, then 71, travelled to Washington to get contracts and designed the first ships that were built by the yard. The first one, the *R. J. Barnes*, not too surprisingly looked rather like a whaleback although she also incorporated some of McDougall's later theories of ship design. Soon,

Seen here at Boston in 1927, the *Lake Benbow* was a typical "Laker," an ocean ship built on the Lakes for U.S. World War I service. Most had the prefix *Lake* in their names. (*—Institute for Great Lakes Research, Bowling Green State University*)

however, the yard was forced to produce the standardized wartime cargo ships being turned out by everyone else. Captain McDougall stayed with his shipyard until the end of the war; then he retired, looking back on a life in which he had "built eight shipyards, four drydocks, and 200 ships."

The Cunard Steamship Co., the famous British line, placed orders with Great Lakes builders for a number of freighters similar to the Frederickstad design. They were called War ships because the first word of each name was "War"; among them were the *War Banner, War Bayonet*, and *War Bugle*. Sometimes the two words came together strangely, as in *War Pansy*. One of these vessels, built by the Detroit Shipbuilding Company at Wyandotte, Michigan, was the *War Fox*, 251 feet long, 43 1/2 feet wide, and of 1948 gross tons.

Five of the War vessels were delivered to the British owners. Then in 1917 the United States entered the conflict, and shortly afterward the U.S. Shipping Board requisitioned for service under the U.S. flag all ships building on the American side of the Lakes. (The War vessels building on the Canadian side were of course not affected.) The Cunard Line and the various other people who had ordered ships were acutely unhappy and much litigation followed, but the ships after that were operated by the American government. Altogether the U.S. took over 99 that were building in Lakes ports for ocean service. (Of the original Frederickstad ships, 26 had already gone to salt water.) The *War Fox* was one of the 99.

The board also awarded contracts to Great Lakes shipyards for 346 more ships, of which 331 were eventually built. Most of these were slightly modified Frederickstad vessels. There were small variations in design, the ships of this class ranging from 251 to 253 1/2 feet in length and varying in depths of hull; all

Greater Detroit, passing the city of Detroit on her way to her dock. (*—Dossin Great Lakes Museum*)

were 43 1/2 feet wide. These were the "Lakers," so called because they came from the Great Lakes and most of them were given names beginning with the word "Lake." Supposedly Mrs. Woodrow Wilson originated this naming system.

Thirty-odd Lakers, however, were given names that did not include the word "Lake." Most notable was the oddly-christened *Crawl Keys*. She was built in 1918 at Ecorse, near Detroit, in 29 days, the record for World War I. In time she was sold to Japanese owners, becoming the *Keizan Maru*. On March 10, 1945, the U.S.S. *Kete*, a submarine built at Manitowoc on Lake Michigan, sank the Ecorse-built *Keizan Maru* in the South China Sea.

The *War Fox*, requisitioned by the government, become the U.S.S. *Lake Forest*, a mine cargo carrier. On March 4, 1919, she was decommissioned by the Navy and turned back to the Shipping Board. She was then sold to Belgian owners and renamed *Venetier*. Through the following years she sailed under many flags and was renamed many times. Successively she became the *Tabakhandel, Este, Chollin, Rafael Aritzia, San Patricio, Mary V.*, and *Kadio S.* Finally she was scrapped in Spain in 1960.

GREATER DETROIT

The Detroit and Cleveland Navigation Company, largest passenger and package-freight operation on the Great Lakes, prospered during World War I despite growing labor problems and wartime priorities on such things as the coal used by its steamers. Only its Mackinac line suffered, and not long after the war the D & C abandoned that division and sold the boats.

Throughout its long life, starting with the original line between Detroit and Cleveland, the D & C relied on traditional Lake Erie sidewheelers. They had many advantages: the sponson construction of the hull with its wide overhang provided more room than there would be on a propeller of equal length; the paddlers were steadier in a choppy Lake Erie seaway; and they had less vibration—all things of value to passenger ships. Further, the shallow waters of Lake Erie tend to shift with the wind, sometimes changing as much as four feet in depth over a short period; paddle vessels generally drew less water than propeller vessels and so were less apt to find themselves suddenly blocked from entering a Lake Erie harbor. Since 1878 the D & C vessels had been designed by Frank E. Kirby, naval architect of the Detroit Dry Dock Company. Kirby attained much fame as the designer of handsome sidewheelers and the D & C gave him many of his design opportunities. In 1907 and again in 1912 a big Kirby-designed steamer joined the fleet, but during the war years no others were built.

As the United States moved into the affluent 1920s, Warren G. Harding was nominated as Repub-

Above: A stern view of *Greater Buffalo* gives some feeling of the size of one of the two largest paddle-driven vessels ever built anywhere.

Right: The grand salon of the *Greater Detroit*, shown here in one of a series of renderings of the ship's interior prepared for the D & C lines. The D & C preferred "grand salon" to the more generally used term, "grand saloon," perhaps because Prohibition forces had managed since the turn of the century to equate saloons with low dives in the minds of the public. The decorations of this big room, though less ornate than those of earlier night boats, are in keeping with the taste of the 1920s, the era of the *Greater Detroit* and her sister *Greater Buffalo*. (—*Both, Dossin Great Lakes Museum*)

A corner of the dining room of the *Greater Detroit*, as depicted in a rendering of the steamer's interior. (*—Dossin Great Lakes Museum*)

lican candidate for president and then elected. Upon his nomination, the president of the D & C Line, A. A. Schantz, who had known the genial Harding since he was a Marion, Ohio, newspaper editor exchanging passes on the D & C for advertising space, wired him, "Accept the hearty congratulations of one of your old Buckeye friends." Schantz spoke for many Americans, not just Buckeyes (Ohioans), who now reacted equally against wartime problems and the liberalism of Woodrow Wilson, and who wanted, in Harding's phrase, to "return to normalcy."

For the D & C, normalcy included more Kirby ships. In 1922 the company obtained bids on two new vessels designed by Kirby, now an elderly man. Over the next two years the steamers were built at Lorain, Ohio, and in the summer of 1924 they became part of the D & C Line. They were the *Greater Detroit* and her sister *Greater Buffalo,* each 518 feet long with a beam of 100 feet. They not only were the largest passenger ships on the Lakes, but also the largest true paddlers ever built. (The British *Great Eastern* of an earlier era, their only possible competitor, had both paddles and a screw propeller.) The two new steamers, each of which had more than 1,500 berths, were put in service on the company's longest run, between Detroit and Buffalo.

One of the many unusual things about these two giants was that the company paid for them directly out of its treasury. No loans, additional stock issues, or other of the normal ways of raising capital were

necessary. The D & C was firmly in the black and, as Mr. Schantz pointed out in a news story upon delivery of the new steamers, it was consciously building for the future.

A. A. Schantz, known to many as "Gus," was a manager from a departing era, one who believed in personal control of his company. He read every letter delivered to it and none of the D & C steamers sailed from Detroit until Schantz stepped out on his office balcony and rang a bell. It had been hard for him to accept the seamen's union and the fact that he no longer was able to deal directly with many of his employees. But now that he had steered his company through the difficult war years and back into what he conceived of as normally prosperous times he felt properly optimistic in accord with this optimistic decade.

The *Greater Detroit,* like the *Greater Buffalo,* rose four decks above the water. The main saloon of each was on the promenade deck and rose through the interior of the ship for two more decks. Galleries along either side gave access to staterooms. The interior decoration was done by the New York firm of W. & J. Sloane & Co. in a free adaptation of Renaissance style. It provided a pleasant, clublike atmosphere a good deal more straightforwardly than the rococo interiors of the prewar D & C steamers; it was more in keeping with the times but somewhat disappointing to admirers of the older ships.

Through 1929 the D & C Line operated at a profit, although by 1928 there were signs of trouble

Rendering of a stateroom of the *Greater Detroit*. (—*Dossin Great Lakes Museum*)

around the Lakes. That year the company carried its greatest freight tonnage and received its greatest freight revenue, but also that year the Cleveland local agent of the Sailor's Union of the Great Lakes noted, "In so far as this port is concerned, all the newspaper talk about prosperity is all wrong. There are thousands of jobless men and women in Cleveland."

In 1928 the line also developed a plan to connect Detroit and Cleveland by Dornier flying boats, but first there were many problems to solve and then the horrifying year of 1930 put an end to any thoughts of expansion; revenue fell over 25 percent.

It fell nearly as much the next year and only a little less the next. The Buffalo-Detroit run, carried on mainly by the *Greater Detroit* and her sister, in 1932 actually carried more freight than in 1929, but the freight revenue was only 62 percent of that in 1929 and passenger revenue was far worse. This was a much better showing than most other ships were able to make; altogether in 1932 only 29 percent of the 1929 freight tonnage moved across the Lakes. That year one freighter sailed with a deck crew of five captains, two first mates, and three second mates, and an engine room crew of eight chief engineers and seven assistant engineers. Another had a deck

Greater Detroit in the white paint that she wore toward the end of her career. (—*Elwin M. Eldredge Collection, The Mariners Museum, Newport News, Va.*)

The *Lemoyne* docking at her home harbor of Midland, Ontario to unload grain at the elevators in the background. In this picture she is beginning to get a new paint job that has not yet progressed very far. (—*Watson's Studio, Midland*)

crew composed of twelve captains. Men of experience and responsibility felt lucky to sail as deck hands; the men who would normally be deck hands had no chance at all.

By 1938 business declined so that the *Greater Detroit* and her sister were laid up for the season. In 1939, however, business began to increase. The big boats went back into service until 1942, when the U. S. Navy took over the *Greater Buffalo* and converted her, like the *Seeandbee*, to a side-wheel aircraft carrier for training Navy pilots. The two vessels were the only ones of the kind ever known, but their big overhanging sponson decks made them ideal for the purpose. During the war the *Greater Detroit* and her smaller fellows ran with freight decks jammed and passenger accommodations reasonably full. Afterward, however, they came once again on evil days. The internal-combustion engine now was king. People travelled more quickly, in better cars, over better roads; as the greater part of the D & C's income had been from passenger travel, that alone was a tremendous blow. Trucks, using those same roads, were faster and more flexible carriers of package

freight. Maritime wages and other costs rose steadily. More specific disasters struck the company: in 1950 one of its steamers collided with a salt-water freighter and not only was damaged beyond repair but also was found to have been at fault; and the City of Detroit, redeveloping its waterfront, condemned the D & C terminal. In 1951 the D & C suspended operations.

After being laid up several years, the *Greater Detroit*, biggest passenger ship on the Great Lakes and biggest sidewheeler in the world, in 1956 was intentionally set afire to gut her wooden superstructure and leave only her metal hull to be scrapped.

LEMOYNE.

The Georgian Bay lumberman and shipowner, James Playfair, in 1916 constructed a shipyard in place of his big mill, thus finally moving completely out of the dwindling lumber business and into the expanding shipping business. The first vessels he built were salt-water freighters for the Imperial Munitions Board—vessels much like the *War Fox*. They were launched too late for war service, however, and there-after the yard turned to building freighters.

Most Playfair ships had names beginning with the prefix "Glen." Some he bought and renamed, others he built at Midland; eventually he owned about forty of them. In 1926 he launched the biggest freighter on the Lakes, christening her *Glenmohr*. At the same time, however, he completed arrangements to sell his fleet and shipyard to Canada Steamship Lines, and so when the big new freighter steamed out of Midland harbor on her shakedown voyage, the name *Lemoyne* was painted boldly over the old name, which still could be seen faintly underneath.

Once again, Mr. Playfair had moved out of a business at the right time, selling his fleet almost at the height of the boom; after 1929 no one wanted to buy a ship, let alone a fleet of them. On that summer day in 1926 when the *Lemoyne* headed out into Georgian Bay on her first trial run, he held a party aboard this last big vessel that he was to build, inviting a number of his friends. (It perhaps should be noted that this was a very decorous party; Playfair, born in Scotland, was a good Presbyterian and a thoroughgoing teetotaler.)

As the big steamer ran in circles, testing her steering gear, the guests sat in deck chairs and ate sandwiches. In the middle of Georgian Bay they seemed an infinite distance from shore. One of them, a doctor, relaxed in comfortable isolation from his normal cares. He was standing near the after deckhouse and suddenly started when a telephone rang near at hand, shattering the illusion of complete separation from the world. In the same way there were beginning to be economic signals that the boom of the '20s was not to be completely isolated from unpleasant fiscal reality.

Since the end of World War I, freighters 600 feet long had become standard on the Lakes. Almost every new carrier built was about 600 feet long with a 60-foot beam and 32-foot depth. The *Lemoyne* changed all that. She was the longest and largest ship on the Lakes, 633 feet in length, 70 feet in beam, and 29 feet in depth. The next year an American steamer was built that was 5 feet 9 inches longer, but 5 feet narrower.

After that the *Lemoyne* was not quite the longest, but she remained the largest. Ships, like houses, are three-dimensional objects. A two-story house is not necessarily larger than a one-story house, nor is a longer ship necessarily larger than a slightly shorter one; in both cases it is the amount of space inside that counts. This is why sailors usually rate ships by tonnage. A ton is, among other things, a measure of enclosed space. The definition of a ton has changed with the years, however. When Commodore Perry's ships were built on Lake Erie during the War of 1812, a ton was 40 cubic feet of enclosed space; today it is 100. There also are several different kinds of tonnage and nearly every seafaring nation has its own formulae for determining them. Thus comparison of tonnage becomes a technical exercise often more confusing than helpful.

It is enough to say that the *Lemoyne* broke all the carrying records on the Lakes for grain and coal and then broke her own records. She held world records for the quantities of those items that she carried. Throughout the Depression years she remained the largest freighter on the Lakes. In 1942, when Canadian vessels were allowed to participate in the U.S. ore trade under stress of wartime conditions, the *Lemoyne* promptly added to her honors a cargo of 17,080 tons of ore, breaking all previous records for that commodity. But in 1942 a number of new bulk carriers were launched on the American side of the Lakes and several of them exceeded the *Lemoyne* in size.

She continued in service for many years, however. Meanwhile the St. Lawrence Seaway was opened; immediately there was a change in the patterns of shipping, especially on the Canadian side of the Lakes, where grain was the primary cargo. The big freighters loaded at the Canadian Lakehead cities of Fort William and Port Arthur (today combined in the one city of Thunder Bay) with grain brought from the prairie provinces; formerly they carried it to ports on Georgian Bay and Lake Ontario for transshipment to Montreal or ports farther east, but now they went directly down the Seaway. Soon the demand was for vessels of the maximum length that could go through the locks, 730-footers. Canada

U.S.S. *Waxwing*, a mine sweeper, one of the many naval vessels built on the Great Lakes during World War II. Here she is in lock No. 1 of the St. Lawrence and Lake Ontario Canal, on August 14, 1945. She was on her way to the Atlantic when VJ Day was accounced. (—*Courtesy Robert Berger*)

Steamship Lines began to equip itself with ships of the maximum Seaway length.

In the later 1960s CSL also began weeding out many of its older vessels and selling them. The *Lemoyne* was laid up at Kingston in the winter of 1968-69, and her owners announced her retirement. In 1969 she was towed across the Atlantic for dismantling in a European shipbreaker's yard. Even in passing she made a record: she was the newest and largest freighter yet to go to such a fate.

WAXWING

Great Lakes shipyards responded to the Second World War even more vigorously than they had to the First. In 1943 and 1944 they turned out 35 N-3 cargo ships, vessels not unlike the "Lakers" of the First World War. In 1944-45 they also built 82 C-1 cargo ships, somewhat larger diesel-powered vessels. But in addition to merchant ships, during this war they produced a number of naval vessels that ranged from the twenty-eight 310-foot submarines that were built at Manitowoc (and floated down the Mississippi) through frigates, landing craft, and motor torpedo boats. Nearly every Great Lakes port of any size built some type of vessel for the war effort.

The American Ship Building Company at Cleveland and Lorain constructed a wide assortment of wartime vessels, over eighty of them altogether.

Among the more specialized ones were the mine sweepers, built there in both 180-foot and 220-foot lengths, the latter being actually 221 feet over all and 32 feet in beam. The 220-footers, called auxiliary mine sweepers, were intended to precede convoys or fighting ships and clear the way in unknown waters. (Ships of this type were later classified "fleet mine sweepers," which more clearly suggests their work.) Altogether 16 of this largest size of mine sweeper were built at these yards. The order for the last eight of them was split between the facilities at Cleveland and those at Lorain, and the final vessels were just being completed when the war ended. (An interesting sidelight is that a number of smaller vessels were built earlier in Canada under U.S. Navy contract and then transferred to the Royal Navy on lend-lease.)

These mine sweepers were all named for birds. On August 6, 1945, the U.S.S. *Waxwing* (AM-389) was commissioned at Cleveland, at the East Ninth Street Pier; on the 11th she sailed for salt water. She carried a crew of 100 men and 5 officers; Lieutenant Commander Rowe was her skipper. Through the Welland Canal she went and across Lake Ontario. Like all mine sweepers she was inclined to roll and pitch in a seaway. Such vessels are designed with rounded, shallow underbodies to that the concussion of an exploding mine will push them up out of

Launching of the *Noronic* at Port Arthur (now Thunder Bay) Ontario, June 2, 1913. (—*National Archives of Canada C 31495*)

the water instead of crushing them. A certain lack of stability results. On one occasion during a trial run on Lake Erie a number of senior officers were on board, and when a civilian electrical engineer felt queasy and headed for the rail he was comforted to find that many of the distinguished visitors joined him.

This engineer, Robert C. Berger, was one of a two-man team. Each mine sweeper going down through the canals carried one engineer representing General Motors Corporation. The vessels were driven by a complex diesel-electric system and had electronic sweeping and other gear; the two engineers were there to make last-minute adjustments if necessary and train the crews in use of the equipment. Berger was the electrical engineer aboard the *Waxwing* on her voyage from Cleveland to Montreal.

This vessel, like all of her 220-foot sisters, had four 800-hp V-16 diesel engines each driving a 750-kw D.C. generator, which in turn was connected to a 750-hp motor. Two motors drove each shaft. There were two engine rooms: the propulsion equipment in the forward one drove the starboard propeller, that in the after engine room the port propeller. In addition she had three 150-hp straight-8 diesels, each driving an alternator to provide electrical power; two were in the forward engine room, one in the after. Much duplication was thus provided to ensure against failure of the system. One engine room could be knocked out entirely and the ship would still be able to operate.

Ships of this class were armed with two twin 20-mm guns, two twin 40-mm guns, a three-inch gun, and depth charge racks. No ammunition was put aboard until the vessel reached Montreal on her way to the sea.

The *Waxwing* was dwarfed by the freighters she met in the Welland Canal and on Lake Ontario, but after she passed through the Thousand Islands she saw few other ships. On the evening of August 13 she tied up at Ogdensburg, N.Y., for the night. Next morning she entered lock No. 1 in the St. Lawrence and Ontario Canal. While locking through, her commander received word by radio that hostilities had ended in Japan: it was VJ Day. Cap-

tain Rowe made the announcement over the ship's public address system: "Now hear this. . . ." He also announced that as soon as the ship reached Montreal, liberty would be declared immediately for the first section.

As they progressed through the Soulange and Lachine locks, the gates of which still were operated by hand cranks, the captain sent the whaleboat ahead with a detail of men to handle the lines, a job normally done by the lockmen, thus saving time. Where possible he shot rapids instead of using canals. When finally they reached Montreal, it was the evening of August 15, but the city was still celebrating madly.

NORONIC

By 1949 the 362-foot passenger steamer *Noronic* was the only ship being operated on the Sarnia-Lakehead service of Canada Steamship Lines. This vessel, of 52 feet beam and 29 feet depth, had been launched in 1913 at Port Arthur (today's Thunder Bay) for the old Northern Navigation Company, latterly the Northern Navigation Division of CSL. The run was no longer an especially prosperous link in the big CSL operation. As a result, the *Noronic* began to end her normal service rather early and go on one or two postseason cruises each year. These were well advertised, the ship usually was quite full, and both the owners and passengers found them rewarding.

In September 1949 the *Noronic* started off on such a cruise. She picked up passengers at Detroit, then at Cleveland, and headed through the Welland Canal to Lake Ontario. There were 524 passengers aboard. After a stop at Toronto she was bound for a cruise of the Thousand Islands area of the upper St. Lawrence. She docked at the foot of Bay Street, Toronto, at 6 p.m. on Friday the 16th; there she was to remain until the next afternoon, giving her passengers an opportunity for sight-seeing and shopping. The captain and most of the crew went ashore.

About 1:15 a.m. a passenger walking along a corridor saw smoke coming from a linen closet. The door was locked. He got a bellboy and the two of them opened the door and made some attempt to fight the flames with hand extinguishers. As another

Above: *Noronic*, as recorded by the noted marine photographer Capt. William J. Taylor. (—*Dowling Collection, University of Detroit Mercy*)

Below: The *Noronic* at Midland on a cruise during the 1930s. The boxy little steamer at lower left is the *City of Dover*, which ran in conjunction with the *Midland City*. (—*National Archives of Canada C 31465*)

Noronic burning in Toronto harbor on the morning of Sepember 17, 1949. (*—Toronto Telegram Syndicate*)

passenger said, they might as well have tried "to put out hell with their fountain pens." The fire spread quickly. The bellboy then rang an alarm which sounded in the officers' quarters, stewards' quarters, and engine room.

The first officer, who was in his quarters, went up to the pilothouse and threw the switch that sounded klaxon horns located throughout the ship. He also blew the whistle; because of some failure in the mechanism it continued to blow on and on, until a lack of steam caused it to falter.

Captain Taylor, returning to his ship at about this time, took charge of the fire fighting. He manned a hose, assisted by one crew member and some passengers; then as this proved useless he and the few crewmen on duty attempted to rouse the passengers. No one seems to have thought of giving the alarm ashore and it was not until 2:38 a.m. that a pier watchmen saw flames and turned in an alarm to the city fire department.

Many of the passengers did not wake up. Those who did reacted in various ways. One man dragged ashore a woman who had collapsed, went back and carried out a man who was badly burned, and was about to go back again. "I saw someone in uniform and heard people shouting at me, and then as I turned to go back in, I was struck on the back of the head. I think someone slugged me to keep me from going back. I could hear people and little children screaming."

In contrast, a woman passenger reported, "A rope was tossed over the rail and I put a hitch knot on it to hold it to a stanchion. As I did so, three men pushed in front of me and shoved some screaming women out of the way. They went down the rope." Another

Noronic still smolders at her Toronto pier on September 17, immediately after the fire. The middle picture shows the port side, toward the bow, and the vessel's gutted condition. At bottom is the litter of the *Noronic*'s top deck, looking toward the stern. (—*All National Archives of Canada, top C31497, center C 31496, bottom C 31498*)

woman commented, "There was so much panic that I don't know how these people found a way to safety."

About a hundred passengers crawled aboard the *Cayuga*, a steamer tied up near the *Noronic*, but then she too started to burn and had to be moved away. Passengers jumped indiscriminately to the dock, injuring themselves, and into the water. One man who did not panic told how he got his family to safety.

> We went to the side of the boat away from the dock. There was one lifeboat not close to the flames. Some of us worked to release it. It was terrible. We didn't know how to do it. There was a young cabin boy who was fine. He helped all he could.
>
> We finally got the boat even with the rail and outside the rail. I pushed my wife and young people in. Some others climbed in. So did I.
>
> It seemed like hours getting down the side of the ship. People kept throwing purses and baggage into the boat. Someone jumped in from another deck and hurt my wife's ankle.
>
> Water came in the boat and half filled it. Finally we were on the water. We got the hook released from one end of the boat, but we couldn't get the hook free at the other end. We found a hatchet, but even that wasn't much help.
>
> People were screaming above us, and the flames were getting worse. A woman jumped from B deck into the water. We got her into the boat, but she was pretty near gone. I helped fish out a man. He was stark naked and bleeding badly down his legs. A boy in pajamas threw us his grip, jumped in the water, and swam to the boat.
>
> Somehow we got the other hook loose. But the boat was so full of people and water it seemed we must sink. Just then a police launch came by and threw us a line with a life preserver on the end. We pulled our boat over to theirs, and everybody climbed on the police boat. By this time the sirens and whistles were drowning out the screams of those still on the ship.

Before long 18 fire engines and 2 fireboats were at the scene. It was five hours before the fire burned down sufficiently that firemen could go aboard. There they found the remains of many people who had been trapped, among them family groups with their arms around each other. The final count of dead was 104 passengers; 14 were missing. None of the crew died.

Passengers, wandering away from the ship, congregated in various places. Many went to the nearby Royal York Hotel. One man who had no clothes whatever was hurriedly given a topcoat from the hotel lost-and-found department. The people of Toronto quickly did whatever they could for the survivors. A clothing store was set up in the Royal York that gave free clothes to the victims. A taxi driver picked up four dazed men, drove them to a clothier's and told the manager to put the bill on his charge account; the manager refused, saying it would be on the house.

On September 28 a government Court of Inquiry into the disaster was convened. It continued to sit, with some recesses, until November 21. In general it found that there was a lack of serious planning for such a fire and that when it did come there was a failure to take effective action to wake the passengers and get them ashore.

The burning of the *Noronic*, the greatest disaster on the Lakes since the *Eastland* capsized, foretold the end of Great Lakes passenger service. The Canadian and American governments began to enforce more and more stringent safety regulations on Lakes passenger vessels. All those in service were old; the passenger business had been declining for years; none of them could meet the new regulations. It was too expensive to rebuild them, let alone build new passenger ships. Over the next few years passenger shipping would be forced from the Great Lakes.

IMPERIAL LEDUC

The brief if active career of the *Imperial Leduc* and her sisters, world's largest fresh-water tankers, illustrates both the hazards of changing conditions and the competitive nature of Great Lakes shipping.

In 1951 the handsome big *Leduc* was built at the Collingwood Shipyards on Georgian Bay. She was 620 feet long, 69 feet in beam, and had a capacity of 125,000 barrels of crude oil. That same year a sister ship was launched at Port Arthur and in the following year another was launched at Collingwood. All three were powered with steam-turbine engines that provided 4,500 hp and all were relatively fast, being capable of 14 1/2 knots.

Imperial Oil Ltd., the Canadian arm of the Standard Oil empire, had been the first company to operate a tanker on the Lakes—the *Imperial* of 1909—and since that time had built up a sizable fleet as

The *Imperial Leduc*, first of what was known as the Leduc Class of tankers, the largest on the lakes. These vessels went out of service when a pipeline was extended from the head of Lake Superior to Sarnia. (—*Courtesy Imperial Oil Limited*)

well as fleets on the Atlantic and Pacific Coasts. Lake tankers primarily delivered petroleum products from refineries to marine terminals, where they would then be distributed to consumers. Thus Imperial Oil was familiar with the operation of tankers, and when in 1949 it became evident that the Leduc oil field in Alberta could produce enough oil to be useful in Ontario refineries, and a pipeline was built from Edmonton to Superior, Wisconsin, Imperial's next move was obvious. The company decided to build tankers that would carry the crude oil from Superior to its marine base at Sarnia, and construction of the three ships followed.

The *Imperial Leduc* in all her glory carried the first cargo of oil from Superior to Sarnia in April 1951, being welcomed by the premier of Ontario, the president of Imperial Oil, and a group of other dignitaries. Television and radio reported the ceremonies. But in December 1951 she made another kind of news. While she was cleaning tanks at Sarnia there was an explosion that injured five men, one of whom later died, and that damaged her hull extensively. The cause is uncertain, but it may have been an electrical defect. The vessel was taken to Toledo, Ohio, for repairs and returned to service in midsummer 1952.

During the navigational season the three ships travelled steadily back and forth between the two ports. They could load about 25,000 barrels per hour at Superior and unload about 20,000 barrels per hour at Sarnia, so their turn-around time was brief. Of course it was to their owner's advantage for them to start work as soon as possible in the spring. The power of their engines and shape of their hulls made them good icebreakers and they were usually among the first vessels in service.

But storm clouds were blowing up ashore; the management of Imperial Oil was beginning to have second thoughts. Although the pipeline ran all year, the tankers only operated during the navigational season. It would have been possible to build large oil-storage facilities, but that did not seem efficient. Instead, the answer seemed to be to extend the pipeline, and this was done. The line now enters the United States south of Winnipeg, crosses the Straits of Mackinac, and recrosses into Canada at Sarnia. From there it goes on to the refining center of Clarkson, just west of Toronto.

As a result, the big tankers were no longer needed. At the end of 1953 the *Imperial Leduc*, barely three seasons old, and her two sisters, one a year younger, were sold. The two other vessels were almost immediately converted to dry bulk carriers; the *Leduc* was renamed *Nipigon Bay* and operated by Canada Steamship Lines for several years as a tanker; and then she too was converted to a dry cargo ship. She ended service in 1982 and after being idle for several years, was scrapped in 1989.

British American Oil, which had also built a tanker to the same plans as the *Imperial Leduc,* had its vessel shortened. Tanker business on the Lakes returned to the business of smaller vessels—from 300 to 400 feet in length—delivering refined products to consumers. The fine big tankers were gone, victims of rapidly changing conditions.

MIDLAND CITY.

In addition to large ships that operated over long distances, through the years many smaller vessels carried passengers and freight on shorter voyages. There were, for example, the *Maud,* a 120-foot sidewheeler launched at Kingston, Ontario, in 1871; the *America,* a 153-foot sidewheeler that operated on the St. Lawrence from 1895 until 1920; and the *Midland City,* a twin-screw diesel vessel that was finally retired from her Georgian Bay run in 1955. Each was a typical small coastal ship, and each was a different name for the same vessel.

As the *Maud* she was built for C. F. Gildersleeve of the noted Lake Ontario shipping family and named for his young daughter. Her iron plates and frames were made in Scotland, then shipped to Kingston and assembled there; outside the iron plates her hull was covered with heavy oak planking. Her steam engine was built by Gildersleeve. In time she was sold, then lengthened and renamed *America.* In 1921 she was again sold to a group of businessmen who named her *Midland City* and put her on the Georgian Bay run between Midland and Parry Sound; in 1933 she was converted from steam sidewheel to twin-screw diesel propulsion; in 1955 she was scrapped.

The latter part of her career is of even more interest than her surprising longevity. It is noteworthy that the final long-distance passenger-and-package-freight services on the Lakes, as provided by the *Noronic* and her Canadian Pacific competitors, and the last short-haul services of the same kind, as provided by the *Midland City* and a few others, were on the Canadian side of the upper Lakes. Among the reasons for this were the northern shores of Georgian Bay, the North Channel, and Lake Superior, which were composed of the ancient, hard, and unfriendly rock of the Canadian Shield. These areas were settled late and are still settled sparsely, and constructing roads through them is a discouraging job. Therefore the car and truck entered later onto the scene along these shores, and small vessels lingered on. Until almost the end of the *Midland City's* life,

The *Midland City,* one of the last small coastal steamers, before her 1933 conversion from a steam sidewheeler to a diesel-driven propeller. (*—Huronia Museum, 1986-20-24-22*)

The *Midland City*, after being converted from a steam sidewheeler to a twin-diesel propeller, carrying an excursion party along the northeastern shore of Georgian Bay. (—*National Archives of Canada C 31609*)

it was simpler to drive one's car aboard her for transport from Midland to Parry Sound than it was to drive over the indirect and bad roads between one place and the other.

She was the last of a series of little steamers that had plied the same route, along the Inside Channel and through the Thirty Thousand Islands of the northeastern shore of Georgian Bay. She was the primary means by which people and provisions moved to the many summer homes along that shore. Each day, a short time before noon, a fast train known as the "Flyer" reached the Midland dock, carrying vacationists bound up the shore. (Today even the name of the train seems quaint.) Shortly after noon the *Midland City* sounded her whistle and pulled away. She travelled all afternoon and evening to Parry Sound, stopping at innumerable small landings. Next morning she returned to Midland.

The vacationists she carried might be an academic party bound to the Madawaska Club, a Toronto University settlement; or they might be a group of teenagers with bicycles and knapsacks bound to the northwoods via Parry Sound. Many passengers reverently carried fishing tackle. Families lined the upper decks. Travellers took photographs of the scenery as canoes and sailboats crisscrossed the channel. Boats converged on landing places ahead of the ship

and their occupants climbed out to wait impatiently on the dock until the mail was delivered.

Before World War II the fast train was discontinued and the track was taken up; a diesel rail car came by a roundabout way, but then it too was discontinued. After the war roads were put into many places along the Bay shore, so that cars and trucks could reach them easily. Motor boats multiplied almost as quickly as the cars, becoming faster, smaller, and less expensive in the process; the internal-combustion engine now could take a summer cottager directly to his island home. The *Midland City* was old and decrepit and apt to sink without warning; often her captain had to run her aground in a sheltered place until she could be repaired. After the *Noronic* disaster it seemed hopeless to try to rebuild her to fit the stricter regulations that were about to be enforced. Then her owners became involved in a strike and sold her to another group that ran her for a year or two from the nearby town of Penetanguishene. Finally she was laid up and scrapped.

The peculiar conditions that sustained the *Midland City* for so long disappeared rather quickly, and as a result what happened to her provided something like a speeded-up film of the demise of all the other little ships. Cars, trucks, and highways first destroyed the rail service that supported her, then penetrated along the shoreline that she followed and

The *Concordia* passing through the newly opened St. Lawrence Seaway. This small German ship has more in common with the vessels that used the older St. Lawrence canals than with the larger freighters that were to follow her, but in her way she is as significant as the *Columbia* of an earlier day. (—*Photo by Malak, Ottawa, courtesy St. Lawrence Seaway Authority*)

destroyed her own traffic. Small, fast motor boats carried people easily from the ends of the roads to their island cottages. Rising wages increased expenses of running the ship at the same time that her income went down. Her age and the stricter fire regulations helped end her career. But if little coastal ships had been economically sound at that time and place, a newer, safer vessel would no doubt have replaced her some years before that.

None did. Probably none ever will.

CONCORDIA

On April 25, 1959, the St. Lawrence Seaway was opened to traffic. One of the first vessels to pass through that day was the *Concordia,* a West German freighter 243 feet long and of 36 feet beam. Her home port was Hamburg although she had been built in Denmark. She was the harbinger of the many salt-water vessels that would follow her in successive days and years, and her presence emphasized the future possibilities for direct shipping through the Seaway between Great Lakes and foreign ports.

The opening of the Seaway that day culminated years of hoping and working. Ever since the Erie Canal, completed in 1825, drained away much of the Lakes cargo that formerly had gone via the rapid-filled St. Lawrence River to Montreal, there had been plans for St. Lawrence canals. But the results always lagged far behind the dreams, and these canals were built slowly and built small. After World War II, when Canada and the United States entered the most prosperous era in history, pressure for a real ship canal increased.

There were two basic ideas. First, an improved St. Lawrence canal system would in effect extend the Great Lakes complex as far as the lower St. Lawrence and at the same time extend the useful range of Lakes shipping. Second, the ports on the Lakes wanted access to salt-water shipping; they long had chafed at the idea of receiving and sending goods overland through Atlantic coastal ports.

The Great Lakes-St. Lawrence chain runs along the southern edge of the two largest Canadian provinces; nearly everyone there stood to gain from an extension of lake shipping. In addition, Toronto and Fort William (now Thunder Bay) welcomed access to salt water. On the American side, the iron-receiving ports on Lakes Erie and Michigan also wanted to extend their reach to the lower St. Lawrence; they were haunted by the specter of diminishing ore resources on Lake Superior and attracted by new ore discoveries north of the Gulf of St. Lawrence. Cities such as Chicago and Toledo very much wanted to reach salt water and then via the oceans reach overseas ports. On the other hand, Buffalo saw itself losing all the traffic that flowed through its harbor en route to New York, and all of the U.S. Atlantic coastal ports saw themselves being deprived of cargoes. Thus while Canadian opinion was solidly in favor of the Seaway, American opinion, even in the Great Lakes ports, was divided.

Actions of the two governments reflected this difference. In 1950 they were able to agree on a secondary matter, that the 160-foot drop of the international section of the St. Lawrence should be harnessed to produce hydroelectric power. But when, the following year, the Canadian Parliament established the St. Lawrence Seaway Authority to build a deep waterway, the United States lagged behind. It was not until 1954 that the U.S. Congress established the St. Lawrence Seaway Development Corporation.

Engineers then started work on a coordinated project site 334 miles long, from Montreal to Lake Erie. Five years later the Seaway was opened. Meanwhile towns were moved house by house and chan- nels dug; locks and dams were built and hydroelectric stations installed. Five new locks were built on the Canadian side, two on the American. The most expensive mile of the entire Seaway lies in Canada. It is the channel between the Upper and Lower Beauharnois locks, constructed in an area of hard, abrasive sandstone. A four-lane tunnel for auto traffic runs directly under the lower lift lock. The construction cost $50 million.

During the 1959 navigational season, 2,152 other vessels followed the *Concordia* through the Seaway; the greatest number, 647, came from the three Scandinavian countries of Denmark, Norway, and Sweden. Next in number were the 520 ships from the United Kingdom; then came the 448 from West Germany. (The novelty of the new passage soon wore off, and the numbers decreased considerably.)

The impact of all these vessels on the Great Lakes was enormous—and chaotic. Rules of the road on the Lakes were different from those on the high seas and ships' officers were often confused. Salt-water vessels, unused to canals and narrow channels, barged into anything they approached: the walls and gates of canals, navigational aids, lake freighters, and rocks. During the first several seasons of Seaway operation, nearly a third of the world-wide marine casualties reported were on the Great Lakes and St. Lawrence. The term "salty"—the lake sailor's term for an ocean ship or an ocean sailor—came to mean someone who could not handle his ship properly in close quarters.

Meanwhile those who lived around the Great Lakes began to worry about all the things people can worry about. Those who lived near the ship channels worried because the whistles kept them awake at night. Summer cottagers worried because the wakes of passing ships might damage their docks and boathouses. Public health officials worried about the added sewage dumped into the Lakes by the additional ships. And people who lived in Duluth worried about the girls from the twin city of Superior who—they said—stayed all night on ships in the Superior-Duluth harbor, while people in Superior worried about those same girls who were—they said— from Duluth.

The bateaux used in building the Seaway were smaller versions of the boats used on the St. Lawrence since early French times. Commonly called "pointers" by English-speaking Canadians, the boats are employed most often in logging activities on the rivers tributary to the Great Lakes. These pictures were taken during a river drive on the Mississauga River of Ontario in 1949. Below, the bowsman of a bateau running the rapids. (—*Both, courtesy Ontario Department of Lands & Forests*)

Ocean ships coming into the Lakes found that from their viewpoint things could be much improved. The Welland Canal became a bottleneck and ships queued up to enter it, as many as ninety of them at a time. Each ocean vessel had to have a pilot to guide her through the Lakes, but there weren't enough pilots and those that were available often were not well trained. Few Lakes ports had made adequate preparation for ocean shipping, outstanding exceptions being Toronto and Milwaukee. Most of the others were like Detroit, where two bond issues for harbor improvements had been defeated and where a German captain asked in irritation, "Didn't you people expect ships?" The cities suddenly if belatedly started to build harbors for ocean freighters, harbors that expanded more and more in the years that followed.

The *Concordia* was relatively small; the largest saltwater cargo ship to sail the Seaway that season was the 610-foot Norwegian tanker *Solviken*, which passed through upbound in late July. The *Concordia* was small, but her significance was enormous. She was small enough to have passed through the old St. Lawrence canals but instead was one of the first vessels to come in through the new Seaway, which made the Great Lakes seem truly part of the global oceans. Thus she represented both the largest type of salt-water ship that could have entered the Lakes before the Seaway and the smallest type that would enter them in future.

THE BATEAU (III)

Building the Seaway required a great deal of the most complex and largest construction equipment that technology could provide. But it also required those most traditional of fabrics, fifty-five bateaux.

The bateau is one of those simple but inspired designs that, like the canoe, has gone on for centuries. It is heavier than a canoe but is less fragile and requires less specialized building techniques. For general freight work on the St. Lawrence and its tributaries, such as the Ottawa, the bateau in more recent times became mainly a work boat in the lumber camps from Maine to Minnesota.

At the height of the Ontario lumbering period, activity centered on the Ottawa River. In the 1850s John Cockburn, an English immigrant from

Newcastle-on-Tyne, a fine boatbuilder and carver of ship's figureheads, settled first in Ottawa, then moved to Pembroke. J. R. Booth, the Ottawa lumber king, persuaded him to turn out boats for river driving. Cockburn produced what English-speaking lumbermen called a pointer, but what was actually a well-built and refined small bateau. His version was extremely popular. For years his shops turned out 200 pointers annually. He was succeeded in the business by his son, John Cockburn.

It was the second John Cockburn who built the boats that were used in construction of the Seaway. Cockburn pointers were still used mainly by lumbermen, but they also were popular with mining, power, and construction organizations, wherever sturdy but responsive work boats are needed. They were used in establishing the DEW line in the far north and two were employed for harbor control at Churchill, on Hudson Bay. It was natural that when boats were needed for Seaway construction, the Cockburn pointers, smaller editions of the old St. Lawrence bateau, were the craft selected.

The boats were built of much the same materials as the early French bateaux. The planking was white pine; the frames were cut from white cedar roots. Oars were made from red pine or white spruce, cut to a standard 10 1/2-foot length; paddles were made from yellow birch or white oak in a 7 1/2-foot length. After the boats were planked they were dressed with a traditional preservative of double-boiled oil and jeweler's rouge that gave them a venetian red color, the mark of a Cockburn product.

The Cockburn boatyard also started building similar craft with a square stern and an inboard jet engine that can travel at 30 mph with a heavy load. Thus when necessary the traditional bateau can even move at a modern speed.

ASSINIBOIA

Competing with the *Noronic* and her predecessors that ran from Sarnia to the Canadian Lakehead, were Canadian Pacific Railway steamers that connected Georgian Bay ports with the Lakehead. This Great Lakes fleet was the oldest CPR marine operation, begun long before either the Pacific or Atlantic

Above: The *Keewatin*, sister ship of the *Assiniboia*, at the Georgian Bay harbor of Port McNicoll, the eastern end of her run. She has just discharged passengers for the Toronto boat train, seen at extreme left. (*—Capt. Ted Belcher Collection, Huronia Museum*)

Right: *Assinboia* at Port Arthur (now Thunder Bay) the other end of the line, after a November voyage in 1913. (*—National Archives of Canada C 31613*)

About 1919 the Canadian Pacific changed the color of its hulls from black to white. Here the *Assiniboia* approaches her Port McNicoll dock. In this picture she is shown at her handsomest, after her wheelhouse was raised to the level of the bridge, but before the three tall masts were removed and twelve feet were lopped from her stack when she was converted from coal to oil burning in the winter of 1953-54. (—*Marine Museum of the Upper Lakes*)

Ocean services of the Canadian Pacific. Until 1912 its southeastern terminus was at Owen Sound; that year the CPR moved to Port McNicoll, where it had built its own docks, freight sheds, and town. The Great Lakes service of the Canadian Pacific ended in 1965.

All but one of the Lakes ships owned by the CPR were built in Scotland. When growing business led the company to order two more ships they again ordered Clyde-built steamers. The new ships followed a precedent set by the first three CPR vessels: they steamed across the Atlantic, were cut in two so they could come through the canals, and then were put together again. In 1908 the *Keewatin* and *Assiniboia* went into service. They were passenger and package-freight steamers each 336 feet long, 43 feet in beam, and 26 feet in depth.

Five CPR steamers continued full service until the middle of World War I. Then the two oldest were retired from passenger runs and used only to carry package freight; when the Depression came they were laid up. During World War II they carried freight to and from Chicago and Milwaukee, but after the war they were retired, and in 1950 a third vessel was scrapped. As a result of the regulations enforced after the *Noronic* disaster, the two remaining and newest CPR ships—by then over forty years old—during the winter of 1949-50 were fitted with steel fire bulkheads, sprinkler systems, and new fire-fighting equipment.

Typical of many of the voyages that the *Assiniboia* made during those forty years was the one that began on November 30, 1936. It was not typical in two ways, however, being the last voyage of the season and the last in the career of her master at that time, Capt. James McCannel, commodore of the CPR fleet who had commanded the *Assiniboia* for twenty-four years. As the captain left the door of his Port McNicoll home at 6:00 a.m. the thermometer registered half a degree below zero and moonlight still touched the snowy streets.

The ship was laden with thirty or forty carloads of jute bags, canned goods, package freight, and general merchandise. On her return trip she would bring back flour in bags. Her crew was happy to make this last trip: it would bring in money to help fill the Christmas stockings. They put on all the clothes they owned and set to work getting her ready to sail.

At 8:00 a.m. they cast off and the ship began to grind her way out through the six-inch ice that extended from Port McNicoll until she reached open water near Hope Island. At 1:00 a.m. next morning she again pushed into ice, this time in the St. Mary's River as she approached the Sault Canal. There she met a steady stream of freighters bound down with the final cargoes of the season. As the *Assiniboia* and the freighters passed, two of the latter froze in and could not move. Captain McCannel used the bow

Assiniboia, with shortened stack and two short masts. This picture by Robert A. Zeleznik shows her in 1959 at Fort William with all flags flying. Note the blue peter, the rectangular blue and white flag at the foremast—the international signal that a vessel is ready to sail. (*—Courtesy Robert A. Zeleznik*)

of his ship to "whittle, hack, and hew" them out, according to the marine journalist and historian C.H.J. Snider, who went along as the only passenger. At noon the captain locked into the Canadian canal after fourteen hours on the bridge. By 1:00 p.m. he headed her out into the gray-green water of Lake Superior. There was not much wind or sea, and the ship moved steadily ahead.

This was in contrast to her previous voyage. Then, with less freight to hold her in the water than this time, she met a mile-a-minute wind and "leaped and ramped like a mare gone mad."

> She had abused everybody that last trip—chased Afternoon Sandy, the water-tender, out of the firehold and into a Fort William hospital, having hurled an anvil after him and caught him in the foot. She threw Miss Thompson, the stewardess, out of her bed onto the washstand and piled a dressing table on top of her. She hurtled one of the firemen into the coal pile and sent another ploughing the steel floor of the firehold with the bridge of his nose. Engineers held the fire doors open and the stokers' shovels aimed at one door registered on another. Half a dozen men were hurt by flying furniture.

On that trip, as Captain McCannel fought to keep her in open water and away from a lee shore, the storm made a shambles of things on board. But on this quieter voyage the *Assiniboia* smoothly approached the twin cities of Fort William and Port Arthur prior to daylight on December 2, and "before the white-collared world had sat down for breakfast" longshoremen were unloading the freight.

Later in the morning the *Assiniboia* shifted docks to load the flour; later yet she took on coal as fuel. Then back down gray Superior went the ship without incident, and the captain got his first full sleep in three days. Nothing untoward happened until on approaching the Sault they found that a turning buoy was missing. Captain McCannel anchored for an hour until the snow cleared enough that he could find his way (this was of course before the days of radar). With ten inches of ice reported in the river ahead he decided to tie up overnight at the government dock.

At 8:00 a.m. on the fourth, they pushed off. The ice in the river was not caked and the steamer passed through easily and went into Lake Huron. Not another ship was in sight and not a plume of smoke; the navigation season was at its end. Down Huron and into Georgian Bay she went. Near Hope Island, about midnight, they met the ice again and learned that the whaleback *John Ericsson* had been stalled in it for thirty hours. By 1:00 a.m. on the fifth they were grinding their way through. At 2:30 *Assiniboia* jammed and stuck, three nautical miles from Port McNicoll.

The captain rang off the engines and waited until it began to be light. Before dawn he backed her up and started forward again. At sunrise he dressed ship with every flag aboard. The ship crept ahead. The last half mile took her two hours. "Louis Belanger, wheelsman, got off and walked home with his laundry under his arm when his watch ended. He just stepped from the passenger gangway and struck across the ice, a quarter of a mile from the dock."

During the winter of 1953-54 the *Assiniboia* was converted to an oil burner and given a new boiler; her stack was shortened twelve feet to provide the right draft for the new fuel. Her sister ship, the *Keewatin*, was scheduled for the same work at a later time, but this was never done; it had begun to be evident that these ships were nearing their end. All other scheduled passenger service on the Lakes had disappeared, but for a time the CPR boats kept on.

The last boat train on the North American continent still ran from Toronto three hours north to Port McNicoll, where it pulled out beside the waiting steamer. Passengers from the train walked to the ship through a carefully tended formal garden; little muzzle-loading cannon pointed out to sea. The *Assiniboia* or her sister lay at the dock with the blue peter flying at the foremast. (This rectangular blue and white flag is the international signal that a ship

U.S.C.G.C. *Mackinaw*, built primarily as an icebreaker. The shape of her bow permits it to ride up over ice, crushing it with her weight. (*—Official Coat Guard photo, courtesy Ninth Coast Guard District*)

The *Mackinaw* in an ice pack. (—*Courtesy Ninth Coast Guard District*)

is ready for sea; on the Great Lakes the CPR vessels were among the few that used it.) Five minutes before sailing time two short blasts of the whistle called the crew to quarters. The uniformed mates stood by the shore lines. At sailing hour on signal from the bridge the lines were let go; the engine room telegraph rang slow ahead; and as the ship moved away from the dock the blue peter was lowered from the mast.

At 6:00 p.m. a bugle sounded the first call to dinner. Waiters stood at attention in the dining saloon; during the summer when passenger travel was at its height many of them were college students. The passengers moved into the Edwardian elegance of the saloon where, amid surroundings of wooden panelling and polished brass, crisp white napery contrasted with the silver sugar and cream dishes and flatwear, and with the brightly colored flowers on each table. In the background an orchestra played dinner music. Later, if the weather was good, the orchestra moved to a sheltered deck area set aside for dancing.

But the Canadian Pacific was in a multiple squeeze. Cars and highways were inexorably growing in number. The Canadian government was inexorably stepping up the safety requirements. The ships were still fast and nimble, but they were old by almost any standard, and they could not easily be altered to meet the new regulations. The thought of new ships became ridiculous when their cost was compared with the dwindling revenue from passenger traffic. Wages grew higher. It seemed that the entire economy of North America was conspiring against the business of coastal passenger traffic.

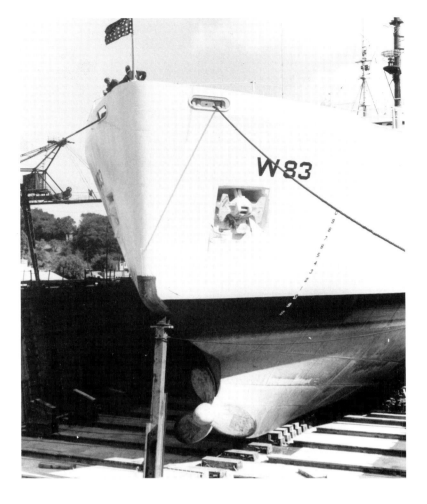

Bow of U.S.C.G.C. *Mackinaw*, showing the bow propeller, which pulls water out from under ice, and the shape of hew bow. She also has two much larger stern propellers that provide her main propulsion. (—*Official Coast Guard photo, courtesy Ninth Coast Guard District*)

The two steamers kept on through the 1965 season. But on November 28, when the *Assiniboia*, under Capt. Ernest H. Ridd, moved out from the Port McNicoll dock, the blue peter fluttered down to mark the beginning of the end. This was not only the last CPR passenger voyage but also the last scheduled passenger voyage by any line on the Great Lakes. On board were two passengers, both representatives of the Great Lakes Historical Society.

MACKINAW

The great demands on industry for the effort of World War II brought great demands on lake freighters to carry raw materials, especially ore, to the mills. But whenever the weather was really cold, the ice in Lake Superior, the Sault, the Straits of Mackinac, and other key points froze so solid that freighters could not push through. Something had to be done to reduce the length of time that ice blocked navigation. It was an accepted governmental responsibility to maintain the waterways; on December 17, 1941, ten days after the attack on Pearl Harbor, the gov-

ernment authorized construction of a Coast Guard icebreaker powerful enough to open these passages.

On December 20, 1944, a 292-foot Coast Guard cutter was commissioned at Toledo, Ohio. The *Mackinaw*, as she was named, was then the most powerful icebreaker in the world. She proceeded to her home port of Cheboygan, Michigan, arriving on December 31. Soon afterward she gained the nickname that has stuck with her ever since, "The Mighty *Mac.*"

The *Mackinaw* has hull plating 1 5/8 inches thick from her keel to above her water line. She is heavily framed. She has six 2,000-hp diesel engines connected to six electric generators. They in turn drive the propulsion motors of 5,000 hp each; and the three motors drive two stern propellers and one bow propeller. (The stern propellers each weight 10.7 tons, the bow propeller weighs 7.2 tons.) The ship breaks ice by riding over it, forcing it downward. Meanwhile the bow propeller weakens the ice by sucking water out from under it and forces a stream of water along the hull, reducing friction between the vessel and the ice through which it is cutting.

In the spring of 1956 prolonged cold weather kept the ice at the eastern end of Lake Superior from softening. On April 2 the *Mackinaw* passed through the locks at Sault Ste. Marie and came out into the frozen expanses of the big lake. She quickly met ice thirty inches thick, but she pushed straight ahead at a steady eight miles per hour. Occasionally she met pressure ridges, thicker bands of compressed ice. Only one of these, a band fifteen feet deep, stopped her. She backed up half a mile, thrust forward again, and chopped into the ice so hard that chunks flew into the air on either side. Gordon Macaulay, a newsman who was on board, reported:

> The worst ice was found in the area between Gros Cap and Parisienne and for the first day the *Mackinaw* made several parallel cuts in this area over a course of five to seven miles. Almost playfully at times she would cut visible figure eights with all the grace of a figure skater across the parallel cuts she had previously made. At other times she would get into one of the cuts and run the length of it at full speed, her wake smashing ice for some distance on either side, and doing considerably more damage than her original passage. With darkness the ship wedged herself into the ice and quietly lay until morning.

The second day of these operations was the first 24-hour period in 187 days that the temperature had not gone below freezing. The ship continued her work, but the weather steadily grew worse and by 9:00 p.m. the wind had risen to 65 mph and there was a violent electrical storm. There was also a thick fog. The vessel kept on cutting away, guided by her radar. "The shrieking of wind, roll of thunder, and crunching and grinding of the vessel through the ice created an unbelievable din and a setting which defies coherent description." After fifteen hours of steady work, Capt. Clifford MacLean pulled the *Mackinaw* into a sheltered spot and waited until morning. Then he found that her labors and the storm had freed the ice; he radioed the Sault that freighters could now be permitted to enter Lake Superior, and the steady procession began.

Three years later, in the spring of 1959, the *Mackinaw* faced a different problem on Lake Superior. This time, after one of the severest winters on record, the ice extended ninety miles westward from the Sault. The stockpiles of ore on the lower Lakes were getting perilously small, and new supplies had to get through. Leaving the ice undisturbed except for the cut she made, the big icebreaker sliced steadily westward. Once in open water she met the first three freighters of the season downbound with ore; they had cleared Two Harbors, Minnesota, at about the time she cleared the Sault. The *Mackinaw* turned around and led the freighters carefully back through the cut made by her outward passage, leading them around the heavier packs, always in communication with them by radiotelephone. Meanwhile the pilot of the helicopter that rode on her afterdeck stood by in his rubber survival suit, waiting for any emergency; luckily none developed. The ship continued breaking ice and leading vessels back and forth for the next two weeks. (Once the ice disappears from the Lakes, the *Mackinaw* turns to the normal police and rescue duties of any Coast Guard cutter, though recently there have been suggestions that she should be laid up during warm weather.)

The *Mackinaw* has continued to be the centerpiece of icebreaking which is carried out by both the U.S. and Canadian Coastguards, who also have smaller icebreakers that they use both to assist her and to clear other areas in the Lakes. The tremendous ice flows that pack up at Buffalo, for example, are broken in the spring by smaller icebreakers. Occasionally the U.S. Coastguard has brought polar icebreakers in from the Atlantic to help.

But in the mid-1990s, the Coast Guard has repeatedly tried to get rid of her, though pressure from shipping lines has so far kept her active. By 1995 she was, after all, fifty years old—an extended old age for most ships. Her age makes her more and more expensive to maintain, and if she continues she will need a thorough overhaul and rebuilding at considerably greater expense. The Coast Guard does not have the money, and assures the shippers that it can do an equally good job with smaller, less expensive icebreaking tugs. Thus far, the skeptical ship owners have won.

Their point was proven in the spring of 1995. Shipping began to move near the end of March after the winter lay-up was over and after a relatively mild winter was past, but northeast winds drove a

The *Grande Hermine*, a maximum-size Seaway freighter, plies the Lakes from Superior to the lower St. Lawrence with bulk cargo. In the middle photograph she loads grain at Thunder Bay, Ontario, to carry it to a port on the Gulf of St. Lawrence. At bottom is a view from the bridge of the *Grande Hermine* while entering a full Seaway lock before being lowered to the next level. Upbound vessels below wait their turns. (—Top, *courtesy St. Lawrence Seaway Development Corp., middle and bottom, photographs by the author*)

ten-foot-thick accumulation of ice into the entrance of Duluth-Superior harbor. Eight vessels trying to enter or leave the port on March 27 found themselves locked in the ice, which reached about seven miles into the lake. The Coast Guard Cutter *Sundew* arrived to help, but was not able to break the jam. Mid-day on the 28th *Mackinaw* arrived and went to work, carving the stranded vessels out of the ice. She remained in the area, continuing to free newly arriving ships, until her help was no longer needed.

A major development over the years also made it worthwhile to break ice in the winter. The steel industry, the driving force behind most Great Lakes shipping, once used natural hematite ores: large hunks of rock that had to be dug out of the ground, carried to ports, and dumped into ships through pocket docks. When the temperature reached freezing, the natural hematite ore froze; it would not drop from rail cars into dock pockets or down chutes from the pockets into freighters. If it was in a freighter's hull and froze there, unloading became a major problem; the vessel with the ore might just be laid up until warm weather. But then in the 1950s, as hematite ores were becoming exhausted, the industry changed to taconite ore. It was processed near the mines and converted into small, dry, metallic pellets. The dry pellets were not subject to freezing, and the ore could be handled in the coldest weather; the ships then needed ice-free water to carry it to the mills.

The shipping season has gradually been extended by cooperation of U.S. and Canadian Coast Guards, shipowners, and ports. Before *Mackinaw* was commissioned, Great Lakes navigation was generally closed by ice for about four and a half months each year. After her arrival on the scene and with the work of others that time was reduced to an average of three months. In 1994 the Seaway closed on December 28, the Sault locks on January 15. Some years shipping can extend into February.

A few vessels may move over limited distances for specialized purposes throughout the winter, but they can not use the major canals. The Baltic Sea, perhaps the nearest equivalent to the Great Lakes elsewhere, has been opened to shipping year around, and there is no technical reason that the Lakes could not be kept similarly open, but there are many objections to working throughout the winter.

The objections come from groups ranging from environmentalists to ships' crews who want the midwinter break from work. Navigation through a cold winter would require considerable investment in bubblers—tubes on the bottom of harbors that emit air bubbles and keep the ice from forming—and ice booms, and there undoubtedly would be extra maintenance of vessels, patching them up after they met heavy ice. Further extension of the season probably will not occur unless there is extreme need, as there was during World War II.

GRANDE HERMINE

Grande Hermine was one of the ships of the explorer Jacques Cartier when he first visited the sites of Quebec City and Montreal in 1534. The *Grande Hermine* was also a maximum-size Seaway freighter built in St. John, New Brunswick, in 1963 for the Papachristidis Co. Ltd., a Montreal-based shipping firm.

The maximum-size Seaway vessels are perhaps most typical of all Canadian ships plying the Lakes today. Their dimensions have been standard: 730 feet in length, 75 feet in beam, and 25 feet nine inches in laden draught. Most typical of their trades is the carriage of grain from the Canadian Lakehead port of Thunder Bay (the city formed in 1970 by combining Fort William and Port Arthur) to the lower St. Lawrence, and the return transport of iron ore to the Great Lakes steel-making cities. The grain originates in the prairie provinces; on the eastern St. Lawrence most of it is reshipped abroad in ocean freighters. The ore comes from mines in northern Quebec or Labrador and most of it goes to U.S. steel mills.

The St. Lawrence Seaway is much more a Canadian enterprise than an American one. Five locks and four channels of the stretch between Montreal and Lake Ontario lie in Canada; two locks and one channel lie in the United States. A few channels are maintained jointly. The entire Welland Canal, which connects Lake Ontario with Lake Erie, is Canadian. Thus it is not surprising that most of the traffic between Montreal and Lake Ontario is Canadian or

The *Grand Hermine* and an ocean freighter pass in the Seaway. (—*Photograph by the author*)

A battery of improved Hulett unloaders at Conneaut, Ohio, unloads vessels carrying ore from the head of Lake Superior and those bringing it from the Gulf of St. Lawrence. Below, late-model Huletts in the hold of a freighter. They differ noticeably from the 1899 Hulett unloaders shown earlier, as the clear, open hold here differs from the cluttered construction of the hold in that picture. With the subsequent major change to self-unloading freighters, Huletts have disappeared from the Lakes. (—*Both, courtesy McDowell Wellman Engineering Co., Cleveland*)

that over half of that through the Welland Canal is Canadian.

Grande Hermine and the four other Great Lakes freighters of the Papachristidis fleet were sold in 1972 to Upper Lakes Shipping Ltd., and at that time her name was changed to *Canadian Mariner.* Like the other four, she is powered by General Electric steam turbines of 9,900 shaft horsepower that drive her at a loaded speed of 15 1/2 knots in open water. In common with several of them she has a bow thruster, a propeller in a tunnel at the forward end of the ship that can push the bow sideways in either direction, thus giving extra maneuverability in passing through locks and in docking.

After the Seaway was opened, and partly as a result of Canadian government subsidies for ship-

building which have since been ended, a number of maximum-size Seaway freighters were built. They were the largest vessels on the Lakes for a number of years. A few ships varied the arrangement, but most of them had the traditional profile, with pilothouse and navigational equipment all the way forward and machinery in the stern, and with a large stretch of open deck between. Such a boat was so big, and her hatch covers so large and heavy, that a standard feature became a travelling electric gantry crane running on tracks on the spar deck to lift and replace the covers.

Seaway-size lake freighters make the longest routine voyages of any Great Lakes vessels. They encounter the cold northern waters of Lake Superior, the short choppy waves of Lake Erie, the narrow congested rivers and canals of the Seaway, and the

Norwegian bulk-freighter motor ship *Rolwi*, designed for the Seaway, shown in the Eisenhower Lock on her voyage from Antwerp to Cleveland. Many of the ocean freighters that come through the Seaway are similar in appearance. (*—Courtesy St. Lawrence Seaway Development Corp.*)

Atlantic coastal traffic of the lower St. Lawrence. Their officers must be adept at responding to a great variety of situations and the ships themselves must answer to the men who guide them. They no longer are the largest vessels on the Lakes, but they probably remain the most able ones.

ROLWI

The Norwegian motor freighter *Rolwi* and her two sister ships, each 709 feet long and of 75 feet beam, built in 1968 and 1969, indicated the shape of things to come. They were specialized bulk carriers built for the Seaway that could bring steel into the Lakes and carry out such bulk cargoes as grain, and these were the primary overseas trades that developed.

It is an anomaly that coils or slabs of steel are classified as general cargo, which one normally thinks of as materials that travel in boxes, bags, or barrels—and often within containers—rather than in vessels designed to carry heavy materials. But that classification means that the same ships often carry general cargo into the Lakes and bulk cargo out of them.

Many small ocean ships have dropped out of the Seaway trade, so that the number passing through has diminished; on the other hand, most of the important ocean vessels are now too large to fit the Seaway. As a result, small-to-medium-sized ocean vessels, some of them built especially to enter the Lakes, dominate the trade. But ocean cargo makes up only a small part of total Seaway traffic, in most years well under ten percent.

Great Lakes cities have adjusted to the foreign vessels. Much of the outgoing grain is shipped from the twin cities of Superior and Duluth. Even the distress of

Periodically the locks of the St. Lawrence Seaway must be emptied of water so that maintenance can be done on them. This picture, taken at such a time, shows the size and construction of a typical lock. (*—Courtesy St. Lawrence Seaway Development Corp.*)

The *Manchester Mercurio*, a small ship designed to carry containers of general cargo through the Seaway, between Montreal and Great Lakes ports. She is shown here unloading at Milwaukee. This service was abandoned in the 1970s and relatively few containers now go through the Seaway. (*—Photograph by the author*)

local burghers that local girls were being smuggled aboard foreign ships to stay overnight has now faded. These days teen-agers are warned off, and as one newspaper put it delicately, "Adult women sometimes are invited aboard with the captain's permission."

Although steel and grain are predominant on the cargo lists, occasionally ocean ships have unusual cargoes. In 1993 the Russian *Viljandi* called at Toronto to unload Russian tractors and to load new and used cars for Poland and Russia. A ro-ro (roll on-roll off) vessel, she merely opened her huge bow so that the tractors could be disgorged and the cars could be driven aboard. At the same time, at another Toronto dock, heavy cargo was being loaded for a Taiwanese power station.

Four vessels especially built for operation through the Seaway are planned by Fednav International, a Montreal-based company. They are to be 656 feet long and 77 feet beam, taking advantage of an expected change in widths permitted in the Seaway; they are being built in China; and they are to be delivered in 1996 and 1997. The expected cargoes are steel coming in and grain and other bulk cargoes going out. These are the first new vessels built specifically for Great Lakes use since 1985, and if they prosper there may be more.

MANCHESTER MERCURIO

Manchester Mercurio was a little ship that tried to answer a question going back at least as far on the Great Lakes as the arrival of the *Madeira Pet*: what is the most efficient way to move ocean cargoes in and out of Great Lakes ports?

Ocean shippers use the term "general cargo" when they are speaking of the same thing that Great Lakes shippers have long called package freight—manufactured or processed goods in bags, bales, barrels, boxes, and similar wrappings. (A large exception is the steel coming from overseas into Great Lakes ports, which also is classified as general cargo.) The package freight business within the Great Lakes has disappeared, but since the opening of the Seaway there has been some general cargo—what in effect is ocean package freight—coming and going.

In the past few years a revolution has taken place on the ocean in the handling of general cargo. Much

227

Most general cargo now going out through the Seaway consists of agricultural and other materials sent by relief programs or to ports that do not have container-handling equipment. They travel in bags, crates, and similar packings. Here in Milwaukee harbor a freighter loads such cargo. (*—Photograph by the author*)

of it now goes in containers, metal boxes of standard sizes that can be carried by truck or rail as well as by ship. Their ease of handling and relative security against pilferage have made them increasingly popular. For a time older ships carried containers on deck and general cargo stowed in the conventional way in their holds, but now worldwide at least eighty percent of general cargo travels in containers. Specially designed container ships on the oceans are too large to enter the Seaway, and in any case would not spend the time required to move through it; to maintain their schedules they move quickly and spend the least possible time in port.

Few Great Lakes ports can provide enough containers to make a shipload, and the possibility of funneling containers from smaller lake ports to bigger ones, for further transhipment to a large ocean vessel would certainly be slower and probably more expensive than sending them overland to the Atlantic Coast.

A possible solution was the *Manchester Mercurio,* a ship designed to take containers in and out of the Lakes. She was built in 1971 in Spain and was 262 feet over-all, 42 feet in maximum breadth, and 18 1/2 feet in maximum draught. She and two similar ships were operated by a British company, Manchester Liners. They picked up containers brought into Montreal by the overseas container ships of the company and carried them to Great Lakes ports; there they picked up outward-bound containers and carried them back to Montreal. They were relatively small vessels with a capacity of about a hundred 20-

The *Huron*, last lightship on the Lakes, was decommissioned late in August 1970 and replaced by a battery-powered automatic buoy. She was third in a series of lightships that had been stationed on Corsica Shoals at the foot of Lake Huron since 1893. This particular vessel was launched in 1921 and was used in various places on the Lakes until 1935, when she was moved to the station where she remained for the next 35 seasons of navigation.

Lightships are traditionally painted red, but because this one marked the port side of the channel, she was painted black—the same color as channel buoys marking the port side. After the opening of the St. Lawrence Seaway, when ocean-going vessels began to enter the Great Lakes in some numbers, she became a conversation piece for startled ocean mariners who never before had seen a black lightship.

In 1949 she was overhauled, given diesel engines, and fitted with a radio beacon and other new equipment. But as the years passed the cost of operating her rose until the Coast Guard estimated that it would take $105,500 to keep her on station in 1971. (Most of that amount was in the salaries of the eleven men who manned her in shifts of six at a time.) *Huron* is now owned by the City of Port Huron, Michigan, the nearest city to her old station, and is on permanent display there. (—*Official U.S. Coast Guard photo, courtesy Ninth Coast Guard District*)

Leola Charles, a modern Lake Erie fishing boat equipped with radar, radio, and echo-sounding equipment to locate fish, and fitted to operate either with gill nets or a trawl. Note the icicle fringe around the wheelhouse. (*—Courtesy Ontario Department of Lands and Forests*)

foot containers each (in contrast to the container ships of the same line, which carried 600 containers each, and to more recent ocean ships that can carry 2,000 or more); thus they could obtain full cargoes in Great Lakes ports.

The service, which started in 1971 with two ships, *Manchester Mercurio* and *Manchester Rapido*, prospered sufficiently that a third one, *Fortuna*, was added later, giving regular service to the United Kingdom and many European and Mediterranean ports. But in the late 1970s the company, Manchester Liners, was sold to Far Eastern owners, who discontinued Great Lakes container service.

Some ports on the Lakes now accept outgoing containers for rail or truck shipment to the Atlantic Coast. Occasionally containers travel as deck cargo on vessels moving into or, particularly, out of the Lakes, but they are relatively few. Cleveland has made particular efforts to increase container shipments,

but the results still are small. Outgoing general cargo usually consists of agricultural commodities going to undeveloped countries under various aid programs and to ports (usually in those countries) that do not have container-handling equipment. Incoming general cargo is mainly iron, steel, and some scrap metal. A small but essential type of outgoing general cargo consists of large things built by the industrial cities around the Lakes—steel mill or paper mill machinery, locomotives, earth-moving equipment, and the like, that must be carried by "heavy lift" ships. Great Lakes ports continue to promote the transit of containerized general cargo in every way they can, but the category still shrinks.

LEOLA CHARLES

Lake Erie became so notorious for its pollution that people often were startled to learn that it produces about as large a quantity of fish as all the other

Iced fish, fish boxes, and Lake Erie fishing boats at Wheatley, Ontario, delivering to the dockside processing plant. (*—Photograph by the author*)

Some commercial fishing exists on the other Lakes. Here a Lake Superior boat returns to harbor at Munising. The aft wheelhouse is typical of Lake Superior fishing boats. (*—Photograph by the author*)

Great Lakes put together. In fact, the more polluted it became, the more fish it produced—but they were fish of ever-diminishing desirability. Now that it is recovering, the catch includes walleye as well as white perch and yellow bass. Smelt, an introduced variety, are also caught in great numbers by trawling.

Commercial fisheries still flourish along the Canadian shores of Lake Erie, thanks largely to one man, the late Leonard Omstead of Wheatley, Ontario. He pioneered the idea of a dockside processing plant to convert wholesome but unglamorous varieties of fish into frozen fish sticks or packages of frozen smelt that find ready sales in this era of convenience foods. Other entrepreneurs have built smaller copies of Omstead's factory—now said to be the largest freshwater-fish packing plant in the world—and as one result, there are many large boats engaged in commercial fishing along the Ontario shore.

On the American side of Lake Erie things are quite different. Sandusky and Port Clinton, where there were

formerly large fishing fleets, today see only an occasional old and dispirited commercial fishing boat. It is true that the big sources of pollution are the cities of the U.S. shore, but that is not the major reason for the difference in fisheries. The Ontario government, while not always acting for the best interests of commercial fishermen, has helped them far more than most of the state governments. Many American commercial fishermen are convinced, with some reason, that their states want to destroy them and turn the fisheries over to sports fishermen. Although most marine biologists feel that a healthy fishery has room for both kinds of fishing, some of the more extreme sportsmen's representatives, who contend that commercial fisheries should be banned, are having a strong influence. Ohio, for example, has forbidden commercial fishing in many of the traditional fishing grounds. Yet in the lakeside towns that adjoin those same grounds, a pleasure fishing industry has grown up; the hundreds of boats that go out from the dozens of marinas would seem to put

The *Roy A. Jodrey* unloading crushed rock at a glass-sand plant in Midland, Ontario. The plant is where the Midland shipyard once stood, and the *Jodrey* lies where many vessels, including the *Lemoyne*—for many years the largest vessel on the Lakes—first slid into the water. The *Jodrey* later sank in the Seaway. (—*Photographed by the author*)

fully as much pressure on the fisheries as commercial fishermen ever could—but they bring in far more money. It is doubtful that most sportsmen really think it would enhance their pleasure if the great majority of taxpayers who help to maintain the Lakes, but who depend on commercial sources of fish, were deprived of their dinners, but their more vocal spokesmen have moved the forces of state government in that direction.

Along the Ontario shore, however, a balance has still been maintained between commercial and sports fishing; and the numerous Detroit residents one sees angling there bear witness that pleasure fishing is still worthwhile. One of the better large commercial fishing boats in use has been the *Leola Charles*, a steel 78-footer, of 22 feet beam and 6 feet draught, launched at Port Dover in 1968. This vessel was built and operated by Don Mummery Fishing Ltd., a firm consisting of three brothers, and was named for their late parents. She usually is operated by a crew of three. Like most of the boats she normally goes out each day between 4:00 and 6:00 a.m. and returns between 3:00 and 5:00 p.m.

The contrast between the *Leola Charles* and the Mackinaw sailing boats used by Captain McDougall a century earlier demonstrates how far we have come in technology during that century. The *Leola Charles* is propelled by a 6-cylinder, 335-hp diesel engine that gives her a cruising speed of 12 mph. She is equipped with radar, radio, and an echo sounder used for fish detection, and has a mechanical gill net lifter and trawling equipment.

ROY A. JODREY

Ever since the early 1900s a few lake freighters have been equipped with machinery enabling them to unload themselves. The equipment has consisted of conveyors that bring the bulk cargo up from the hold and, mounted on deck, a skeletal metal boom that carries an endless belt. When the vessel is under way, the boom is secured on deck; when she is unloading, it is swung out beyond the dock to carry the cargo ashore and dump it there. Such freighters have been used mainly to take coal and crushed rock into places where there is no dockside unloading equipment. Many lakeshore power plants, for example, are brought their coal directly by self-unloading bulk carriers.

Over the years, self-unloaders grew in popularity because of their flexibility. Unlike the standard freighters, they were not limited to docks that were already provided with unloading equipment such as Huletts.

The *Stewart J. Cort*, first 1,000-foot-long freighter on the Great Lakes, upward bound at Detroit on her initial voyage, is being welcomed by a fireboat and pleasure craft. (*—Courtesy Bethlehem Steel Corporation*)

As they became more popular, self-unloaders also became larger. One modern ship of this category was the *Roy A. Jodrey*, a motor vessel launched at Collingwood, Ontario, in 1965 for the Algoma Central Railway. The *Jodrey*—named for a former director of the Algoma Central—was 640 feet in length, 72 feet in beam, and 40 feet in depth. Her boom was 250 feet long.

Such vessels, though normally used for loads of stone or coal, are versatile and can carry almost any bulk cargo that is provided. On November 20, 1974, the *Jodrey*, carrying a cargo of ore, grounded on a shoal in the Seaway. Wisely, she was abandoned. Next day she teetered off the shoal and sank in 150 feet of water.

STEWART J. CORT

In 1969, on June 26, the new Poe Lock connecting Lakes Huron and Superior was dedicated at Sault Ste. Marie. The limiting dimensions of the lock are 1,200 feet in length and 110 feet in width, but at that time there were no vessels on the Lakes that even approached those dimensions. On June 28, however, another ceremony was held on another part of the Lakes. At Erie, Pennsylvania, a division of Litton Industries called Erie Marine held the grand opening of its new shipyard, a $20 million plant, designed especially to build a new generation of giants for

234

the ore trade. Shortly after the opening, the yard started to build the first 1,000-foot freighter, designated Hull 101—later to be named *Stewart J. Cort.*

The new shipyard embodied a new idea in vessel construction for North America (similar ideas had already been tried out in Europe and Japan); the plant could accurately be called a ship factory. It contained assembly lines on which steel panels and steel frames were fabricated, an assembly shop where they were put together to form 48-foot sections of the hull (each section was built on end to make the best use of automatic welding equipment and then the 700-ton unit was turned hydraulically onto its bottom), and a 1,250-foot graving dock—the largest on any coast of the United States—in which the sections were joined together when they were completed. Each time a section was attached the dock was flooded, the hull moved 48 feet farther out, and the dock again pumped dry. The final result was that the hull protruded out of the as-sembly shop into the open graving dock, getting longer and longer as each section was added, for all the world like a sausage being ground out of a giant sausage machine. At the same time men within the hull installed pipes, wiring, and other essentials in perfect shelter from outside weather—which in winter, in the Great Lakes region, can be pretty bad.

Meanwhile the extreme bow and stern sections were built elsewhere, by Ingalls Shipbuilding, also a division of Litton Industries, at Pascagoula, Mississippi. The finished vessel has the classic profile of the Great Lakes freighter, with the pilothouse and navigational equipment in the extreme bow and the power plant in the extreme stern (it departs from the standard arrangement by having all living quarters in the forward structure). When these two sections were completed they were welded together, producing a strange little ship consisting of scarcely more than power plant and pilot house.

Newer ore docks designed to handle only pellets made from taconite have belt conveyors that can load thousands of tons in a few hours in ships of almost any size. Here such a dock is loading a freighter at Silver Bay. (—*Photograph by the author*)

One of the short self-unloading booms of the *Stewart J. Cort*. When not in use it retracts into the after structure of the ship. In this demonstration, taconite pellets are being deposited on the dock, but in actual service they would be unloaded at a rate of 20,000 tons per hour into a dockside hopper device. Adjusting the unloading system so that it would operate as intended took an extra year before delivery of the vessel to her owners. (*—Photo by North American Films, courtesy Litton Industries*)

It was dispatched up the Atlantic Coast and through the Seaway to Erie, where it was cut into its two sections again. Tanks were added to the sides of both bow and stern sections to round them out so that they fitted smoothly onto the 818-foot-long cargo hull, and the ends of the big vessel were welded in place.

The first 1,000-foot-long freighter on the Great Lakes, the *Stewart J. Cort*, was christened on May 4, 1971. Because of the method of her construction, one cannot say that she was ever launched, for she was water-borne intermittently from the earliest period of building. The new freighter, named for a former director and vice president of Bethlehem Steel Corporation, which owns the vessel, can carry twice as much as the biggest freighter on the Lakes before she was built; she made everything else look tiny. But it took a year to fit her out and tune her systems; she left Erie and headed up the Lakes for the first time on May 1, 1972. She was the first and essentially the last big ship to be built in that yard.

The only other thing built there was the hull body of an unusual integrated barge-and-tug combination that has a total length of a thousand feet, the *Presque Isle*, which was built immediately after the *Cort* and is still operating on the Lakes. The tug is locked into a space-consuming notch in the stern of the barge which reduces its carrying capacity. Supposedly offsetting this, the integrated tug-barge unit in theory (and legally) needs a crew of only nine, as opposed to a normal freighter's twenty-seven. The idea that two attached vessels need less crew than only one vessel is at best dubious. When two vessels are locked together as are the tug and barge, they become a more complicated item than does a single, solid hull, and the interlocking mechanism requires frequent inspection and maintenance; such a small crew would have difficulty enough finding time to maintain the normal equipment of any freighter, before adding the extra connecting machinery. And there are questions of safety when a large unit of this kind is under way, manned by a small crew, especially in narrow waters. In addition most ship operators have labor agreements that do not permit greatly reduced crews. The *Presque Isle* carries a larger crew than was first planned. No more thousand-foot tug-barges have been built, but a few smaller ones have been tried more successfully, and in some protected waters there is limited use of the barge-towboat system seen on the inland rivers—an arrangement better suited for small crews.

In constructing the *Cort*, the yard had a cost overrun reported at $18 million. Bethlehem Steel refused delivery until the self-unloading system, a newly

236

Ore docks at Superior, Wisconsin, were the ultimate development of the type of dock seen on the Great Lakes for a century. These pocket docks, the largest in the world, still were too small for the 1,000-foot freighters. The dock second from left was the last wooden piling dock on Lake Superior and has been dismantled since this picture was taken. The others still stand at this writing, but have been stripped of machinery and no longer are used. (*—Wisconsin Natural Resources Department*)

designed mechanism, could be made to work, and the freighter lay at Erie for a year until it was revamped. A penalty for late delivery began in September 1970; the amount was $12,000 per day and in time it reached $1,200,000, but eventually it was renegotiated. Then the yard refused to build additional ships for Bethlehem at a price it once had suggested for up to five of them; Bethlehem sued, but after six years lost the suit. By then Erie Marine had attracted no other customers and had closed the yard.

The *Stewart J. Cort* and the *Presque Isle* began the modern era of thousand-footers, but neither of their designs prevailed.

8

Fewer but Larger

In 1950 there were 665 bulk carriers on the Great Lakes. In 1995 there were 129.

During that time a major force behind Great Lakes shipping, the iron and steel industry, went through a revolution, many of its plants closing permanently, others changing and shrinking; today it has one fifth the number of employees it had in the 1970s. At the height of the turmoil, in 1982, vessels on the Lakes carried less ore than at any other time since the Great Depression. The center of the industry has shifted from Pittsburgh to the Indiana shoreline of Lake Michigan. Domestic producers are under constant pressure, but at this writing their exports have risen to several million tons each year. Steel from overseas, coming in largely through the Seaway, has declined to about 20 percent of the market. Electric furnace minimills, established with relatively small capital, rework scrap—rather than using ore—and produce another 30 percent domestically. The constant changes in the market are hard to forecast.

But it is unlikely that the integrated domestic iron-and-steel industry that carries the process from the mines to the final metal will ever again be as potent an economic force as it was during the 1950s. For that reason the steelmakers need fewer ore carriers; and in seeking ways to cut costs they realized also that larger vessels could move more cargo for less money. Some vessels were lengthened to take advantage of the Poe Lock at Sault Ste. Marie; these enlargements did not approach the maximum size permitted by the lock, but carrying capacity of the ships was improved. The primary decision, however, was to build freighters that took real advantage of the lock size, and as a result shipyards began to turn out thousand-footers, following the lead of the *Stewart J. Cort*, though not her design. Terminals for the thousand-footers had to be huge and specialized, which meant that the ships were limited to fewer ports. These new vessels were diesel powered and could carry 63,000 gross tons of cargo, as opposed to perhaps half that amount by some of the larger vessels that preceded them.

Capacities of bulk freighters on the Lakes are usually measured by the weight of the cargoes they are able to carry, which in the U.S. is expressed in gross tons of 2,240 pounds—the normal ton that is used ashore. The nautical space-measurement term "gross tonnage," which has a completely different meaning, can generally be ignored in this context. The ton employed here is the everyday ton.

In the 1950s, as the natural soft, red hematite ore near Lake Superior began to run out, a process was developed to take the much poorer taconite ore and concentrate it near the mines into small pellets of good ore. Soon the taconite pellets became the standard. Unlike the hematite, they were easy to load. They were dry and did not freeze in cold weather, and they did not have to be loaded by dropping globs of ore into dock pockets which then sent them through chutes into the vessels' holds; instead they could be loaded by conveyor belts. Taconite did not need to be unloaded by machinery that lifted a bite at a time out of the holds. Some relatively large self-unloaders had already been built to carry the limestone used as flux to remove impurities during steel making, and they demonstrated to the steel makers that self-unloaders could handle sizable amounts of dry cargo such as pellets. Just when the owners began to wish for big ore carriers that would, however, loom higher than the loading docks and be too large for Hulett and other unloaders, ore pellets made it possible to load and unload big ships by different means.

It was not necessary to build larger and more expensive Huletts. The biggest ships became self-unloaders. So did the medium-sized ones. Many "straight-deckers"—the old, standard, bulk carriers that did not have their own unloading equipment—

The first "standard thousand-footer," the *James R. Barker*, under construction at the American Ship Building Company yard in Lorain, Ohio in 1976. (—*Photograph by author*)

were converted to self-unloaders. Sometimes the conversions made them look even more ungainly than vessels originally built as self-unloaders, and there were few cheers over the appearance of almost any self-unloading ship; but the owners cheered at more flexible and quicker unloading schedules, and the dock superintendents cheered that they no longer had to maintain unloading equipment or worry about employing longshoremen who could only be put to work when a vessel came in. The Huletts soon disappeared from the Lakes and almost all bulk freighters became self-unloaders.

The coal trade, like the ore trade, was changing. In 1923 the 12.6 million tons of coal moving through the Duluth-Superior port was all eastern coal from Appalachia ("soft" coal that burned with considerable air pollution) moving westward for industrial and domestic use; by 1994, 13.5 million tons moved through the port, all of it western coal from the Great Plains ("hard" coal that contained little sulphur and burned with little pollution) moving eastward, pri-

marily to electric generating plants. The demand for Appalachian coal, which once provided backhauls for freighters that brought ore down the Lakes, has faded steadily since the end of World War II.

The majority of the American Great Lakes vessels began to be landlocked, too big to go through either the Welland Canal or the Lake Ontario-Montreal stretch of the Seaway. U.S. owners of that fleet had little interest in going through the Seaway. The economies of scale they gained by the larger vessels on the upper Lakes met their interests and they could easily forget any occasional trips to Lake Ontario or to salt water. What they did need to accommodate their big ships was a second lock at Sault Ste. Marie as large as the Poe Lock, and they began to ask for that.

But Canadian shipowners needed the Seaway. One of their most productive trades was the carriage of grain out of the Lakes to lower St. Lawrence ports and the carriage of ore back again. For this purpose they maintained a small fleet of older straight-deckers, though all of their new ships—which also were intended to carry grain and ore—were self-unloaders and many of their older ones were converted to self unloading. Whatever the type of vessel, it had to be within the length acceptable to Seaway locks, which was 730 feet. (Then the admissible size was stretched a few more feet, and vessels could be admitted that measured up to 736 feet, 6 1/2 inches; now the limit is 740 feet.) These vessels could go many places on the Lakes, carrying such cargoes as coal or stone or salt into ports the thousand-footers could never enter, but they did not have the economic advantages of single cargoes of very large size, and when both ore and grain cargoes through the Seaway lessened, there was further economic pressure.

At one time it seemed that there might be a Canadian thousand-footer to carry ore from Lake Superior to a new steel mill that was built at Nanticoke, on the northern shore of Lake Erie. The Collingwood Shipyards, the major Canadian yards on the upper Lakes, optimistically sketched out the relatively few yard changes they needed in order to construct such a ship. But she was never built, and the Collingwood Shipyards closed forever in September 1986. On the Lakes, Canadian shippers in the foreseeable future will have only 730-40 footers and smaller vessels.

Since the early 1980s in the U.S. and the mid-1980s in Canada, no new self-propelled bulk carriers (and few barges) have been built on the Lakes. We are unlikely to see any new vessels until conditions change. The railroads have emerged from their languor of a few years past and are competing fiercely, using long unit trains with two-man crews to carry large amounts of ore, coal, or grain. The steel industry that changed to taconite in the 1950s could change again to some completely different raw material or technology. The future of Great Lakes shipping is unpredictable.

The *Niagara*, built in 1897, passes the thousand-footer *Edgar B. Speer* soon after the latter was built in 1980. (*—Photograph by the author*)

Above: The *J. W. McGiffin*, launched in 1971 at the Collingwood Ship-yards and seen here in the Welland Canal, was the first lake freighter built with the now standard cylindrical bow and extreme box shape. (—*Institute for Great Lakes Research, Bowling Green State University*)

Below: Stern view of the *McGiffin* emphasizes the boxlike shape that set the pattern for vessels built later. (—*Institute for Great Lakes Research, Bowling Green State University*)

It does seem probable that the ships will not become much larger. We know that every past era had the biggest ships until then, and that in each there were people who forecast that nothing larger could be built. But in our age of thousand-footers on the Lakes, and of vessels 730-40 feet long passing through the Seaway, it would be difficult indeed to enlarge locks and channels enough to make them substantially more useful. And a vessel much larger than the thousand-footers could scarcely maneuver on the Lakes; it probably would be the powered equivalent of the *David Dows,* which demonstrated that large sailing vessels were too clumsy for these restricted waters. Today shipowners, instead of thinking of bigger vessels, are considering how to make their present vessels competitive with railroads through such things as more efficient equipment, reduction of crew sizes, and improvement in methods of propulsion.

J. W. McGIFFIN

The *J. W. McGiffin* is as important in the history of Great Lakes ships as the *R. J. Hackett* was eighty years earlier. Both vessels became the pattern for the bulk carriers that followed them.

The 730-foot *McGiffin* was launched at the Collingwood Shipyards on Georgian Bay in December 1971 and began service in April 1972. She looked much different from the freighters that Collingwood had turned out up to that time, and the response to her appearance was somewhat like that of earlier mariners to McDougall's whalebacks—by current standards she was notably unbeautiful. She had all deck structures aft, forming a control tower that looked forward the length of the ship. This was a cost-saving move that had been seen occasionally at least since the whalebacks and that was now in use on many ocean freighters. She had no sheer, another cost-saving feature. She had a self-unloading boom mounted immediately in front of the after structure. But most important, she had a boxlike hull with a cylindrical bow unlike anything previously seen on the Lakes.

Over the years freighters on the Lakes had become more and more boxlike, a shape forced on them by the canals and narrow passages they had to navigate. The *McGiffin* seemed the ultimate floating box. The block coefficient of a vessel tells how nearly the submerged part of its hull resembles a flat-sided, square-cornered box (or block); the higher the coefficient, the more carrying space there usually is in the hull. *McGiffin* has a block coefficient of about 90 percent. Her designer, Stewart Thoms, had arrived at the boxlike shape—which some of his design associates referred to as "the brick"—but could not find a bow form that parted the water smoothly for it. The same restrictions that make vessels boxy and limit their length to that of canal locks (in this case, the locks of the Seaway) prevent them from having the bulbous projections at the bow that part the water more smoothly for many ocean freighters.

Thoms drew up a conventional sharp bow and had it tested at the Netherlands Ship Model Basin; it worked miserably on the extreme box form that he wanted. Casting about for a solution with the help of Professor Michelsen of the University of Michigan, he thought of the cylindrical bows that were being adopted for box-shaped ocean tankers. He drew up three cylindrical bow forms and sent them off to the Netherlands. It turned out that the bigger the radius the less resistance was offered by the bow, and all were superior to the traditional sharp bow.

Great Lakes vessels have to navigate in ice, however, and so the bow could not be too blunt. A middle form with a radius of 17 1/2 feet was adopted. It eventually turned out that *McGiffin* does have a little trouble steering in ice, but that is a small trade-off for the advantages in reducing the shoulder wave caused by the traditional bow.

The *McGiffin*—which originally was to be given the Indian name of *Nakouba*—was named for the chairman of the board of Canada Steamship Lines, for whom the vessel was built. She was the first of a new class of self-unloaders for CSL. But much more important, she was the first of a whole new pattern of Great Lakes vessels that would be built both in Collingwood and on the U.S. side of the Lakes in following years.

The *Charles E. Wilson*, U.S. freighter with cylindrical bow, boxy hull, and all deck structures aft, was built in 1973 at Sturgeon Bay, Wisconsin. Here she unloads ore at Lorain, Ohio. (*—Photograph by author*)

CHARLES E. WILSON

Bay Shipbuilding Co., at Sturgeon Bay, Wisconsin, in 1973 brought out the *Charles E. Wilson*, 680 feet over all. Bay Shipbuilding had followed the tests at the Netherlands Ship Model Basin and then applied them to the *Wilson*, giving her a high block coefficient and a cylindrical bow.

Thus far there were only two thousand-foot vessels on the Lakes, the *Stewart J. Cort* and the tug-barge combination, the *Presque Isle*. Few shipyards were yet prepared to build thousand-footers; not until 1976 could Bay Shipbuilding even launch the 770-foot *St. Clair*, designed specifically to bring western coal eastward. Few loading or unloading docks were yet prepared to ship or receive the 50-to-60-thousand gross ton cargoes that thousand-footers carried. Vessels in the *Wilson* class could operate efficiently—and still are useful today for working into smaller harbors or carrying special loads. Their versatility often brings them more cargoes and partly offsets the economic advantages of the big ships, which seldom have backhauls.

Like the *Wilson*, most freighters now were built with deck structures consolidated in aft towers and with hulls of high block coefficiency, and increasingly they were built with cylindrical bows. New vessels were changing in other ways. Almost all were diesel powered; welded hulls replaced riveted ones; all freighters were self-unloaders.

CHI-CHEEMAUN

The railroad car ferries of the Great Lakes were early examples of vessels with cargoes that rolled on and rolled off—what today are called "ro-ro" ships. The car ferries gradually faded from existence with the exception of one that has been converted to carry autos across Lake Michigan. But in Europe, perhaps sparked by the landing craft of World War II, there began to develop ferries that were designed to permit numbers of trucks and cars to roll on and roll off. The concept gradually expanded until today an entire class of ocean-going ro-ro ships carry cargoes that are not necessarily vehicles but that in one way or another roll on and roll off.

On the Lakes since the 1930s small vessels carried people and autos back and forth between Tobermory at the tip of the Bruce Peninsula and South Baymouth on Manitoulin Island, across the exposed and reef-strewn gap, once notorious for its many wrecks, between Lake Huron and Georgian Bay. Manitoulin, said to be the largest freshwater island in the world, gradually became a popular recreation area. Autos multiplied; the vessels in use were not of the best design for carrying vehicles and were too small to handle the growing load; long lines of cars waited for interminable periods to get aboard what had become a weak link in the highway system. Eventually

The *Algosoo*, launched at the Collingwood Shipyards in 1974, is at this writing the only Great Lakes freighter combining the cylindrical bow and boxy hull with the traditional forward deck structure, and the last freighter built on the Lakes with the forward structure. (—*Great Lakes Historical Society*)

Chi-Cheemaun (Indian term for "Big Canoe") approaching Tobermory harbor. One of the few "roll-on roll-off" vessels on the Lakes, she carries autos and passengers between Tobermory and Manitoulin Island. (—*Photograph by the author*)

The *Chi-Cheemaun* at her Tobermory dock. Her bow is open to permit rapid unloading and loading of cars and trucks. (—*Photograph by the author*)

View of the *James R. Barker*, showing the cylindrical bow and the power of the ship behind it. Low-flying air photograph by Wayne Farrar. (*—Courtesy Interlake Steamship Company and Wayne Farrar*)

the Ontario government stepped in and had a much larger ferry built at Collingwood.

The *Chi-Cheemaun* (an Ojibway name meaning "big canoe") went into service in 1974. The 365 x 62 x 12.6-foot vessel can carry nearly 150 cars and over 600 passengers on the crossing, which takes about two hours. She has passenger lounges and a cafeteria but no passenger staterooms, although her crew live aboard (she has two complete crews—including two captains—who work alternate shifts). One of the few ro-ro vessels now on the Lakes, she can load and unload cars and trucks quickly, so that in midsummer, at the peak of the tourist season, she makes four round trips daily, cruising at a maximum speed of over sixteen knots.

Those trips are not always routine. Bad weather comes often, and the vessel's course is exposed to the full sweep of waves coming down Lake Huron. She prudently stops for major storms, but not for lesser winds and fogs. She is equipped with stablizers: fins that can be folded out from her hull under water, that are controlled by gyroscopes, and that move like the ailerons of an airplane to keep the vessel level. The bridge deck is 55 feet above the waterline, and at times water has gone over the bow and the wheelhouse.

On occasion freighters cross her course, sometimes assuming the right of way when it is not theirs, knowing that the ferry's captain will take no chances with all the lives he carries. Once, the fleet of sailing yachts that were heading up Lake Huron in the Mackinac race were blown off course; instead of turning at the usual point and going up the Lake they came into the straits—and when it happened there was a fog. As Captain Schreiber, who commanded her on that trip, put it, "We just had dots all over the place on our radar." The ferry has twin screws and twin rudders, and her officers of necessity are skilled at navigating with radar. "We kept going, but just altered course a little bit here to pass one and back the other way to go around another one."

JAMES R. BARKER

In 1883 the new firm of Pickands Mather & Co. bought shares in the *V. H. Ketcham,* then the largest vessel on the Lakes. In 1976 the Interlake Steamship Co., the descendent of the same organization, took delivery of then the largest, the *James M. Barker,* named for the president and board chairman of Interlake. The *Barker* is 1,004 feet over all and has a capacity of 63,300 gross tons, compared to the largest preceding vessel, the *Stewart J. Cort,* which is 1,000 feet over all and can carry 58,000 tons.

The *Barker* was built by the American Ship Building Company at Lorain, Ohio. She was built in the traditional way, rather than the innovative—and costly—construction that built the *Cort,* but unlike the *Cort,* which has the traditional Great Lakes profile with deck structures both fore and aft, the *Barker* has all deck structures aft with a self-unloading boom mounted just ahead of them, a high block coefficient, and a cylindrical bow. In effect, she is a much larger version of the *J. W. McGiffin*.

Over the following years Interlake built two more thousand-footers (a term that includes vessels of slightly greater length). The *Mesabi Miner* has the same measurements and capacity as the *Barker;* the *Paul R. Tregurtha,* at present the largest on the Lakes, is 1013.5 feet long and has a capacity of 68,000 gross tons. And the company now manages a fourth thousand-footer, the *George A. Stinson*, which has the same measurements as the *Barker* but is owned by Stinson, Inc.

Most of the major American fleets now own thousand-footers. Among them is the USS (formerly U.S. Steel) Great Lakes Fleet, which still has the red hulls and the black-and-silver funnels that marked the "tin stackers" of its predecessor, the old Pittsburgh fleet. Beginning in 1979 it acquired three of the big vessels, but still, like Interlake, it also operates a few others that can enter smaller harbors.

Including the *Stewart J. Cort* and the *Presque Isle,* there are thirteen ships on the Lakes that measure a thousand feet or slightly more. The eleven that came after the first two vessels are all "standard thousand-footers" of the same pattern; all have high block coefficients, deck structures consolidated aft, self-unloading equipment, and cylindrical bows.

Vessels so large can be difficult to operate in narrow spaces and must be handled with care. There naturally are occasional incidents when they nudge the side of a dock or even run aground. But one such vessel, the *Indiana Harbor,* was involved in what is probably the most incredible accident on the Lakes. She collided with a lighthouse.

The *Indiana Harbor,* on September 9, 1993, having left the Sturgeon Bay shipyard, was running light on a clear night in upper Lake Michigan, at 3:30 a.m., traveling at 14 knots, when she ran into the Lansing Shoals light. Apparently the third mate, who was on watch, did not change course to pass through the Straits of Mackinac but let the ship continue straight ahead into the light. We can imagine the captain's remarks as he came on the bridge after the smash. Later the more measured language of the Coast Guard and others suggested that the mate was perhaps in the wrong profession.

Indiana Harbor, which had a 50-square-foot hole in her bow, managed to back off the shoal, turned around, and proceeded back to Bay Shipbuilding, nine hours away, arriving there to the considerable surprise of shipyard workers who had seen her leave the day before. She suffered $1.9 million damage. The 69-foot-tall lighthouse suffered $112 thousand, but continued to blink away.

ALGOPORT

Relatively small Canadian lake vessels have from time to time made lengthy ocean voyages; in

A picture that shows the great length of the *James R. Barker,* first of the "standard thousand-footers," with cylindrical bow, box-shaped hull, and all deck structures aft. She began service in 1976. Photo by R.J. MacDonald. (*—Institute for Great Lakes Research, Bowling Green State University*)

Algoport just before launching at Collingwood in May 1979. She was the first sizable modern vessel to be designed for interchangeable lake and ocean trade, but now is used mainly on the ocean. At 658 feet in length, she is shorter than the Seaway locks and her projecting bow is able to fit within them. Later ocean-lakers of full Seaway size have cylindrical bows. (—*Institute for Great Lakes Research, Bowling Green State University*)

1979, for example, the 355-foot *Ontadoc* carried bentonite from Chicago to Holland. Interest in such voyages was growing. That same year the *Algoport*, a 658-foot vessel designed for both Great Lakes and ocean service, was launched at Collingwood.

Canadians in the Great Lakes region have long considered the St. Lawrence Seaway and the canals that preceded it as their means of access to the oceans and the world beyond, and have used them accordingly. In earlier years many of the steamers owned on the Canadian side of the Lakes were built in the British Isles and brought through the canals to fresh water; more recently some relatively small lake-and-coastal freighters such as the *Ontadoc* have gone regularly from the Lakes through the Seaway to ports in the Canadian maritime provinces or to summer work in the Arctic.

Even before shipbuilding paused in the 1980s, it was evident to Canadian shipowners that the flow of grain from the prairie provinces to Atlantic coastal ports through the Seaway and the backhauls of ore from the lower St. Lawrence to Great Lakes steel mills were becoming problematical. Grain sales to overseas customers such as Russia were irregular, the Canadian government was encouraging grain produc-

ers in the prairie provinces to send their crops to the Pacific rather than the Atlantic coast, and there were recurring labor problems at Thunder Bay, the major grain shipping port on the Lakes. The near collapse of the North American steel industry and its slow recovery lessened the demand for ore. These developments could idle ships.

So in the late 1970s and early 80s Canadian owners began to build some vessels of Seaway size, considerably larger than the *Ontadoc*, that could easily go beyond the Great Lakes, St. Lawrence, and maritimes into extended ocean trade; they could carry cargoes between the Lakes and more distant ports, or they could work in the Lakes and St. Lawrence in warm weather, then carry ocean cargoes when the Lakes closed in winter.

One of the first of these was *Algoport*, perhaps built slightly smaller than full Seaway length because she still was considered an experiment. Evidently it was a successful experiment because *Algobay*, a full Seaway-length vessel that had been launched the previous year for the same owners, was later upgraded for ocean work and then even sailed for a time under the Liberian flag. As time passed, the class of ocean-lakers, which belonged to various Canadian

The *Ontadoc* was one of the first Canadian Great Lakes vessels in recent years to enter the ocean trade. She carried bentonite from Chicago to Holland in 1979, the year the larger *Algoport* was built for lake-ocean service. (—*Photograph by the author*)

owners, began to find major use on the oceans, maybe in part because many were self-unloaders and vessels so equipped were then almost unknown on salt water, maybe in part because they carried so much cargo for their size. Ships from the Lakes were particularly handy at such chores as delivering stone for construction of the tunnel linking England and France or unloading gypsum in small European ports.

Another ship, launched at Collingwood in 1983, began life as the *Prairie Harvest*, named for the grain that she carried out through the Seaway. But then after refitting in 1988 *Prairie Harvest* became more involved in ocean trade and became the *Atlantic Huron*, a name symbolizing her connection with both the Lakes and the ocean. In 1994, after she had been absent from the Lakes for a time, her symbolic connection was severed entirely and she became *Melvin H. Baker*.

Others went quickly into ocean service. *Atlantic Superior*, completed in 1982, during her first summer moved in and out of the Lakes with ore and grain as did most Seaway vessels. (It should be noted that many vessels still follow the pattern of trade between the Lakes and the lower St. Lawrence, in the manner of the *Grande Hermine*–later renamed *Canadian Mariner*–and *J. W. McGiffin*.) Then during the following winter she sailed from the Bahamas to Longview, Washington, and back to Baltimore. By 1985 she was in continous ocean service, operating mainly in Europe, and now she is registered in the Bahamas rather than in Canada. The concept of vessels that can trade in both fresh and salt water seems to be changing, with more emphasis today on ocean work.

These vessels grow older, and ships do not last as long on salt water as they do on fresh water. When the time comes to replace them, the shipowners may no longer care whether their vessels fit the Seaway. Algoma Central—the company that launched the *Algoport*—is now to operate six ocean ships of a Canadian-Danish-German consortium. The two belonging to Algoma, the first new ones ordered by the company in thirteen years, will be built in Gdansk, Poland. The ships are to have the boxy shape and high block coefficient that has become standard on the Lakes—but they will be too large for the Seaway.

Above: The *Fort William*, the last long-distance package freighter built and one of the last still working when the service ended in 1981. (*—Photograph by the author*)

Center Right: Inside the Canada Steamship Lines package-freight terminal at Hamilton, Ontario, showing many of the kinds of articles that were shipped by package freight. (*—Photograph by the author*)

Lower Right: The *Fort William* unloading newsprint at Toledo, Ohio. These vessels were unloaded quickly by forklifts working through the side ports. Note also the deck cargo of trucks. (*—Photograph by the author*)

Even if shipowners build new freighters to Seaway dimensions they probably will not build them on the Lakes or the St. Lawrence; the Canadian government no longer subsidizes shipbuilding and most Great Lakes shipyards have closed. Fednav Ltd., an ocean shipping company based at Montreal, has announced that it will build four ocean ships of a type that can trade through the Seaway, and that it will build them all in Shanghai.

FORT WILLIAM

The year 1981 was the ending date for a service that had existed on the Great Lakes almost since steamers began. Canada Steamship Lines, which had operated package freight services with specially built vessels for many years, were the last still to carry package freight on a major basis. CSL had package freight terminals strung out from Montreal to Thunder Bay (the merged city formed by the combination of Port Arthur and the vessel's namesake, the city of Fort William), with intermediate stops at many strategic points.

In the final years of CSL's package freight operation, it consisted of six vessels, the newest of which was the *Fort William,* launched at the Davie yard, Lauzon, Quebec, in 1965. She was 488 feet, 6 inches long, and had four cargo doors in each side to permit dockside loading and unloading, which usually could be done speedily by longshoremen with fork lifts. Because the major cities of Ontario and Quebec were stretched along the edge of the St. Lawrence-Great Lakes system, and because Canada did not have many super highways paralleling that system, package freighters were able to compete for a considerable time against truck lines hauling boxed, baled, and barreled small goods.

Truck competition began to tell, however. In 1979 the handsome package freighter *Fort Henry,* the last such vessel with the traditional fore-and-aft cabins, was retired because, although she was the fastest, she was for the same reason the largest consumer of fuel and thus the most expensive to operate. Then two more CSL package freighters were laid up, another one on that same year and one on the following year.

In 1981 the company still had six package freighters on its roster, but only three were in operation, each of the more recent design with all deck structures aft. But at the end of the 1981 season, Canada Steamship Lines ended its package freight line; the three vessels that still remained in service were retired. *Fort William,* being the newest, was sold, taken to Collingwood, and converted to a cement carrier renamed *Stephen B. Roman,* which works between ports mainly on Lake Ontario but at times as far west as Windsor.

On the Lakes today small ferries or similar vessels may still carry package freight to island communities or for some other particular reason, but the end of specially designed long-distance package freighters and their sizable cargoes came, essentially, at the end of 1981.

AMERICAN REPUBLIC

As development of the the thousand-footers continued, various problems were foreseen. There was a steel plant well up the Cuyahoga River in Cleveland which was supplied with ore by relatively small vessels; how could taconite be taken up the winding river (whose Indian name is usually translated as "snake" because of its twists and turns) if taconite were travelling only in the big new freighters? During the early planning it was suggested that the thousand-footers could unload on the Cleveland waterfront and a conveyor belt then take the ore to the plant, but that would disrupt so many other activities along the river that the idea was soon discarded. The next suggestion was to have the big boats unload at Cleveland and have smaller vessels carry the ore up the river (while all this was going forward, relatively small freighters did continue to bring ore all the way from Lake Superior and carry it to the plant), but it then developed that Cleveland didn't want an ore storage yard on its waterfront and was not even enthusiastic about having thousand-footers in its harbor.

The eventual answer was to establish a taconite storage facility at Lorain, Ohio, not far along the lake from Cleveland; for the thousand-footers to unload there; and for smaller vessels to carry the ore from there to Cleveland and up the Cuyahoga to the plant. These vessels were suited for general Great

Stern view of the *American Republic*. Designed to carry taconite ore on the Lake Erie shuttle between a storage yard at Lorain, Ohio, and steel mills on the Cuyahoga River in Cleveland, she is particularly maneuverable in the river. Her wheelhouse not only looks forward over the length of the hull but also has duplicate controls that look over the stern, so that she can more easily back down the Cuyahoga. Here she loads ore at Lorain. (*—Photograph by the author*)

Lakes use, but were 634 feet long, a practical length for the Cuyahoga, and so were called the river class. After unloading, a freighter that went up the river usually had to move slowly backwards down it with the help of a tug, and some needed a tug to help them up the river in the first place.

Planners began to think about a vessel that could load ore at Lorain, carry it to Cleveland and up the Cuyahoga, unload, and then move stern-first down the river to the lake without using any tugs or losing any time. Thus was conceived the *American Republic,* launched by Bay Shipbuilding at Sturgeon Bay in 1981 and owned by the American Steamship Company which is based near Buffalo. She is considered the most nimble vessel of her size in the world.

She is 634 feet long by 68 feet wide, which makes her one of the river class, though the others are by

no means as technically advanced. Her pilot house faces both forward and aft, with two sets of controls. She has eight rudders, her thousand horsepower bow and stern thrusters can easily move the ends of the vessel sideways, and she has two diesel engines driving twin controllable pitch propellers mounted in nozzles, giving maximum control.

Built as a highly specialized vessel to work on the shuttle between Lorain and the Cleveland steel plants, the *American Republic* is reinforced by other ships of the river class during peak demands for ore. She spends about two-thirds of the time on this run, but at times is taken away for other assignments while other river class vessels substitute for her or if there is a lull in the need for ore. All those rudders, bow thrusters, stern thrusters, and other specialized items of equipment that let her almost dance in the water do not deter her from general Great Lakes service and may sometimes make her useful elsewhere.

PAUL R. TREGURTHA

Built in 1981 and launched as the *William J. Delancey*–later renamed the *Paul R. Tregurtha*–at this writing the largest vessel on the Lakes, 1013.5 x 105 x 56 feet, can carry 68,000 gross tons of iron ore. An advertising drawing by her owners, Interlake Steamship Company, shows her standing on end beside the Empire State Building, almost reaching the top of that tower's 1,250 feet. A long, thin vessel, nearly ten times as long as she is wide–the proportions forced on her by the locks and narrow passages of the Lakes–she has the slightly flexible hull that has been the mark of Great Lakes freighters ever since lessons were learned from the loss of the *Western Reserve*. Those in the aft wheelhouse atop her deck tower can see the hull that stretches ahead of them flexing slightly as she rides the bigger waves.

The appeal of having one's name inscribed on the bow and stern of a vessel, making it a sort of waterborne monument, must be overwhelming to many chief executive officers or chairmen of boards. Relatively few ships are given such names as *Burns Harbor* or *Algosoo;* many receive the names of people. But there is a problem. Vessel names can be changed, as often happens when a ship is sold to another owner. Consider the *William K. Field,* which became the *Reiss Brothers,* which became the *George D. Goble,* which became the *Robert S. Pierson,* which became the *Spruceglen.* In such cases does the human owner of the erased name feel as though the engraving on his tombstone has been changed? Such alterations may also be made when there are more subtle adjustments. The largest ship on the Lakes was launched in 1981 as the *William J. Delancey,* named for the

The biggest vessel and most efficient ore carrier on the Lakes, the *William J. Delancey* (later renamed *Paul R. Tregurtha*) unloading ore at Lorain, Ohio. Smaller vessels such as the *American Republic* that can navigate the Cuyahoga River will carry the ore from here to Cleveland mills on the Cuyahoga. (*–Great Lakes Historical Society*)

The largest vessel on the Lakes, here named *William J. Delancey* (she has since been renamed *Paul R. Tregurtha*), was launched in 1981. She is 1,013 feet, 6 inches long. Built with boxy hull and cylindrical bow, she can carry 68,000 gross tons of cargo. (*—Great Lakes Historical Society*)

chairman and chief executive officer of Republic Steel, which then had a contract with the Interlake Steamship Company to carry ore for Republic. In 1990, still owned by Interlake, she was renamed *Paul R. Tregurtha*, for the vice chairman of the Interlake board.

The *Tregurtha* is a giant box with a cylindrical bow—what one marine historian has dismissed as "a diesel barge." It is sad that the designers of big new lake vessels did not give them a few additional shiplike touches: a little sheer, perhaps? Yet now many ocean vessels are built without sheer, which apparently has become a luxury. Lake freighters' high block coefficient and their long, narrow hulls do make them surprisingly seaworthy; as a naval architect has pointed out, a plank on edge moves through the

water quite well, yet it has a block coefficient of 100 percent. The "diesel barge" description is not entirely apt.

Today our thousand-footers are the most efficient carrying devices on the Lakes, and shipping is always under pressure to be more efficient. The *R. J. Hackett* and her immediate descendents were less attractive to look on than most sailing vessels, but they were more efficient and their pattern prevailed. Labor costs at present comprise roughly half the cost of operating a ship; the current standard crew of twenty-seven using the *Tregurtha* can deliver more ore than with anything else on the Lakes. The last of the present series of thousand-footers to be built and the largest is at least for now the ultimate.

Hulett unloaders at Lackawanna, N.Y. Huletts have since disappeared form the Lakes. (—*Courtesy McDowell Wellman Engineering Co., Cleveland*)

Afterword

The late Rowley W. Murphy, distinguished marine artist and historian, recalled an incident that took place in August of 1910. His father, his cousin, and he were cruising at the western end of Lake Ontario. After a late start from Toronto they anchored their yawl for the night in the little harbor at the mouth of the creek at Etobicoke. Two other yachts were also anchored there; the three crews totaled eleven men.

All hands turned in earlier than usual, there being no distractions ashore, and by midnight were deep in happy dreams, helped by the quiet ripple alongside. At what was about 1:30 A.M. the writer was wakened by four blasts on a steamer's whistle. After waiting for a repetition—to be sure it was not part of a dream—he put his head out of the companionway.

There, flooded by moonlight, was a steamer heading about WSW—at about half speed, and approximately half a mile offshore. She had a good chime whistle but not much steam—like *Noronic* on that awful night of September 17, 1949, who also repeated her four blasts many times.

———

In this appearance off "Toby Coke" (a variant of spelling), the starboard light, deck lights and some seen through cabin windows, had the quality of oil lamps; and her tall mast, with fitted topmast, carried a gaff and brailed up mainsail. Her smokestack was all black and she had no hog beams—but appeared to have four white boats. Her chime whistle was a good one, but was reduced in volume as previously mentioned, and was sounded continuously for perhaps ten minutes. Very soon all hands now watching on the beach decided that something should be done. So a dinghy was quickly hauled over from the basin, and with a crew of four made up from some of those aboard the three yachts, started to row out with all speed to the vessel in distress, to give her what assistance might be possible.

As the boys in the dingy reached the area where something definite should have been seen, there was nothing there beyond clear and powerful moonlight, a few gulls wakened from sleep—but something else, impossible to ignore. This was a succession of long curving ripples in a more or less circular pattern, which just might have been the last appearance of those caused by the foundering of a steamer many years before on a night of similar beauty . . . .

Most of the vessels in this book are similar creations of another age that we view, if less dramatically, through moonlight from a distance. Most of them could have existed only during a short span of history. A wooden passenger steamer, for example, could be built only at a time when wood was an acceptable material, when there were passengers to be carried, and when steam engines were both available and economical. As we look at each vessel we can conjure up around her the period in which she was built and the way that people then lived.

But there are exceptions. The bateau and the canoe belong to the entire history of the Great Lakes; when an idea is simple and good and meets a basic need it can last for a long time. And there are even more acute exceptions, the modern ships that we can go and look at today. The ships of these inland seas continue to mirror the people who live around them, but we are too close to our present vessels to be able to say accurately what they tell of our own time. True, they are bigger and more complex than any before, but every previous generation could have boasted the same thing.

Bibliography and Notes

ABBREVIATIONS USED:

AHR	*American Historical Review*
B	*The Beaver*
BEHS	Buffalo and Erie County Historical Society
BHC	Burton Historical Collection, Detroit Public Library
CH	*Chicago History*
CHR	*Canadian Historical Review*
CHS	Chicago Historical Society
DHSB	*Detroit Historical Society Bulletin*
DMH	*Detroit Marine Historian*
GG	*Greenwood's Guide to Great Lakes Shipping*
GLHS	Great Lakes Historical Society
GLL	*Great Lakes Log*
IOFN	*Imperial Oil Fleet News*
IS	*Inland Seas*
JC	*Journal of Commerce*
JEH	*Journal of Economic History*
MD	*Mer Douce*
MH	*Minnesota History*
MHM	*Michigan History Magazine*
MTCL	Metropolitan Toronto Central Library
MVHR	*Mississippi Valley Historical Review*
NAC	National Archives of Canada
NF	*National Fisherman*
ODLF	Ontario Department of Lands and Forests*
OH	*Ontario History*
PBHS	*Publications of the Buffalo Historical Society*
PM	*Professional Mariner*
PR	*Papers and Records*, Ontario Historical Society
PUNI	*Proceedings, U.S. Naval Institute*
RC	Runge Collection, Milwaukee Public Library
SB	*Steamboat Bill*
SHSW	State Historical Society of Wisconsin
SR	*Seaway Review*
T	*The Evening Telegram* (Toronto)
WMH	*Wisconsin Magazine of History*

*The department no longer exists. Most of its functions are now in the Ministry of Natural Resources.

Certain works have been used for general guidance and interpretation. If they also provided more specific information they are cited again in the appropriate place:

American Lakes Series: Harlan Hatcher, *Lake Erie* (New York, 1945); Fred Landon, *Lake Huron* (New York, 1944); Grace Lee Nute, *Lake Superior* (New York, 1944); Arthur Pound, *Lake Ontario* (New York, 1945); Milo M. Quaife, *Lake Michigan* (New York, 1944).

George A. Cuthbertson, *Freshwater* (Toronto, 1931).

Ronald L. Heilmann, Harold M. Mayer, and Eric Schenker, *Great Lakes Transportation in the Eighties* (University of Wisconsin, 1986).

Erik Heyl, *Early American Steamers* (Buffalo, 1953-69), six volumes.

IS, Volumes I (1945) - .

J.B. Mansfield (ed.) *History of the Great Lakes* (Chicago, 1899), two volumes.

C.H.J. Snider, "Schooner Days," a series of articles that appeared in *T* from January 31, 1931, to October 8, 1955.

Richard J. Wright, *Freshwater Whales* (Kent State University, 1969).

Standard references on economic and political history were used. They are cited, however, only if they contain specific material on the Great Lakes.

Chapter 1

INTRODUCTORY MATERIAL and general background. D.C. Creighton, *The Commercial Empire of the St. Lawrence, 1750-1860* (New Haven, 1937). Bernard De Voto, *The Course of Empire* (Boston, 1952). J. Mackay Hitsman, *The Incredible War of 1812* (Toronto, 1965). Minnesota Historical Society, *Aspects of the Fur Trade* (St. Paul, 1967). Harold A. Innis, *The Fur Trade in Canada* (Toronto, 1956). C.H.J. Snider, *In the Wake of the Eighteen-Twelvers* (reprint edition, London, 1969) gives a fictionalized account of the naval war on the Lakes, which includes some traditional but unverified stories; it provides useful background and flavor. Ernest Voorhis, *Historic Forts and Trading Posts* (Ottawa, 1930).

INDIAN CANOE. Arthur T. Adams (ed.), *The Explorations of Pierre Esprit Radisson* (Minneapolis, 1961). Edwin Tappan Adney & Howard I. Chapelle, *The Bark Canoes and Skin Boats of North America* (Washington, 1964). H.P. Biggar (ed.), *The Works of Samuel de Champlain* (Toronto, 1922-36), six vols. J. Herbert Cranston, *Étienne Brûlé, Immortal Scoundrel* (Toronto, 1949). Kenneth G. Roberts & Philip Shackleton, *The Canoe* (Toronto, 1983). Reuben Gold Thwaites (ed.) *The Jesuit Relations and Allied Documents* (Cleveland, 1896-1901), 73 vols.; *New Voyages to North America by the Baron de la Hontan* (Chicago, 1905), two vols.

GRIFFON. George A. Cuthbertson, *Freshwater* (Toronto, 1931). Frank A. Severance, *An Old Frontier of France* (New York, 1917), two vols., *PBHS*, XX & XXI. Reuben Gold Thwaites (ed.), *A Discovery of a Vast Country in America* by Louis Hennepin (Chicago, 1903)

BATEAU (I). Howard I. Chapelle, *American Small Sailing Craft* (New York, 1951). Nathaniel Shurtleff Olds (ed. & transl.), "Journal of the Expedition of Marquis de Denonville Against the Iroquois: 1687" by Chevalier de Baugy, *Rochester Historical Society Publications*, IX (1930). M. Pouchot, *Memoir Upon the Late War in North America*, Franklin B. Hough, ed. & transl. (Roxbury, Mass., 1886), two vols. Thwaites (ed.), *Jesuit Relations* LXIII. John Gardner, "Bateaus Played Key Role in American History," *NF*, April 1967; "Famous Boat Type in Transitional Stage," *NF*, May 1967; "Construction Details of Old Bateaux Show Basic Design With Variations," *NF*, June 1967; "Old Sketch Provides Clue to Bateau Shape," *NF*, July 1967; "Bateau 'Reconstructed' From Remains, Drawing," *NF*, August 1967. Thwaites (ed.), *New Voyages . . . de la Hontan.*

OSWEGO AND *LA MARQUISE DE VAUDREUIL*. E. A. Cruikshank, "Notes on the History of Shipbuilding and Navigation on Lake Ontario," *PR*, XXIII (1926). Cuthbertson, *Freshwater*. Severance, *Old Frontier*. Letter, Broadley to Bascawen, *Oswego* sloop at Oswego, 15 September 1755; Public Records Office, London, Adm 1/480; Letter, Broadley to Cleveland, *Oswego* sloop at Oswego, 19 June 1756; Public Records Office, Adm 1/1487. Letter, Broadley to Cleveland, *Oswego* sloop at Oswego, 20 June 1756; Public Records Office, Adm 1/1487. The last-cited letter contains the passage quoted.

OUTAOUAISE. Cruikshank, "Notes . . . on Lake Ontario." Cutherbertson, *Freshwater*. Malcolm MacLeod, "Fight at the West Gate, 1760," *OH* LVII (1966); "*HMCS Onondaga*–The Heritage," an unpublished paper made available by courtesy of the author.

MICHEGON AND *HURON*. "Proceedings of a Court of Enquiry unto the Conduct of Mr. Nicholas Newman Master of the Huron Schooner on his way to Niagara in May 1763," NAC, MG 12, B99, Vol. 49. Letter, Ensign Price to Colonel Bouquet, Fort Erie, 26 June 1763, NAC, MG 21, Series A, Vol. 19-1. "A List of Vessells on the different lakes in North America," Capt. Joshua Loring, Nov. 1762, NAC, WO 39, MG 12, B 111, Vol. 65. Correspondence regarding wreck of the sloop *Michegon*, Aug. & Sept. 1763, NAC, WO 34, MG 12, B 72, Vol. 22. Some secondary accounts say that both vessels were schooners built by the British in 1762, but the above references show clearly that the *Michegon* was rigged as a sloop and was so old that she probably was built by the French.

ONONDAGA. Cruikshank, "Notes . . . on Lake Ontario." Cuthbertson, *Freshwater*. Malcolm MacLeod "Simcoe's Schooner Onondaga," *OH*, LVIII (1967); *HMCS Onondaga*–the Heritage."

NANCY. E.A. Cruikshank, "An Episode in the War of 1812," *PR* IX (1910); (ed.), "The John Richardson Letters," *PR* VI (1905); "Notes. . . on Lake Ontario." Cuthbertson, *Freshwater*. ODLF, *HMS Nancy* (Toronto, 1963). "Timothy Pickering Manuscript," *IS*, I (1945)

DETROIT. James P. Barry, "The Sloop Detroit," *IS*, XXVI (1970) gives complete references.

FUR-TRADE CANOE (I). Daniel William Harmon, *A Journal of Travels in the Interior of North America* (Andover, 1820). Grace Lee Nute, *The Voyageur* (St. Paul, 1955). Eric W. Morse, *Canoe Routes of the Voyageurs* (St. Paul & Toronto, 1962); *Fur Trade Canoe Routes of Canada* (Ottawa, 1969). See also previous references for Indian Canoe.

BATEAU (II). Sir Richard Bonnycastle, *Canada and the Canadians* (London, 1846). Patrick Campbell,

Travels in the Interior Parts of North America in the Years 1791 and 1792 (Toronto, 1937). Francis Hall, *Travels in Canada and the United States in 1816 and 1817* (London, 1818). Thomas Hamilton, *Men and Manners in America* (Philadelphia, 1833) contains the passage quoted without attribution. George Heriot, *Travels Through the Canadas* (London, 1807). John Howison, *Sketches of Upper Canada* (Edinburgh, 1821). *The Diary of Mrs. John Graves Simcoe*, John Ross Robertson, ed. (Toronto, 1911). Edward Allen Talbot, *Five Years' Residence in the Canadas* (London, 1824). Isaac Weld, *Travels Through the States of North America and the Provinces of Upper and Lower Canada During the Years 1795, 1796, and 1797* (London, 1807). See also previous references for Bateau (I).

NIAGARA. James P. Barry, *The Battle of Lake Erie* (New York, 1970) gives detailed references.

PRINCE REGENT. Howard I. Chapelle, *History of the American Sailing Navy* (New York, 1949). E.A. Cruikshank, "The Contest for the Command of Lake Ontario in 1814," *PR*, XXI (1924). C.P. Stacey, "The Ships of the British Squadron on Lake Ontario, 1812-14," *CHR*, XXXIV (1953).

Chapter 2

FRONTENAC. Cruikshank, "Notes . . . on Lake Ontario." Cuthbertson, *Freshwater.* Anna G. Young, *Great Lakes' Saga* (Owen Sound, Ont., 1965).

WALK-IN-THE-WATER. Heyl, *Early American Steamers,* II. Grace Hunter, "Life on Lake Erie a Century Ago," *IS*, XXII (1966). Joe L. Norris, "The Walk-in-the-Water," *DHSB*, XIX (1963), Mary A. Witherell Palmer, "The Wreck of the Walk-in-the-Water," *PBHS*, V (1902). Capt. Augustus Walker, "Early Days on the Lakes," *PBHS*, V (1902).

CANOE OF GOVERNOR CASS. Francis Paul Prucha, S.J., *Lewis Cass and American Indian Policy* (Detroit, 1967) contains the Cass statement quoted. Henry R. Schoolcraft, *Narrative Journal of Travels Through the Northwestern Regions of the United States Extending from Detroit through the Great Chain of American Lakes to the Sources of the Mississippi River in 1820*, Mentor L. Williams, ed. (East Lansing, Mich., 1953); *Summary Narrative of an Exploratory Expedition to the Sources of the Mississippi River in the Year 1820* (Philadelphia, 1855). Charles C. Trowbridge, "The Journal of Charles C. Trowbridge," Ralph H. Brown, ed., *MH*, XXIII (1942).

MICHIGAN. George B. Catlin, "Oliver Newberry," *MHM*, XVIII (1934). Heyl, *Early American*

can *Steamers,* II. Hunter, "Life on Lake Erie." Walker, "Early Days." Ivan H. Walton, "Developments on the Great Lakes, 1815-1943," *MHM*, XXVII (1943)

RAMSEY CROOKS. Norman Beasley, *Freighters of Fortune,* (New York, 1930). "Calendar of the American Fur Company's Papers," *Annual Report of the American Historical Association*, 1944, II & III (Washington, 1945).

UNITED STATES. Roy F. Fleming, "St. Lawrence River Pilot," *IS*, XVII (1961). H. O. Frink, "The Van Cleve Book," *SB*, Mar. 1948. Erik Heyl, "Captain James Van Cleve," *SB*, Dec. 1953; *Early American Steamers,* II. John Ireland, "Andrew Drew: The Man Who Burned the *Caroline*, *OH*, LIX (1967). William Kilbourn, *The Firebrand* (Toronto, 1956). George F.G. Stanley, "Invasion: 1838," *OH*, LIV(1962). Capt. James Van Cleve, manuscript book (copies at BEHS and CHS).

OSCEOLA. A.T. Andreas, *History of Chicago*, II (Chicago, 1885). Catlin, "Oliver Newberry."

ERIE. James O. Brayman, "Burning of the *Erie*," *IS*, IV (1948). "Burning of the Steam-Boat *Erie*," *IS* , I (1945). Heyl, *Early American Steamers,* II.

VANDALIA. Cuthbertson, *Freshwater.* Frink, "The Van Cleve Book." Heyl, "Captain James Van Cleve." Van Cleve, MS book.

Chapter 3

INTRODUCTORY MATERIAL and general background. Hugh G. J. Aitken, *The Welland Canal Company* (Cambridge, Mass., 1954). Cuthbertson, *Freshwater.* Charles Dickens, *American Notes* (London, 1892). John Forster, *The Life of Charles Dickens* (Philadelphia, 1886) contains the letters quoted.

GREAT WESTERN. Heyl, *Early American Steamers,* II. Margaret Fuller Ossoli, *Summer on the Lakes* (Boston, 1843).

U.S.S. *MICHIGAN.* "The Armaments of the Great Lakes, 1844,"*AHR*, XL (1935) reprints British internal documents expressing alarm at the building of the *Michigan.* Frank M. Bennett, *The Steam Navy of the United States* (Pittsburgh, 1897). Lt. Commander Walter E. Brown, "The Daddy of 'Em All," *PUNI*, Oct. 1924. Carlos C. Hanks, "An Iron Patriarch Passes," *PUNI*, Aug. 1942. Herbert Reynolds Spencer, *USS Michigan–USS Wolverine* (Erie, Pa., 1966). W. R. Williams, "The *Mohawk*," *IS*, VII (1951).

CHIEF JUSTICE ROBINSON. Bonnycastle, *Canada and the Canadians.* Heyl, *Early American Steamers,* VI. Van Cleve, MS. book.

TIMBER RAFT (I). D. D. Calvin, *A Saga of the St. Lawrence* (Toronto, 1945). T. R. Glover and D. D. Calvin,

A Corner of Empire (Toronto, 1937). Edwin C. Guillet, *Early Life in Upper Canada* (Toronto, 1963).

LAFAYETTE COOK. Aitken, *The Welland Canal Company.* Calvin, *A Saga of the St. Lawrence.* Cuthbertson, *Freshwater.* Public Archives of Canada [now NAC] Memo No. 975 L, July 14, 1969, abstracting records of *Lafayette Cook.* C.H.J. Snider, "Two Sheep for $1.00," *T,* Aug. 17, 1935. The *Cook* was built by Louis Shikluna, the noted Maltese shipbuilder of St. Catherines who is credited, perhaps optimistically, with building 200 vessels between 1836 and 1884. See C.H.J. Snider, "Mighty Maltese of Shipman's Corner," *T,* Aug. 9 & 16, 1947, reprinted in *IS,* XXV (1969).

EUREKA. Jewell R. Dean, "Lake Brig's Trip of '49 Recalled," *Plain Dealer* (Cleveland), Feb. 27, 1944. Robert Samuel Fletcher, *Eureka; From Cleveland by Ship to California* (Durham, N.C., 1959). Florence M. Gifford, "The *Eureka's* Voyage to the Gold Fields, 1849-1850," *IS* XIII (1957). James Gilmore, "The St. Lawrence River Canals Vessel," *IS,* XIII (1957). H.A. Musham, "Ships that Went Down to the Seas," *IS,* II (1946).

CHALLENGE. Henry N. Barkhausen, "William Wallace Bates," *Anchor News,* XIX Nos 3 & 4 (1988). Chapelle, *History of American Sailing Ships; The Search for Speed Under Sail, 1700-1855* (New York, 1967). *Daily News* (Manitowoc) Dec. 1, 1911, obituary of William Bates. *Herald* (Manitowoc), Dec. 1, 1911, obituary of William Bates. *The Marine Weekly Journal,* II, "Captain William W. Bates." Isacco A. Valli, "William Wallace Bates," *Anchor News,* XIII (1982) *The U.S. Nautical Magazine and Naval Journal,* Jan. 1856, contains a description and plans of the *Clipper City.* Chapelle's *History* contains plans of the *Challenge;* his *Search* contains plans of the *Clipper City.* The *Anchor News* is published by and in the files of the Wisconsin Maritime Museum; *The U.S. Nautical Magazine* is in the files of the New York Public Library; all other periodicals are in the files of the SHSW, Madison. Plans and construction details of this and other Bates vessels are in the Wisconsin Maritime Museum, Manitowoc.

SAM WARD. Heyl, *Early American Steamers,* III. Laurence Oliphant, *Minnesota and the Far West* (London, 1855). Ralph D. Williams, *The Honorable Peter White* (Cleveland, 1907).

FUR-TRADE CANOE (II). See references for previous canoe sections plus Henry John Moberly and William Bleasdell Cameron, *When Fur Was King* (New York, 1929). For background on law courts in Hudson's Bay Company territory see Roy St. George Stubbs, "Law and Authority in Red River," *B,* Summer 1969.

COLUMBIA. John N. Dickinson, *To Build a Canal* (Miami U., Ohio, 1981). Sarah V. E. Harvey (compiler), *Jubilee Annals of the Lake Superior Ship Canal* (Cleveland, 1906). Clarence S. Metcalf, "The Brig *Columbia,* Justis Wells, Master," *IS,* I (1945). Charles Moore, *The Saint Marys Falls Canal* (Detroit, 1907). Irene D. Neu, "The Building of the Sault Canal: 1852-1855," *MVHR* (June 1953-Mar. 1954). Oliphant, *Minnesota and the Far West.* Williams, *The Honorable Peter White.* Mrs. Harvey's book contains Harvey's own narrative of the background and building of the canal; having outlived all his contemporaries, he was able to give a glowing account of his own accomplishments without fear of contradiction. Dickinson and Neu in their treatments greatly discount his claims. The most complete coverage is Dickinson's.

MADEIRA PET. "Direct to Europe," *CH,* V (1959) Musham, "Ships that Went Down to the Seas."

Chapter 4

INTRODUCTORY MATERIAL and general background. Douglas McCalla, "The Commercial Politics of the Toronto Board of Trade, 1850-1860," *CHR* L (1969) summarizes the view of Upper Canada businessmen toward westward expansion of Canada. Frederick Merk, *Economic History of Wisconsin During the Civil War Period* (Madison, 1916). C. P. Stacey, "The Myth of the Unguarded Frontier," *AHR,* LVI (1950). Robin W. Winks, *Canada and the United States: the Civil War Years* (Baltimore, 1960).

WESTERN WORLD. Heyl, *Early American Steamers,* II & IV (IV contains an article on the *City of Buffalo* that gives much background on palace steamers). Mansfield (ed.), *History of the Great Lakes,* I. Samuel Ward Stanton, *Great Lakes Steam Vessels* (Meriden, Conn., 1962) is an extract from the original *American Steam Vessels* (1895). John Disturnell, *A Trip Through the Lakes of North America* (New York, 1857). Some accounts say that the *Western World* and *Plymouth Rock* were built in sections at Greenpoint, N.Y. (on Long Island) and shipped to Buffalo for assembly. Yet at that time the difficulty of sending large prefabricated structures over long distances, the availability of much good wood in the Great Lakes region, and Buffalo's fame as a shipbuilding center, all suggest that the vessels were built at Buffalo. The machinery did come from N.Y. City, and the more elaborate vessel fittings were probably sent from the East Coast, perhaps giving rise to an exaggerated idea of what came from there. The vessel's construction is discussed in letter to me, C. Patrick Labadie, April 19, 1995.

LADY ELGIN. Heyl, *Early American Steamers,* II. Dr. John L. Mahar, "One Hundredth Anniversary of the *Lady Elgin,*" *IS,* XVI (1960). Mansfield (ed.), *History of the Great Lakes,* I; the quotation from a survivor appears in Mansfield. C. E. Stein, "The Saga of Darius Nelson Malott," *IS,* XXV (1969). Records show that *Lady Elgin* was built for U.S. owners, but some accounts say that she was built for the Grand Trunk Railway, a Canadian company. In either event, she apparently was named for the popular wife of the Governor General of Canada.

COLLINGWOOD. Henry Youle Hind, *Narrative of the Canadian Red River Exploring Expedition of 1857,* I (London, 1860); "Report," *Journals of the Legislative Assembly of the Province of Ontario, Session 1858,* Appendix #2, XVI. Hind notes in Hind Papers, MTCL. Capt. James McCannel, "Shipping on Lake Superior," Thunder Bay Historical Society; "Shipping Out of Collingwood," *PR,* XXVIII (1932).

RESCUE. William Gibbard, "The First Trip of the Rescue," letter dtd. July 19 in the *Daily Globe* (Toronto), July 21, 1858 (NAC). McCannel, "Shipping on Lake Superior"; "Shipping Out of Collingwood." Thunder Bay Historical Society, *Fourteenth Annual Report,* 1923, "An Interview with Captain Dick of the S.S. *Rescue.*"

MERCHANT. Beasley, *Freighters of Fortune.* Heyl, *Early American Steamers,* III. Mansfield (ed.), *History of the Great Lakes,* I. Stanton, *Great Lakes Steam Vessels.*

PHILO PARSONS. Martha Mitchell Bigelow, "Piracy on Lake Erie," *DHSB,* XIV (1957). Charles E. Frohman, *Rebels on Lake Erie* (Columbus, Ohio 1965). "Northwest Conspiracy," *Southern Bivouac* (Louisville, Ky.), II. Richard J. Wright, "Stars and Bars Over Lake Erie," *IS,* XX (1964). Cole told more and more fantastic stories about the plot to anyone who would listen; some of these stories found their way into print and still are sometimes repeated as though true.

IRONSIDES. Heyl, *Early American Steamers,* III. Guy MacLean, "The *Georgian* Affair; an Incident of the American Civil War," *CHR,* XLII (1961). Kenneth N. Metcalf, "Detroit—steelmaker to the Nation," *DHSB,* XVIII (1962). Janet Coe Sanborn (ed.), *The Autobiography of Captain Alexander McDougall* (Cleveland, 1968). Stanton, *Great Lakes Steam Vessels.* Richard J. Wright, "A History of Shipbuilding in Cleveland, Ohio," *IS,* XIII (1957).

JAMES F. JOY. Henry N. Barkhausen, *Great Lakes Sailing Ships* (Milwaukee, 1947). Dana Thomas Bowen, *Memories of the Lakes* (Daytona Beach, Fla., 1946). Arthur A. Markowitz, "Joseph Dart and the Emergence of Buffalo as a Grain Port, 1820-1860," *IS,* XXV (1969). Neu, "The Building of the Sault Canal." RC, data sheet, *James F. Joy. Telegraph* (Ashtabula), Oct. 28, 1887. Anthony Trollope, *North America,* I (London, 1862). Williams, *The Honorable Peter White.*

BRITOMART. J. A. Bannister, "Port Dover Harbour," *OH,* XLI (1949). James P. Barry, "The U.S. - Canada Great Lakes Border Frictions," *IS*, XLV (1989). W. G. Hardy, *From Sea Unto Sea,* (New York, 1960). F. M. Quealey, "The Fenian Invasion of Canada West," *OH,* LIII (1961). Richard J. Wright, "Green Flags and Red-Coated Gunboats," *IS,* XXII (1966).

CHICORA. James P. Barry, "The Wolseley Expedition Crosses the Great Lakes," *IS,* XXIV (1968) gives a full account of that event with complete references. Henry C. Campbell, *Early Days on the Great Lakes: The Art of William Armstrong* (Toronto, 1971) contains many of artist-engineer Armstrong's drawings and paintings of the regions traversed and installations set up by the Wolseley Expedition. "Chicora," *DMH,* VI (1953). Hardy, *From Sea Unto Sea.* Heyl, *Early American Steamers,* V. John Kinsey Howard, *Strange Empire* (New York, 1952). McCannel, "Shipping Out of Collingwood."

Chapter 5

R.J. HACKETT AND *FOREST CITY.* Beasley, *Freighters of Fortune.* William D. Ellis, *The Cuyahoga* (New York, 1966). "Freight Carriers of the Great Lakes," *Marine Review* , June 2, 1904. H. L. Polk & Co., *Marine Directory* (Detroit, 1884) at GLHS. Lawrence A. Pomeroy, Jr., "The Bulk Freight Vessel, *IS,* II (1946). Wright, "A History of Shipbuilding in Cleveland, Ohio." The Ellis book contains a chapter on Eli Peck and his vessels that is semi-fiction and must be used with care, but that conveys something of the atmosphere at the time the ships were built. The vessels were discussed in letter to me, C. Patrick Labadie, April 19, 1995.

FUR-TRADE CANOE (III). See references for previous canoe sections, plus the following. Judge F. W. Howay, "Building the Big Canoes," *B,* Dec. 1939. Grace Lee Nute, "Voyageurs' Artist," *B,* June 1947.

JAPAN. "Alaska", *DMH,* V (1952). "Anchor Line," *DMH,* III (1946). Bowen, *Memories of the Lakes.* Wayne H. Garrett, "What Makes a Steamboat Go? Single

Crankshaft Engine," *DMH*, XLVIII (1995). Dr. Thomas H. Langlois, "Jay Cooke and Gibralter Island," Toledo *Blade Pictorial*, March 4, 1951. Ernest H. Rankin, "Steamer *Japan* Weathers October Storm," *IS*, XXIII (1967). Sanborn (ed.), *Autobiography of Captain McDougall*.

MACKINAW BOAT. James P. Barry, *Georgian Bay, the Sixth Great Lake* (3d ed., revised, Toronto, 1995); *Georgian Bay, An Illustrated History* (Toronto, 1992). Paul James Barry, "Mackinaw Boats and Collingwood Skiffs,"*Yachting*, LXVIII (1940). Chapelle, *American Small Sailing Craft*. Sanborn (ed.), *Autobiography of Captain McDougall*. The two books on Georgian Bay give more complete treatments of the boats' development; the *Yachting* article (also written by me under a youthful combination of names) a more technical one. The boats, though probably descended from ships' boats or other craft built by Watts in Ireland, were closely related to some Atlantic Coast types; see William A. Baker, *Sloops and Shallops* (Barre, Mass., 1966). William Watts, son of the boatbuilder, wrote several letters to me during the 1930s, giving background and history; copies are in the files of the Collingwood Museum and the Institute for Great Lakes Research, Bowling Green State University. The spelling of the tug name appears as *Siskiwit* in most records; McDougall's *Autobiography* actually spells it *Sisquit*.

MOONLIGHT. Barkhausen, *Great Lakes Sailing Ships*. Dana Thomas Bowen, *Shipwrecks of the Lakes* (Daytona Beach, 1952). Chapelle, *History of American Sailing Ships*. Cuthbertson, *Freshwater*. Stewart Holbrook, *Holy Old Mackinaw* (New York, 1938). RC, data sheet, schooner *Moonlight*. C. H. J. Snider, "Another Old Red Elevator Bites the Dust," *T,* June 26, 1937.

LETTIE MAY. Barkhausen, *Great Lakes Sailing Ships*. H.C. Inches and Chester J. Partlow, "Great Lakes Driftwood Schooner-Scows," *IS*, XX (1964). Willis Metcalfe, *Canvas & Steam on Quinte Waters* (Picton, Ont. 1968) tells of Minerva Ann McCrimmon. RC, data sheet, *Lettie May*. C.H.J. Snider, "Inside and Out of the 'Pioneer's' Passing," *T,* Aug 20, 1938.

V.H. KETCHAM. *DMH*, VI (1953). Walter Havighurst, *Vein of Iron* (Cleveland, 1958). H.C. Inches, *The Great Lakes Wooden Shipbuilding Era* (Vermilion, Ohio, 1962). H.C. Inches to editor of *IS*, XVIII (1962). Polk, *Marine Directory*. Williams, *The Honorable Peter White*. The name of the vessel is spelled *Ketcham* on the bow of the vessel in the painting hung in the Interlake board room, but *Ketchum* in the title plate on its frame, according to letter, Christine R. Hilston of Interlake Steamship Co., April 6, 1995. Mansfield gives the spelling as *Ketcham*.

GEORGE M. CASE. Barkhausen, *Great Lakes Sailing Ships*. A.E. Coombs, *History of the Niagara Peninsula* (Montreal, 1950). Cuthbertson, *Freshwater*. C.H.J. Snider, "The Albatross, Timber Drogher," *T,* June 22, 1946.

CHAMPION. Detroit Dry Dock Co., *Around the Lakes* (Detroit, 1894). William A. McDonald, "Tugs Triumphant," *IS,* XX (1964). Lauchlen P. Morrison, "Recollections of the Great Lakes, 1874-1944," *IS,* IV (1948). Loudon G. Wilson to editor of *IS,* XXV (1969). C. Patrick Labadie, letter to me, April 19, 1995.

ASIA. Canada, *Sessional Papers,* XVI (1883). *Enterprise* (Collingwood) Sept. 21, 1882. Fred Landon, "The *Asia*," *DMH,* VI (1953); *Lake Huron*. Mansfield (ed.), *History of the Great Lakes,* I. *Advertiser* (Owen Sound), Sept. 21 & 28, 1882. Dunk Tinkiss, "Dunk Tinkiss Tells His Story," *MD,* I (1921). "The Wreck of the Asia," *MD,* I (1921). The stories in the *Advertiser* gave the accounts by Tinkiss and by Christy Morrison; they were widely printed in other Canadian papers of approximately the same dates. The name "Tinkiss" in some references is spelled "Tinkis"; the former spelling seems to be correct.

DAVID DOWS. *Blade* (Toledo), April 21, 1881; May 17, 1881. Bowen, *Memories of the Lakes*. "The David Dows," *Federal Reporter,* St. Paul, Minn., XVI, reprinted in *The Telescope*, Aug., 1959. Inches, *Wooden Shipbuilding Era*. John F. Miller, "The *David Dows*," *The Telescope*, Mar. 1961. C.H.J. Snider, "Great Ones of the Great Lakes," *T,* Nov. 12, 1949; "Two 'Barques' and their Finish," *T,* Dec. 5, 1936.

IRON DUKE. L.W. Burch, "Reminiscences of My Sailor Days," *WMH,* XVIII (1934). Detroit Dry Dock Co., *Around the Lakes*. Polk, *Marine Directory*. Loren W. Burch, after sailing on the Lakes for several years, became a travelling salesman, then an electrical contractor in Madison, Wis. His lifelong hobby was painting. He lived to the age of 88, dying at Madison in 1951. *Wisconsin State Journal,* Madison, Aug 20, 1951, SHSW files.

ONOKO. Pomeroy, "The Bulk Freight Vessel." Ellis, *The Cuyahoga*. W.A. McDonald, "Composite Steamers," *IS,* XV (1959). Wright, *Freshwater Whales;* "A History of Shipbuilding in Cleveland, Ohio." The *Harvey H. Brown* was the steel freighter that had her bottom sheathed in wood in 1894.

ALGOMA. The Rev. Edward J. Dowling, S.J., "Canadian Pacific Railway," *DMH*, XV (1962). Fred Landon, "Disaster on Isle Royale," *IS*, XXI (1965). Lorenzo Marcolin, "Canadian Pacific Railway Company Steamship Lines—Last of an Era," *IS*, XXII (1966). *Daily Sentinl* (Port Arthur), Nov. 10 & 14, 1885. Young, *Great Lakes Saga*. The fact that there were two different *Algomas* running over essentially the same route at two different periods has caused some confusion; of course the earlier wooden paddle steamer and the later steel propeller had little in common but their names.

CORA A. Barkhausen, *Great Lakes Sailing Ships*. C.H.J. Snider, "Barges and Barges," *T*, Oct. 6, 1934; "Canada's Largest Lake Schooner," *T*, Nov. 19, 1949; "Why the Topmasts Were Sent Down," *T*, Sept. 1, 1945.

Chapter 6

INTRODUCTORY MATERIAL and general background. Penelope Hartland, "Factors in Economic Growth in Canada," *JEH*, XV (1955). The quotation that in the Edwardian era the sun always shone comes from a literate author of mystery stories, the pseudonymous Amanda Cross, in *Poetic Justice* (New York, 1970).

WESTERN RESERVE. Bowen, *Memories of the Lakes*. Fred Landon, "Loss of the Western Reserve," *IS*, XX (1964). Mansfield (ed.), *History of the Great Lakes*, I. Wright, *Freshwater Whales*.

CHARLES H. BRADLEY AND TOW. Dana Thomas Bowen, *Lore of the Lakes* (Daytona Beach, 1940); *Shipwrecks of the Lakes*. Harold M. Foehl & Irene M. Hargreaves, *Logging the White Pine in the Saginaw Valley* (Bay City, 1964). Holbrook, *Holy Old Mackinaw*. Inches, *Wooden Shipbuilding Era*. Chester J. Partlow, "Charles Bradley," *DMH*, XVII (1964). C.H.J. Snider, "Barges and Barges." Dr. Julius F. Wolff, Jr., "A Lake Superior Lifesaver Reminisces," *IS*, XXIV (1968). I am indebted to Robert J. MacDonald for relating a conversation he had with Captain Inches about the centerboard in the *Bradley*. A few lumber steamers were built with all cabin structures and the pilothouse aft, and with an unbroken deck forward; they were commonly known as "rabbits."

TIMBER RAFT (II). See references for previous timber raft section. The book by Glover and Calvin contains the passage quoted.

CHARLES W. WETMORE. The Rev. Edward J. Dowling, S.J., "The story of the Whaleback Vessels and of their Inventor, Alexander McDougall," *IS*, XIII (1957).

Leonard Gray & John Lingwood, *The Doxford Ships* (World Ship Society, England, 1975). Fred Landon, "Turret Boats," *IS*, XXIII (1967). George Carrington Mason, "McDougall's dream: The Whaleback," *IS*, IX (1953). Sanborn (ed.), *Autobiography of Captain McDougall*. Jesse Lynch Williams, "The Workers of the Great Lakes," *The Outing Magazine*, XLVII (November, 1905), reprinted in *Tales of the Great Lakes* (Secaucus, N.J., 1986). The quotation about the discomforts of the vessels is from Williams; the other quotations are from the *Autobiography*.

CHRISTOPHER COLUMBUS. See references for *Charles W. Wetmore* plus the following. James L. Elliott, *Red Stacks Over the Horizon* (Grand Rapids, 1967). Elliott Flower, "Chicago's Great River-Harbor," *The Century Magazine*, LXIII (February 1902), reprinted in *Tales of the Great Lakes*. Herman Kogan & Lloyd Wendt, *Chicago: A Pictorial History* (New York, 1958). Ernest H. Rankin, "The *Christopher Columbus*," *IS*, XXIII (1967). James R. Ward, "Harbor Disaster," *IS*, XVI (1960). Flower gives the harbor tonnage comparisons. The final quotation from an "old timer" is from a letter, April 14, 1976, to me from Ernest H. Rankin, Sr.

LOG RAFT. James Elliot Defebaugh, *History of the Lumber Industry of America*, I (Chicago, 1906). Robert C. Johnson, "Logs for Saginaw," *IS*, V (1949). W.R. Williams, "Big Tugs and Big Rafts," *IS*, III (1947); "Wreck of the Cambria," *IS*, XV (1959).

NORTH WEST. Bowen, *Lore of the Lakes*. Francis Duncan, "The Story of the D & C," *IS*, X (1954). Mansfield (ed.), *History of the Great Lakes*, I. James Gilpin Pyle. *The Life of James J. Hill*, 2 vols. (New York, 1917). Ken Smith, "*North West* and *North Land*," *DMH*, II (1948). Stanton, *Great Lakes Steam Vessels*. Robert D. Wallace, "Mark Twain on the Great Lakes," *IS*, XVII (1961). Jesse Lynch Williams, "The Workers of the Great Lakes." The descriptions of the vessel that are quoted come from Mansfield. Walter C. Cowles in a letter to IS, *LI* (1996), written after inspecting the original plans of the *North West* and *Northland*, notes the arrangements for the lower decks. The plans are now at the Institute for Great Lakes Research, Bowling Green State University.

CITY OF ERIE. Bowen, *Lore of the Lakes*. Herbert W. Dosey, "Sidelights on the *Erie-Tashmoo* Race," *IS*, VIII (1952). A. T. Zillmer, "The *Erie-Tashmoo* Race," *IS*, VIII (1952); "History of the Cleveland & Buffalo Transit Company C & B Line," *IS*, II (1946).

UNITED EMPIRE. Fred Landon, "In Rock Harbor for Shelter in 1901," *IS,* XII (1956); *"United Empire,"* *DMH,* V (1952); letter to me dtd. London, Ont., July 8, 1969. "Monarch," *DMH,* VIII (1954). Young, *Great Lakes Saga.* The letter from Dr. Landon written less than a month before his death, contains the first material quoted. The description of the ship in the storm is from the *IS* article. The Beatty Line competed directly with Canadian Pacific steamers that ran from Owen Sound to the Lakehead and that had been conceived and were managed by Henry Beatty, another member of the family. The C.P.R. operated steel, Scottish-built steamers that had been a radical departure for Great Lakes service; the Beatty line operated wooden, Canadian-built steamers that were the final evolution of a traditiional Lakes type. The Canadian names of Indian origin used by the C.P.R. also contrasted with the patriotic British names of the Beatty ships.

BANNOCKBURN. "Bannockburn," *DMH,* VIII (1955). Dwight Boyer, *Ghost Ships of the Great Lakes* (New York, 1968). James Gilmore, "The St. Lawrence River Canals Vessel." Fred Landon, "The Loss of the *Bannockburn,*" *IS,* XII (1957).

J. PIERPONT MORGAN. Beasley, *Freighters of Fortune.* The Rev. Edward J. Dowling, S.J., "The 'Tin Stackers,'" *IS,* IX & X (1953 & 1954). Walter Havighurst, *Vein of Iron.* Roger M. Jones, "The Rockefeller Fleet," *IS,* III (1947). John D. Rockefeller, *Random Reminiscences of Men and Events* (New York, 1909). Williams, *The Honorable Peter White.* Richard J. Wright, "Conneaut Harbor," *IS,* XV (1959).

IMPERIAL. "Great Lakes Fleet of Imperial Oil, Ltd., *DMH,* X (1957). "Imperial's First *Imperial,*" *IOFN,* Summer 1955. John T. Saywell, "The Early History of Canadian Oil Companies: A Chapter in Canadian Business History," *OH,* LIII (1961). Capt. F. C. Smith, "Imperial Ships," *IOFN,* Summer 1963 & Fall 1963.

ANN ARBOR NO. 5. George W. Hilton, *The Great Lakes Car Ferries* (Berkeley, 1962). Earl J. Fillian, "Car Ferries Across Lake Michigan," *IS,* XXIII (1967). Registry lists.

SEEANDBEE. Comdr. John D. Alden, U.S.N., "When Airpower Rode on Paddle Wheels," *IS,* XVIII (1962). Bowen, *Lore of the Lakes.* George H. Hilton, *The Night Boat* (Berkeley, 1968). Capt. John J. Manley, "Great Lakes Lady Bares Her Fangs," *IS,* XIV (1958). A. T. Zillmer, "The Great Ship *Seeandbee,*" *IS,* XIII (1957); "History of the Cleveland & Buffalo Transit Company C & B Line"; "Incidents—Amusing, Tragic and Otherwise," *IS,* XX (1966).

Chapter 7

EASTLAND. Jack J. Billow, "The Tragedy of the *Eastland,*" *IS,* XIV (1958). Bowen, *Memories of the Lakes.* Arthur Jackman, "3 Survivors Recall Day of Horror on *Eastland,*" *Tribune* (Chicago) July 25, 1966. Capt. Merwin S. Thompson, "Just What Was the Cause of the Steamer *Eastland* Disaster?" *IS,* XV (1959). *Tribune* (Chicago) July 25, 1915. The comment that some Clevelanders refused to sail on the vessel is from a letter, April 14, 1976, to me from Ernest H. Rankin, Sr. who, when he lived in Cleveland, did ride on her but was scared by her behavior.

WAR FOX. Evans Burtner, "Some Experiences with Ship Operation in World War I," *SB,* Fall 1970. The Rev. Edward J. Dowling, S. J., *The "Lakers" of World War I* (Detroit, 1967). "War Fox," *DMH,* XIV (1960). Sanborn (ed.), *Autobiography of Captain McDougall.* Material on the brief naval career of the U.S.S. *Lake Forest* (CSP 2991) was provided by the Director of Naval History, U.S.N. A few "Lakers" were built with machinery, cabin structure, and bridge aft rather than midships; they were commonly called "stemwinders."

GREATER DETROIT. Francis Duncan, "The Story of the D & C," *IS,* VII (1951)–*IS,* XIV (1958). Hilton, *The Night Boat.* Lawrence A. Pomeroy, Jr., "Great Lakes Calendar" (entry for Apr. 27, 1966), *IS,* XXII (1966) discusses changes in the level of Lake Erie.

LEMOYNE. Bowen, *Lore of the Lakes.* "Changes in Name and Operation," *IS,* XXV (1969), Nos. 1 & 3. Bernard E. Ericson, "The Evolution of Great Lakes Ships," *IS,* XXV (1969). Fred Landon, *Lake Huron;* "Shipbuilding at Midland, Ontario," *IS,* VI (1950). The first three vessels built by the Midland yard were the *War Fiend, War Levet,* and *War Fury.* As an eight-year-old I was taken by my parents on the shakedown cruise of the *Lemoyne* that is described. The name *Lemoyne* has been used again on at least one more recent but less distinguished vessel.

WAXWING. Robert C. Berger, Erie, Pa., letters to me, Sept. 21, Oct. 4, Dec. 6, 1969. Normal McKellar, "The C1-M-AVL Type Coastal Freighter Built on the Great Lakes During World War II," *DMH,* XI (1958). Leatham D. Smith, "War Shipbuilding on the Great Lakes," *IS,* II (1946). William DuBarry Thomas, "Ships of the N-3 Type Built on the Great Lakes," *DMH,* XI (1957). Much background was also provided by the Director of Naval History, U.S.N.

NORONIC. Canada, Department of Transport, *Report of a Court of Investigation Into the Circumstances*

Attending the Loss of the S.S. Noronic (Ottawa, 1949). The *Plain Dealer* (Cleveland), dispatches telling of the disaster published on Sept. 18, 19, & 23, 1949. *DMH,* VI (1953). Young, *Great Lakes' Saga.*

IMPERIAL LEDUC. "Canadians Push Tanker Renewals," *JC,* May 20, 1969. Skip Gillham,*The Ships of Collingwood* (St. Catharines, 1992). G.S. Robertson, Supt. Operations, Marine Division, Imperial Oil, letter, Toronto, Dec. 2, 1969. Capt. F. C. Smith, "Imperial Ships," *IOFN,* Spring 1964. "20 Years Ago," *IOFN,* Winter 1969.

MIDLAND CITY. Fred Landon,"The End of Coastal Steamer Service on Georgian Bay," *IS* , XI (1955); "The *Midland City,*" *IS,* VIII (1952). John M. Mills, *Canadian Coastal and Inland Steam Vessels 1809-1930* (Providence, R.I., 1979). Young, *Great Lakes' Saga.* Much of the material about the *Midland City* is drawn from my own recollections.

CONCORDIA. Canadian Imperial Bank of Commerce, Commercial Letter, Toronto, May-June 1969. Carleton Maybee, *The Seaway Story* (New York, 1961). St. Lawrence Seaway Authority, *1967 Annual Report* (Ottawa, 1968); Ottawa, letter to me, Oct. 9, 1969. St. Lawrence Seaway Development Corporation, *Annual Report 1959* (Washington, 1960).

BATEAU (III). Chapelle, *American Small Sailing Craft.* H.R. Morgan, "Steam Navigation on the Ottawa River," *PR,* XXIII (1926) contains material on early Ottawa River bateaux. ODLF, *The Pointer Boat* (Toronto, 1963). According to tradition, the first John Cockburn "invented" the pointer, but the wide use of bateaux on the Ottawa and throughout the Great Lakes region in lumbering, plus the fact that the bateau was unknown in Cockburn's native England, make it evident that he actually adapted and refined the native North American type.

ASSINIBOIA. John A. Burke and Cletus P. Schneider, letter, *IS,* XXII (1966). Dowling, "Canadian Pacific Railway." Marcolin, "Canadian Pacific . . . Last of an Era." C.H.J. Snider, "Up Superior in December," *T,* Dec. 12, 1936; "Down Superior in December," *T,* Dec. 19, 1936. David Plowden, *Farewell to Steam* (Brattleboro, Vt., 1966) contains detailed photo of the *Keewatin* and *Assiniboia.* Some of the information in this section was kindly provided by the Canadian Pacific; some of it is based on my own recollections of the vessel and of Port McNicoll, her Georgian Bay base.

MACKINAW. "Alexander Henry," *DMH,* XVII (1964). K. N. Black, "Icebreaking in Lake Erie," *IS,* XX (1964). *GLL,* April 17, 1995 (ice jam at Duluth-Superior in late March 1995). Gordon Macaulay, "Coast Guard Cutter *Mackinaw,*" *IS,* XV (1959); "The Mighty Mac," *IS,* XII (1956). George H. Palmer, Jr., Carlton E. Tripp, Richard Suehrstedt, and Joseph Fischer, "Rebuilding the Great Lakes U.S. Cargo Fleet and the Metamorphosis of the Self-Unloader," in *A Half Century of Marine Technology 1943-1993* (Jersey City, N.J., 1993) contains a discussion of extended season operation. U.S. Coast Guard, *Welcome Aboard U.S.C.G.C. Mackinaw* (Cleveland, n.d.).

GRANDE HERMINE. Stephen M. Aug, "The Seaway After 10 years—Tempered Optimism," *The Sunday Star* (Washington, D.C.), June 29, 1969. James P. Barry, *The Fate of the Lakes* (Grand Rapids, 1972) contains a number of photos taken aboard *Grande Hermine* and an extensive bibliography on the Seaway. "Changes in Name and Operation," *IS,* XXIII (1967); IS, XXVIII (1972). Ronald L. Heilmann, Harold M. Mayer, and Eric Schenker, *Great Lakes Transportation in the Eighties* (U. of Wisconsin, 1986) contains much about the Seaway. Phrixos B. Papachristidis, letter to me, Montreal, Nov. 28, 1969. Lawrence A. Pomeroy, Jr., "Great Lakes Calendar" (entry for Jan. 1966), *IS,* XXII (1966). In October 1966 the vessel's name was changed from *New Brunswicker* to *Grande Hermine;* in 1972 it was changed to *Canadian Mariner* when she was sold to Upper Lakes Shipping.

ROLWI. See above Seaway references, plus the following. Cleveland-Cuyahoga Port Authority, *Cleveland World Port,* (Cleveland, 1969). "Cleveland Seaman's Service." *Cleveland Calling,* Oct. 1969. *Port of Cleveland* (Newsletter), June, July & Sept. 1969. *Port of Toronto News* (Vol XXXX, Nos. 2 & 3, 1993). Edward Schaefer, "Seaway's Effect—Duluth is not yet a Boom Town," "It's Official: Fednav Will Build Four New Ships," *SR* (XXII, Apr.-June 1994). *The Star* (Minneapolis), June 27, 1969.

MANCHESTER MERCURIO. "Growth Potential in a Surprising Area: Containers," *SR* (XXII, Apr.-June 1994). J. L. Haskell, Deputy Port Director, Milwaukee, letter, March 27, 1973. Ronald L. Heilmann, Harold M. Mayer, and Eric Schenker, *Great Lakes Transportation in the Eighties* (U. of Wisconsin,1986). Craig Howard, "Lakes Feeder Service Slated,"*JC,* June 26, 1971. "More Seaway News," *Lake Log Chips,* Mar.15, 1973. "On the Waterfront," *Port of Toronto News,* Nov. 1972.

LEOLA CHARLES. Norman S. Baldwin and Robert W. Saalfeld, *Commercial Fish Production in the Great*

Lakes, 1867-1960 (Ann Arbor, 1962, with supplement, 1970). F. Graham Bligh, "Great Lakes Fish as Human Food," *Limnos*, Spring 1971. Canada, Department of Transport, Marine Services, letter, Nov. 18, 1969 (data on *Leola Charles*). Timothy C. Lloyd and Patrick B. Mullen, *Lake Erie Fishermen* (U. of Illinois, 1990). A. B. McCullough, *The Commercial Fishery of the Canadian Great Lakes* (Ottawa, 1989). George H. McIvor, *Report of Commission of Inquiry into Freshwater Fish Marketing* (Ottawa, ca. 1965). "Ohio Fish," *Lake Log Chips*, Mar. 15, 1973. ODLF, *Commercial Fishing in Ontario* (Toronto, n.d.); letters of Sept. 29 and Nov. 5, 1969 (Lake Erie fishing boats and fisheries).

ROY A. JODREY. Skip Gillham, *The Ships of Collingwood* (St. Catharines, Ont., 1992). John O. Greenwood, *Namesakes of the Lakes* (Cleveland, 1970); *GG*, 1973.

STEWART J. CORT. "*Cort* Cargo Sets Record for Lakes," the *Plain Dealer* (Cleveland), May 6, 1972. Patrick C. Dorin, *The Lake Superior Iron Ore Railroads* (Seattle, 1969) contains much about ore docks. Erie Marine, pamphlet, "Grand Opening, Saturday June 28, 1969." Lake Carriers' Association, *Great Lakes Shipping: The Story of the Lakes Vessel Industry* (Cleveland, n.d.) Stanley Mantrop, "New Litton Shipyard is Opened," *JC*, July 1, 1969. T. A. Sykora, "1972–A New Era in Great Lakes Transportation," *IS*, XXVIII (1972). The staff of Erie Marine kindly provided detailed information and a tour of both their shipyard and the *Stewart J. Cort.* The problems faced by the shipyard are covered in Erie, Pennsylvania newspapers for Dec. 30, 1971; Aug. 30, 1974, and February 24, 1985, all in the collection of Robert J. MacDonald of Erie; further information was gained in discussion with Mr. MacDonald. George J. Ryan, President, Lake Carriers' Association, letter to me, April 17, 1995 discusses tug-barge combinations such as the *Presque Isle.*

Chapter 8

INTRODUCTORY MATERIAL. "Full Circle," *SR* (XXIII, Jan.-Mar. 1995), tells of coal movements through Duluth-Superior. *GG* issues for 1950 and 1995 give the fleet totals of those years. Heilmann, Mayer, and Schenker, *Great Lakes Transportation in the Eighties."* Patrick A. Manley, "Radical Changes are Required for the Great Lakes to Succeed," *SR* (XXIII, Oct.- Dec., 1994). Palmer, Tripp, Sueherstedt, and Fischer, "Rebuilding the Great Lakes U.S. Cargo Fleet," in *A Half Century of Maritime Technology 1943-1993* (Jersey City, N.J., 1993).

George J. Ryan, President, Lake Carriers' Association, letter to me, April 17, 1995 (overall situation). There have been improvements in navigational equipment; Canada Steamship Lines, which has one of the larger fleets, has pioneered adoption of digital charting, which projects on a computer screen both a navigational chart and the ship's exact position as read from satellites—probably the greatest navigational advance since radar. See the *Globe and Mail* (Toronto), July 18, 1995. This introduction and the chapter that follows owe much to discussions with Daniel J. Cornillie, Manager, Fleet Operations, Inland Steel Company.

J. W. McGIFFIN. Gillham, *The Ships of Collingwood.* Most of the information in this section was provided by Maurice Smith, director of the Marine Museum of the Great Lakes at Kingston; he obtained it from Canadian Shipbuilding and Engineering, the parent company of the now defunct Collingwood Shipyards.

CHARLES E. WILSON. Palmer et al., "Rebuilding."

CHI-CHEEMAUN. James P. Barry, *Georgian Bay: The Sixth Great Lake,* (3d ed., revised, Toronto, 1995); "A Unique Great Lakes Operation," *IS*, XXXVIII (1982). *GG* 1995. Charles Zeien, "Development of Large Commercial Roll On/Roll Off Ships, Trailerships, and Car Carriers," in *A Half Century of Maritime Technology 1943-1993* (Jersey City, N.J., 1993).

JAMES R. BARKER. Heilmann et al., *Great Lakes Transportation.* Palmer et al., "Rebuilding." "Responding to Change," *SR*, XXIII (Oct.-Dec, 1994). "Still a Major Force," *SR*, XXII (Apr.-June 1994), tells of the USS Fleet. The *Indiana Harbor* incident is reported in "Ore Carrier Smashed into Lighthouse on Lake Michigan," *PM* February 1994; "Third Mate Charged with Negligence after Piloting Ship into Lighthouse," *PM*, March 1994. As an indication of occasional lesser problems for thousand-footers, *PM*, February/March 1995 tells of the *Presque Isle* grounding in the Detroit River in Nov. 1994, and *PM*, June/July 1995 of the *Edwin H. Gott* grounding in the St. Mary's River in Apr. 1995.

ALGOPORT. Collingwood Shipyards, pamphlet distributed at the launching of *Algoport* (in GLHS Inland Seas Museum files). *DMH*, IIL (1995) tells of Algoma partnership in ocean vessels. *GLL*, June 26, 1965, also tells of that arrangement. *SR*, XXII (April-June 1994) considers the problems of shipping grain. Norman Eakins, *Ships on the Great Lakes in 1994* (Point Edward, Ont. 1995). *GG*, 1976-1995. Gillham, *The Ships of Collingwood.* "It's Official: Fednav will build four new ships," *SR*, XXII (April-June 1994). As noted, the *Grande Hermine* has been renamed *Canadian Mariner;* she still trades through the Seaway between the Gulf of St. Lawrence and the Lakes.

FORT WILLIAM. James P. Barry, *The Fate of the Lakes* (Grand Rapids, 1972) describes Canada Steamship Lines package freight operations at that time. Skip Gillham, "Farewell to the Package Freighters," *Steamboat Bill* (No. 191, Fall 1989) gives the most complete history of package freight operations by CSL and predecessors on the Canadian side of the Lakes. Gillham, *The Ships of Collingwood*, gives information about *Fort William* being rebuilt as *Stephen B. Roman*. A general reference that lists and describes CSL package freighters of the day is *GG, 1981.*

AMERICAN REPUBLIC. Palmer et al., "Rebuilding." "The Innovators," *SR*, XXI (July-Sept. 1992). Ned A. Smith, President and CEO, American Steamship Co., letter to me, May 16, 1995.

PAUL R. TREGURTHA. *GG*, 1995. Palmer et al., "Rebuilding." Palmer et al. gives the comparison of the long, thin hull with a plank on edge. Material on launching of vessel as *William J. Delancey* is in files of GLHS Inland Seas Museum.

Afterword

The quotation from Rowley W. Murphy is taken from his article "Ghost Ships," *IS*, XVII (1961).

Most photos of the Great Lakes vessels depict them either in port or under way in good weather. This one shows the other side of the coin. A view from the after structure of the freighter *William H. Truesdell*, looking forward, during heavy weather on Lake Erie in the 1930s. (—*Institute for Great Lakes Research, Bowling Green State University*)

Index

Boldface indicates picture

271